Four Musical Minimalists

The American composers La Monte Young, Terry Riley, Steve Reich
and Philip Glass are widely regarded as pioneers of the aesthetic and
the techniques of minimalism in musical composition during the
1960s and early 1970s. This book offers the most detailed account so
far of their early works, putting extensive discussion of the music into
a biographical perspective. The true musical minimalism of these
years is placed in the wider context of their musical output as a whole,
and considered within the cultural conditions of a period which saw
not only the rise of minimalism in the fine arts but also crucial changes
in the theory and practice of musical composition in the Western
cultivated tradition.

KEITH POTTER is a Senior Lecturer in Music at Goldsmiths College,
University of London, and is a regular contributor to *The Independent*.

Music in the Twentieth Century

GENERAL EDITOR Arnold Whittall

This series offers a wide perspective on music and musical life in the twentieth century. Books included range from historical and biographical studies concentrating particularly on the context and circumstances in which composers were writing, to analytical and critical studies concerned with the nature of musical language and questions of compositional process. The importance given to context will also be reflected in studies dealing with, for example, the patronage, publishing and promotion of new music, and in accounts of the musical life of particular countries.

Recent titles

James Pritchett   *The Music of John Cage*

Joseph Straus   *The Music of Ruth Crawford Seeger*

Kyle Gann   *The Music of Conlon Nancarrow*

Jonathan Cross   *The Stravinsky Legacy*

Michael Nyman   *Experimental Music: Cage and Beyond*

Jennifer Doctor   *The BBC and Ultra-Modern Music, 1922–1936*

Robert Adlington   *The Music of Harrison Birtwistle*

Keith Potter   *Four Musical Minimalists: La Monte Young, Terry Riley, Steve Reich, Philip Glass*

Carlo Caballero   *Fauré and French Musical Aesthetics*

Peter Burt   *The Music of Tōru Takemitsu*

David Clarke   *The Music and Thought of Michael Tippett: Modern Times and Metaphysics*

M. J. Grant   *Serial Music, Serial Aesthetics: Compositional Theory in Post-War Europe*

Philip Rupprecht   *Britten's Musical Language*

Four Musical Minimalists:
La Monte Young,
Terry Riley,
Steve Reich,
Philip Glass

Keith Potter

CAMBRIDGE
UNIVERSITY PRESS

CAMBRIDGE UNIVERSITY PRESS
Cambridge, New York, Melbourne, Madrid, Cape Town, Singapore, São Paulo

Cambridge University Press
The Edinburgh Building, Cambridge CB2 2RU, UK

Published in the United States of America by Cambridge University Press, New York

www.cambridge.org
Information on this title: www.cambridge.org/9780521482509

First published 2000
First paperback edition, with minor revisions 2002
Reprinted 2004

A catalogue record for this publication is available from the British Library

Library of Congress Cataloguing in Publication data
Potter, Keith
    Four musical minimalists / Keith Potter.
        p.   cm.
    Includes bibliographical references (p. 365) and discography (p. 360).
    Contents: La Monte Young – Terry Riley – Steve Reich – Philip
Glass.
    ISBN 0 521 48250 X (hardcover) – 0 521 01501 4 (paperback)
    1. Young, La Monte, 1935– .   2. Riley, Terry, 1935– .   3. Reich, Steve,
1936– .   4. Glass, Philip, 1937– .   5. Composers – United States –
Biography.   6. Minimal music – United States – History and criticism.
I. Title.
ML390.P759   2000
780'.92'273 – dc21   00–11736   CIP

ISBN-13 978-0-521-48250-9 hardback
ISBN-10 0-521-48250-X hardback

ISBN-13 978-0-521-01501-1 paperback
ISBN-10 0-521-01501-4 paperback

Transferred to digital printing 2006

For Kay,
and David Huntley (in memoriam)

Contents

Acknowledgements

First and foremost, I am indebted to the four composers who are the subjects of this book for their extensive assistance and considerable patience over the years during which it has been put together. Between 1984 and 1998, they have submitted themselves variously, but always generously, to many hours of interviewing and – in a field in which there are relatively few published sources, and in which the secondary source materials are frequently patchy, inaccurate and seldom scholarly – have additionally provided written and taped documentation on a sometimes extensive scale. Whenever their views and memories differ, I hope I have interpreted their collective statements sensitively as well as done justice to each of them individually; in several respects, they have been the ideal counterbalance to each other in the attempt to produce a fully informed historical account. Having stayed at the homes of three of my 'victims', I should also acknowledge their hospitality. Both in this respect, and for participating in interviews and spending many hours collecting and photocopying material and helping to check several versions of the chapter on Young, I must also thank Marian Zazeela, whose husband regularly enjoys the benefits of an unusually close artistic as well as personal partnership.

Among many others who have also submitted to interviewing, corresponded with me and in many others ways assisted, directly or indirectly, with research, I should like in particular to mention Jon Gibson. The only musician to have worked regularly with all four composers under scrutiny here, and himself a composer of minimalist music as well as one of its most talented and staunchest champions as a performer, he has been unfailingly and selflessly helpful. Among others, many of them participants in the early history of musical minimalism, whose knowledge and perspective – the latter sometimes very different from that of my subjects – have been shared with me directly, modifying and improving my understanding of the subject, John Adams, JoAnn Akalaitis, Glenn Branca, Rhys Chatham, Tony Conrad, Hugh Davies, Ruth Dreier, Paul Epstein, Henry Flynt, Daniel Goode, Tom Johnson, Jack Kripl, David Lang, Ruth Maleczech, Phill Niblock, Pauline Oliveros, Michael Parsons, Ann Riley, Howard Skempton and Janis Susskind must receive particular mention. Of those others who have offered assistance or advice at various stages, and in some cases commented on drafts of individual chapters, I should like to mention

Mark Cromar and Robert Davidson (whose unpublished dissertations have additionally proved considerable stimuli to my own work), Jeremy Peyton Jones and Andrew Poppy (the last two being chief among many former students with whom I have maintained an ongoing debate concerning the past practice and present state of musical minimalism), Dave Smith and Mark Swed. David Allenby, of Boosey and Hawkes, and Ramona Kirchschenman, of Dunvagen, are among many others who have helped in various ways. I should also like to place on record my gratitude to David Huntley, also of Boosey and Hawkes, whose unstinting advice and hospitality whenever I was in New York during the ten years before his untimely death in 1994 were a source of special pleasure to me.

Thanks must go, in addition, to Goldsmiths College, University of London, my long-time employers, who have not only given me the time to research and write this book but also provided a travel grant, as did the University of London itself. I should particularly thank Stanley Glasser, for many years Head of Music at Goldsmiths, for his faith that my endeavours in this area would eventually yield fruit in book form. As General Editor of the series of which this volume is part, I am pleased to acknowledge the patient advice of Professor Arnold Whittall, and also proud to admit to being his student many years ago. Penny Souster at Cambridge University Press has been equally persistent in her efforts to see this book through to completion; Ann Lewis, my copy editor, and Karl Howe, production and design manager, are among several others at CUP whom I should also thank. My parents – Ronald and Betty Phelps – will be surprised, and perhaps even pleased, that I have produced offspring of any kind after so many years of waiting. Many friends, both in London and in Dorset (where much of this book was written), have been encouraging and consoling, as appropriate. Finally, I should like to thank Kay Potter, my wife, for being the most supportive and long-suffering of all.

Music examples (some of them in the composers' own hand) are published either entirely by permission of the composer himself (in the case of La Monte Young and Terry Riley) or as follows:

Chapter Three: Examples 3.1–3.7, 3.12 and 3.15: copyright by Steve Reich, reproduced by kind permission of the composer. Examples 3.8, 3.16–3.18 and 3.20–3.25: copyright by Boosey and Hawkes Inc., New York, reproduced by kind permission. (Examples 3.16–3.18 reset for this edition by Marc Mellito.) Examples 3.9–3.11, 3.13–3.14 and 3.19: copyright by Universal Edition, London, reproduced by kind permission.
Chapter Four: Example 4.1: copyright by Novello, reproduced by kind permission. Examples 4.2–4.8, 4.10, 4.11, 4.13–4.15 and 4.17–4.21: copyright by Dunvagen Inc., reproduced by kind permission.

Preface

This book is a story of four American composers all born within eighteen months of each other. Their pioneering roles in musical minimalism are alone sufficient to single them out. A degree of overlap in their associations and their activities makes it sensible to consider them as in some sense a group. The fact that such associations mainly involve the earlier parts of their lives, as tends to be the case with any group of composers termed a 'school' by music historians, is not, however, the only reason why this volume tells their story in detail only to the middle of the 1970s. More significant in this decision is an interpretation of their work which argues a gradual move away from what can reasonably be regarded as music driven by a minimalist aesthetic towards a diversity – not only of underlying intentions, but also of style and technique – that makes it almost impossible to consider their outputs of the last quarter of a century as a meaningful whole. Though this diversity is observable more clearly in the developments of Steve Reich and Philip Glass than of La Monte Young and Terry Riley, there is sufficient evidence in the outputs of the latter pair to make sense of their stories in this rather truncated form as well.

Young, Riley, Reich and Glass have been singled out as a group by other writers, though many leave out the admittedly more controversial Young. Of those who include all four names, several – including Tom Johnson and Michael Nyman, discussed below – have written insightful journalism about them, and in 1974 Nyman brought them together in the final chapter of his seminal book, *Experimental Music: Cage and Beyond*. In his own volume, *American Minimal Music*, originally published in 1980, Wim Mertens (a composer, like Johnson and Nyman) confined his discussion of actual compositions to these four Americans, though the most interesting parts of his text are probably those which discuss wider aesthetic issues. More recently, other writers mentioned in what follows here have brought the four together, sometimes expanding their lists with further, chiefly American names. Of these, Edward Strickland's 1993 volume, *Minimalism: Origins*, imaginatively structured as an A–Z of minimalism in art and music, is the only book-length study. References to articles by several other authors – some tackling the problems of defining musical minimalism more directly, and certainly more succinctly – are made in the present text and bibliography.

My own efforts naturally overlap in intention with those of Strickland. Like him, for instance, I stress the origins and early development of American minimalist music, allowing this to influence not only the cut-off date of *c.* 1976 but also my discussions of the outputs of Young and Riley, in particular, which concentrate on their earliest, pioneering work at the expense of what followed it. I devote much less space than Strickland does, however, to Minimalist art. By dealing with each of these four figures separately, I have tried to give more comprehensive accounts of their early lives. And, in particular, I also offer more detailed musical analysis, considering that the compositions concerned have previously not received the scrutiny I would argue they deserve. Such an approach strengthens the suggestion that each composer, while undeniably playing his part in a wider scenario, is ultimately to be understood as an individual with quite different personal and musical characteristics from those of his colleagues. This book is thus simultaneously a single story and four individual stories.

Given the negative connotations of its connecting aesthetic subject matter, it seems more than usually appropriate to make clear what this book strips away from a truly comprehensive account of musical minimalism. It makes no more than occasional references to the prehistories and 'proto-minimalisms' which others have, sometimes rightly, identified, whether in the music of past composers (Vivaldi, Satie, Ravel) or more recent ones (György Ligeti, Giacinto Scelsi). It does not attempt to deal with the range of other Americans who were in some sense part of the same movement as the four considered here: composer-performers such as Meredith Monk, to give just one example. It does not encompass the variety of possible interpretations of the origins, nature and purposes of minimalism in European musics. It does no more than hint at the growth of European, American or other territories of minimalism, or post-minimalism, since the mid-1970s, or give more than brief suggestions as to whether any or all of these can be considered part of a genuine diaspora emanating directly from the work of Young, Riley, Reich and Glass. It is neither comprehensive nor up-to-the-minute.

It is, rather, an attempt to write – while its subjects are available for extended consultation – a slice of history which seems, to its author, of peculiar fascination, both for itself and for what it tells us about the wider currents of musical, and cultural, development in the twentieth century. When compared to more recent activities, its stories may be likened in some respects to the Old Testament. Limited in provenance and applicability, their subjects' sometimes painful discoveries – and prophecies – nevertheless became vital building blocks for the more encompassing and more widely accepted – though in certain quarters also frequently challenged – revelations of a New Testament enshrined in the musical culture of our own time. Before I begin, however, a little further context for these four stories must be established by examining the term that ostensibly binds them together.

Introduction

What is minimalism in music? Why has a term borrowed from the language of art historians been applied by many writers to music? To what range of work have they actually applied it? How might the use of the term illuminate our understanding of the music involved? Do the composers involved see themselves as in any sense 'minimalists'? What are the term's disadvantages? And what aspects of the wider cultural context – the compositional movements arising at the point in musical history at which these concerns surface, the phenomenon of Minimalist art itself, the move from modernism to post-modernism – help put the stories unfolded here into a wider perspective? Such questions are addressed frequently in the four main chapters that follow and, for the moment, they can be introduced only briefly. Please also note that I have attempted to suggest the rather looser connotations of the term's deployment in a musical context by reserving the upper-case 'Minimalist' for the fine arts, and generally using the lower-case 'minimalist' for musical references. I have also preferred the epithet 'minimalist' (whether upper or lower case) to the overly reductive 'minimal'. Let us begin with the earliest-known applications of the term to music.

Unsurprisingly, most composers described as minimalist are impatient with the term. Of the four subjects of this book, only Young is reasonably happy with it, and then only as applied to his earliest efforts.[1] This is perfectly understandable, even merely on the grounds that no creative artist likes to be defined, and limited, by any term. In an essay entitled 'Paragraphs on Conceptual Art', to which further reference is made below, the artist Sol Le Witt somewhat naughtily concluded that all the labels currently in use to describe Minimalist art – his list also includes 'primary structures, reductive, rejective, cool, and mini-art' – were all 'part of a secret language that art critics use when communicating with each other through the medium of art magazines'.[2] An additional problem attaching to Minimalism arises from its already derogatory sounding suggestion of 'less than usual'. As the art critic Lawrence Alloway has pointed out, '[b]ecause there is no consensus on what is Enough, or Too Much, one cannot accurately characterize [such art] as minimal. . . . It is a weakness of "minimal" as a critical term that it assumes, or rather memorializes, a point in time when such work was less than expected'.[3]

Two music critics who themselves subsequently renounced commentary in favour of composition following a minimalist approach have vied for the dubious honour of being the first to adopt the word 'minimalist' for musical purposes. In March 1972, the American writer Tom Johnson used the term to describe a concert given by his compatriot Alvin Lucier.[4] Lucier's explorations of acoustic and psycho-acoustic phenomena are, in both provenance and sonic result, very different from the music of Riley, Reich and Glass, though they have more in common with Young's rigorous and scientific investigations of sound. But some of the aspects which Johnson identifies in this 'minimal, slow-motion approach' – here not only of Lucier himself, but also of his British pupil Stuart Marshall and his wife, the artist Mary Lucier – are also characteristic of the aesthetic informing the early works of Reich and Glass, in particular. In addition to the fact that 'very little happens in any of the pieces', Johnson notes that 'the most striking thing about the concert as a whole was its coolness'.

An early champion of Riley, Reich and Glass (though oddly less enthusiastic about Young), Johnson had, at the time of this Lucier article, recently covered the première of Reich's *Drumming*: a review he subsequently assessed as 'probably the first occasion that any of the minimalist composers were taken seriously by any of the New York press'.[5] Yet his articles on the music of these figures take a while to settle for minimalism as his term of choice to describe what they do. Just a week after the Lucier notice, a review of the latest sections of Philip Glass's *Music in Twelve Parts* to appear begins with the suggestion that '[o]ne of the most important new trends in music is the area I like to refer to as "hypnotic music"'.[6] A few months later – in a review which must represent one of the first occurrences of the names of Young, Riley, Reich and Glass together in a published article[7] – Johnson relates having heard the term 'New York Hypnotic School' several times, though he includes 'minimal' among his list of such music's attributes, along with 'flat, static . . . and hypnotic'. By June 1977 – when he wrote 'What Is Minimalism Really About?'[8] – Johnson had been deploying the term more regularly for some while, and it is clear that its use had caught on in the New York community in which he operated, as it had by then done elsewhere. The list of epithets in this now classic article forms a good basis for a more detailed consideration of musical minimalism's chief attributes: 'repetition . . . tiny variations . . . hyper-clarity . . . encouraging more subtle perceptions . . . making music less dramatic . . . [stemming] partly from certain Asian and African attitudes'. As one of the few composers besides Young to accept the 'minimalist' label willingly, Johnson has himself consistently celebrated his fascination with numbers, clearly audible processes and what may be called a self-reflexive approach in music combining a high degree of systematisation with a ready wit.

In October 1968, three-and-a-half years before Johnson's Lucier article, the writer Michael Nyman had employed the term 'minimal' in a round-up review, entitled 'Minimal music', including his fellow Englishman Cornelius Cardew's work then known as *The Great Digest*; the word 'minimal' is, though, in fact applied directly only to the also mentioned Henning Christiansen's *Springen*.[9] Cardew had espoused an aesthetic owing a good deal to John Cage, though his activities also engaged improvisation: something his mentor avoided as too redolent of self-expression, of what he called 'individual taste and memory'.[10] Again, the sound world of what later became known as *The Great Learning* and its provenance are far removed from most of the music covered in the present volume. The debt to Cage is, however, some connection in itself, as we shall see; while improvisation has been central to the work of Young and Riley.

Likewise an early champion of Young and the others – in his case, particularly of Reich, whose work he was among the first to present in Britain – Nyman eventually used the term 'minimalist' to describe not only the output of the Americans, but also the work of his own colleagues in the English 'experimental' movement: composers such as Gavin Bryars, Christopher Hobbs, Michael Parsons, Howard Skempton and John White, most of them at one time close associates of Cardew. In an interview which Nyman conducted with Reich in the summer of 1970,[11] when the composer was on his way to study African drumming in Ghana, there is some discussion of labelling, in the course of which Reich reveals a preference for 'pulse music', also the title of a then still fairly recent piece. Though he is described as working 'with an absolute minimum of musical material,' the term 'minimalism' is never used. In October 1971, Nyman suggested that some of the techniques used in English 'experimental music' of the period – the so-called 'systems music' influenced by Riley and Reich, in particular – had analogies with, among other movements, 'Minimal Art'.[12] Four months later, however, he managed to write an introduction to Reich's *Drumming* without ever mentioning 'minimalism'.[13]

Nyman's book *Experimental Music: Cage and beyond* – now a classic of twentieth-century compositional aesthetics, first published in the summer of 1974[14] – devotes a chapter to 'Minimal music, determinacy and the new tonality', in which Young, Riley, Glass and Reich (an order apparently based on their increasing importance as then perceived by the book's author) have pride of place. Nyman makes no attempt here to relate their music to any other movement besides Fluxus. But in putting these composers into a post-Cageian context, he raises the pertinent question of their precise relationship to Cage himself.

Cage was famously critical of musical minimalism, notably of its more rock-orientated manifestations. When Glenn Branca's earthily insistent – and I would say 'post-minimalist' – music for an orchestra of electric guitars was performed at the 1982 New Music America festival in Chicago, this now eminent experimental composer reportedly called it 'fascist':[15] an accusation which has also been levelled at earlier American minimalism – including that of Reich, notably, and rather interestingly, in Germany. Yet Cage's early, pre-chance compositions seem proto-minimalist: in their composer's search for a music based on rhythm and, more generally, lengths of time rather than pitch, for instance, and in their evident borrowing from non-Western musics equally concerned with timbre as well as the vitality of pulse-based methods.

More importantly, Cage's espousal of non-intention, which supplied the philosophical force that propelled his use of indeterminate techniques, links him with the aesthetic of minimalism, both in art and in music. The composer's associations with Abstract Expressionist painters such as Willem de Kooning, Franz Kline and Jackson Pollock have confused many accounts of where Cage's aesthetic preferences really lay. The 'action painting' of Pollock, for instance, represents a mid-twentieth-century *angst* with strong roots in the more 'Romantic' of earlier twentieth-century art forms, notably Cubism and Surrealism. For all its dalliance with automatism – which suggests comparisons with the minimalists' development of processes independent of their creator's control – the Abstract Expressionists' espousal of an essentially non-figurative, (post-)surrealist, aggressively abstract mode is the outcome of attempts to express the individual, often tortured, would-be unique personality of each artist. At least two painters associated with the movement – Barnett Newman and Ad Reinhardt – did, however, prefigure aspects of minimalism: Newman's so-called 'stripe' paintings, for example, clearly deal in drastic reduction.

Cage's artistic preferences were with Marcel Duchamp and Dada, and, in particular, with Jasper Johns and Robert Rauschenberg, probably the composer's closest friends in the art world. All these artists share one crucial concern with Cage which sets them apart from Abstract Expressionism, and which also makes both composer and artists significant, if not often acknowledged, models for Minimalist artists and composers. Like his artist friends, Cage devoted himself to finding ways of bypassing the already mentioned 'individual taste and memory' in order to discover something new and unpredictable to which access could not be gained through the application of the human imagination alone. In connection with this, it may be observed that Johnson's 'encouraging more subtle perceptions . . . making music less dramatic . . . [and] [stemming] partly from certain Asian and African attitudes' are as apt in application to Cage as they are to the minimalist composers.

With Cage, indeterminacy proved the key technique. The artists with whom he was most closely associated were similarly concerned with exploring new perceptions by expunging old values, especially the expressive ones; though, if anything, their work pointed up even more than Cage's the contradictions brought into play by drastic reduction. Rauschenberg's 'White Painting' of 1951 prefigured later minimalists not only in its reductiveness, but also in its use of commercial materials, by rolling house enamel on to a set of identical canvas panels. It was Cage himself who described the results as 'airports for lights, shadows, and particles',[16] drawing attention to the way in which they reflected back to the viewer not the singular, and illusory, void of their original conception but the multiple reflections of everyday life. Acknowledging the influence of Rauschenberg, in 1952 Cage produced what must in some sense be regarded as the ultimate minimalist statement; his infamous 4′33″ similarly reflects the world it confronts but over which it has no control.

Cage acted as a crucial father-figure both to younger composers in the 1950s and, more pervasively, to the artistic culture that flourished with particular vitality in the downtown Manhattan of the 1960s and 1970s that formed the seedbed for much of the musical developments described in this book. Of his better-known immediate associates, Morton Feldman had the closest connections with the painters who went beyond Abstract Expressionism, and the most immediately apparent links with the minimalist composers. In what is probably the most extended examination, in article form, of the relevance for music of the Minimalist aesthetic in art, Jonathan Bernard warns against interpreting '[t]he ostensibly sparse "event-density"' of the music of Feldman – or of Cage and Earle Brown – as minimalist, 'for in reality, the small number of events over time tends to focus the listener's attention intensely on each event, in all its particularity, thus resulting, from the minimalist point of view, in a music of parts rather than a whole'.[17] We shall explore later in this book some of the ramifications of what Bernard calls 'the opposition between arrangement and composition'[18] in minimalist music: in terms, for instance, of the dialectic between the continuing audibility of what I call the Basic Unit of a composition and the perceptual consequences of its working out.

Feldman's earlier compositions, meanwhile, with their deregulation of sounds from the periodicity of a beat, offer a world of unusual purity, in which technique was subordinated to sound, and the pieces became 'time canvases . . . prime[d] . . . with an overall hue of music'.[19] His later scores are not only sufficiently long to subvert their listener's sense of the passage of time while retaining developmental features, but also have a tendency to lock sounds into clearly audible, repeating metrical patterns: sometimes diatonic, often subtly changing, and thus creating ambiguities of musical time analogous to those found in Reich and Glass. The former was aware quite early on of Feldman's *Piece for Four Pianos* of 1957, the first of several pieces by its composer to release a freely unravelling multiple canon suggestive of a free kind of phasing. Reich feels, though, that only much later, after the composer's death in 1987, did he belatedly see the full significance of Feldman. Christian Wolff's early exercises in reductive rigour with only three notes in a whole piece (his Trio for flute, clarinet and violin of 1951, for instance, confines itself to a 'short stack' of perfect fifths, E, B and F♯) seem to have gone largely unrecognised by the subjects of this volume. This is somewhat surprising in view of the fact that several of their early associates – David Behrman, Tony Conrad, Henry Flynt and Frederic Rzewski among them – knew the composer and his music when they were Harvard students and Wolff himself a young Classics professor, during the early 1960s; some of them performed in pieces of his at that time.

Three consequences of the avoidance of 'individual taste and memory' help not only to expand Nyman's definition of an 'experimental' aesthetic built, in particular, upon Cage's example, but also to make additional connections with a working definition of musical minimalism. These are, firstly, the concern to avoid the creation of conventional time-objects by stressing process rather than product; secondly, the avoidance of previous notions of musical expression, in particular of music being in some sense about the composers themselves, their own preconceptions and predilections; and thirdly, the reconsideration of what we may call narrativity. The balance of these concerns varied from composer to composer. Reich and Glass, for instance, might well be argued to have been more involved, even in their early minimalist compositions, with the notion of a 'time-object', even with narrativity, than Young and Riley. But all four composers shared with Cage and other experimentalists the belief that their music should somehow go beyond what their own imaginations were inherently capable of inventing. Importantly, this applied to structure, in their case more than to material.

The art historian Irving Sandler is very clear that a seismic shift occurred in the arts around 1960. 'During the period from Johns's first show, in 1958', he writes, 'to the emergence of Pop Art, in 1962, the sensibility of the avant-garde underwent a pervasive change'.[20] A crucial contributor to this changing sensibility was the painter Frank Stella, whose black-stripe abstractions, also first exhibited in 1958, proclaimed a highly influential form of anti-Expressionism, and whose slogan '[w]hat you see is what you see'[21] became a watchword of the Minimalist sculptors in the 1960s. The art critic Kenneth Baker elaborates on this in ways which suggest close comparisons with both Cageian non-intention and the aesthetics of musical minimalism: 'Stella', he writes, 'shifted emphasis from the artist's activity as a metaphor for human self-definition to the viewer's activity of studying art objects for clues to the metaphysics of experience'.[22]

Yet any attempt to characterise briefly the cauldron of creative activity that followed Sandler's 'seismic shift' immediately comes up against its evident diversity. To confine matters to the so-called fine arts alone, a list of 1960s movements offered by Sandler himself includes 'Pop Art, New Perceptual Realism, Photo-Realism, Op Art, Minimal Art, Process Art, Earth Art and Conceptual Art'.[23] To these we should add the Fluxus movement and the wider range of performance-art activities with which it is frequently considered synonymous; as we shall see, Fluxus provides a further, and notable, 'hinge' between, in particular, Cage and Young. Despite this sometimes contradictory diversity, connections of many kinds can be made between individual items here, starting with the link between the Cage/Johns/Rauschenberg aesthetic and Pop Art. Johns famously took the American flag, targets and numbers as his departure points: 'things the mind already knows', as he put it, which 'gave me room to work on other levels'.[24] The Pop artists, such as Roy Lichtenstein and Andy Warhol, took more obviously commercial subject matter likewise redolent with meanings for their viewers, and made a whole movement out of its exploitation as potential art objects.

Pop Art's critiques, both of the modernist project and of the still new consumer society in which it functioned, should not be underestimated. Warhol and others may have 'contributed to the legitimation of . . . [the consumer] system through its aggressive appropriation of the images, techniques, and strategies associated with the ideology of consumption'.[25] Yet it did so not only by challenging modernism's insistence on purity and the new, but also via two other strategies which call into question the nature of its relationship with consumer society as well as the modernist art that rejected that society more clearly and wholeheartedly. One of these was Pop Art's rejection of narrative rhetoric while using materials – notably the comic strip – previously closely associated with narrative structure: a stance which has clear points in common with that of early minimalism. The other was Pop's blurring of the boundaries between the avant-garde and kitsch, to employ the terms used by the critic Clement

Greenberg in the course of his famous championing of a modernist art unsullied by commerce or the vernacular.[26] This led both to a questioning of the conceptual framework on which modernism and its continued existence was based, and, perhaps paradoxically, to a greater consciousness on the part of artists and their viewers of their historical position and roles. Here, close comparisons with musical minimalism are probably unwise, though, as we shall see, some regard even the early compositions of Riley, Reich and Glass as kitsch.

Neither should we underestimate a certain unity of purpose among at least some of the movements on Sandler's list in aesthetic projects related either to Cageian non-intention or to Minimalist refusal of reference, or to both. In 1967, Gene Davis declared that 'coolness, passivity and emotional detachment seem to be in the air. Pop, op, hard-edge, minimal art, and color painting share it in some degree'.[27] But in their negation of both aesthetic and social values, the Minimalist sculptors such as Carl Andre, Donald Judd, Robert Morris and Richard Serra pushed at the frontiers of art in ways which, again, only Cage equalled for sheer confidence in dismantling preconceived notions of what art should be.

One movement missing from Davis's list above with evident connections both to Minimalist art and minimalist music is the Conceptual Art of Sol Le Witt, who should be mentioned here due not least to his close association with Reich and, later, with Glass. Credited with the coining of the term 'conceptual art' – ironic, given his castigation of labels mentioned above – Le Witt developed his treatment of ideas as opposed to substances not only in his familiar grids of hollowed-out cubes but also in the already mentioned 1967 'Paragraphs on Conceptual Art', with which Reich's 1968 essay 'Music as a Gradual Process'[28] – a now classic statement of the minimalist aesthetic in music – has some parallels. Confronted, by Nyman in 1976, with the similarity, for instance, between his statement that 'once the process is set up and loaded it runs by itself' and Le Witt's 'all the planning and decisions are made beforehand' – both echoes of the Minimalist artists' 'elimination of transformative labor' – Reich argues that his own 'decisions weren't all made beforehand':[29] something which will be examined later, in my chapter on the composer. Both essays are, however, notable as statements of hard-line positions arguably already abandoned – in the composer's case, at least – by the time of writing.

In its instigation of developments which have led it to be considered the leading art movement of the 1960s, Minimalist art focused directly on the object itself. It experimented with the limits of art by asking how many of the elements traditionally associated with it could be taken away to leave something which could still be considered art. By 'eliminating transformative labor from his work',[30] as Baker puts it, Andre – perhaps the most widely known, and widely denigrated, Minimalist sculptor – presents his rectangular arrays of metal plates, modular sequences of blocks of wood (or even single blocks) and infamous piles of bricks for contemplation as art only because they are offered *as* art in a gallery space. In proposing that '[t]he thing . . . is not supposed to be suggestive of anything other than itself',[31] Minimalist art attempted to eliminate not only conventional notions of expression but also referentiality.

Frances Colpitt begins her book on what she calls 'Minimal art' with an unusually clear and concise set of defining and contextual characteristics, summarising the position outlined above:

> Minimal art describes abstract, geometric painting and sculpture executed in the United States in the 1960s. Its predominant organizing principles include the right angle, the square, and the cube, rendered with a minimum of incident or compositional maneuvering. Historically a reaction to what young artists saw as the autobiographical, gestural excesses of Abstract Expressionism, Minimal art, at the same time, pursues the formal innovations of Abstract Expressionism, particularly as laid out by the paintings of Jackson Pollock and Barnett Newman. Although Minimalism shares with Pop art anonymous design, deadpan flatness, and unadulterated or industrial color, and was in fact described as 'Imageless Pop' in 1966, the Minimalists eschewed any form of comment, representation, or reference.[32]

After so many artistic upheavals earlier in the twentieth century, Minimalist art succeeded, by doing away with all expressive baggage, in calling into question once again, yet at the same time freshly, just what the viewer was supposed to get out of art. The absence not only of conventional social symbology, but also of psychological symbology, was crucial. If Minimalist art had no subject matter – no social, practical or psychological value – did it indeed have any aesthetic value at all? Minimalist art's commitment to formal innovation throws down challenges which are heightened rather than cushioned by such art's resistance to metaphorical, as opposed to metaphysical, interpretation. Its focus on sensations based on the direct perception of objects forces the viewer to a radical reconsideration of those objects. Minimalist art also appears antagonistic to a capitalist culture based on values derived entirely from what is perceived to sell most easily. Even its reliance on the mass-production techniques of industrial technology must be viewed, in Duchampian terms, as the only valid response to the apparently inevitable subjection of art objects created with the artist's own imagination and own hands to the values of the market place. Minimalist art's hard-line stance of negation suggests that it operates as an alternative to the excesses of Abstract

Expressionism, but an alternative that is decidedly modernist in its stance.

All this suggests that the early phases of American musical minimalism described in the present book can likewise be interpreted as essentially modernist, along the radical, 'alternative' lines developed by Nyman's definition of an 'experimental' aesthetic. Like Cageian indeterminacy, they represent an American reaction to the serial models of modernism offered by European composers such as Pierre Boulez and Karlheinz Stockhausen, and by American serialists such as Milton Babbitt. All four subjects of this volume have criticised serialism, in particular, as irrelevant not only to their own concerns but also as a musical, and cultural, mistake; Reich and Glass have been particularly vitriolic in their comments on what might be called the establishment modernism of the European serialists working after the Second World War, and on the validity of pursuing, either aesthetically or technically, the achievements of the Second Viennese School. In 1986, Reich protested to Tim Page: 'Don't get me wrong. Berg, Schoenberg and Webern were very great composers. They gave expression to the emotional climate of their time. But for composers today to recreate the angst of "Pierrot Lunaire" in Ohio, or in the back of a Burger King, is simply a joke'.[33] In 1991, Glass was more directly critical of the activities of Boulez and the European serialists in the 1960s, speaking of 'a wasteland, dominated by these maniacs, these creeps, who were trying to make everyone write this crazy creepy music'.[34]

Such dismissals have been frequently paralleled by the denigrations poured on musical minimalism by composers, critics and others from the Western classical tradition. The aesthetic starting points for these sometimes even more barbed criticisms are wide-ranging. Conservative and anti-modernist commentators such as Samuel Lipman suggest that minimalism is 'merely a pop music for intellectuals'.[35] Adherents of high-modernist tendencies such as the so-called New Complexity would probably agree with one of their chief spokesmen, Richard Toop, when, quoting Roland Barthes, he asserts that '[t]he "transparent impenetrability" of recent music by composers such as Glass and Adams is, I believe, a result of their having acquiesced to the culture industry's demand for consumable objects, finished products, for "an art that inoculates pleasure (by reducing it to a known, coded emotion)"'.[36] It is true, though, that Toop's strictures are not meant to apply to all so-called minimalist compositions: he himself makes exceptions of 'the stubbornly nonconformist work of La Monte Young or Philip Corner'.[37] But even more open-minded writers like William Brooks have interpreted Riley's *In C* – still the emblematic example of musical minimalism – as an affirmation of mass culture comparable to Warhol,[38] whose initial rise to fame coincides with the period in which many other compositions discussed in this book were written. Not only, however, is it possible to interpret Warhol's Pop Art aesthetic quite differently (see above), but Riley's cunningly contrived lack of control over the materials he unleashes – in his earlier tape pieces as well as in his own improvisations – surely makes his explorations of sound dangerous as well as delightful.

Besides, matters are not as simple as such polar oppositions suggest. As we shall see, the minimalism of all four composers discussed here has some of its roots in European modernist achievements. While Riley's enthusiasm for free-atonal Schoenberg and the early works of Stockhausen, surprising though it may be, can be argued as merely a stage on the road typical of any composition student attempting to find an individual path, Young drew directly on both free-atonal and twelve-note Webern in the formation of the pioneering minimalism with sustained sounds which strongly influenced Riley's development of a modal, pulse-based style. And while Glass's extensive pre-minimalist output is mostly couched in a rather conservative brand of what is usually called neo-classicism, both his very earliest minimalist efforts and some of the music Reich was writing on the way to his own mature style deploy a dissonance level and technical procedures which owe clear debts to the Second Viennese School.

Just as Boulez and Cage found common ground in the late 1940s and early 1950s in their use of procedures the details of which were generated by forces outside their conscious control, so it is possible to make connections between integral serialism and minimalism: a commitment to the consequences of rigorous application of processes independent, to a significant degree, of the composer's note-to-note control is evidently the key here. Taking these ideas further, Parsons, an English 'experimental' composer with a serial pedigree, has developed a long-standing interest in exploring the relationships between systems in music and an English tradition of 'Systems art', in the work of artists such as David Saunders and Jeffrey Steele. Parsons has pointed to the new kinds of unity between material, sound and expression that such rigorous and, to some, fundamentally unmusical concern with process can bring about. 'The system liberates the medium', he quotes his close associate, Skempton, as saying, adding that 'the expressive quality of the sound itself is revealed'.[39] The involvement of these and other British composers and artists with repetition remains sufficiently severe to exclude the exploration of psycho-acoustic effects: the illusions conjured by the combination of fast repetition and high dynamic level in Glass's music, or the optical illusions of Op Art such as Bridget Riley's. Op Art is denounced by Parsons as 'degenerate': an opinion with which Reich, despite his interest in psycho-acoustic phenomena, would seem to concur.

The most rigorous of the four American composers, Reich was likewise fascinated by a formalism generated by processes discovered and fed with musical material but then left to run their course. Transcending the limitations which inevitably conditioned the human imagination's ability to come up with new structures, as well as materials, this approach led naturally – indeed, with an inevitability clearly attractive to such a composer – to an acceptance of the results, just as Cage was happy to do with the consequences of indeterminacy. But while the processes Cage used were, like those of serialism, 'compositional ones that could not be heard when the piece was performed',[40] as Reich put it, what he himself wanted was 'a compositional process and a sounding music that are one and the same thing'. Minimalist music's purchase on perception is in this case a highly structural one, closely integrated with the process of composition itself. This is the main reason to agree with Bernard when he argues that 'the music of chance ultimately served the minimalists as a negative ideal, an example of what not to do, in their efforts to create a viable alternative to (what they came to see as) the needless and overly intellectual complexities of serialism'.[41] 'I don't know any secrets of structure that you can't hear',[42] wrote Reich, delighting in the transparency of his musical procedures. 4'33" itself, though, cuts through the elaborate chance-derived schemes Cage devised for many of his other works to make the listener's perceptions operate with a different kind of focus. And Reich's discovery of phasing in fact has much in common with Cageian musical practice: the use of raw material drawn from everyday life, for instance, and its roots in the observation of a process happening independently of its composer's conscious control.

In the late 1960s, Glass shared a similar formalist concern, and neither he nor Reich was happy with the results of what he was doing until he had discovered a process of his own with a sufficient degree of rigour to be closely followable by the listener. Young's kind of rigour is different, but his obsession with exploring the innards of a complex sound continuum makes him the most uncompromising of the four composers; the fact that he is 'wildly interested in repetition, because [he thinks] it demonstrates control'[43] offers a further insight into his special and extreme position. As suggested above, the modernist credentials of Riley – whose early music comes nearer than that of anything Reich or Glass composed before the mid-1970s to suggesting a celebratory spirit untinged by more cerebral challenges – are perhaps less easy to argue. As we shall see, however, the critical dimensions inherent in his work go beyond obvious matters such as the transcendence, and subversion, of established modes of listening posed by his all-night concerts of the late 1960s and early 1970s.

Robert Carl[44] and Kyle Gann[45] provide a persuasive amplification of the view that the musical minimalism under discussion here can valuably be viewed from a modernist perspective. More recent interpretations – such as that of Björk, who celebrates minimalism's ability to 'shake off that armour of the brain'[46] which has, for her, constricted so many twentieth-century developments – suggest different origins and functions for musical minimalism. Again, though, distinctions between the minimalism of the 1960s and the (post-)minimalism of the 1990s need to be borne in mind; Björk was referring specifically to Arvo Pärt, whose religious aspirations for his work are shared by many other composers today – Henryk Mikołaj Górecki and John Tavener being just two of them – but, among the four subjects of this book, only by Young and Riley. Even the idea of minimalism as a necessary antidote to the ills of late twentieth-century society, however, has some common ground with another approach to the matter, despite the background of what follows in theories of modernism.

A further modernist interpretation of such early minimalism can be developed with the aid of a Formalist critique dating from much earlier in the twentieth century. In the 1920s, the Russian Formalist Viktor Schklovsky suggested that the goal of all art is its 'defamiliarisation' of things which have lost their impact, and even become invisible to us, through habit. 'Habitualisation', he wrote, 'devours objects, clothes, furniture, one's wife and the fear of war. . . . Art exists to help us recover the sensation of life, it exists to make us feel things, to make the stone *stony*. The end of art is to give a sensation of the object as seen, not as recognised. The technique of art is to make things "unfamiliar", to make forms obscure, so as to increase the difficulty and duration of perception'.[47]

Both serialism and indeterminacy had already sought to encourage new perceptions through the search for new kinds of musical material and its manipulation, and Cage's openness to the familiar as well as the unfamiliar had complemented this search for new vocabularies and grammars with something akin to Schklovsky's 'sensation of the object as seen, not as recognised'. Minimalism goes much further, however, in taking a fresh and more focused look at single pitches, modal fragments, regular rhythmic structures and – in its later developments – chords and simple chord progressions. By selecting some of the oldest and most familiar building blocks of music, and subjecting them to the radical scrutiny afforded by remorseless repetition, it takes on the challenge of revitalising the most hackneyed and debased musical currency available. Minimalism forces its listeners to reinterpret the familiar not only through the microscope of their own perceptions and sensations, but also via the energies generated by processes driven by the same forces – regular pulse and apparent forward motion – which had underpinned the goal-directed approaches of Western tonal musics of the previous few centuries.

Interpreted – by Mertens, for example – as fundamentally different from post-Renaissance Western music of the cultivated tradition in its activation of rhythmic repetition to reject teleology altogether, such music already has the potential to 'make forms obscure, so as to increase the difficulty and duration of perception'. Interpreted – as I would prefer to do – as encoding a much more complicated set of clashes and contradictions of the grammars available for such a simple vocabulary – of which this potential non-teleology is but one – musical minimalism has the capacity to harness the development of active modes of listening in order to 'complete the work'. Such a 'metaphysics of experience', to requote Baker, forces a radical reappraisal of familiar musical objects, conquering habit to make the aural equivalent of the stones *stony*. It also makes common cause with the arguments – probably first advanced, again, by Mertens – connecting the evolution of musical minimalism with post-modernist and post-structuralist concerns such as Barthes' declaration of the 'death of the author'.[48] While Glass's recent music reminds Toop of Susan Sontag's depiction of works 'to which the audience can add nothing',[49] perhaps even he would acknowledge the different approach which this composer's early music encourages. Some would say, however, that Glass's early scores require their listeners to make a contribution to the business of 'completing the work' so large as to call any meaningful input by their author into serious question, though I myself would not go that far.

Just as Minimalist art acted as a critique of a commercialised society and challenged its viewers to adopt new modes of perception, so minimalist music – whether excavating the innards of sound, like Young's work, constructing rigorously assembled sound objects, like the early works of Reich and Glass, or offering counterpoints in textures often sufficiently dense to frustrate any attempt to untangle them, as in Riley's output – required new modes of listening. Even Brian Ferneyhough – a scourge of musical minimalism, like many other kinds of modernist composers and their adherents – acknowledges a certain kinship based on the fundamentals of musical perception and on the greater focus modernists, and post-modernists, from Duchamp onwards have offered on the necessity for the viewer or listener to 'complete the work'. 'All music', as he points out, 'is many-layered. . . . Our ears impose upon us, with any listening process, a number of possible strategies which we're constantly scanning and assessing, and . . . finding a new distance or new perspective in relation to what we're hearing at that particular moment. It's one of the few possible justifications for minimalist music, for instance: that the maximalisation comes through the individual, rather than through the object'.[50]

Mertens' insistence on a fundamentally anti-teleological interpretation of such music seems, as I have already suggested, to limit its potential, despite what I have said above concerning the advantages of the new musical structures which the rigours of process have helped create. The harnessing to his argument of the view that, unlike the dialectical music of the Western classical tradition, minimalist music is 'non-representational and is no longer a medium for the expression of subjective feelings'[51] leads him, however, into some interesting, and wide-ranging, discussion of post-structuralist and post-modernist ideologies of the kind raised above, which could valuably be pursued in ways for which there is no space here, particularly in the context of more recent music.

In a 1990 article, Elaine Broad begins some elaboration of Mertens' position in terms of an aesthetic characterised by 'the conception of the *non-narrative work-in-progress*'.[52] Suggesting that '"stasis" is precisely the wrong word to describe a music that . . . depends so heavily upon time as a vehicle',[53] Bernard suggests, on the other hand, that – like those Minimalist artists (he cites Morris, Jo Baer, Dan Flavin, Agnes Martin and Le Witt) who deal with temporality via gradual and/or systematic progress through a series of possibilities – the minimalist composers draw attention to the passage of time by 'composing out' the possibilities of their material in a followable manner. Though he acknowledges the fact that what he calls 'the more recent work of Glass, Riley, and Reich' is 'brand[ed] "Post-Minimal"', Bernard himself does not seem to see the distinction being made with this label. He refers to it only to suggest that what he calls the 'serial principle' involved in such composing out applies equally well to the later music as to the earlier, and uses this as the justification for continuing to apply the term 'minimal' to both.

Arguments concerning the changing focus of these composers' music up to, and beyond, the mid-1970s are advanced at least somewhat by Timothy A. Johnson's 1994 attempt to discuss the term minimalism as aesthetic, style and technique. His suggestion that 'minimalism may be defined most fruitfully as a technique'[54] allows him to take technical aspects such as 'continuous formal structure' and 'repetitive rhythmic patterns' and trace their use in the music of Reich and others beyond the mid-1970s, surviving the abandonment of minimalism as he defines it aesthetically and stylistically. While his discussion runs into difficulties – for example, that of confusion between 'style' and 'technique' – his argument does something to clarify the notion of a 'post-minimalist' approach.

For the present writer, the differences between the work of these composers, and even of the more single-minded and maverick Young, from the mid-1970s onwards and what they produced in the years before that period is sufficiently significant to make the mid-1970s the cut-off point for the stories told here. While continuing to activate their music with the crucial ingredient of repetition – or, in Young's case, more often sustained sounds – all four composers have, in their more recent outputs, found ways of recuperating aspects which what we might call their earlier, hard-line minimalism had deliberately negated. Melodic profile, timbral variety and sheer sonic allure all added new dimensions that made their music richer and deeper, at least from a conventional Western classical perspective. While the first two of these aspects in principle encouraged the cultivation of a cleaner textural profile – a clear separation into melody and accompaniment, for instance – the increasing interest in texture *per se* brought with it less chance of hearing whatever processes were controlling its note-to-note details. Most significant of all, however, in this 'post-minimalist' music, is the arrival of a kind of harmonic motion: a development which naturally interacts in a variety of ways with the other new aspects, and with the ongoing energy of repetition itself, but which tends towards musical results in which harmonic progression, and sometimes a more encompassing narrative development across broader spans of time, becomes more important than audibility of the sorts of note-to-note processes more characteristic, in any case, of the earlier music.

At this point in the story, Young proves himself capable of highly idio-syncratic feats of fantasy with the melodies and chord sequences which he incorporates into a minimalist idiom still quite evidently his own. Riley's work takes on a surprising variety of styles, some redolent of the jazz to which he has always been closely attached, some more indebted to classical traditions, Western as well as his beloved Indian. Reich retains his contra-puntal concerns, dovetailing them with considerable ingenuity into the new forms he creates with this clearer harmonic profile. Harmonic motion and melodic ingenuity have allowed the especially prolific, and sometimes undiscriminating, Glass to write everything from large-scale operas to pop songs.

While it certainly seems necessary to distinguish these developments by the use of a different term – whether 'post-minimalist' or even 'post-mod-ernist' – the extent to which even the earlier, more truly minimalist, output of the composers can be called 'static' has already been called into ques-

tion. My own view is that the role of harmonic motion, of however putative a kind, proves crucial to an understanding of the music which these
composers were writing in the early 1970s, and that various notions of
hierarchy even play a part in their earliest minimalist compositions. The
analyses which follow are designed, in part, to test out the arguments of
Mertens and others for this music's essentially anti-teleological status.
Particularly interesting here is Jonathan Kramer's concept of a 'vertical
music' free of hierarchies as well as teleology.[55]

In deciding on just how to place such early minimalism in the context of
twentieth-century musical history, the approach adopted by the Prague
School of Linguisticians may assist us, in conjunction with Schklovsky's
already mentioned 'defamiliarisation'. Experimentation with any particular new materials or ideas in itself over time becomes dulled by familiarity:
a process which generally involves adding layers of increasing complexity
to the original. To employ the terminology of these 1930s Czech successors
to 1920s Russian Formalism, fresh stimulation will then need to be sought
by placing in the background what had previously been foregrounded. The
early outputs of Young, Riley, Reich and Glass may thus be interpreted as
foregrounding the modal materials and repetitive formal schemes set aside
by the fragmented discourses of serialism and indeterminacy, and also
challenging the capacity of such materials and structures to come up with
something quite different from the reassuring continuities of a neo-
classicism which, surviving until beyond the 1950s, had long ago lost its
cutting edge. Once this had been accomplished, a so-called 'post-minimalism' was then similarly required to counter the modernist reductiveness of
early minimalism, foregrounding extended melodic materials and harmonic progressions more readily associated with earlier Western musics,
and more obviously narrative structures.

Attention must be drawn to the vital significance for the development of
all four of these composers of musics outside the Western classical tradition. Most obvious among these are the non-Western traditions to which
Tom Johnson makes reference, which have had a powerful influence on the
spiritual development, and lifestyle, of Young and Riley, and which have
also influenced Reich and Glass. Jazz – in particular the so-called modal
jazz developed by John Coltrane and others around the time that the four
subjects of this book were finding themselves, musically speaking – has
been a significant influence on all of them except Glass.

Minimalism – at least of the kinds being examined here, in both the fine
arts and in music – is rooted in American culture. Among many others,
John Rockwell has campaigned for the necessity of treating the history of

music in the USA as 'a dialogue between the "cultivated" and the "vernacular"';[56] though he suggests that '[b]efore the 1960's, by and large, the vernacular side of the dialogue was mute, silenced by the academic, cultivated view of what music was and should be'. Russell Jacoby has argued that the Beat Generation of 1950s American writers (Allen Ginsberg, Jack Kerouac and so on), soaked in the jazz of their time, had a crucial role in the popularisation of High Art for Americans;[57] they certainly helped to produce the cultural climate in which Young and Riley first flourished in late 1950s San Francisco, just as they had also contributed to the Greenwich Village 'alternative' culture of a decade earlier.

Sally Banes argues that it was only when the work of the early 1960s artists of a younger generation 'circulated transgressive ideas in what would ultimately become acceptable packages'[58] that a true counter-culture was created by 'the first generation of postmodern artists':[59] her initial list includes the Judson Dance Theater and Poets' Theater, the Living Theater, Warhol and the film-maker Kenneth Anger. It is here – in the so-called 'downtown' scene of New York's Greenwich Village and SoHo in the 1960s and 1970s, and in the extent of its overlaps with the so-called hippie culture of which it formed part – that we find the wider cultural context of most immediately impinging relevance for the work of all four composers discussed here. The Manhattan artistic community that spawned many of the artistic developments which have fed into the continuing story of musical minimalism and 'post-minimalism' in part owed its existence to purely practical aspects: the low rents for large loft spaces available in downtown Manhattan in the 1960s and 1970s, for instance, and the (relatively) high technology that was beginning to become available, and affordable.

With its new version of the 'happy babble of overlapping dialogues – not just cultivated and vernacular, but European and American, white and black, male and female, East Coast and West Coast, Occidental and Oriental . . '.[60] that Rockwell identifies as the story of America's musical history, this 'downtown' community offered much more than radical art practice spiced with the *frisson* easily gained via a few 'vernacular' borrowings. As part of this wider range of endeavours, musical minimalism confronted the contradictions between the 'cultivated' tradition in its more radical guises and the 'vernacular' roots with which so many of its practitioners felt perfectly at ease.

More widely still, of course, there is the context of a specifically 'Sixties' counter-culture with roots on the USA's West Coast and ramifications which are international in scope, even though many of the hippie trappings famously associated with the Haight-Ashbury district of San

Francisco percolated out to give a powerfully American flavour to the developments which followed in the wake of this radical critique of capitalism. Ironic in the manner in which it helped spread specifically American values as well as fashions and mannerisms to an international community already primed by the Americanisation of the 1950s, and too quickly compromised by its remarkably easy commodification by the very institutions it had set out to undermine, that so-called counter-culture was nevertheless a very real force in a climate primed for change of every kind: social and political as well as cultural in the narrower senses of the term.

Though nurtured by the hothouse artistic community of 1960s and 1970s downtown Manhattan, musical minimalism was actually spawned in Young's California, while Riley, who brought about its second phase, has spent most of his life on the West Coast. It is typical of the contradictions seemingly inherent in this 'happy babble of overlapping dialogues' that it is the latter composer who simultaneously seems responsible for the early commercial breakthrough of minimalism via its assimilation into late 1960s rock culture, and today – along with the still less well-known Young – continues most evidently to uphold the spiritual values of a 1960s ethos engulfed by the subsequent waves of attack on its principles and practice.

In a cultural climate such as this, it might be argued that only those – like the already mentioned Greenberg or, to take a famous example from musical discourse, Theodor Adorno[61] – who preach an aesthetic completely antithetical to commercial contamination or who practise an art totally untainted by worldly constraints, such as the serialism of Milton Babbitt, can claim to be the true proponents of a critically modernist stance. Discussions of cultural realignment, meanwhile, to say nothing of such accusations of pre-emptory commercial capitulation, might suggest the characterisation of early, as well as later, minimalism as post-modernist rather than modernist in character.

A willingness to engage with 'vernacular' traditions is one of the few aspects widely accepted as a defining characteristic of post-modernism. We should be wary, however, of the conflicting arguments which continue to rage around any attempt to characterise post-modernism more fully, and in particular of the gulf that exists between what Hal Foster has called a 'post-modernism of reaction' and a 'post-modernism of resistance'.[62] While the former might involve an uncritical re-embracing of such matters as the commodification of culture, the latter, which Foster argues is the genuine post-modernism, requires the kinds of radical engagement characteristic – as I have argued elsewhere[63] – of Nyman's theory of 'experimental music'. Such a 'post-modernism of resistance' offers potentially fertile territory for any future that 'experimental music' might have. Already mentioned concepts such as that of the listener 'completing the work' would here extend naturally to others, such as Barthes' famous, and already mentioned, argument regarding the 'death of the author'.

For a composer of a younger generation, such as the American David Lang, the musical minimalism of the 1960s and 1970s which is the subject of this book can best be defined in political, rather than aesthetic, terms. His vision of it is as a weapon with which to challenge the hegemony that had been constructed around the serialism from which I argue minimalism itself in part derived. While it offers another perspective for viewing what that downtown culture, and musical minimalism itself, now represents, it also attempts to confront the consequences for those who come after it. Minimalism, he says,

> was a historic reaction to a sort of music which had a stranglehold on
> American musical institutions, and which none of us really liked. . . . What
> most people really hated was the way that this other world had theorised that
> it was the only music possible . . . I look at minimalism . . . as being just the
> battleground that was necessary to remove those forces from power: not to
> obliterate them or destroy them, but . . . to loosen up the power structure in
> America. And I think that [one reason why] Glass's music and Reich's music
> came out so severe, and so pared down, was that . . . it was a polemical slap in
> the face. . . . That battle's been fought. . . . My job is to sift among the ashes
> and rebuild something.[64]

1   La Monte Young

La Monte Young's career divides geographically into three parts: his child-hood and undergraduate years mainly in Los Angeles; his time as a gradu-ate student at Berkeley, in the San Francisco Bay Area; and the period that saw his establishment as both composer and performer, as well as concert organiser, teacher and much else, following his move to New York City. Young was almost twenty-three when he went to Berkeley; just twenty-five when he moved to settle permanently on the East Coast. In terms of his output as a minimalist, the story begins while he was still an undergradu-ate, and becomes of substance with a composition he took with him when he went to northern California to begin graduate studies. Young is not only the first true musical minimalist, but was producing radically innovatory work at a much younger age than Riley, Reich and Glass: some of his most important compositions were written when he was twenty-one and twenty-two.

Central to Young's development is his tendency to combine an involve-ment with improvisation – an involvement so extensive that the distinc-tion between composition and improvisation sometimes becomes hard meaningfully to preserve – with a concern to establish a firm theoretical base for his music. The latter contributes to his slow rate of creative output as much as it productively intertwines with it. Not least among the effects of these things is a tendency to work on a composition over many years: extending its theoretical investigations, adding to its material, and testing ideas through improvisation. The best example of this is *The Well-Tuned Piano*, which originated in a tuning devised in 1964 and some improvisa-tions made using it, and which, over thirty years later, is still open-ended, at least in principle. It makes little sense to abandon consideration of this in the mid-1970s; accordingly, the story of this major work will be taken beyond the present book's official cut-off date. Young also continues to use material originally conceived for use with the famous group he had with John Cale, Tony Conrad, Terry Jennings, Terry Riley, Marian Zazeela and others in the mid-1960s, which makes it difficult to establish clear lines of chronology and closure. Some aspects of Young's development – for instance, his move away from ensemble work and towards solo per-formances, to which the first sustained and successful period of work on *The Well-Tuned Piano* in 1974–5 contributes an important statement –

mark the mid-1970s as something of a watershed in his development. Yet many of the essentials of Young's aesthetic, style and techniques were firmly established by the mid-1960s, thus making detailed commentary beyond this period less important to an understanding of his significance.

Wim Mertens divided Young's output into the customary three periods.[1] Though not an entirely accurate reflection of the composer's development, they provide a useful point of departure. Mertens characterises the compositions of 1955–8 as 'serial music'; Young discovered what came to be called 'sustenance',[2] the use of long sustained sounds, while working with serial principles as a basic framework. Mertens' 'second period' covers the years 1959–61; this was the period when, under the influence of John Cage, Young moved away from conventionally notated compositions and into a range of performance art works that are commonly – though in Young's view erroneously – included as an integral component of the Fluxus movement which flourished in the early 1960s and beyond. The third and final period begins in 1962, characterised by Mertens as the 'actual repetitive period'. Mertens was writing in 1979, and other ways of dividing what is now a period of over three decades are available besides that which pinpoints the mid-1970s. One could, for example, argue that Young's more recent return to ensemble work – with The Forever Bad Blues Band and Big Band, both reincarnations of The Theatre of Eternal Music newly inspired by his old love, jazz – represents a new 'period', beginning in 1990. Yet it still seems sensible to view the obsessive concern with 'sustenance' and drones, which dominates almost everything the composer has done since the early 1960s, as one long development: emerging from his discovery of long tones in the 1950s, and separated from this by a short period of more theatrical – but still crucially related – activities.

No scores by Young are published in any conventional sense and few commercial recordings of his work exist.[3] For many years, he habitually made access to would-be interviewers extremely difficult and, to this day, all private tapes can be listened to only in his loft, while scores and documentation are lent extremely selectively. That documentation is extensive: no activity in his daily life, whether musical or otherwise, is too insignificant to escape the tape recorder, the photocopier or the filing cabinet. Between 1979 and 1985, the Youngs took advantage of the lavish sponsorship bestowed on them by the Dia Foundation in the ordering, notation and copying of some of this material. While the archive he jealously guards with the help of Zazeela – his constant companion – and several assistants is not as thoroughly catalogued as it would be in the hands of a professional librarian, it could form the basis of an extensive biography far beyond the aims of the present book.

Early years

La Monte Thornton Young was born in a log cabin in Bern, a Mormon hamlet in Bear Lake County, Idaho, on 14 October 1935. His parents – Dennis and Evelyn – were poor; when the composer was born, his father was a shepherd. Young relates that 'the very first sound that I recall hearing was the sound of the wind blowing under the eaves and around the log extensions at the corners of the log cabin'.[4] In an earlier interview, he describes this as 'very awesome and beautiful and mysterious; as I couldn't see it and didn't know what it was, I questioned my mother about it for long hours'.[5] Continuous sounds – man-made as well as natural – fascinated Young as a child: the humming harmonics of the step-down transformer at the local power plant; train whistles across the river; lathes and drill presses; wind, insects, water, trees. The telephone poles in Bern produced a continuous chord from which, much later, he recalled the four pitches he named the 'Dream Chord', basing many of his mature works on it. Southern California, in general – with its 'sense of space, sense of time, sense of reverie, sense that things could take a long time, that there was always time'[6] – helped Young to conclude from an early age, well before he encountered the ideas of Cage, that the external world was quite possibly more fascinating than art.

Young's early years in this Idaho dairy community dominated by Mormon values was not, however, bereft of musical experiences. The composer says that the harmonica was the first instrument he ever played; 'however, at the age of two, this was soon followed by singing and guitar lessons from my Aunt Norma, who sang in the local high-school operettas [and rodeos]. The songs I learned to sing at that time were cowboy songs'.[7] He played his maternal grandparents' piano a little. When he was aged three or so, the family moved to Montpelier, the nearest town to Bern, where he also had tapdancing lessons; at the age of four, he was singing and tapdancing at Montpelier's Rich Theater. The family moved to Los Angeles when Young was five, to Utah when he was ten, and then back to settle finally in the Los Angeles area when he was about fourteen. Young did not learn to read music until he was seven, when he began learning the saxophone, taking lessons from his father. His first performing experience on this instrument came via Mormon services. The saxophone – first alto, later tenor and, particularly, sopranino – was, though off and on, his main performing outlet until 1964. Between 1951 and 1954, he had lessons on the clarinet as well as saxophone with William Green at the Los Angeles Conservatory of Music.

Between September 1950 and June 1953 Young attended the

John Marshall High School in Los Angeles, a rough school which was nevertheless known for its music making and was capable of attracting at least a few artistic and intellectual high fliers. His harmony teacher, Clyde Sorenson, turned out to have been a pupil of Schoenberg at the University of California, Los Angeles; Sorenson, who played a recording of the Six Little Piano Pieces, op. 19, first introduced Young to Schoenberg's music. While in high school, he accompanied the dancing of an Apache friend, encountering native American music for the first time. As he points out, American Indian music, like the cowboy songs he learned in early childhood, is essentially static. But Young's most important high-school musical experiences came through jazz.

Jazz was Young's first love, and though not a direct influence on most of the first compositions he would now regard as his own, it dominated his musical activities as a teenager. It was later to have a considerable influence on his music. Almost the first thing he did on returning to Los Angeles in 1950 was to join a Dixieland band that played outside every morning before school classes began. He played extensively in his high-school and early college days; jazz was, he says, 'the burning thing'. John Marshall High School had a strong jazz tradition and high playing standards. Young's jazz-playing schoolfriends included Pete Diakinoff, a tenor saxophonist who advised him to study with Green and introduced him to the latest trends in bebop and cool jazz; and David Sanchez, known as 'Gordo', a precocious trombonist – and local gang leader – who had already been on the road with Perez Prado's band by the time he was in tenth grade (aged about fifteen). Young and his friends were often hired to play for dances, but never asked back since they were considered too modern. 'I stopped playing in dance bands for money, accepting dance gigs . . . because I only wanted to play pure jazz', he says.

From September 1953 – by which time he had moved out of the family home to live with his paternal grandmother – to June 1955, Young attended Los Angeles City College, studying counterpoint and composition both in school and privately with Leonard Stein, who had been Schoenberg's disciple and assistant. In February 1956, after further private work with Stein, he registered for a year at Los Angeles State College, additionally returning to Los Angeles City College for the fall semester of 1956. In January 1957, he enrolled for three semesters at the University of California at Los Angeles; here he majored in music, taking music theory, composition and ethnomusicology, and some English, finally obtaining his BA in June 1958. Composition studies were undertaken with Boris Kremenliev and John Vincent; Lukas Foss, then running one of the earliest free-improvisation groups, also encouraged him. He was, in addition, a pupil of Robert Stevenson, who taught him Baroque and sixteenth-century counterpoint and keyboard harmony.

At UCLA, Young encountered a fellow student called Dennis Johnson when he heard him practising Webern's Piano Variations, op. 27; the two became firm friends. Johnson – whose own compositions (only rarely publicly performed after his student days) would, for a while, also be influenced by Young – was to become, says Young, the only person in the late 1950s besides Jennings and Terry Riley to understand his music. Johnson's role, Young says, 'along with that of Terry Jennings, was extremely important in the formative years of minimalism in the late 1950s through 1961 and 62. Dennis developed some of the most original and feelingful ideas about music, including the social implications of concerts and venues, of anyone I had ever met'.[8] Johnson's idealism was to lead to the withdrawal of his work from public performance, since he ceased to believe that the concert arena had any worth for the presentation of serious music. In 1959 or 1960, he once described to Young an outline for a piece to be 'staged in some far away wooded countryside . . . heard only by those who just happened to come across it by happenstance'. The overall conception of this – and in particular the plan for the musical material to consist of a perfect fourth 'which would sound for a long time from some far away undiscoverable place' before falling a minor third and continuing at the new pitch – was evidently influential on Young's subsequent development.

At Los Angeles City College Young had continued his involvement with jazz, competing successfully against Eric Dolphy for the second-alto chair in the award-winning City College Dance Band; the first alto was a brilliant player called Lannie Morgan. (In the College Symphony Orchestra, Dolphy played first clarinet, Young second.) Young additionally played in the College Jazz Combo. He was invited by the pianist Don Friedman to join his trio, which ultimately led to the formation of Young's own group with the guitarist Dennis Budimir, the drummer Billy Higgins, and the bassist Hal Hollingshead, which played regularly at Studio One in downtown Los Angeles. Others sat in from time to time, including the trumpeter Don Cherry, whom Young already knew, and guitarists Buddy Matlock and Tiger Echols, the latter of whom became an important influence on Young's early blues playing. The earliest surviving recording of Young performing appears to be a 'demo' disc of 'All the things you are', made in the summer of 1955, on which he plays with this group. By that time, he was living in Hollywood with friends, plus his step-uncle Kenny Young, who moved in a social circle which included James Dean and Vampira.

Other jazz experience gained at this period included occasional performances as featured soloist with the Willie Powell Big Blues Band. Also playing in this primarily black and Mexican band was another white alto saxophonist, the then thirteen-year-old Terry Jennings: a pianist and clarinettist, but ultimately most brilliantly a saxophonist, who had recently entered John Marshall High School and whom Young had already heard on tape. Jennings was to become a close associate for many years. During jam sessions around Los Angeles, Young played sets with Ornette Coleman; both Cherry and Higgins later became members of Coleman's original free-jazz quartet.

When in school and college, Young had at first intended making a career in jazz. Stylistically, he seems to have been ahead of many of his playing colleagues; he favoured an approach, influenced in particular by the saxophone playing of Lee Konitz and Warne Marsh, which tended to fragment the beat. Though surviving tapes of his playing at this time suggest a move towards the kind of 'free jazz' Coleman was shortly to pioneer, Young began to feel jazz's limitations: 'Jazz is a form, and I was interested in other forms'.[9] His involvement with jazz peaked in 1955–6; Young's decision not to register for the fall semester of 1955 at City College was due partly to his wish to play more jazz sessions. A piece called *Annod* – a twelve-bar blues in a style influenced by the playing of Konitz and Miles Davis on George Russell's *Ezzthetic* (1948) and *Odjenar* (1949), and perhaps particularly by Johnny Carisi's 'Israel', one of Capitol Records' landmark 'birth-of-the-cool sides' with Davis, recorded in 1949–50 – was written some time between 1953 and 1955. *Annod*, which spells the name of a girlfriend (Donna Lee Lathrop) backwards, includes a ten-bar bridge that abandons melody and regular beat and employs a degree of polytonality; its composer claims it as a precursor of both his later use of sustained sounds and what he came to call the 'Dream Chord'.

By the time Young moved to UCLA in January 1957, he had for the moment abandoned serious saxophone playing 'and was really headed into composition. I never took up jazz in the same way ever again'. Jazz nevertheless returns as a direct influence on his work from about 1962, when he took up the sopranino. And he considers that 'many things about jazz absolutely never left me: for instance, the fact that I became so interested in improvisational forms'. In addition to the better-known influence of jazz on his later saxophone playing, he also began to develop a style of piano improvisation based on the standard twelve-bar blues. Called 'Young's Blues' by the composer, it was characterised at this stage by a continuous alternation of the chords in the left and right hands – for example, in a left-*right*, right-left, right, right-left pattern – which Young

Example 1.1 'Young's Blues', characteristic rhythmic structure

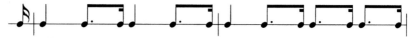

describes as 'ka chunk chunka chunk chunka':[10] see Example 1.1. The detailed evolution of this 'Young's Blues' style is far from clear. Riley recalls that Young's blues playing in the practice rooms at Berkeley in 1958–9 was at first in the form of 'funky bebop in the right hand over some sort of walking bass in the left hand'. Then, one day at Riley's house on Potrero Hill, he recalls Young playing in the later characteristic 'ka chunk chunka chunk chunka' style and saying, 'This is something new I'm working on'; after this, Riley never heard his friend play blues in any other way. Other evidence – for example, the testimony of the tenor saxophonist Michael Lara, a friend of the composer's from his Los Angeles City College days – suggests that 'Young's Blues' originated some four years earlier, or even as far back as 1953. But it was only fully developed much later when he began playing regularly with Jennings in New York.

The significance of jazz was in any case shortly to become intertwined with an influence equally compelling, and arguably even more important, in Young's later development: that of non-Western musics in general and North Indian classical music in particular. The realisation that a classical art form could also involve improvisation helped feed an interest in the creative potential of performing that had initially been nourished by jazz. In addition, the approach to harmony in both jazz and a variety of non-Western musics – very different from that of Western classical music – is clearly an important influence on Young's development of 'static' structures.

Young's education on the West Coast allowed him at least some contact with non-Western musics as early as 1957. Strolling one day, he heard Indian music broadcast across the UCLA campus: an experience which sowed the seeds of what was to become important to him a decade later, and eventually an overwhelming preoccupation. Young cites an early recording by Ali Akbar Khan (sarod) and Chatur Lal (tabla) – of two ragas, *Sind Bhairavi* and *Piloo* (heard on the radio and then purchased) – as particularly influential, since it 'essentially introduced the longest example then available of masterfully played Indian music'.[11] Perhaps at least as importantly, it provided him with his first opportunity to hear the drone instrument, the tambura, with its timbral harmonic array, played solo at the beginning of the recording by Shirish Gor. Young says that this experience had a profound effect on him, furthering his interest in sustained sounds and harmonics; the tambura eventually became the instrument he played in his studies of vocal music under Pandit Pran Nath. In 1961–2, two other Indian musicians – the shenai player Bismillah Khan and the South Indian flautist T. R. Mahalingam – became the major influences, along with John Coltrane, on Young's sopranino saxophone playing.

UCLA had a particularly good ethnomusicology department, with its own student gagaku orchestra and Japanese instructors; Young listened a lot, but did not attempt to play. The combination of precision and serenity found in gagaku, in the context of a sense of musical time quite different from that of most Western musics, has been acknowledged by him as a significant influence on *Trio for Strings*, in particular. Quite early on, he also heard plainchant and organum on records. Later, while at Berkeley, he visited a local Dominican monastery to hear chant. This, however, was only after he had pursued – to quite new, and extraordinary, conclusions – the dominant modernist musical aesthetic and technique of the day: serialism.

Towards serialism, and away from it

Young's earliest compositions were, he says, written in the style of Bartók, with some additional influence from Debussy. These include Variations for String Quartet (1954); 'after that', the composer reports, 'Leonard Stein announced to people that I was a composer'. He had also been attracted to serialism; he says that his schoolteacher's association with Schoenberg made him 'predisposed to the twelve-tone technique'.[12] Like Pierre Boulez and Karlheinz Stockhausen, however, Young preferred the freely atonal compositions of Schoenberg to his twelve-note ones. 'Farben', no. 3 of the Five Orchestral Pieces, op. 16, was singled out for comment: not surprisingly, since what he called its 'mirage-like motifs disappearing and reappearing over recurrent droning textures'[13] exhibit precisely the qualities – static, drone-based, essentially repetitive – of Young's later music. He had little interest in the more conventionally thematic approach of Schoenberg's twelve-note works.

It was Webern who was more useful to Young in pointing the way forward to a new 'static' music. On going to college, Young came to Webern largely through Stein, and investigated a post-Webernian idiom for himself. Webern's integration of serial technique and motivic materials interested Young more than the sorts of integral procedures being developed 'out of Webern' by the Europeans; so did the extent to which Webern's serial processes were audible. But it was the apparent contradiction between an aesthetic still rooted in the dynamism of classical forms and a resulting music that was often essentially static that probably fascinated him most. One technique of significance to Young, as to others, was Webern's tendency to repeat pitches at the same octave, as found, for instance, in the Symphony, op. 21, and the Variations for Orchestra, op. 30; though he seems not to have appreciated the potential of this until after he composed *Trio for Strings* in 1958. This brought greater structural clarity; it also suggested the constant repetition of material to create what Young saw as a non-developmental form of striking economy. Thinking along these lines, twelve-note music easily became understood as 'the same information repeated over and over and over again, in strictly permuted transpositions and forms, which recalls the thirteenth-century use of cantus firmus';[14] European Renaissance music had, after all, also been a strong influence on Webern. The latter's influence on Young was not, however, confined to the twelve-note works; in Webern's Six Bagatelles for String Quartet, op. 9, he heard 'little static sections, like a chime, or a music box, or time ticking off'. Webern and, more selectively, Schoenberg turned out to offer models as potent for the development of a 'static' music as did jazz and non-Western musics.

In developing his idea of minimalism using serialism as a direct inspiration in the creation of an innovative static style, Young by no means ignored the twelve-note method's usual function of generating non-tonal pitch material. As a result, his early but already highly individual approach to minimalism has more in common with other, more conventionally non-tonal, modernist musics than does the early minimalism of Reich or Glass. Yet while Young's compositions of 1956–8 adopt the basic principles of the twelve-note method, they soon depart quite radically from any of the styles to which the method had previously given rise. Webern may have used sparse textures; but Young quickly takes economy of material to such an etiolated extreme that the term 'minimalist' becomes the most natural word to describe it. The most striking difference between Young's music and earlier twelve-note and serial practice is its increasing reliance on sustained notes. His choice of intervallic vocabulary – rejecting thirds and sixths in favour of perfect intervals and major sevenths – is, however, also important. These tendencies culminate in *Trio for Strings*, the most remarkable work of this period; its extremity alone should guarantee its place in the history of musical minimalism.

In the evolution of Young's serial compositions from exercises in Second Viennese twelve-note music to the establishment of 'sustenance' as his own mature minimalism's chief concern, the extent and function of sustained sounds provide the main point of reference. These already play a role in the Five Small Pieces for String Quartet (2–16 November 1956), the

earliest of Young's compositions to receive more than very occasional performance today. Young says that the Five Small Pieces, written when he
'was deep into my studies with Leonard Stein . . . were the first works that I
composed using twelve-tone row technique'.[15]

The pervasive atonality of the Five Small Pieces, in which individual
intervals nevertheless emerge as prominent, shows an obvious debt to
Webern. But they also include, in their composer's own words, '[l]onger
static sections of pulses and ostinato figures, and even a hint of the sustenance to come in my later works'. Interestingly, the subtitle of the Five
Small Pieces – 'On Remembering a Naiad' – suggests the Romantic
imagery conjured by Schoenberg's op. 16, no. 3 (subtitled 'Summer
Morning by a Lake'), or by Webern himself in his own accounts of his
compositions, rather than post-Webernian abstraction. Variations for alto
flute, bassoon, harp and string trio (11 February 1957), apparently
inspired in particular by the palindromic variation structures of the
second movement of Webern's Symphony, op. 21, emphasises the perfect
fourths and fifths and major sevenths that were to become characteristic of
Young's later music; significantly, too, these intervals can be contemplated
in the silences that surround them.

Young had not yet abandoned more conventional idioms. Other pieces
from 1957 are simply exercises: the Prelude in F minor for piano, for
instance (24 March), was written as 'a personal assignment in $\frac{5}{8}$ meter' for
Stevenson's Baroque counterpoint class at UCLA; yet in 1989 Young numbered it among his favourite compositions. A Canon for two instruments
(24 April), an assignment for Kremenliev, demonstrates the fledgling composer's 'enthusiasm for the contrapuntal disciplines as applied to serial
technique and developed in the works of Schoenberg and Webern'. It was
played on two pianos at UCLA by the composer and Johnson, but it can be
performed by almost any two melodic instruments, or even as a piano solo.
Even after he went to Berkeley, Young was responding to his teachers'
requests to write, for example, 'a work in a Baroque dance form, but using
a "modern" scale'. The result in this case – a Sarabande for piano (late 1958
or early 1959) using major-seventh chords with a minor third – actually
emphasises the very intervals, major and minor thirds, which he had
already made a characteristic of avoiding. This mixture of works is hardly
surprising in a twenty-one-year-old or even twenty-three-year-old
student. What is surprising is the significance Young today ascribes to even
so obviously exercise-like a piece as the Prelude: it is a good example of his
obsession with the significance of everything he does.

for Brass (the lower case f is deliberate), completed only four months
after the Variations, is already a much more independent statement.

Example 1.2 *for Brass*, bars 54–66

*- Harmon mute with plunger extended

Finished in June 1957, this is a single movement lasting, according to the score, thirteen-and-a-half minutes for an octet consisting of a pair each of French horns, trumpets, trombones and tubas. It is the first of Young's works to use sustained notes as more than an incidental feature. According to its composer in 1966, the middle section of *for Brass* introduces 'notes sustained easily for three or four minutes . . . [N]othing else would happen except other occasional long notes overlapping in time, and there would be rests for a minute or, at any rate, a few beats, and then another long note or chord would come in'.[16] Inspection of the score and a performance on tape reveal that this is rather an exaggeration. In the section in question, single notes, dyads and trichords, even a single four-part chord – presented just twice – are characteristically held for between twenty and thirty seconds, though some are shorter (see Ex. 1.2). Silences, too, vary only between about five and eight seconds in length.

Throughout *for Brass*, the intervals of the perfect fourth and fifth and the major seventh predominate, frequently presented by the pairs of the octet's instrumentation. The set on which the work is based emphasises these intervals. The opening two pairs of pitches (G♯, A, G♯ and D) also form what the composer was later to call the 'Dream Chord', and it is this which becomes the real building-block for the whole work; 'throughout the work', he has written, 'numerous examples of the Dream Chords are stated at various transpositions for the first time in my music'.[17] This was the chord inspired by his childhood experiences of the hum of telephone-pole wires. Young in fact formulated four 'Dream Chords', described in more detail below with respect to *The Four Dreams of China* (1962). Their characteristics – stress on secundal and quartal intervals, and avoidance of thirds, both major and minor, but particularly major – now became the basis of Young's harmonic vocabulary, as he began to formulate his 'own musical mode'. 'I began to realize', he has said, 'that this interval of a major third didn't convey any of the feelings that I was interested in'.

In the context of major sevenths such as C B, omission of the major third – either as E above C or G below B – also permitted what Young argues is 'the true character'[18] of the equal-tempered major seventh (eventually to be translated into the ratio 17:9 in *The Four Dreams of China*) to emerge unencumbered by 5:4 associations above the dominant G, or 3:2 associations above the major third E. (There is a difference of only 1.05 cents between the equal-tempered and the just-tuned 17:9 major sevenths, even less than the 1.96 cents' difference between the equal-tempered and the just-tuned 3:2 perfect fifths.) Either, or both, of these associations tend to establish the more conventional tonally functional leading-note character of the 15:8 major seventh. The notion that 'the major third sounded worn out and used up' was later to receive theoretical justification when Young began to investigate just intonation and the expression of intervals as ratios using prime numbers. More generally, the particular qualities contained in the simplest of intervallic relationships had, for him, already taken the place, both structurally and expressively, of those aspects of music – thematic, tonal, serial or whatever – which most other composers regard as their basic building-blocks.

Though the outer sections framing the slower middle one – forming what is basically a three-part arch structure with coda – are durationally less extreme, these basic methods obtain throughout. While even the held notes of the middle section, which forms an exact palindrome, are not as consistently long as those of the later *Trio for Strings*, they already signal the adoption of a technique which turns Webern's pulverisation of musical grammar to quite new ends. Though *for Brass* also fails to exploit low dynamics with the bare-faced consistency that characterises their use in the *Trio*, it remains an unusually radical and reductive statement for its time.

The other composition of significance in the evolution of the *Trio*'s style is *for Guitar*, completed on 21 June 1958, just before work on the *Trio* began. While not actually longer than those of *for Brass*, the long notes and silences of *for Guitar* are more consistent and pervasive. The application of these for the first time to an instrument incapable of sustaining a note for any length of time without fast repeated attack causes a quite different relationship to develop between sound and silence. *for Guitar* makes ingenious use of the possibilities the acoustic guitar offers for resonance; as a result, the work perpetually hovers in the territory between the decay of a sound and its total absence. The composer's own description of the work stresses the extension of what he calls 'my concept of abstract musical form which included identical and similar pitch constellations set in durational permutations occurring at points sometimes separated by long periods in expanded time structures'.[19] The outer main sections of *for Guitar*'s four-part-plus-coda structure may still be audibly relatable, partly through the use of the same registers on repetition; and the second section (much longer than the first) is another exact palindrome. But the use, particularly in the third section – which extends the 'abstraction' of *for Brass* without the aid of a palindromic structure – of similar overlapping techniques to those of the earlier composition frees both repetition and silence to work more comprehensively to confound any attempts to make sense of the music as a balanced, goal-directed whole.

In a work for a single instrument, Young is almost bound to focus on fewer pitches at once; in general, *for Guitar* is more reductive and more rigorous. As before, he tends to avoid thirds and sixths, though the bottom E and open G string of the guitar inspire the occasional minor tenth. While *for Brass* had formed 'Dream Chords' from pairs of characteristic intervals, *for Guitar* generates what its composer calls 'three-pitch subsets' of the 'Dream Chords' by dividing the basic set – of eleven notes this time – into small groups, rather as Webern did. The outer sections focus almost exclusively on secundal dissonances: both narrow seconds and wide sevenths and ninths. Young himself sees the beginning and end of *for Guitar* as being in E-Phrygian, though as Example 1.3 illustrates, foreign notes are soon added. The third section introduces a perfect fourth (G♯ C♯), a perfect fifth (C♯ G♯) and a range of longer single pitches. Despite the potential these offer for establishing a modality, the prevailing impression is much more elusive.

Young did not find a performer for *for Guitar* at the time of its composition and it remained unplayed until 1979, when Ned Sublette, who had

Example 1.3 *for Guitar*, bars 1–3

practised this extremely difficult work for three years, gave its première. A version using just intonation, made the year before this, was eventually performed by Jon Catler in 1986.

Trio for Strings

Trio for Strings was composed in Los Angeles with the help of experiments made on the pipe organ at UCLA's Royce Hall, one of the city's main concert venues, and copied in Berkeley, where the date of 5 September 1958 was added to the score. The work is cast in a single movement; an accurate observation of its metronome markings implies a performance of fifty-eight minutes. The most striking aspect of the work is, of course, its reliance on long sustained notes. Young has written that the *Trio* 'is the first work that I composed which is comprised almost entirely of long sustained tones. It is probably my most important early musical statement, and I feel it actually influenced the history of music since no one had ever before made a work that was composed completely of sustained tones'.[20] While long notes – and their counterpart, silences – had been important components of *for Brass* and *for Guitar*, in *Trio for Strings* they constitute the work's material and essence.

The opening viola note C♯, for instance, has been timed from an actual performance at 4'23";[21] and though it lasts longer than the two notes by which it is surrounded – the first on violin, the second on cello – it proves to be by no means 'eccentric' in the context of the work as a whole. (Example 1.4 reproduces the first two pages of the score.) Silences, too, punctuate the texture quite frequently; though they are much shorter than many of the sustained notes, some last as many as forty seconds. As with *for Brass*, each instrument's sequences of pitches in the *Trio* are not designed to be played 'as individual "parts", but as contributions to a chordal unit whose components are of different durations'.[22] This makes the function of the lengthy silences clearer: they separate the chordal units so that they may be experienced as individual, isolated phenomena.

Some *scordatura* is necessary to achieve the full range; both viola and cello are required to tune to the B♭ a tone below their usual bottom pitch. Though the *Trio* employs, according to the score, 'an absolute scale of eleven perceptible dynamic gradations (*pppppp* to *fff*)', much of the work is extremely soft, as well as slow. Another important aspect of the *Trio* is the method of performance: '*senza* vibrato. Vibrato should not be used at any time, *ever!*' says the score. The effect should thus consistently be of a timbre from which all colour has been bleached. This is but one of many special challenges for the players that the *Trio* creates; the range of less familiar techniques includes *flautando* and *col legno*, as well as quite extensive use of harmonics. Young also requests 'the production of a smooth, steady bow stroke while also minimizing the audibility of the change of bow direction so that the long sustained tones sound as uninterrupted as possible'. Even – or perhaps especially – in this context, the instruction to make 'the difference between adjacent dynamic markings (e.g. *ppp* to *pp*) just perceptible' seems a tall order. The focus and concentration the work requires also has an effect on the listener's experience of the *Trio* in concert. 'The sculptural qualities of the sound', as Dave Smith says, 'are reinforced in performance by the statuesque appearance of the players'.[23]

The entire pitch material of the *Trio* is derived from a twelve-note set, the subdivisions of which form two-, three- and four-note groupings based on the 'Dream Chord'. Within these groupings, Young confines himself almost entirely to the intervals of the minor and major second, the perfect fifth and the possible inversions of these, again avoiding the major third. The only interval included in the work's articulation of these groupings besides those given above is, Young says, 'a very occasional augmented eleventh'. Such thirds as occur between groupings play no part in the harmonic articulation, and are in any case separated by substantial silences.

The basic pattern is established at the outset. A single note (in this case, the viola's C♯) is sustained throughout the unit; to this are added a further two notes (in this case an E♭ on the violin and a D on the cello), disposed in a strict durational symmetry about the held C♯. (See Ex. 1.5 for a graphic representation of this.) Examination of Examples 1.4 and 1.6 will show the sort of variations on this pattern which Young immediately establishes. The opening trichord (C♯ E♭ D) is followed by a group of four notes (F♯ B F♮ E). Here, an initial dyad (rather than a single note) is sustained throughout, while the third of the four pitches, F, is repeated prior to the entry of the final one, E, and again later. Then we have another trichord (B♭ A♭ A♮), consisting of an initial dyad to which a single pitch is added; and finally a fourth group consisting of a dyad (C G) on its own.

Example 1.4 *Trio for Strings*, pages 1–2

Subsequently, this set is fragmented into further representations of the 'Dream Chord' in a variety of ways. The next statement of the set, for example, presents an inverted form (I-9), whose initial trichord (B♭ A♭ A♮) turns out to be identical, in pitch-class, to that of P-0's third unit; each note enters separately according to a new, overlapping durational scheme. The second unit is also of three notes this time (F C F♯), returning to the simple symmetry of the opening. Instead of completing the presentation of I-9 with two further trichords, the F♯ from group 2 is repeated, overlapping with G♮ to form group 3. We are now left, again, with five pitches, divided, as before, into three (E♭ C♯ D; again, identical in pitch-class to the first group of P-0) and two (B E) to complete the statement of I-9 without the

Example 1.4 (*cont.*)

aid of any further durational symmetry. It should be observed that, like the rest of the *Trio*, this statement frequently fails to respect the registral dispositions of the set's initial presentation.

In a variety of spacings and transpositions, this set and its attendant 'Dream Chord' divisions provide all the material needed to fill out the whole structure of the *Trio*, each group of long sustained notes unfolding in turn for the listener's contemplation before a silence separates it from the next. While the means of elaboration vary considerably, the constant alternation of chordal unit and silence increases the audibility of a structure devoid, like Webern's, of tonality or modality. A music is offered in which a minimum of material is slowly laid out before the listener in such

Example 1.5 *Trio for Strings*, duration structure of first trichord

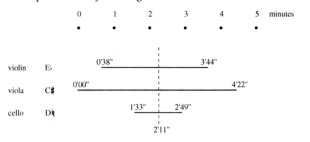

Example 1.6 *Trio for Strings*, twelve-note procedures

"Exposition"

"Recapitulation"

an extended form, the connections between units becoming in the process so fragile, that a totally new form of listening must be developed. *Trio for Strings* seems to be the ultimate 'static' music.

Or is it? When asked about the structural audibility of the *Trio*, Young talks not of allowing the listener to meditate on the minutiae of each unit's 'perfect' deployment of pitch stripped to bare essentials and suspended in time on a potentially endless stream of symmetries and asymmetries, but of the extent to which it may be heard in terms of the formal thinking which apparently helped him compose it: sonata form. He insists that the work has 'extraordinarily deep roots in Classicism, both of the West and of the East', and that it was conceived as an exposition–development–recapitulation–coda structure articulated not so much by the twelve-note organisation as by pitch centres and by development as well as repetition. To suggest that the 'exposition' consists of the first twelve notes, the initial unfolding of the set itself, certainly makes sense in terms of sheer duration, since the music moves so slowly that these notes take more than ten minutes to play. (Example 1.4, in fact, includes this 'exposition', reproduced complete.) And since this does indeed lay out the *Trio*'s basic material, it may not seem too far-fetched to describe the ensuing twenty minutes or so in terms of what Young calls 'a long kind of variations type of development section,' and the last fifteen or twenty minutes as 'a recapitulation of the exposition in a special set of permutations', followed by a coda which includes the thirty-one bars' duration of the concluding C G dyad in the cello – the longest single note or chord in the entire work.

We have already examined the opening of Young's 'development' section in analysing the statement of I-9. As an example of how the basic material of the 'exposition' is reworked in the 'recapitulation', let us take the opening's first and third chordal units. The first unit of the 'exposition' (Ex. 1.6a) consists of a 'major-second' dyad (C♯ E♭) underpinned by the note (D) a major seventh below its lower pitch ('one of my favourite voicings', says Young). The third unit (Ex. 1.6b) already presents this in a different, and transposed, form: the 'major-second' dyad has now become a minor seventh (B♭ A♭), and the underpinning note (A) is now just a semitone below. At the beginning of the 'recapitulation' (see Ex. 1.6c), the opening 'major-second' dyad has become a minor seventh (E♭ D♭), underpinned by the original pitch-class D now just a semitone below: in other words, the pitches of Example 1.6a in the voicing of Example 1.6b. Similarly, in Example 1.6d – the third unit of the 'recapitulation' – the minor-seventh dyad has become a 'major second' (G♯ B♭), underpinned by the original pitch-class A now a major seventh below: in other words, the pitches of Example 1.6b in the voicing of Example 1.6a.

If this hardly suggests the kind of evolutionary structural manoeuvres to be found in Beethoven, it surely makes it less surprising to learn that Milton Babbitt apparently admired Young at about this time, though he may not have seen any of the *Trio*. But its composer makes other claims for the work's links with the Western classical tradition. The *Trio* is, he avers, 'a rather tonal piece. It's in some sort of C . . . probably . . . C-minor . . . . It doesn't start there, but it gets there: in the cadence of the exposition and in the cadence of the recapitulation and in the cadence of the coda'. The first of these 'cadences' can be seen towards the end of Example 1.4: concluding on the C G open fifth of the cello. This is certainly the work's first clear consonance; Young himself speaks of it as concluding 'a kind of modal cadence', in which the preceding B♭ A♭ dyad, to which A is then added, produces an effect 'a little bit like a Landini cadence'.

While the glacial progress of this exposition in actual performance will be likely to produce an effect drastically different from its effect on the eye in the form of little more than a page of manuscript, the very attenuation created by the music's speed must surely help blur the listener's ability to distinguish between 'atonality' and 'modality'. Yet the result will, of course, hardly resemble the dynamic tonality of sonata practice. More interesting than the above details themselves, perhaps, is the fact that Young apparently thought about the material of *Trio for Strings* in this way. One might have expected that the purveyor of ideas as radical as those he was about to unleash on the New York avant-garde could have created a work of such stunning originality only by jettisoning the baggage of 'tradition' entirely. We should not forget the continuing influence in the *Trio* of jazz and Indian music and, in particular, that of Japanese gagaku, as well as whatever influence Western classical music still exerted on his thinking at this time. Modality, not atonality, was to provide Young with the key to his mature development, but his ability to synthesise elements from a wide range of musical traditions into multifaceted compositions is a hallmark of his development.

Now 'refined and perfected', as its composer calls it, the approach already identified in *for Brass* and *for Guitar* is here taken to extremes. In excluding 'almost any semblance of what had been generally known as melody', Young may not have entirely purged his music from past associations. But he had certainly created music with a degree of reductive focus – both of means and of expression – unusual, if not unique, in Western composition of the time. Edward Strickland has suggested that the 'dodecaphony' of the *Trio* could be argued as 'exclud[ing] the harmonic stasis theoretically afforded by tonal organisation'.[24] Yet the models Young had selected from the output of the Second Viennese School suggested that both free atonality and the twelve-note method could produce music much more static than anything propelled by the dynamism properly implied by 'tonal organisation'. Besides, Young had shown that it is possible to 'freeze out' the linearity implied in twelve-note theory, and often used as a prop in twelve-note practice, while continuing to use its basic techniques. Even the long silences, which Strickland also argues '[interrupt] the musical continuum',[25] call linearity into question in a context so removed from that of traditional musical discourse – not least in dynamic level – that what he calls a 'reciprocity' between sound and silence allows a new kind of continuity to develop. The *Trio for Strings* is undoubtedly Young's most important composition of this period, and the work which firmly establishes his place as the first composer to discover a truly minimalist language and to develop it in a totally individual way.

Young himself has described this revolution in terms of a move from 'ordinal' to 'cardinal'.[26] Serial technique, he argued, was essentially 'ordinal', being based on a linear sequence of pitches. The increasing emphasis 'on concurrent frequencies or harmony in my work', on the other hand, 'implied the possibility of the organization of the cardinal values both in regard to how many frequencies are concurrent and the relationship of the frequencies to each other'. The first stage, accomplished by the *Trio for Strings*, was to release the twelve-note method from its linear origins. The second was to continue the search for an 'absolute music . . . evolving from the universal truths of harmonic structure'[27] without the shackles that method inevitably imposed.

This 'cardinal' thinking was to lead to Young's investigation of tuning systems and new kinds of harmony in the 1960s. And though some of the thrust of this acoustic research appears very theoretical – Young has a firmer grasp of acoustic theory than most composers – it was rooted in the search for music one could unravel to an unusual extent by ear. The twelve-note compositions of Schoenberg, even Webern, and certainly those of the emerging younger generations had serial structures resistant to aural identification. By contrast, Young's emphasis on longer notes made 'harmonic analysis by ear a reality'.[28] And it was this desire to get inside the harmonies he was creating that led him to become dissatisfied with the imprecisions and limitations of the equal temperament which he had up to now accepted as the foundation for his work as a composer. The use of a circumscribed number of intervals – and in particular, his natural predilection for perfect fourths and fifths – was already leading him towards a Pythagorean approach to the harmonic series, and its attendant aesthetic. By investigating the possibilities of just intonation, Young was eventually to discover new 'integral relationships' which 'soon sound much more beautiful and harmonious and correct than their irrational equal-tempered approximations'. In 1984, he even produced a version of *Trio for Strings* using just intonation.

Could a modal, rather than Webernian, approach to pitch materials combine with the other elements Young had already selected from musics both Eastern and Western to provide a more permanent way forward for a new music? In the long term, the answer was emphatically yes. The use of long sustained notes and modal pitches derived from just intonation inspired by non-Western models gave Young 'other organizing factors' which became 'more interesting and pertinent' to his work. In the short term, however, Young became occupied with – and in certain respects sidetracked by – other concerns. The main influence on his output over the next two or three years was Cage.

Berkeley and Darmstadt: towards Cage, and away from him

In September 1958, Young moved north to the Bay Area and enrolled as a graduate student at the University of California at Berkeley. (He had seriously considered going to Princeton to study with Babbitt who, through the intervention of Stein, had apparently been enthusiastic about *for Brass* and *for Guitar*. Babbitt, though, had a bad car accident that year and was unable to teach for a while.) For two years, he studied composition – first with Seymour Shifrin, later with Charles Cushing and William Denny – as well as analysis (with Andrew Imbrie). For his first year Young had received a Woodrow Wilson Fellowship, and in his second year he became a teaching assistant.

He took with him to Berkeley the *Trio for Strings*, which he had been composing during the summer vacation. It was the first score he showed to Shifrin who – though more open-minded than some of his academic composing colleagues – was, not surprisingly, highly critical of its radical reinterpretation of Webernian principles and, given his own Schenkerian predilections, presumably doubtful about Young's attempts to create a music so patently devoid of voice-leading. He was sufficiently concerned for his new pupil, however, to arrange for a performance of the *Trio* at one of the 'musicales' for graduate composers held in his own home. Shifrin seems to have been unconvinced that Young could hear his own composition's structure; the performance was designed as a demonstration of the piece's unworkability.

The première of *Trio for Strings* was accordingly given privately that autumn by student players – Oleg Kavelenko, John Graham and Catherine Graff – to a very small audience. Nearly all its members were Young's fellow composition students in Shifrin's class, several of whom would later become well known for very different kinds of music; these included David Del Tredici (especially admired as a pianist at this time), Jules Langert, Pauline Oliveros and Loren Rush. 'Almost everyone thought that I had gone off the deep end',[29] Young recalls. Few of his colleagues, and none of his teachers, subsequently took Young very seriously; though it should be pointed out that Oliveros subsequently developed her own style of minimalism based on sustained sounds.

The only friend of Young who appears to have developed any real understanding at the time of what he was doing missed the *Trio*'s première. Terry Riley didn't register officially at Berkeley until the spring of 1959; though he visited the campus, at the suggestion of Rush, some time in October or November to check out its suitability for his own studies, he wasn't present at the performance. It was through this visit that Young and Riley first met; their friendship began to develop even before Riley officially became a fellow student. Riley's sympathetic recollections of Young at this time make clear that his image, as well as his music, was strikingly, bafflingly innovative. Young, he says, 'had one of the weirdest images of anybody I'd seen. You have to remember this is the '50s, when everybody was very straight-looking, and La Monte looked like he'd just drifted in out of the '60s . . . So he was the most psychedelic-looking person in the class'.[30]

By 1957–8, Young says, he 'was beginning to discover reasons for moving beyond the twelve-tone system'. At Berkeley, however, he continued to write several more fully notated scores in a style now owing much to 1950s serialism. The titles of his solo piano pieces of 1958–9 – *Studies I, II* and *III* – suggest the impact of Stockhausen, with whose work he was starting to become familiar. *Study I* (finished on 18 January 1959, and written for Del Tredici to play) was circumscribed by the conditions imposed by Shifrin, who had told Young after hearing the *Trio for Strings* that he was 'writing music like an eighty-year-old man',[31] and that he 'should be writing music with lines and climaxes, vitality and youth' in order to receive a grade. The piece used serial methods and sharp contrasts in order to show his teacher 'that I could indeed write music that more overtly included elements that have come to be considered the conventions of our tradition', but still contained sections of more spare, sustained sounds, as well as fast music 'somewhat inspired by Stockhausen's "as fast as possible" writing'. *Study II*, begun in the spring of 1959, also for Shifrin, remained unfinished.

Meanwhile, other interests were compelling Young's attention, and contributing to his 'reasons for moving beyond the twelve-tone system'. Between his two years at Berkeley, he went to Europe. On his way east, he stopped over in New York. There he met Richard Maxfield, whose tape music especially impressed him; Maxfield was shortly to become his teacher. But the object of Young's quest that long vacation was the 1959 Darmstadt Summer School, where he was to participate in Stockhausen's composition class. Stockhausen, Young says, 'had made a very powerful impression on me', and he wished to find out more. He had intended to go to Darmstadt with Dennis Johnson who, having accompanied him to New York, contracted pneumonia and had to abandon the trip. Young took with him scores of *Trio for Strings* and *Study I*.

Stockhausen, according to Young, praised the *Trio*, though – perhaps rather untypically – its composer waited nervously until his last day in Darmstadt before producing it for his inspection. Young does not seem to have been viewed very seriously by many of those at Darmstadt, though he got on well with a few of his fellow students, including Sylvano Bussotti, Cornelius Cardew (then Stockhausen's assistant), Friedrich Goldmann, Heinz-Klaus Metzger and Ernstalbrecht Stiebler. Stockhausen, however, seems to have approved of both *Study I* and of *Study III*, the latter of which Young composed during the course (it is dated 3 September 1959).

Stockhausen's ideas about the integration of pitch and time, in particular, seem to have struck Young as having greater potential than, say, Babbittian serialism. *Study III*, at some twelve minutes, was his longest and most substantial piano piece so far. It follows on from *Trio for Strings* in its use of sustained notes and long rests in conjunction with a serial structure, to which the Webern-influenced technique of repeating pitches at the same register is now rigorously applied. As with *Study I*, though, this texture is several times broken up by short, faster sections which reveal the influence of Stockhausen and make the piece far less minimalist than some of its predecessors. Even its Stockhausen-influenced aspects – the 'entire work is based on the number seven'[32] – failed to gain *Study III* anything more than a rather cool reception from apparently sophisticated colleagues, who considered it 'somewhat radical and abstract'. David Tudor was supposed to play the piece during a student composition concert, but the score mysteriously disappeared – and was only rediscovered too late. Tudor, though, began to perform Young's compositions in New York and in Europe the following year.

Young's major discovery at Darmstadt was in fact not Stockhausen but Cage. In what now seems a generous gesture – considering, not least, the battle then being waged between Stockhausen and Boulez for domination of the European avant-garde scene – Stockhausen devoted much time to Cage in his composition seminar that year. Though Cage himself was not present, he had made a significant impression at Darmstadt the year before; and in 1959, Tudor was again on hand to play his work, as well as that of Bussotti and others. Curiously, Young had not come to grips with either Cage's ideas or his music before. 'In those days', he said in 1966, 'there was no Cage on the West Coast, except on records. Dennis Johnson had played the recording of the Sonatas and Interludes for Prepared Piano for me maybe once, and Terry Jennings had a record of the String Quartet which we used to listen to, but I had to go to Europe to really discover Cage'.[33] In a later interview, he stressed the importance of the First String Quartet, 'Cage's best piece'.[34] Darmstadt even provided Young with his first exposure to Cage's lectures, in written form. The recording of the première of *Concert for Piano and Orchestra*, completed the previous year, was 'played on an impressive sound system'.[35]

In Young's 1966 interview with Richard Kostelanetz, Cage's influence on him is acknowledged by the composer himself in the form of two specific matters: 'the use of random digits'[36] and 'the presentation of what traditionally would have been considered a non- or semi-musical event in a classical concert setting'. To these we should add Cage's concern with the discovery of new sound sources. *Vision* and *Poem for Chairs, Tables,*

Benches, Etc. (or other sound sources) – two of the four main works Young composed during his final year in California before beginning the *Composition* series – use random numbers 'as a method for determining the inception and termination of the sounds'. They also constitute the composer's first 'algorithmic scores', as he calls them: rule-based compositions in which words, and sometimes other forms of notation, provide the instructions to the performers. The idea of 'live friction sounds', as he refers to it, used in *Poem*, is further explored in the other pieces of this period, notably *2 Sounds*. In all these, the influence of Cage manifests itself in aesthetic, as well as technical, matters.

Vision (12 November 1959) consists, according to its composer, 'entirely of unconventional sounds articulated on conventional instruments';[37] the work is scored for an ensemble of twelve instrumentalists, including a recorder player and four bassoonists. Its performers are ranged around the perimeter of the auditorium and the work is played in darkness. Each sound is precisely described in the score, but the duration and spacing of these sounds within a total time of thirteen minutes must be calculated with the aid of a random number book or telephone directory. Silence, with which the piece begins and ends, continues to be an important feature. The composer's tape of the Berkeley première in December 1959 bears out his assertion that *Vision* 'created a major stir with the audience and the faculty, since apparently nothing quite so radical had ever been heard at the University'.[38]

Poem (21 January 1960) was, in the mid-1960s, 'probably the most widely performed of all La Monte compositions', according to Cardew;[39] Cage and Tudor introduced it to New York before Young's own arrival there. The initial inspiration for the piece may have occurred in the Berkeley laundromat. 'I vividly remember trying out the large, heavy wooden benches', Young has written, 'which when pulled or pushed across the cement floor produced unimaginably beautiful sustained tones'.[40] One can detect Cage's influence on this work in Michael Parsons' observation that 'sounds of the kind specified in *Poem*, sometimes regarded as an affront to the ear, can actually be quite beautiful if one concentrates on listening to them'.[41] The score specifies in detail the techniques required for pushing and dragging 'ordinary, readily available furniture . . . across an engaging floor surface'. As in *Vision*, random numbers determine the number of events ('any number including zero'), the duration both of each event and of the performance as a whole ('any length including no length'), the points at which events begin and end, and the relationship of available sound sources to the duration scheme.

In the instructions for *Poem*, we can also see the influence of Cage on

Young. What is missing is almost as telling as what is prescribed. Since no rules are given concerning the size of the unit to be used to measure the duration of the events, this could, as Michael Nyman points out, be 'quarter of a second, hours, days, years',[42] thus enlarging the potential field of perception considerably. But since the composition may be 'any length including no length', chance may, as Nyman says, determine that nothing at all is perceived, thus taking the work into the realm of the purely conceptual. As Cardew observed, *Poem* 'developed into a kind of "chamber opera" in which *any* activity, not necessarily even of a sounding variety, could constitute one strand in the complex weave of the composition, which could last minutes, or weeks, or aeons. In fact it was quickly realized that all being and happening from the very beginning of time had been nothing more nor less than a single gigantic performance of *Poem*'.[43] *Poem* is then, as its composer suggests, 'the forerunner of my 1960 conceptual word pieces'[44] and of all Young's subsequent 'algorithmic scores' too.

The moving furniture of *Poem*, its composer discovered, was 'but one subset from an entire genre of live friction sounds, such as gong on cement, gong on wood floor, metal on wall, with which I worked at that time'. In *2 Sounds* (April 1960), Young extended these ideas with the aid of tape. The following account was given by Cardew in 1966, based on performances of the work for Merce Cunningham's ballet *Winterbranch* (1964) in London two years earlier. (Cage selected *2 Sounds* for Cunningham: evidence of Cage's continuing enthusiasm for Young's work.)

> The composer had provided two sounds on separate tapes, to be started at different points during the ballet. When the first sound starts you cannot imagine that any more horrible sound exists in the whole world. Then the second sound comes in and you have to admit you were wrong. That is an exaggerated account of the piece given by one of the managers of the dance company.[45]

Though the work could have used other 'friction sounds', the tape of *2 Sounds* recorded by Young consisted of tin cans scraped across window panes (which he improvised with Riley), and a drum stick scraped around a gong (which he improvised alone).

This single-minded attention to 'friction sounds' also marks the beginning of Young's attention to harmonics as the central, or even sole, focus of a musical experience. *Poem* and *2 Sounds* – both, when under their composer's control, frequently producing an ear-splitting roar – make possible the production of 'very unusual sets of harmonics', he says, 'which I enjoyed listening to for long periods of time'. Begun in earnest in *Trio for Strings*, and followed up in the compositions of 1959–60, Young's concern to 'give ourselves up to [sounds]',[46] to get 'inside of them to some extent so that we can experience another world', was occasionally to be deflected by other concerns over the next couple of years. But the work done with live friction sounds eventually contributed a great deal to the essential characteristics of Young's output from the early 1960s onwards.

2 Sounds, in particular, provides a link to another important dimension of Young's activities during his student years at Berkeley: his work with the choreographer and dancer Ann Halprin. In 1959–60, Young was musical co-director of her company, providing music for her dances in collaboration with Riley. Halprin made use of *Trio for Strings* for a dance entitled *Birds of America or Gardens Without Walls*, premièred in San Francisco on 29 November 1960, after Young had left for New York. But the music Young and Riley produced for her consisted largely of live friction sounds, *2 Sounds* being but one example. According to Riley, 'we were dragging things across glass to make these sounds. . . . Then we also used to drag garbage cans down stairs and stuff like this when she was dancing, to make really incredible clatters'.[47]

The many performances, both formal and informal, which they gave with Halprin's company included a concert at UCLA's Schoenberg Hall on 22 April 1960. On this return trip to Los Angeles, Young also played piano at a session at the home of Jennings's parents which was important for the further development of 'Young's Blues'; the group on this occasion consisted of Young on piano, Jennings (alto saxophone), Johnson (hichiriki) and Lara (tenor saxophone). Among the performances Young organised at Berkeley was a pair of concerts shortly after this – on 2 and 6 May 1960, entitled 'Collaboration Event: To' – mounted in conjunction with the Department of Architecture. These programmes included a performance, in an open courtyard, of *2 Sounds* with a further, subsequently discarded sound, that of triangles in buckets. The third performer, in these events, with Young and Riley, was the sculptor – and drummer – Walter de Maria, who had also played jazz with Young in the Bay Area.

One composition produced by Young in the context of his work with Halprin made a small but significant departure from this employment of continuous sounds. *Arabic Numeral (any integer), to H. F.* is also widely known as 'X for Henry Flynt', to whom it is dedicated. (A Harvard-trained mathematician, Flynt became a significant member of the circle around Young in New York.) The score requires a pianist to repeat a single loud cluster, using the forearms, a large number of times, at equal intervals of between one and two seconds. The curious title thus refers to the number of repetitions selected by the performer. This decision should be made in advance, the number then forming part of the title: for instance, '1698 (to

Henry Flynt) (April 1960)', to choose a taped performance of 3 March 1961 by the composer himself with which he seems especially happy. Though the piano is specified in the score, Young first performed the piece – in April 1960 at one of Halprin's rehearsals – using a drumstick on a gong. It may, according to the composer's worklist, be played by 'piano(s) or gong(s) or ensembles of at least forty-five instruments of the same timbre, or combinations of the above, or orchestra'.

In performance, it becomes clear that what are usually regarded as sounds of indefinite pitch in fact contain a rich variety of both acoustic and psycho-acoustic phenomena: harmonic partials, combination tones and so on. A further dimension of the piece's interest lies in 'the stress imposed on the single performer and through him on the audience',[48] as Cardew has put it. 'What the listener can hear and appreciate are the *errors* in the interpretation. If the piece were performed by a machine this interest would disappear and with it the composition'. *Arabic Numeral* is one of only two works by Young to use repetition, the method favoured by all the other composers discussed in this book, rather than the sustenance for which he has become famous; its employment of repetition predates Riley's early tape compositions by over two years and his *In C* by two more. Despite its untypical aspect, it is a particularly fine and characteristic example of Young's tendency 'to concentrate on and delimit the work to be a single event or object'[49] in contradiction to Cageian multiplicity.

In the summer of 1960, Young and Riley taught composition at Halprin's summer school in Marin County. Not surprisingly, their course was somewhat unconventional: Young says, for instance, that he required the students 'to go out and collect bugs and things, and put them in paper bags'. Here, he also delivered 'Lecture 1960'. This rather Cageian mixture of philosophical pronouncements and anecdotes – featuring Riley, Jennings and Johnson – is perhaps most notable for a statement that Cage would not have made:

> Often I hear somebody say that the most important thing about a work of art is not that it be new but that it be good. . . . I am not interested in good; I am interested in new – even if this includes the possibility of its being evil.[50]

Among those attending this summer school were Trisha Brown, Simone Forti (at that time married to Robert Morris) and Yvonne Rainer, all of whom subsequently became important choreographers and dancers. Forti's husband Morris – later to become a famous sculptor – was also present at the Marin County summer school; his own interest in performance art had been stimulated by Halprin and continued for several years. A tendency towards disciplinary 'crossover', encouraged by

Halprin's example, characterised all the members of this group. Young himself had been interested in poetry for some time, partly as a result of his relationship with the poet Diane Wakoski, with whom he lived for some while both in Berkeley and after he moved to New York. On 16 September, Wakoski and Young shared a poetry reading at the Millard Bookstore in San Francisco, at which he read some 'simultaneous poems' of his own, and also poems by Morris and others. Within weeks, Young together with a number of these colleagues had moved to New York City to seek their fortunes in the avant-garde art world there.

New York

In the autumn of 1960, not yet quite aged twenty-five, Young moved with Wakoski to New York City, which became his permanent home; after staying for a while in Brooklyn with the composer Joseph Byrd, whom Young had known from northern California, they found an apartment on Bank Street in the West Village. Young was still a student, having won the Alfred Hertz Memorial Traveling Scholarship (which he is sure Berkeley awarded him in order to get rid of such a subversive pupil); he had officially gone to New York to study electronic music with Cage and Maxfield. Yet Flynt is quite clear about the true motive for Young's move to New York. '[T]he avant-garde', he has written, 'was conducted in a messianic way. . . . In 1960–61 in New York, the role of solidifying the new wave was assumed by La Monte Young'.[51]

Besides, Cage was out of town; that autumn, Maxfield had taken over Cage's teaching at the New School for Social Research. Young studied with him for about a year. Maxfield was mainly a composer of tape music, and technically very much at the forefront of this field; he was a leading recording engineer at Westminster Records and also acted as musical director for the James Waring Dance Company. Disillusioned, apparently, by his lack of public success, he committed suicide in 1969. Young himself seems to have had little trouble achieving recognition in New York almost immediately. To some extent this was a matter of image: 'psychedelic' before such things existed, he was soon dressing in a black velvet suit and black cape. To some extent it was a matter of circumstance: early on, he fell in with other leading practitioners of the downtown avant-garde, including the artist George Brecht, the lighting designer Nic Cernovich, the composer and pianist Toshi Ichiyanagi, the poet Jackson MacLow, the graphic designer and avant-garde impresario George Maciunas, the film-maker and conceptual artist Yoko Ono (then Ichiyanagi's wife) and the artist Larry Poons; Flynt – a philosopher, violinist and commentator on the avant-garde, among other things – also became an important member of this community. It was now enlarged by Young's Californian entourage.

Within scarcely two months of his arrival, Young became the founding musical director of the concert series in Ono's loft at 112 Chambers Street, having been introduced to Ono by Tudor. According to Young, this series 'was perhaps the first to take place in a loft in New York City, thus representing one of the beginnings of alternative performance spaces'. Eight pairs of programmes were presented by him between December 1960 and June 1961, with two concerts each devoted to a single composer or artist.[52] In only six months, Young helped establish a significant presence for several new kinds of music on the wider New York avant-garde scene. The first pair of programmes was devoted to the music of Jennings. Besides music, theatrical events and even installations were also included. Later programmes featured both musicians – including Maxfield and Ichiyanagi, as well as Young himself – and others, including Forti, MacLow and Morris. After this series, however, he resigned as Ono's concert organiser due to disagreements with her over programming.

By the time he arrived in New York, Young had already written several of the works which soon helped establish him as a leader of the avant-garde. These include not only *Arabic Numeral (any integer), to H. F.*, given its first public performance in New York on 14 May 1961, but also half the pieces eventually grouped under the title *Compositions 1960*. The theatrical and conceptual dimensions of these pieces were, in fact, partly a response to the stifling atmosphere of Berkeley, where Young's activities had been widely treated with derision. Together with the three *Piano Pieces for David Tudor* (which the composer has also included as part of *Compositions 1960*), the two *Piano Pieces for Terry Riley* (both sets also 1960), the *Compositions 1961* – all composed in New York – and a few other lesser-known works, these 'word pieces' or 'performance pieces' are probably Young's most famous, or infamous, creations.

Several of the fifteen *Compositions 1960* emphasise how what might at first appear essentially theatrical or conceptual may also be considered musical. *Composition 1960 #5* (8 June; some pieces are precisely dated, others not) – inspired by a trip to Mount Tamalpais, in Marin County – requires the performer to 'Turn a butterfly (or any number of butterflies) loose in the performance area'. In interview with Kostelanetz, Young agrees that performing this activity in a concert situation makes clear that even a butterfly makes a sound. More importantly, he says that 'a person should listen to what he ordinarily just looks at, or look at things he would ordinarily just hear'.[53] Other pieces go further in redefining the relationship between the audience and the performer. In *Composition 1960 #4* (3 June), the lights are turned off for a period of time previously announced; when they are turned back on, the audience may be told that it is they who have been the performers, though the score says that 'this is not at all necessary'. In *Composition 1960 #6* (2 July), performers onstage pretend to be the audience. Still other pieces seem more viable as poetry than as performance instructions. *Composition 1960 #15* (9:05 A.M., 25 December) reads: 'This piece is little whirlpools out in the middle of the ocean'. *Piano Piece for David Tudor #3* (14 November 1960) suggests merely that 'most of them were very old grasshoppers'. According to Cardew,[54] Cage once suggested that Wakoski was at least partly responsible for these pieces, a view Young attributes to the fact that Wakoski transcribed some of them for him. Wakoski now recalls that 'for La Monte, words, including poetic language, were sound events. I didn't influence him to write poetry – he was already describing ordinary events as poetry. We simply inspired each other to follow our own imaginations'.[55] Both she and – later and to a much greater extent – Zazeela worked tirelessly to help him realise his ideas and to promote himself. The pieces for Tudor were composed out of admiration for 'the foremost performer of new music',[56] who was now championing Young's work after encountering it at Darmstadt.

In *Piano Piece for David Tudor #1* (October 1960), the performer is asked to '[b]ring a bale of hay and a bucket of water onto the stage for the piano to eat and drink. The performer may then feed the piano or leave it to eat by itself. If the former, the piece is over after the piano has been fed. If the latter, it is over after the piano eats or decides not to'. The initial stage is simply – if, in a concert context, amusingly, even shockingly – theatrical. But then things become more complicated: whichever option is taken (and for that matter whichever option the piano may be deemed to have taken), the piece quickly moves into a surreal, unreal or conceptual space in which the piano itself is simultaneously the focus of an entirely new attention and the piece's only link with 'music'. *Composition 1960 #13* (9 November) instructs the performer to 'prepare any composition and then perform it as well as he can': an apparently straightforward activity. Flynt, however, once performed *#13* by selecting *#13* itself as the composition to be performed: an altogether more 'conceptual' response.

Other pieces from *Compositions 1960* offer direct connections to Young's more purely musical activities, both before and since. Probably the best example is *Composition 1960 #7* (July), which consists of the perfect fifth B F♯, notated on a staff, plus the words 'to be held for a long time'. The link with the composer's concern with sustained sounds is obvious, right down to the choice of a 'pure' interval which allows the listener to focus on aspects otherwise unnoticed. More clearly, because even more reductively, than any of Young's earlier works, #7 opens up the world of psycho-acoustic events behind a simple acoustic phenomenon: combination tones, for instance, and the possibility of hearing the balance of partials within each note of the interval quite differently in different parts of the room. As Smith has said, the piece 'emphasises the harmonic series through the purity and reduction of material and points to Young's later work with precisely-tuned sinewave drones and voices'.[57] Just as the world had become conceptualised as 'a single gigantic performance of *Poem*', so *Composition 1960 #7* can be considered to encompass Young's entire output.

This can also be said of *Composition 1960 #10* (October) – dedicated 'to Bob Morris' – which consists of the instruction 'Draw a straight line and follow it', and its companion, *#9* (October), the score of which is a horizontal line drawn on a card. Though even more conceptual than *Composition 1960 #7*, these are readily translatable into everyday, theatrical or musical terms. Young's own realisation of *#10* involved sighting with plumb lines and making a chalk line along the floor. Howard Skempton once performed the piece by sustaining a single chord on the accordion for two-and-a-half hours. Young used to play *#9* by sustaining a single note. 'People said I was playing one note', he says, 'but I was trying to make it very clear that even if you try to play the same thing over and over, it will always be different'.

The following year, Young decided to translate the already apparent universality of 'Draw a straight line and follow it' into the direct working terms of his own output. Reckoning that in 1960 he had averaged completion of a new piece every thirteen days, he composed a similar quota for 1961 at a single sitting, on 6 January, by writing out 'Draw a straight line and follow it' twenty-nine times, giving each a date between 1 January and 31 December, and publishing the result in a miniature volume entitled *LY 1961*. This 'single, all-embracing metaphor',[58] as Nyman calls it, takes Young and his audience yet further into the realms of what Young termed the 'Theatre of the Singular Event', and towards what is often called 'conceptual art'. His metaphor of the 'line' can be taken as representative of the 'potential of existing time',[59] expressed in directly musical terms in the held B and F♯ of *Composition 1960 #7*. But in 'Draw a straight line and follow it', a line can also be taken, more ambiguously and even more provocatively, 'as a condensation of any number of mono-directional, undeviating linear activities – walking, education (perhaps), marksmanship, Catholicism, La Monte Young's career, etc'. He also performed all twenty-nine pieces by drawing a line and then attempting to draw over it twenty-eight times; 'and each time it invariably came out differently. The technique I was using at the time was not good enough'. While not the total triumph of perception over conception – this performance took place on 21 March 1961 at Harvard University, arranged by Flynt: that is, before most of these pieces had been 'composed' – this certainly demonstrates that Young was as willing to deal with challenging approaches to the passing of time as some of his other avant-garde colleagues, such as Cage and Dick Higgins.

Such matters may seem to connect Young with Cage once again; and indeed Cage was a potent influence on his junior colleague's abandonment, not merely of serialism, but of note-against-note composition in any conventionally understood sense in favour of a fresh look at what music might be and might signify. Neither does the influence all flow in one direction. Flynt argues that Cage's 0′ 00″ (1962) and Variations III (1963) can be seen as attempts to keep up with the example set by Young's word pieces, and even by Flynt's own anti-art lectures, such as the one he gave on 5 July 1962, on New York's Avenue D, which Cage attended.[60]

Young's move into conceptual art may have sprung from a Cageian base, but it already occupied new territory. Cage himself said in 1961 that 'La Monte Young is doing something quite different from what I am doing, and it strikes me as being very important. Through the few pieces of his I've heard, I've had, actually, utterly different experiences of listening than I've had with any other music'.[61] As Flynt has it, '[Cage's] compositions, and those of his colleagues, presupposed a quasi-scientific analysis of music as nothing but a collection of sounds defined by frequency, amplitude, duration, and overtone spectrum'.[62] 'Young', he claims, 'overthrew Cage's definition of new as extravagent [sic] confusion'. The composer's own view of the matter, at the time, was that (to quote a longer version of a statement already included above) whereas Cage's pieces 'were generally realized as a complex of programmed sounds and activities over a prolonged period of time with events coming and going, I was perhaps the first to concentrate on and delimit the work to be a single event or object in these less traditionally musical areas'.[63] The conceptual, in other words, was being investigated with newly minimal means.

Douglas Kahn expresses the issues with explicit reference to the two composers' relationship to conceptual art. For Cage, 'everything we do is music. . . . By means of electronics, it has been made apparent that everything is musical'.[64] Young, according to Kahn, 'was beginning to say, with respect to Composition 1960 #5 [the butterfly piece], that any sound could be music as long as the existence of sound was conceivable; in other words, the arbitrary limitations of the human ear or technology (imagine the difficulty of placing a microphone on the butterfly) should not define the bounds of music'. Cageian multiplicity, focusing on perception and aided by electronics and chance operations, had given way not only to Youngian singularity, in which the conceptual played a much more important role; chance and, for the moment, electronics were replaced by an audacious imagination positively enlivened by practical restrictions. According to Flynt, by the time Young came to New York, 'For him Cage was already history then'.[65]

Young's 'unitary activities' had a certain amount in common with the Fluxus compositions of those such as George Brecht and Maciunas. Five of Young's 'conceptual word pieces' were performed at the Fluxus festival in Wiesbaden in September 1962, including what was billed as '566' for Henry Flynt and a string quartet version of Composition 1960 #7, the held-fifth piece, following a realisation for strings at the AG Gallery in New York the previous year. Several of his works – including Trio for Strings as well as Compositions 1961 – were published by Fluxus from 1963 onwards.[66] Since then, his output of 1959–61 has been played all over the world in Fluxus-related contexts, including the periodic revivals that the movement has spawned; and his name frequently appeared on Maciunas's lists of Fluxus associates. Overlapping with the end of Young's series at Ono's loft, Maciunas mounted his own short but more intensive series, plus a show of Ono's paintings, at the AG Gallery. Young, according to his own account, had some influence on the choice of contributors to its fourteen events. Those not already represented at Ono's included Cage, de Maria and Higgins; Young had two programmes to himself, including the aforementioned 1960 #7 as the sole content of one.

By 1963, however, Young had largely detached himself from Fluxus, feeling much the same as Morris, who left the movement a year later: that Fluxus performances 'were nothing more than vaudeville, shallow revivals of the Dadaist performances of Hugo Ball and Tristan Tzara'.[67] The programming of his compositions in Fluxus contexts, by Maciunas and others, was done without their composer's consent. The work of Young and his circle in 1960–61 is, in any case, arguably pre-Fluxus and not part of Fluxus itself; Flynt suggests that the work of both Young and Cage 'has been submerged by Fluxus expansionism'[68] by subsequent chroniclers, including Maciunas himself, who seems to have been desperate to unite the whole post-Cage movement under his command, and thus set himself up as a rival to Young.

Cage, Young and Maciunas all made what Flynt calls a 'screaming claim to be new (along with an attempt to dictate the definition of the terms "new" and "avant-garde")'.[69] But the 'conceptual' aesthetic of Young and Flynt 'had nothing of the demand for political reconstruction of culture, or for unpretentiousness, which Maciunas incorporated in Fluxus'.[70] It was more sophisticated: Flynt argues for independence from the emotions, and, in his 'Essay: Concept Art', characterises this approach by referring to 'refinement, elegance, intellectuality'.[71] The titillation of Fluxus was to be avoided in favour of a fresh look at the potential of boredom: 'prolonged monotony in art – the position which would later be called minimalism'.[72]

Young remained, however, in sympathy with the belief – expressed at various times by both Cage and several Fluxus artists, though it is another matter whether they have acted on this – that 'art should aim for self-sufficient exploration and not for the saleable product'. This determined how he came to feel about those of his close associates – whether musicians or other artists – who, the composer believes, have 'made themselves saleable'. Young well understands the need to make a living, as befits someone who grew up in a family in which, he says, his father even had trouble finding the rent for a log cabin. From the mid-1960s, lists circulated of the composer's charges for performing his music: the shorter the proposed performance, the more astronomical was the fee. ('A purely conceptual business', he comments dryly.) In the early 1980s, as we shall see, he cultivated his own sources of funding his art with spectacular success. But Young remains in certain respects curiously purist, by conventional standards, despite his constant financial need not only for the technology to develop his work but also for assistance both professional and personal. The Youngs' present home – their old loft on Church Street – is close to one of the busiest road junctions in downtown Manhattan, and a stone's throw from the offices of Wall Street. Yet Young and Zazeela live there like hermits, largely aloof from the teeming world around them.

Young fairly soon relinquished the role of impresario, deciding that life was too short to spend so much time away from presenting his own work. The position of influence in the New York avant-garde art world that went with that role was in the process inevitably affected too. But before this, he responded with enthusiasm to the writer Chester Anderson's suggestion, some time in 1961, that he guest-edit a special issue of *Beatitude East* magazine (of which Anderson was editor) devoted to an anthology of the avant-garde art with which he was associated. *Beatitude East* folded and Anderson disappeared. The project itself suffered other vicissitudes too, but *An Anthology of Chance Operations/Concept art/Meaningless work/ Natural disasters/Indeterminacy/Anti-art/Plans of Action/Improvisation/ Stories/Diagrams/Poetry/Essays/Dance/Constructions/Compositions/ Mathematics/Music* – to give it its full title – was finally published in 1963 by Young himself and Jackson MacLow, it was designed by Maciunas. A second edition appeared in 1970 under the auspices of Heiner Friedrich, a supporter of Young's work since the previous year, when this Munich-based gallery-owner underwrote the publication of the composer's *Selected Writings.*[73]

There were eventually twenty-five contributors to *An Anthology*, ranging from subsequently established Fluxus artists already mentioned, to Cage and his close associates, and several of Young's own circle including Flynt, Jennings, Johnson and Riley. Flynt's seminal 'Essay: Concept Art' – substantially revised in the second edition – has already been quoted. Morris withdrew his own contribution when the as yet unbound volumes of *An Anthology* were stored in his loft. Young himself is represented by ten of the *Compositions 1960: #2–7, 9, 10, 13* and *15*, as well as the three pieces dedicated to David Tudor and one of the two dedicated to Riley. David Farneth's assessment of *An Anthology* as being 'among the most influential collections of music and performance art of the 1960s . . . represent[ing] an unprecedented breaking down of barriers between artistic media that had an important influence on the FLUXUS movement'[74] appears fully justified.

Amidst this 'conceptualism', Young's only other composition to rely on reductive repetition, besides *Arabic Numeral*, sits somewhat oddly. *Death Chant* (23 December 1961) was written in memory of the daughter born to MacLow and his wife Iris, who died when she was only three days old. It consists of a spare and bleak three-note dirge based on the minor mode on G, subjected to brief processes of addition and subtraction very similar to those used from around five years later by Glass. *Death Chant* is reproduced as Example 1.7. The work is scored for male voices, with percussive thigh slaps on the last, and later the first, beat of each bar; alternatively, a carillon or large bells may be used, transposed as necessary. It remains Young's only piece of 1960–62 to use staff notation except *Composition 1960 #7*, and was the composer's last fully notated work until *Chronos Kristalla* in 1990.

From composition to improvisation?

By the summer of 1961, Young was improvising regularly on the piano to accompany the alto saxophone playing of Jennings, who was now also living in New York. In doing so, he not only began the process of returning to music *per se*, but also began to establish the musical concerns which would occupy him from then onwards: in particular, the attempt to discover new ground on which composition and improvisation might meet with the aid of structures and approaches borrowed, at least in part, from the music of his youth – jazz. Jennings' abilities as an improviser especially impressed Young, causing him to develop a particular style of piano playing to accompany Jennings' saxophone. He also used a different form of this in more occasional performances with Flynt on violin.

As we have already seen, Jennings and Young had first experimented with this style of improvisation at least a year earlier. 'Young's Blues', as the composer called it, took the basic I–IV–I–V–IV–I blues structure, but prolonged each chord for as long as required; Young then provided a continuous, regular rhythmic accompaniment on each chord in turn, using the 'ka chunk chunka chunk chunka' manner he had already begun to use at least two years before that. Jennings, meanwhile, improvised a continuously flowing stream of notes over this in a manner influenced by Coltrane and shortly to be explored further by Young himself. 'The concept in that style of blues', Young has written, 'was to spend long periods of time on each chord change to emphasize the modal drone aspects of the music'.[75] The result was a 'static, modal, drone-style' combining the sustained approach of Young's early notated compositions with a jazz structure articulated through improvisation. *Young's Aeolian Blues in Bb with a Bridge* – an improvisation by Jennings and Young, recorded that summer – appears typical. Sometimes the basic material of their improvisations is credited to Jennings, notably his *Tune in E* (1961), first recorded at the same session.

An important result of this was to suggest to Young that he could now return to the concerns first successfully explored in *Trio for Strings*, and pursued at least intermittently in the performance-art works, but now in the context of a modal form of pitch organisation. The change of pitch commitment proved crucial. By forsaking both Webernian atonality and serialism, and Cage's dismissal of harmony, and by returning to modality, he finally discovered an approach rich in potential precisely because of the accessibility it allowed to 'the profound feelings that have to do with these universal structures which consist of vibrational systems'. This essentially Pythagorean aesthetic was to serve Young as the basis for his work to the present day.

Playing piano for Jennings paved the way for Young's return to the saxophone in the spring of 1962. While his previous saxophone playing had been firmly based on the jazz of its time, the new approach, using a sopranino, followed the 'static, modal, drone-style' of his keyboard style; 'the piano', as Kyle Gagne puts it, 'in a sense was a transition between [Young's] reed styles'.[76] Coltrane's move from tenor to soprano saxophone a year or so earlier had popularised this instrument almost overnight.

Example 1.7 *Death Chant*, complete score. The composer's captions read:
Line 1: Statement of The Theme with All Motivic Elements;
Line 2: Statement of The Theme with All Motivic Elements Plus Retrograde;
Lines 3–5: Statement of The Theme With All Motivic Elements Followed by
Additive Permutations in Which The First Measure is Followed by The First and
Second Measures, Which Are Followed by The First, Second and Third Measures,
Which Are Followed by The First, Second and Third Measures, Which Are
Followed by The First, Second, Third and Fourth Measures, and Then at The
Unison, The Retrograde of All of The Material to This Point

Young had been an alto player; thus the choice of sopranino was more
natural for him, since both these instruments are in Eb (tenor and soprano
are both in Bb). The essential ingredients of Young's sopranino saxophone
improvisations were the repetition of modal pitch sequences at an
extremely fast tempo over a continuous drone. The sopranino proved especially persuasive for this kind of playing, being even more redolent than

Example 1.7 (*cont.*)

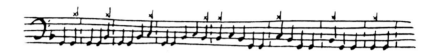

to be repeated
many times
or ad infinitum

Any of the above may be
played on carillon or
large bells. If carillon,
use the pitches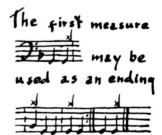
If bells, use any low
pitches with the proper
interval relationships.
The carillonist or bell
ringer should find the
best way to produce
the percussive sound
for each performance
situation.

Slower tempos may
be used, especially
in the case of
bells.

The first measure
may be
used as an ending

Coltrane's soprano of the Indian double-reed shenai; Dolphy, Young's
student colleague, who now played with Coltrane, may have been another
influence. To provide the drone he required, Young now set about establishing a regular group of like-minded performers around him, with whom he
could work extensively: recording every rehearsal, listening and learning,

modifying, elaborating. Though he usually now played saxophone, Young also continued to employ his piano blues style with this ensemble.

Byrd, de Maria, Jennings and Johnson – in any case only occasional members – were the sole musicians in this group who had been part of Young's original 'entourage' from California. All the others were new. Angus MacLise – a poet and composer of music for underground films, as well as a percussionist – was in fact the first to participate in Young's sopranino saxophone improvisations, in the spring of 1962; usually playing hand-drums, he was a regular member of the group until he left New York in February 1964, initially to go to India, eventually to Morocco. The earliest recorded example of Young's sopranino improvisation dates from 11 June 1962, when he was accompanied by MacLise and Forti, who sang what they called the 'drone tone'. Within days of this recording, however, Marian Zazeela – a painter, calligrapher and light artist recently graduated from Bennington College, whom Young got together with through working with MacLise – had moved into the composer's Bank Street apartment; she now replaced Forti as vocal drone in the group. Young and Zazeela were married on 22 June 1963, exactly a year after they began living together. Zazeela subsequently established her innovative and exquisite lighting designs as an indispensable dimension of all Young's concerts and, later, of their 'sound and light environments'.

This trio gave a series of seven concerts at the 10-4 Gallery on Fourth Avenue and 10th Street in the summer of 1962, joined towards the end by Billy Linich – also known as Billy Name, later an assistant to Andy Warhol – who remained in the group until some time the following year. Tony Conrad – who had met Young while visiting Berkeley a few years earlier – attended several of these concerts and joined the group as a violinist the following May, after he moved from Harvard to New York. His training as a mathematician was soon to prove useful to Young in establishing the theoretical basis for his work in just intonation. John Cale, who joined the group in September 1963, was a viola player from South Wales; he had gone to the USA to study with Aaron Copland at the Tanglewood Summer School. He decided to settle in New York, where he investigated the avant-garde scene and quickly became part of Young's ensemble.

The range of pitches covered by Young's sopranino playing was very wide – more than two octaves; but he sometimes employed just a few notes in a narrow microtonal range, using alternative fingerings. The intention behind both approaches was to create 'the impression of a sustained chord'. The speed of his playing – creating the effect of a continuous stream of sound, though in practice separated into bursts of wild, breathless tremolo lasting between about four and ten seconds, separated by

short pauses and divided into sections by longer ones – is quite extraordinary; despite the influence of Coltrane, Young's performances have a character all their own.

The choice of modality employed and the ways in which it is spun out
over what may seem exorbitant spans of time play important parts in this.
The natural improviser's sheer joy of improvising is significant, too. 'I
went more and more in the direction of improvisation as a creative outlet',
Young says of this period. He himself refers to the style of these improvisations as a 'combination/permutation technique on one set of tones'.
Ultimately, these performances are compelling because the fantasy of
improvisation is held in tight check by highly reductive repetition. 'I am
wildly interested in repetition', Young told Kostelanetz, 'because I think it
demonstrates control'.[77] MacLise's drumming, also very fast, gives the
music a rather fierce tension, though it, too, gives the impression of being
highly controlled, in spite of its metrical freedom. The drone-based
accompaniment – in which pitches are sustained for long periods, usually
by upper strings and voices – makes a significant contribution as well.
Most important, however, is Young's concern with exploring the innards
of sound over extended time-periods.

In August 1963, Young and Zazeela moved from Bank Street in the West
Village to a loft on Church Street, at the edge of the area later to become
known as TriBeCa. Their loft – among the earliest of the artists' lofts of
downtown Manhattan – was ideally suited for rehearsals and occasional
private concerts, both sometimes taking all night: perhaps the beginnings
of Young's interest in the even longer time-spans involved in the Dream
House projects and the twenty-seven-hour day which he and Zazeela
began observing in the 1960s and have now developed to a more flexible
twenty-eight to thirty-six hours. (This routine – originally eighteen to
nineteen hours awake, eight or nine hours sleeping – is, they argue, more
in line with their natural body clocks.) This nucleus of musicians provided
a vehicle not only for Young's improvisations using the sopranino
saxophone – which turned out to be a fairly brief, if intense, obsession –
but for the wider range of group work conducted under the title The
Theatre of Eternal Music.

The Four Dreams of China *and the move towards just intonation*

The work that really began to bring Young's concerns into a new, much
sharper focus was *The Four Dreams of China*. This marks the composer's
discovery that the harmonic material which he had been using in his
instrumental compositions of 1957–8 could be further rationalised to

form four chords, each consisting of four pitches. The story goes that Young first notated these chords on a restaurant paper napkin during a car trip from San Francisco to New York City on 10 or 11 December 1962.

Example 1.8 reproduces the chords in full. Their simplest interpretation is in the form of four different orderings of the pitches C, F♮, F♯ and G (though of course any transposition could also be used). The third and fourth 'Dreams' present the pitches in close position, spanning a perfect fifth; either can be interpreted as an inversion of the other, the cluster of semitones being attached to the lower or the upper pitch of the larger interval. The first and second 'Dreams' spread the pitches out to span the interval of a tritone displaced by an octave, leaving a major-second cluster either closer to the lower pitch or the upper; again, these chords are related by inversion. *The Four Dreams of China* thus clarifies the harmonic basis upon which Young's early works using sustenance, notably *Trio for Strings*, had been written by a rigorous ordering of the intervals already emphasised in those compositions: the minor and major second, and the perfect fourth and fifth. Once again, the major third is avoided; even the interval framing the first and second 'Dreams', the augmented eleventh, is comparable to the occasional augmented elevenths to be found in *Trio for Strings*.

The Four Dreams of China, its composer has written, 'forms a structural, stylistic and harmonic link between my earlier, fully notated works composed of long sustained tones from the late 50s, and later works combining improvisation with predetermined rules and elements'.[78] The connection with *Trio for Strings* is especially close. 'As I listened to one of these sustained chords while composing the *Trio for Strings*', he writes, 'I received a powerful image of the sound and timelessness of China'. On 12 October 1962, the *Trio* received its live public concert première in New York's Judson Hall, performed by LaMar Alsop, Jack Glick and Charlotte Moorman.

As a concept – open-ended in its potential realisation and of no fixed duration – *The Four Dreams of China* forms a link with the 'conceptual' performance-art pieces of the previous few years. In performance, it becomes the first composition in which Young combined the style based on long sustained notes and silences with his, still new, re-embrace of improvisation. It could only be realised as group improvisations based on algorithmic scores which extrapolated particular characteristics of the chordal vocabulary it set out, and which provided both the materials and the structures from which those improvisations could proceed. This increased Young's concern to establish on a firmer footing the group with which he had already been playing sopranino saxophone. *The Four Dreams of China* not only provided the basis of much that he and the ensemble did

Example 1.8 *The Four Dreams of China*

over the next few years, but also led to the 'eternal music' of the Dream House installations.

One more element, however, was necessary to complete the ingredients for Young's mature style: the move into just intonation. His experimentation with this emerged naturally out of his involvement with modality and drones which had, in turn, arisen from a considerable experience of sustained sounds. 'What I found', he says, 'was that I was deeply and profoundly moved by great modal music, and that I really wasn't by harmonically unstructured music, equal-tempered music in particular'. A full appreciation of the possibilities inherent in tuning systems less compromised than equal temperament, he found, was complemented perfectly by his already established concern for sustained sounds, since the ear needs the time allowed by a drone to get inside a sound in the ways which interested him. Coltrane's exploration of freedom within harmonically well-defined limits in his modal period had an important effect on his developing style of harmonic-based music; Young cites the famous improvisations on 'My Favorite Things' as particularly important to him at this time, but has also argued that Indian classical music was an even more significant influence.

It was his increasing commitment to just intonation that caused Young's decision to give up the sopranino saxophone in favour of the voice. The fixed-pitch structure of the saxophone posed considerable problems for anyone wishing to break free of equal temperament. For a while, Young investigated the possibilities of adapting the instrument to his new musical needs. He bought some double reeds and attempted to turn his sopranino into a kind of shenai, which it already somewhat resembled. He considered having a modified version of the instrument specially built to incorporate the new tunings he wanted. Ultimately, though, he realised that the saxophone could never provide him with the flexibility of pitch he needed. '[W]ith the voice', on the other hand, he once wrote, 'I could sing anything I could hear'.[79] On 23 March 1964, he also began tuning the first piano to which he had ever had permanent access to a system of just intonation and improvising the earliest versions of what turned out to be another major project, *The Well-Tuned Piano.*

The move into just intonation caused Young to become something of a specialist in areas of acoustic theory which remain a closed book to many musicians. It is not possible to detail these investigations here, but their central relevance to the composer's thinking and his output to this day should be stressed, not least since it may do something to counter the impression of dilettantism given by casual acquaintance with the infamous pieces of 1959–61. Since the longer a note is sustained, the more its overtones become clear to the listener, it is hardly surprising that Young should have become obsessed with such theorising. Other matters of acoustic fact, too, relate the theory of acoustics directly to the concerns the composer had earlier developed quite intuitively: his distaste for the major third, for instance, is well founded, scientifically speaking, in that while equal temperament modifies the perfect fifth by only two cents, it alters the major third by 13.69 cents.

Young's adoption of ratio numbers soon began to focus and clarify his approach to intervals. 'I was beginning', he has written, 'to understand the musical implications of the overtone series more specifically as a set of rational numbers and that there were ways of getting around in the series by ear'.[80] The theoretical potential inherent in conceiving intervallic structures in terms of their Pythagorean base in prime numbers allowed him to develop those areas of particular interest to him – secundal and quartal harmonies based on the primes 2, 3 and 7, later also 31 – and to avoid the third-based areas based on the number 5. Ratios also nicely accommodate the composer's already established preference for 'algorithmic scores', which – in the later works – not only allow space for improvisation but can also be extremely precise in those areas of most interest to him. The exploration of intervallic relationships over sustained periods of time thus encourages close connections between theory and practice, 'inspiring a new vision of composition evolving from the universal truths of harmonic structure'.

The framing augmented elevenths of the first and second 'Dream Chords' as notated in Example 1.8 can only be considered the exact equivalent of the augmented elevenths to be found in *Trio for Strings* in equally tempered terms. As his preference for expressing the pitches of these 'Dream Chords' in ratios suggests, however, Young soon began to think in terms of just intonation, in which the precise quality of these intervals could be appreciated in ways which corresponded more closely to the 'universal truths of harmonic structure'. Thus the four pitches C, F♮, F♯ and G become 24:32:35:36, later becoming refined in the ratios 12:16:17:18. This permits the exploitation – in works such as *The Second Dream of The High-Tension Line Stepdown Transformer* (the 'Harmonic Version', 1962; the 'Melodic Version', 1984) – both of ratios which are further reductions of these to the simplest and purest intervals – 18:12 becomes 3:2, for example – and of ratios which remain reducible no further – 18:17, for example.

As the date of the 'Harmonic Version' of *The Second Dream* suggests, the basic materials, as well as the founding inspiration, of much of the composer's work in the last thirty-five years were conceived in the early 1960s. Two decades later, Young was regrouping the 'Dream Chords' to make *The Subsequent Dreams of China* (1980), and using this as the basis for *Orchestral Dreams* (1985), which exploits the octave displacements available with orchestral resources. The only commercially recorded performance of *The Second Dream* is of a realisation of the 'Melodic Version' for eight trumpets made in 1990. In 1966, he began work on a theoretical treatise entitled *The Two Systems of Eleven Categories* which remains unfinished and unpublished, just like the compositions *The Tortoise, His Dreams and Journeys* and *The Well-Tuned Piano*, both begun two years earlier. A mass of other theoretical explication – most of it published, if at all, only in the form of programme notes, etc. – has accompanied many of his musical projects.

Extended duration is not the only requirement for the exploration of the innards of sound along these lines. Young has also sometimes found it necessary to use levels of amplification which reach the threshold of pain in order to appreciate these harmonic partials with full clarity and intensity. In the autumn of 1967, the taped drones he had provided for three of Warhol's films to be shown at the New York Film Festival proved too loud for the Lincoln Center authorities. Young withdrew his music rather than turn down the volume: a good illustration of the commercial opportunities lost through his refusal to compromise. The following February, encountering his solo performance of *Map of 49's Dream* (see below) at the Barbizon Plaza Theater was described by one reviewer as 'like being hit in the face with a blast of hot wind or like walking into a room full of brine and discovering that surprisingly enough it was still possible to breathe'.[81] While such high dynamics have proved crucial, 'creat[ing] a world of feelings which can't be achieved in any other way',[82] Young's severe loss of hearing in recent years may well be due to such extended exposure to loud sounds; he himself, though, argues that this may be hereditary, at least in part.

While theorising has been crucial to his practice, Young was also keen to pursue his musical endeavours with the help of other experimental aids. The connections his thinking had to the taking of hallucinogenic drugs must be mentioned here, since it seems unlikely that Young's – and, as we shall see later, also Riley's – musical development in the 1960s and beyond would have taken the form it did without these experiences. Though he has previously said little in public concerning the matter, drugs had played an important part in Young's life from the mid-1950s onwards. He says that 'everybody I knew and worked with . . . – especially because of my background as a jazz musician – was very much into drugs as a creative tool as well as a consciousness-expanding tool'. He was introduced to them by Jennings and Billy Higgins in about 1954; in the late 1950s, Young himself seems to have been responsible for Riley's first experiences of LSD, marijuana and peyote. As a listener, Young used drugs from early on: 'it was under the influence of cannabis', he says, 'that I first heard certain structural relationships in Stockhausen's *Gruppen für drei Orchester*'. While alcohol was central to the social milieu of Cage and his circle in the 1950s and 1960s, as it was to that of the Abstract Expressionists and Post-Expressionists with whom they mixed, different drugs helped define the artistic, as well as the social, experiences of many of Young's minimalist generation.

Understandably, the composer is concerned to emphasise the creative potential of drugs: chiefly, for musical purposes, cannabis. 'These tools can be used to your advantage if you're a master of [them]. . . . If used wisely – the correct tool for the correct job – they can play an important role'. He considers that 'there was something in the cannabis experience that probably helped open me up to where I went with *Trio for Strings*'. With the later, improvised and modal music, cannabis sometimes proved a disadvantage when performing anything which required keeping track of, or actually counting, the number of elapsed bars; smoking it, in particular, also apparently restricts the voice, so Young has seldom used it either in his own vocal improvisation or when singing Indian music. On the other hand, both his sopranino saxophone improvisations and the whole work with The Theatre of Eternal Music benefited from drugs: with the latter, he says, 'we got high for every concert: the whole group'. And Young has never performed *The Well-Tuned Piano* without being high on cannabis, though he often practised the piece without it.

When asked directly whether his music would have developed in the same way without the influence of drugs, Young says that he 'would have done, probably, everything I did had I never taken a drug'. He adds that 'many people have taken drugs, but I was the only one to compose the *Trio for Strings*'. In general, however, his comments make it clear that, at least in the past, he has valued their potential as both creative and listening 'tools'. The more 'experimental', extra-personal aspects of the Pythagorean aesthetic are certainly encouraged by this: 'I try to present the music as it flows through me from this higher source of inspiration', Young says, 'and to make a concrete physical manifestation of the information that's going through me that is as true as possible to the information itself. And to make it available, and not to try to temper it for this audience or that audience . . . just to let it be'. He also argues the case for the drug experience as a stimulus to listening to his music: 'It allows you to go within yourself and focus on certain frequency relationships and memory relationships in a very, very interesting way', he states. 'Things happen that allow you to hear frequency structures over time in a different way'. Young is mindful, though, of the disastrous effects that drug dependency, and dealing, can have. MacLise died a possibly drug-related death, in 1979; in 1981, Jennings was murdered, apparently on the wrong side of a bad deal. These days, Young says, he confines himself primarily to alcohol – or abstinence – but also says that he will never lose his appreciation for cannabis.

The Theatre of Eternal Music and the expansion of Young's reputation

Though not called The Theatre of Eternal Music until February 1965, and then disbanded the following year, some of the musicians involved had worked closely together from the summer of 1962 – initially with Young playing sopranino saxophone. The group embodied, in a more focused and particular way than had been possible before, the ideas about 'universal structure', harmony and the effect of sound on both mind and body which have already been discussed. The Theatre of Eternal Music's activities, too, had repercussions reaching well beyond the establishment of

Young's position as a composer and improviser in the mid-1960s, being crucial to the development of the Dream House concept as well as much of his later work besides his solo playing, some of it involving the same musicians with whom he had collaborated in the period 1963–6.

In 1963 and early 1964, Conrad, MacLise, Young and Zazeela, joined shortly by Cale, formed the group's core. While continuing to play modal and blues-derived improvisations with Young on saxophone, its next major project was a realisation of part of *The Four Dreams of China*. This was *The Second Dream of the High-Tension Line Stepdown Transformer from The Four Dreams of China*, listed as being 'for any instruments that can sustain four-note groups in just intonation'; in this 'Harmonic Version', though, each performer plays only a single pitch. The work's title relates to the power-plant transformer that had so attracted the composer as a child. According to Young's worklist, the composition was written in 1962, but its essentially improvised nature means that *The Second Dream* did not really exist as such until the group began rehearsing it in May 1963. Eight musicians were involved, the core members playing instruments different to their usual ones: Conrad on viola, MacLise on violin, Zazeela on violin, and Young on bowed mandolin. The other four performers all had associations with the New York avant-garde: Poons played viola; and the other three – Byrd (guitar), Dottie Moskowitz (lute) and the film-maker Jack Smith (mandola) – like Young, bowed the guitar-related instruments in which Conrad subsequently specialised. An outdoor performance at George Segal's farm in North Brunswick, New Jersey, on 19 May contributed to George Brecht and Robert Watts' YAM Festival, which seems to have been a day of avant-garde mayhem. As Alan Licht argues, it was here that 'the concept of eternal music was born'.[83] This 'Harmonic Version' of *The Second Dream* was subsequently performed by musicians besides those of Young's ensemble; and since 1984, The Theatre of Eternal Music Brass Ensemble, led by the trumpeter Ben Neill, and The Theatre of Eternal Music String Ensemble, led by the cellist Charles Curtis, have presented the already mentioned 'Melodic Version' in which all four pitches of each chord may be played, according to strict rules, by each performer.

The original Theatre of Eternal Music then set about attempting to give more concerts, though many of the group's activities were confined to the Youngs' new loft. Improvisations involving sopranino saxophone continued to occupy much of the group's time in its early stages. Surviving tapes, made between 1962 and 1964, each have a title prefaced by date (sometimes also the time) and place, and also by the names of the days MacLise used in his 'calendar poem', *Year*: for example, '12 I 64 AM NYC the first twelve *Sunday Morning Blues*' is a twenty-nine-minute tape in three sections which features some particularly subtle drumming from MacLise. This performance also gives an idea of the typical instrumental line-up: Young played sopranino saxophone, MacLise played hand drums, and the drone was provided by Cale (viola), Conrad (bowed guitar and plucked mandola) and Zazeela (voice). But performances naturally varied: sometimes, for instance, a set would begin with Young on saxophone over string and vocal drones, followed by a gong duet (Young and Zazeela); then Young would play piano, followed by another gong duet and then a return of the opening saxophone-and-drones line-up to complete the symmetrical, arch-form structure.

Harmonically, these tapes almost invariably apply the 'combination/permutation technique,' referred to above to a single chord, or to a very few closely related chords, throughout. The aforementioned *Sunday Morning Blues*, for instance, is typical in being rooted in an E♭⁷ chord. Because of the sopranino saxophone's structure, Young favoured the Dorian mode on B♭; as a consequence, he tends to refer to the E♭⁷ chord of *Sunday Morning Blues* as IV⁷ of B♭ Dorian. Similarly, on the tape '24 XII 63 NYC third day of yule *Early Tuesday Morning Blues*', a single E♭⁷ chord forms the basis for a whole improvisation. In dramatic contrast, '19 X 63 NYC fifth day of the hammer *B♭ Dorian Blues*' applies the 'Young's-Blues'-style chord-expansion technique to drone tones outlining the chord changes of a typical twelve-bar blues in B♭ (Dorian): B♭⁷ E♭⁷ B♭⁷ F⁷ E♭⁷ B♭⁷. Eventually, the music comes to rest on an E♭⁹ chord (E♭ B♭ D♭ F) and develops a familiar 'combination/permutation' sequence on this alone. As a result, this *B♭ Dorian Blues* is less static than the others; Young likens its structure to that of an Indian classical improvisation. Though the context is entirely different from that of *Trio for Strings*, the tendency to create something potentially dramatic out of the apparently static is similar.

In *Studies in The Bowed Disc*, first worked on during the autumn of 1963, Young and Zazeela improvised as a duo on a five-foot steel gong, painted in black and white like a target and suspended on a wooden frame. Specially constructed by Morris, this was played, not with sticks as used on a gong in many realisations of *2 Sounds*, but with double-bass bows. This permitted much greater control and continuity in the production of its rich range of overtones. As with practically all Young's projects from this time on, *Studies in The Bowed Disc* was the subject of much experiment and many improvisations over a period of several years. Its performances also took on a characteristically spiritual and ritualistic quality. Wakoski describes a private performance in which Young and Zazeela, their large white gloves contrasting with their black uniforms, 'appeared to be priests of an esoteric order performing a sacred ritual'.[84] At first, the slow bowing of the gong's rim created the effect of 'a train . . . passing a room with a cello in it, and the strings were beginning to vibrate without hands touching them'. Once the space was filled with the sound of the gong, 'the room was like glass'. A section of the work, entitled *The Volga Delta*, was recorded in 1964; sounding, as Smith puts it, 'a bit like distant aeroplane engines with certain pitches booming through above the rest',[85] it formed one side of the composer's first commercial disc, the so-called 'Black LP', issued in 1970.[86]

With the departure of MacLise in February 1964, the group abandoned the rhythmic aspect altogether in the absence of drumming. The drone-based dimensions of its work were now developed more single-mindedly. Melody was forsaken in favour of a continuous stream of sound; Young started holding longer notes on the saxophone. From late 1964, Cale and Conrad began using contact microphones; Conrad played a variety of instruments – guitar, mandolin and mandola (usually bowed, occasionally plucked) – in addition to the violin. The need to balance the volume of the string drones with that of the saxophone encouraged the group to use amplification, and a high volume level soon became an important component of the total sound. But by the summer of 1964, Young had finally given up the saxophone altogether in favour of the voice: singing, as did Zazeela, in a 'nasal' style which uses the nose and throat to control the production of harmonics. Young's vocal improvisations slide from note to note of the drone frequencies, elaborating complex, rhythmically free patterns around them. While this 'nasal' style is familiar from its use by Indian vocalists – which helped make the Youngs' serious study of Indian music from 1970 a natural progression – Smith also suggests connections between the composer's use of it in conjunction with a consistent emphasis on the fourth and fifth above a tonic, and both Greek Byzantine chant and the Temiar Dream music of Malaysia.[87] The increased importance of voices allowed the group's involvement with just intonation to proceed to a new level.

These developments led to Young's *magnum opus* for the Theatre of Eternal Music: *The Tortoise, His Dreams and Journeys*, begun in 1964 and officially still, like *The Well-Tuned Piano*, a work in progress. As a symbol of static evolution and longevity, the tortoise could hardly be bettered. Young and Zazeela kept pet turtles at this time; by 26 March 1966, the drone from the motor that powered their aquarium was amplified and now provided the fundamental pitch to which the group tuned, and which sounded continuously throughout a set. (The group had used a sixty-cycle hum as a frequency reference as early as 6 June 1965.) This was to become one of several electronic drones in actual performances. The basic frequency ratios of the first *Tortoise* music were written down on 29 February 1964, and represented Young's first efforts at notating frequency ratios in just intonation. As with *The Four Dreams of China*, however, *The Tortoise* only exists in performance in the form of a variety of realisations based on a central harmonic idea. What Young calls 'a characteristic melodic pattern' was, though, also played by him on the saxophone, while the other members of the group sustained pitches from this melody as drones.

While these ideas were still coming into focus, the group improvised several proto-*Tortoise* performances. The earliest of these to survive on tape is a private performance given on 2–3 April 1964 for Harry Kraut of the Tanglewood Festival, in the hope of an engagement there. Later known as *Pre-Tortoise Dream Music*, this now included Young and Jennings (sopranino and soprano saxophone, respectively), Zazeela (voice) and the string drones of Cale and Conrad. This was a realisation based on Young's original frequency ratios. Only on 9 October that year were amplified string drones introduced, in a concert performance given the title *Prelude to the Tortoise*, at the Philadelphia College of Art.

The first mature realisations of *The Tortoise* took the form of one- to two-hour 'sections' in 1964, at which the musicians would begin playing before the audience was allowed to enter, thus enhancing the impression of continuity. The first realisation of *The Tortoise* proper was given on the weekends of 30 October–1 November and 20–22 November (either side, as it happens, of the première of Riley's *In C* on the opposite side of the continent), in two groups of three performances each at the Pocket Theater on New York's Third Avenue (the scene in the previous year of Cage's performance of Satie's *Vexations*). By this time, Cale had devised a highly individual approach to his new instrument. He had flattened the bridge in order to be able to bow several strings simultaneously, and used electric-guitar strings on the viola, which helped to create 'a drone like a jet engine!'[88] when fed through the high amplification; he also occasionally played drones on the sarinda, an Indian classical string instrument.

The title given these performances – *The Tortoise Droning Selected Pitches from The Holy Numbers for The Two Black Tigers, The Green Tiger and The Hermit* – alludes to the composer's poem later published in *Selected Writings*;[89] this refers, respectively, to Young and Zazeela (who had begun dressing in all-black denims soon after they first met), and to the string duo of Conrad and Cale. Young and Zazeela sang in front of the Morris gong, which they also bowed; all the musicians were amplified. On 12–13 December, at the same venue, there were two further performances, this time called *The Tortoise Recalling The Drone of The Holy Numbers as They were Revealed in The Dreams of The Whirlwind and The Obsidian*

Gong and Illuminated by The Sawmill, The Green Sawtooth Ocelot and The High-Tension Line Stepdown Transformer. As the music of *The Tortoise* evolved, so did the length and obscurity of each section's title, assembled collectively by the group along stream-of-consciousness lines.

Subsequent realisations of *The Tortoise* became the vehicle for much more detailed explorations of the harmonic series and its musical potential. *Map of 49's Dream The Two Systems of Eleven Sets of Galactic Intervals Ornamental Lightyears Tracery* – its major 'section', on which work was begun in 1966 – had developed to between three and four hours by the time of the 1975 concert performances. (*49* was a pet turtle.) Though the *Tortoise* project remains officially unfinished to this day, these performances – with a Theatre of Eternal Music ensemble by now rather different from that of the original – represent one culmination, at least, of the years spent exploring the potential of the original frequency ratios to sustain long spans of musical time.

Zazeela's lighting designs, on which work had begun in 1964, were first used to full effect at a performance of *The Tortoise* on 4 and 5 December 1965 at the Filmmakers' Cinematheque Festival of Expanded Cinema in the old Wurlitzer building on 41st Street, for which she devised a series of slides that were projected on to the players' silken robes. Kostelanetz's assessment of *The Tortoise*, as early as 1968, as 'among the most admired works in the new theatre'[90] suggests the importance of Zazeela's achievements to the Theatre of Eternal Music's performances. Subsequent developments in her work with light – which continues to provide the visual context for all the composer's performances and installations to this day – included an early predilection for green and, in particular, magenta theatrical gels, used to colour both slides and, later, the shadows cast on ceilings and walls by the elegant, Minimalist, white aluminium mobiles that have become a regular feature of Zazeela's highly imaginative, sculptural use of light.

The Filmmakers' Cinematheque concert marked the beginning of The Theatre of Eternal Music's demise in its original form. During 1965, Cale had already divided his time between Young's ensemble and the group that eventually became The Velvet Underground; Conrad and MacLise were other members of its chief predecessor, The Primitives. After the Cinematheque concert – feeling increasingly dissatisfied with what he regarded as the esoteric and extremist atmosphere surrounding The Theatre of Eternal Music – Cale left to devote all his attention to the other group. His place was taken by Riley, newly arrived in New York, who sang with Young until August 1966. Though Riley performed in public only twice during his involvement, his contribution was telling: with three voices in the group, the 1966 performances of *The Tortoise* relied less on the wall of sound produced by string drones and more on a vocal counterpoint in which Riley, Young and Zazeela 'soared past one another like stars shooting through space'.[91]

Despite these hopeful developments, this incarnation of The Theatre of Eternal Music came to a swift end. Riley's departure to concentrate on solo performances left only Conrad, Young and Zazeela as core members. It was at this point that existing differences between Conrad and Young over the issue of who made the musical decisions erupted into open dispute. Conrad considered that the contributions he and Cale had made to the group's improvisations 'were just much, much more central than I think La Monte would like to admit, or has'.[92] 'There was no composer, but group consensus. La Monte worked out some things that he wanted to do, but this was tangential to the main enterprise'.[93] He says that Young 'has always secreted the material that best shows the contributions of anyone other than himself' and even that he manipulated recordings 'to make him dominate'.

Young, unsurprisingly, views the matter differently, stressing his role as both the originator of the basic aesthetic and as the composer of the music which The Theatre of Eternal Music performed. The essence of *The Tortoise*, most notably, may be argued to have been the notion of 'eternal music' itself, rather than any collection of musical material as such. 'I really like to improvise', he has said, 'and I only like to write down broad, powerful, theoretical constructs'. He responded, indeed, to the demise of The Theatre of Eternal Music by concentrating for some while on his theoretical treatise *The Two Systems of Eleven Categories*, begun in August 1966. Yet Young states that he was largely or entirely responsible both for the codification of pitches in ratio form and for the musical structures involved in their elaboration. The issue of whether the music in the many surviving recordings of the group constitutes compositions by Young or improvisations in which all the performers made important creative contributions beyond the embellishment normal to musical performances remains unsettled to this day. As a consequence, the release of these recordings – something all concerned would basically welcome – is, as of this writing, still prevented by legal wrangling over the rights to the material they contain. Conrad has gone so far as to picket Young's concerts during the last few years. It may simply be that, as Young puts it, Conrad was 'more of a free spirit', while Young himself was interested in a more controlled and limited tonal palette, obsessively devoted to his chosen prime number ratios. But the dispute carries aesthetic as well as practical significance, as we have already seen.

Day of The Antler

What precisely did Young notate for these works, and to what extent can they reasonably be considered his own compositions in addition to – or even rather than – group improvisations? As an illustration of what Young has written down and how notation might be used to analyse the music after the event, let us take the single page of 'score' for the improvisation entitled *Day of The Antler 15 VIII 65 The Obsidian Ocelot, The Sawmill and The Blue Sawtooth High-Tension Line Stepdown Transformer Refracting The Legend of The Dream of The Tortoise Traversing The 189/98 Lost Ancestral Lake Region Illuminating Scenes from The Black Tiger Tapestries of The Drone of The Holy Numbers from 'The Tortoise, His Dreams and Journeys'* (see Ex. 1.9). This was actually transcribed not for performance but in order to apply for a Guggenheim Fellowship, a condition of which was that scores must be submitted.

As the title suggests, this tape was made on 15 August 1965, when the core group of performers improvising as a quartet consisted of Young and Zazeela (voices), Cale (voice and five-string viola) and Conrad (violin). These are indicated by name in the left-hand margin, and by initial in the first column, 'Articulating Instrument(s) or Voices'. As the heading of the sixth column indicates, the improvisation used a range of three octaves (represented by the ratio 512:64). For those unused to notation in frequency terms, the final column offers the easiest way in. This gives the pitches in equal-tempered *solfège* notation. One can read these *solfège* symbols off against the cent tables of the sixth column (where the pitches to be used have been precisely calculated) and the seventh column (presented as a guiding grid) with reference to the semitones and tones of the major scale. The fundamental turns out to be E at 80 cycles per second; thus the dominant is 60 or 120 cycles per second.

In the second column, these pitches are given in the form of cycles per second, presented as a single big chord. This shows, not surprisingly, that the pitches based on the fundamental E constitute not the equally tempered scale perhaps suggested by the *solfège*, but an unclassifiable mode in just intonation including flattened fourths and sevenths, very flat sixths, plus very sharp fourths and sevenths – as written in against the more precise cents of the sixth column, tuned in just intonation. While the fundamental E could be considered the tonic, B can also be heard as the basis of this mode. In the third column, each partial is given in its lowest common terms, making clear, for example, which intervals are septimally related. In the fourth column, their factorised equivalents are given for calculation purposes; this reveals that all the pitches in *Day of The Antler*

Example 1.9 ... *the day of the antler* ..., complete score

La Monte Young

System of Frequencies Used on the day of the antler · 15 VIII 65 (Tape of "The Obsidian Ocelot, The Sawmill And The Blue Sawtooth High-Tension Line Stepdown Transformer Refracting the Legend of The Dream of The Tortoise Traversing The 189/98 Lost Ancestral Lake Region Illuminating Quotients from the Black Tiger Tapestries of The Drone of The Holy Numbers") "The Tortoise, His Dreams And Journeys"

Articulating Instrument(s) or Voice(s)	Cycles per Second	Lowest Binary Form of Partials	Partials of The Partials Within the Three Octaves 512/64	Partials Within the Three Octaves 512/64 (frequencies in ratio)	Cents of The Partials Within The Three Octaves 512/64	Cents		Major Scale in Equal Temperament (3/2)
π	640 / 630	63	2^9 / $7 \times 3^2 \times 2^9$	512 / 504	E 3600 / D## 3572.74	3600	E	do
						3500	D#	ti
						3400	D	
π	560	7	7×2^6	448	D↓ 3368.83	3300	C#	la
						3200	C	
π	490	49	$7^2 \times 2^3$	392	C↓↓ 3137.66	3100	B	so
π	480	3	3×2^7	384	B 3101.96			
π	472.5	/89	$7 \times 3^3 \times 2$	378	A## 3074.70	3000	A#	
π	420	21	$7 \times 3 \times 2^4$	336	A↓ 2870.11	2900	A	fa
						2800	G#	mi
						2700	G	
						2600	F#	re
						2500	F	
MZ/πC	320	1	2^8	256	E 2400	2400	E	do
						2300	D#	ti
						2200	D	
MZ/LY(3rd)	280	7	7×2^5	224	D↓ 2168.83	2100	C#	la
						2000	C	
JC	236.25	/89	7×3^3	/89	A## 1874.70	1900	B	so
						1800	A#	
						1700	A	fa
						1600	G#	mi
						1500	G	
						1400	F#	re
						1300	F	
LY/JC(3rd)	160 / 157.5	63	$7 \times 3^2 \times 2$	128 / 126	E 1200 / D## 1172.74	1200	E	do
						1100	D#	ti
						1000	D	
LY	140	7	7×2^4	112	D↓ 968.83	900	C#	la
						800	C	
LY / JC(3rd)	122.5 / 120	49 / 3	$7^2 \times 2$ / 3×2^5	98 / 96	C↓↓ 737.66 / B 701.96	700	B	so
						600	A#	
						500	A	fa
						400	G#	mi
						300	G	
						200	F#	re
						100	F	
	80	1	2^6	64	E 0	0	E	do

Code: LY = La Monte Young voice; MZ = Marian Zazeela voice; TC = Tony Conrad (Tony) Violin; JC(3rd) = John Cale 5-string drone; JC = John Cale Gong voice; π = πC

are factors of 2, 3 or 7. The fifth column presents all the partials laid out within the same octave range in the form of frequency ratios, which is to say in their proper ratios to each other in the improvisation itself.

This algorithmic score thus confines itself purely to pitch and instrumentation. Clearly, the detailed structure of the performance – including all matters of duration and proportion – as well as its style were established by a combination of reference to previous practice, rehearsal and the inspiration of the improvised moment. The musical results depend on the way in which intuition and imagination go to work on given material. It may be asserted that Young provided the material; but others may also have had an input into this, especially at the earlier stages of such music's conceptualisation. The group clearly provided the elaboration of it, each performer being ultimately responsible for his own part. But the interaction not only included Young as one of the protagonists but was also, on the available evidence, driven by someone who acknowledges that he is 'very authoritarian' and – in an oddly characteristic moment of self-deprecation – 'not fit to be collaborated with'. While such an approach may be said to contradict the spirit of the Pythagorean aesthetic that lies behind The Theatre of Eternal Music, it led to music of an unusually individual creative certainty.

Dream Houses and Indian classical music

Young disbanded The Theatre of Eternal Music in its original form following a performance at the Sundance Festival in Pennsylvania on 20 August 1966; after turning for a while to theoretical work, he began to perform again alone or with Zazeela. While Young's uncompromising conditions for the dissemination of his art have frequently hindered its commercial exposure, Young and Zazeela made annual tours throughout the USA and Europe between 1969 and 1975. It was during this period, in fact, that Young's music received its widest exposure. The creation of Dream Houses and other installations in art galleries and museums was now complemented by solo performances by Young, duo performances with Zazeela and, from the late 1960s, the revival of The Theatre of Eternal Music as an ensemble along lines similar to that of the mid-1960s. Some members of the original group, including Conrad, returned; musicians who now performed with the composer for the first time included Alex Dea, Jon Gibson, Jon Hassell, Lee Konitz, Garrett List and David Rosenboom.

Some of the Theatre of Eternal Music's performances, both in Europe and the USA, took place in Dream House installations. Notable among these are the ones for the Maeght Foundation in the south of France in the summer of 1970, at the invitation of Daniel Caux, and the run of performances at major international cultural exhibitions: Documenta 5 in Kassel and the Munich Olympics (1972) and Contemporanea in Rome (1973). American performances included a Dream House installation with concerts at the University of Illinois in 1973 and a week-long series of events at The Kitchen in New York, beginning on 28 April 1974, the latter announced with a Sunday feature in the New York Times by Tom Johnson[94] which, Zazeela says, 'drew crowds that circled the block waiting to get in'.[95]

The exposure of Young's music, particularly in Europe during the first half of the 1970s, was assisted by the composer's first commercial recordings. A 1969 realisation of a 'section' of *Map of 49's Dream* appeared on the West German Edition X label in 1970 – on the already mentioned 'Black LP', with *The Volga Delta* from 1964 on the other side – with Young and Zazeela singing over a sine wave drone. Another – in which sine wave drones accompanied Hassell's trumpet and List's trombone as well as the voices of Young and Zazeela once again – was released on the French label Shandar in 1974, together with a version of *Drift Studies*; both sides of this LP were recorded in the previous year. Though these recordings were issued on small, independent labels, they were quite widely disseminated, expanding the reputation of a composer whose work had already become known in France, West Germany, Italy and elsewhere in Europe (though very little in Britain) in the late 1960s.

The more obvious manifestations of 'eternal music' are most immediately appreciated in the Dream House projects and 'Sound and Light Environments', one of which – on the floor above the Youngs' loft, begun in 1993 – was scheduled to run for seven years, their longest to date. Young and Zazeela characterise what they call these 'extended exhibitions',[96] in which visitors may move about freely, as 'time installation[s] measured by a setting of continuous frequencies in sound and light'. Frequencies tuned to the harmonic series, generated by electronically produced sine waves creating continuous chordal drones of periodic composite waveforms, constitute the entire aural material of these installations; yet, by moving around the space, the listener is able to experience not only different relationships among the frequencies emphasised by the audible standing wave patterns, but also the combination tones brought about by the interaction of the harmonically related sine wave frequencies themselves, including the phenomenon known as 'acoustical beats'. Change may thus be experienced in the extended contemplation of apparently unchanging, or only slowly changing, acoustic situations. Zazeela's contributions – both 'environmental' (pure light) and sculptural mobiles and wall sculptures – share the concern with symmetry which has increasingly characterised Young's work with frequencies. More importantly, they are crucial to the Dream Houses' aim of encouraging their visitors 'towards self-reflection and a meditative state'.

The frequencies selected for these sound environments have sometimes been taken from Young's concert works; thus *The Tortoise*, for instance, provided chords for *Intervals and Triads from Map of 49's, etc.* (1967). The original idea of the Dream House incorporated live musicians, but this proved far too expensive. (In recent years, the exploration of new frequency relationships in sound environments has fed into the concert output.) The investigation of psycho-acoustical effects without performers was taken up as an independent 'work' in *Drift Studies* for two or more sine wave drones, precisely tuned on oscillators which must be highly stable. Like *The Tortoise* and *The Well-Tuned Piano*, this dates from 1964. The version that appeared on the already mentioned Shandar disc ten years later is typical of the sets of frequencies devised for the Dream Houses, which are also to be found in *The Two Systems of Eleven Categories*. Here, Young exploits the consequences of the instability inherent in combining waveforms generated by older 1960s and 1970s model analogue sine wave oscillators and their relationship to the 'universal truths of harmonic structure'. As the phase relationship between the sine waves alters, due to the change of air pressure within a space, both pitch and volume vary according to one's location in the room; this 'allows the listener to actually experience sound structures in the natural course of exploring the space'.[97] When 'the composite waveform of the combination tones of the two sine waves gradually, internally and organically, shifts', explains the composer, '. . . [t]he body intuitively recognizes that information having to do with basic universal structure is coming in as sound'. At high volume levels, one also 'begins to have a sensation that parts of the body are somehow locked in sync with the sine waves and slowly drifting with them in space and time'.

The idea 'that a piece could be forever, if you let the concept happen'[98] emerged in 1962, inspired by *The Four Dreams of China*. But the first of these sound installations was not established until September 1966, in the Youngs' own loft, where it continued almost without interruption until January 1970. Though not all its successors have used extremely high volumes, this early example, with which the couple lived almost continuously, was often amplified to the high levels required to 'get inside of the sound', and to hear all the components of the envelope generated by the harmonically related sine waves. The first public Dream House was opened at Friedrich's Munich art gallery in July 1969. Several others have since been set up, both in the USA and Europe, including an important one at Rice University, Houston early in 1970. A more prominent one at New York's Metropolitan Museum of Art, in the autumn of the following year, included performances in which the composer's regular musicians were joined by Konitz, who was then studying, like Young and Zazeela, with Pandit Pran Nath (of which more below). Tapes from the latter, plus 1964 recordings of *The Well-Tuned Piano* and *Sunday Morning Blues*, were broadcast on the radio in France and Germany; this led, in 1992, to the release of a two-disc bootleg recording.

The most ambitious Dream House occupied the enormous church-like space of the old Mercantile Exchange Building at 6 Harrison Street, not far from the Youngs' loft. Here, between 1979 and 1985, Young and Zazeela established themselves in splendour, financed by the Dia Foundation with the intention of providing a permanent research centre and public outlet for their activities. This came the nearest among such projects to Young's utopian vision of continuous sound which would 'last forever in Dream Houses where many musicians and students will live and execute a musical work. Dream Houses will allow music which, after a year, ten years, a hundred years or more of constant sound, would not only be a real living organism with a life and tradition of its own but one with a capacity to propel itself by its own momentum'.[99] Though funded – with oil money from the Schlumberger heirs – with a magnificence almost unparalleled in late-twentieth-century sponsorship of the arts, this project came to an abrupt end after six years when the oil market collapsed.

In the evolution of Young's work after the mid-1960s, one other biographical aspect is paramount. In 1970 Young and Zazeela both became disciples of the North Indian master singer Pandit Pran Nath. Young had already come under his influence in 1967, when Shyam Bhatnagar, already a disciple, played some tapes for him, which impressed Young with the profundity of their expression. In January 1970, the Youngs helped Bhatnagar bring Pran Nath to the USA. In the manner of the students of such spiritual as well as musical mentors, they devoted all their time and energies to him for certain periods over twenty-five years; for fifteen years their guru spent half his time in the Youngs' loft. Pran Nath died on 13 June 1996. The Youngs had maintained a close spiritual relationship with him, and continue to regard him as their musical and spiritual master. Such an involvement is scarcely surprising in the context of Young's previous concern with the connections Indian classical music had with his own: his listening to recordings by major masters, which were an important formative influence on the early development of the composer's 'static' approach; and his development of a style of saxophone playing owing something to the characteristics of the Indian shenai with which the sopranino instrument, in particular, has something in common. Closest of all, of course, is the adoption, by both Young and Zazeela in the mid-1960s, of a style of singing already owing much to the timbre and general approach of Indian singers, even though they had not yet made a systematic study of any Indian vocal style.

The influence of Pran Nath has, inevitably, been at least as much spiritual as musical. Indian theory and practice foster close connections between the two, which emerge in Pran Nath's teaching, for instance, in the form of analogies between tuning one's voice and drawing closer to the deity. 'When the voice becomes perfectly in tune with the drone, with the tambura', Young says, 'it's like leaving the body and meeting God'. The composer has said that 'while there are many profound relationships and differences between my work and Indian music', he has tried 'to keep the two forms as distinct and pure as possible'. One significant influence of Pran Nath on Young's own music, however, has been the organically evolving form of improvisation to be found in the Kirana style of which his guru was a leading practitioner. This has influenced all Young's work since the early 1970s, but in particular *The Well-Tuned Piano*.

The most important aspect of Young's activities in the period 1974–5 was his return to work on *The Well-Tuned Piano*, which now became his main project of the 1970s and 1980s, and the chief focus of his solo performances during that time. The story of his compositional development, as well as performing career, in this period is largely the story of the evolution of *The Well-Tuned Piano*, which correspondingly forms the final section of this chapter.

The Well-Tuned Piano

Though *The Tortoise, His Dreams and Journeys* may in several respects be accounted Young's *magnum opus*, it is *The Well-Tuned Piano* which has occupied the lion's share of his attention for significant periods of time since the 1970s. The work is, however, significant not only in the context of his output as a whole but more widely: in the contexts of musical minimalism, of musics working at the interface between composition and improvisation, and of twentieth-century music for solo piano. It does not seem too far-fetched to say, as Gann does in the opening sentence of the most important article so far published on the piece, that '*The Well-Tuned Piano* may well be the most important American piano work since Charles Ives's *Concord* Sonata – in size, in influence, and in revolutionary innovation'.[100] Since even its most recent performances relate intimately to the basic principles and methods conceived for the work in 1964, it seemed appropriate to extend the discussion of it beyond the cut-off date established for this book as a whole.

Work on *The Well-Tuned Piano* began in 1964, though it was not until ten years later that any version of it was performed live. Being an improvised 'composition' – though in ways somewhat different from those of the ensemble music – *The Well-Tuned Piano* is flexible both in content and structure, indeed seemingly infinitely expandable. The 1974 Rome world première realisation paved the way for all subsequent endeavours on what Young has called 'the work which has since completely captivated me and has become the source and inspiration for some of my most creative developments'.[101] *The Well-Tuned Piano* has been performed in public over sixty times. In addition to the important performances in New York in 1975, following fairly closely on the four in Rome, two series of performances – both also made in New York – are culminating, if not yet 'definitive'. Those made in 1981 include the five-hour performance on 25 October, the recording of which, issued by Gramavision in 1987, is the only realisation of *The Well-Tuned Piano* to have become widely available; the booklet notes for this are commendably informative and include a detailed structural breakdown of the performance itself. In 1987, Young performed a further series, adding much new material and extending the average length to around six hours. The last two performances in this series, and in particular the final one, represent, at least for Young himself, the present state of the work. While, as usual, every performance was recorded, the last three 1987 realisations were also videotaped; among the advantages of releasing a version of one of these would be to make Zazeela's lighting design for *The Well-Tuned Piano* more widely appreciated. Since 1987, *The Well-Tuned Piano* has never been performed. Young now wonders if it ever will be again.

The chief reason for this is the demands Young makes, on himself and others, when proposals are made to perform the work. He considers that it takes 'at least a week or two' to tune the piano properly; meanwhile, the instrument must remain *in situ*: thus, he considers, making the space, as well as the piano itself, largely unusable for other performances. In fact, he asks for three months 'on location', in the first month of which, ideally, a whole Dream-House-style environment is constructed around the constantly tended piano, allowing Young unlimited preparation and the audience the best possible conditions in which to appreciate a continuous performance of some five or six hours. Even the size and position of the audience can change the acoustic sufficiently, for instance, to affect whether specific psycho-acoustic effects discovered earlier while working in the space would actually sound in the concert itself. What he most wants, with each engagement to play *The Well-Tuned Piano*, is the opportunity to add more to it, to experiment, to compose, as well as to rehearse: the improvisational nature of the work clearly blurs the distinctions between these activities anyway. 'I get no satisfaction unless the piece grows', he says. He will only practise *The Well-Tuned Piano* during intensive periods of preparation for concert performances, free of day-to-day concerns.

Two other matters have for years prevented even a single one of the performances Young has given of *The Well-Tuned Piano* – each one meticulously taped – from being analysed with the thoroughness the work deserves. The first is the system of just intonation it uses, which for years Young kept a secret, until Gann reconstructed much of it, thus persuading the composer 'to release the tuning into public discourse'.[102] There is, considers Gann, 'virtually no way to analyze the piece without it'. The second is the nature of the musical material upon which Young constructs his improvisations, which for years Young also kept secret, though some of it was written down in the form of themes, chord structures and scales, and what Gann calls 'ornamental patterns'.[103] Though still not published, a copy of this 'score' has been obtained by the present author – who, like all those not part of the composer's own immediate circle, has in the past had to rely purely on the evidence of his own ears, plus a few tantalising glimpses of tiny portions of the material in notated form. Young says that he developed his tendency to be secretive about his ideas before they were actually published because he found that other composers liked his ideas 'so much that they felt the need to avail themselves of them'.

It is not my intention here to provide a comprehensive analysis of *The Well-Tuned Piano*, least of all with detailed regard to the issue of tuning; Gann, in any case, has already accomplished this task quite brilliantly. What follows attempts merely to establish the nature and estimate the significance of the work, in terms of Young's evolution of minimalism, by charting a little of its history, and giving some examples both of its basic material and of the structural context into which the improvisational elaborations of this material are fitted. This discussion draws not only on the 'score', but also on hearings of a number of recordings of *The Well-Tuned Piano*, going back to the 1964 tapes – not only the commercial recording of 1981, on which Gann's article is largely based. And though the booklet notes to the Gramavision release of the 1981 recording give an account of the evolution of the work to that date, they do not include the advances made in 1987.

In the spring and summer of 1964, when Young made the first tapes of *The Well-Tuned Piano*, he only had a small spinet-type piano that he had recently been given by Zazeela's parents; though almost thirty years old, the composer had never had regular access to a piano of his own before. On 23 March, he began to retune this instrument in just intonation, and soon began to play short improvisations on it. The justly tuned modality which is central to *The Well-Tuned Piano* establishes a natural link with Young's sopranino saxophone improvisations of 1962–4, on concluding which, work on this composition began. *The Well-Tuned Piano* takes as its fundamental, its 'tonic', the E♭ on the seventh chord of which he had built so many saxophone improvisations. The choice has already been explained in terms of the sopranino saxophone's structure itself; in applying this to the keyboard, Young was also following an established trend in blues playing developed over many decades. Using this E♭ as his fundamental, he devised a tuning of twelve frequencies evolved from the six used in *Pre-Tortoise Dream Music* which, earlier in 1964, had been the basis of the first sopranino saxophone improvisations to attempt just intonation. This tuning is also based on the same ratios factorable by 2, 3 and 7 used in such improvisations with the Theatre of Eternal Music as the already discussed *The Day of the Antler*.

A further connection with the saxophone improvisations is made via the 'fast combination/permutation' techniques Young now again employs on the piano, based on those he used in the work with saxophone. In *The Well-Tuned Piano*, these were to become what the composer calls 'clouds'. On the 1964 tapes, these 'clouds' are already present, if in vestigial form, as fast permutations on a single handful, sometimes two handfuls, of notes. Only later, though, does Young introduce a dimension crucial to the impact of these 'clouds': the *sostenuto* pedal lacking on the original spinet piano.

In other respects, too, the first attempts at *The Well-Tuned Piano* are, not surprisingly, more in the nature of experiments than fully formed structures. While three main 'chordal areas' – which Young calls 'The Opening Chord', 'The Tamiar Dream Chord' and 'The Early Romantic Chord' – were established in 1964, their articulation was achieved mainly by means of the fast permutation technique with fairly primitive results. By the time Fabio Sargentini arranged the first public performances of *The Well-Tuned Piano*, in Rome ten years later, Young had modified the tuning and, more importantly, obtained a Bösendorfer piano, which Sargentini purchased for his exclusive use. In 1976, the Dia Art Foundation purchased for Young a large Imperial Bösendorfer which, after custom work done under the composer's direction, was flown to New York, and between 1979 and 1985, housed permanently at Harrison Street.

Young had also begun to develop a much wider range of material. Though in 1974/5 this was still essentially in the form of 'chordal areas', the following years – culminating in the performances of 1981, which took place in Harrison Street – saw the invention of fully fledged themes, as well as greater and greater elaborations of the basic chords, proliferating into sets and subsets with exotic names such as 'The Deep in the Rainforest Chord' and 'The Ethers Churn (The Dinosaurs Dance)'. Already in 1981, Young had assembled themes with a surprising, and post-modernist, range of references to other musics, as their titles also hint at: 'The Homage to Brahms Variation of The Theme of The Dawn of Eternal Time', 'Young's Böse Brontosaurus Boogie', 'Scheherazade'. By the time of the 1987 performances, a further category of themes – 'Orpheus and Eurydice in The Elysian Fields' – had been added. Some of the material of *The Well-Tuned Piano* dates back as far as the improvisations Young used to perform in his late teens on his maternal grandmother's piano. One category of material, in particular – what the composer calls 'the more classic-sounding themes' – derives, at least in part, from this source. Example 1.10 illustrates something of the range of the material, both chordal and thematic, on which *The Well-Tuned Piano* is based.

The ideal conditions in which the piano was eventually housed permitted the further development of one of the most important discoveries that work on *The Well-Tuned Piano* had thrown up. The combination of increasingly precise tuning and the fast combination/permutation finger techniques Young had by now perfected allowed some of the composite waveforms to become audible. 'Extraordinary periodic acoustical beats became suspended in the air like a cloud over the piano', writes the composer, 'sometimes even filling the entire space during the energy accumulations of the longest passages'.[104] One development which significantly enhanced the range and impact of the 'clouds' was Young's discovery – in 1975, during a three-month-long Dream Festival at Dia's Wooster Street space – that he could synchronise the rhythms of the piano mechanism's hammers with the acoustical beats produced by his fast repeated playing. The result is 'a type of resonance system' in which the pulses of the hammer rhythms combine with those of the waveforms in a symbiotic sort of feedback; 'a controlled, audible, acoustical synchronization between rhythm and frequency in live performance (without the aid of electronics) for the first time in the history of music', Young argues.

Certainly, those who have most thoroughly investigated and exploited the connections between rhythm and frequency – Stockhausen, for example – have not only researched this with the aid of electronics but also employed tape or live electronics in realising its potential in actual compositions. Even if the claims seem a trifle hyperbolic, the effect of this synchronisation, cunningly exploited at length in the course of a slowly unfolding overall structure, is extremely powerful. The 'clouds' are central to *The Well-Tuned Piano*, leading the listener to experience a wide range of psycho-acoustic effects: French horns, saxophones and voices have all been heard on the 1987 tapes by the present author. In one of the Rome performances, Young even experimented with singing, using his own voice to provide a further dimension – acoustic this time, not psycho-acoustic – to

Example 1.10 *The Well-Tuned Piano*: (a) 'The Magic Opening Chord'; (b) 'The Romantic Chord'; (c) 'Theme for Orpheus and Eurydice in The Elysian Fields'; (d) a 'Blues Break from Young's Böse Brontesaurus Boogie'; (e) 'The Homage to Brahms Variation of the theme of the Dawn of Eternal Time'

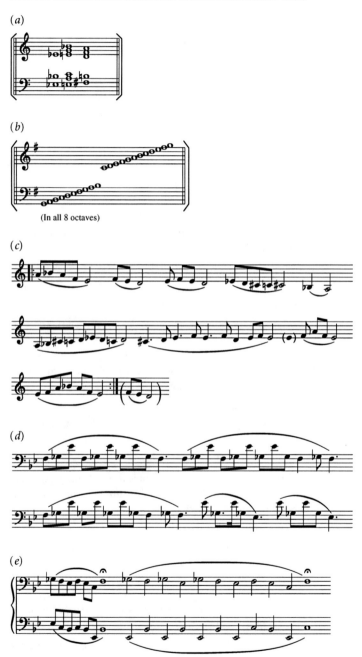

the experience. But although it was well received, he quickly found that it was very difficult, and he felt that it would be necessary to interweave the singing more systematically throughout the work to achieve a sense of timbral balance, which would have been even more difficult. Finally, he concluded that *The Well-Tuned Piano* was so complete in itself that, if anything, the addition of other timbres detracted from the achievement of the work as a piano solo. Though he tried it again in rehearsal at Harrison Street, he never repeated the experiment in a concert.

For each series of performances, Young has developed a clear notion of 'the current macro-structure', on which each individual performance will be based. Playing entirely from memory, he then improvises on a range of the material introduced above with reference to this overall scheme. With the 'piece in its present state of affairs', the structure would unfold along the following lines:

The Well-Tuned Piano: basic structural plan

'The Opening Chord'; E♭; mid-range, close position; simple statement

transition; adds notes to prepare for

'The Magic Chord'; A D; no pitches in common with 'The Opening Chord'

transition to

'The Magic Opening Chord'; E♭ B♭ and D A; mixes 'The Opening Chord' and 'The Magic Chord'; gradually unfolds in the setting of 'The Magic Harmonic Rainforest Chord' (most of the notes of the original E♭ key in a rising harmonic series, with 'The Magic Chord' added in); the longest section, with much new material added, including the major new section, 'Blues for Eurydice'

transition; unusual harmonic departures mixed with 'Baroque sequences'

'The Romantic Chord'; G-Dorian; from which 'The Magic Chord' is derived, since 'The Magic Chord' is a subset of 'The Romantic Chord'

'The Elysian Fields'; D-Aeolian

'Orpheus and Euridice in The Elysian Fields'; E♭ B♭ and D A, fused to create two new hyper-modes – one on D and one on E♭ – composed of similar-sized but not identical intervals, omitting the fourth degree

returning eventually to E♭ for

'The Ending', with a final statement, an octave lower, of the first two dyads of 'The Theme of The Dawn of Eternal Time'

Each of these main sections has many subsections within it, allowing many possibilities for varied development both of material and structure. But Young's intention is to allow the music to grow out of the opening notes 'in a way that to me sounds compositionally realistic and lifelike'. In part, this is achieved through statement, variation and restatement of the thematic material already discussed. But the structural evolution of *The Well-Tuned Piano* also owes a good deal to the key scheme which lies behind it. Beginning in E♭, this extends its way up into the harmonic series and eventually returns to the opening mode. Important in this unfolding of modal centres is the note D, which recurs throughout the work as an alternative to E♭, a procedure made more subtle and even ambiguous by the close proximity of these pitches in Young's tuning: the ratio of 64:63, or 27.26 cents. The prominence of the 'dominants' of these two pitches further complicates matters, making the mixed modality of 'The Magic Opening Chord', for example, ultimately describable only as E♭ B♭ with D A.

In addition, E♭'s seventh partial, notated as C, is used as a common pitch to link the original E♭ to the G-Dorian mode, in which this C now becomes the fourth degree. Present in 'The Opening Chord', but absent from 'The Magic Chord', C becomes crucial in the process of modulation away from and back to E♭. Its close relationship to G – which is present in 'The Magic Chord' – helps make these modulations possible, using not only common notes but those closely related to them to achieve smooth changes of mode. Modulation is generally considered problematic in just intonation. For Young, however, it is 'an exciting adventure more than a problem'. The basic difficulty he faces is the number of keys on the keyboard which, combined with the unusual nature of his chosen tuning, makes what might have appeared as closely related areas (modes a perfect fifth apart, for instance) linkable only with difficulty or compromise. Since both the D and D♭ keys were used up on other vital parts of Young's tuning, the flat minor seventh he required had to be played by the C key, already mentioned. This in turn led him to avoid using B♭ – the 'dominant' of the fundamental E♭ – as much as might have been expected, since the dominant of *its* dominant (C, a perfect fifth from F) is now already in use. This makes chord V in B♭ unavailable, and thus also its tonicisation, at least in the same way as E♭ could be tonicised. Some of the 1987 version's 'Boogie' material, which the composer describes as 'a kind of blues in B♭', is in that key, using E♭ as its IV in a typical blues manner, but using chord V sparingly and without sounding its fifth, C.

It would be foolish to deny that minimalist elements can be found even in the 1987 realisations of *The Well-Tuned Piano*. Its use of combination/permutation techniques on sets of pitch clusters, and more generally of both extended repetition and modality, represent some of the classic minimalist traits as defined both by this book and by Young himself, who employs the term with respect to *The Well-Tuned Piano* almost as cheerfully as he does with respect to *Trio for Strings*. But the work is much more besides. It confronts the challenge of building an extended musical edifice with the aid of themes and their development, which involves variation, extension and combination, not merely repetition. In particular, it employs a sophisticated large-scale formal approach that has significant evolutionary tendencies which listeners to *The Well-Tuned Piano* are encouraged to appreciate over audaciously long spans of time, and which bring to the work not only a sense of grand design but also of tension and growth, dynamism, climax and resolution. As we have seen, this is achieved through pitch structure as well as thematically. It is influenced, perhaps particularly, by Young's deeper experience of Indian classical music through his studies with Pran Nath, who taught him that modal music need not be purely static, but could change and evolve in dramatic spans of cumulative power.

In its concern for the drama of development and contrast, the overall form of *The Well-Tuned Piano* – at least in its realisations of 1981 and 1987 – is not minimalist at all but, as Daniel Wolf has said, 'maximal'.[105] In 1964, however, this structural sense was as lacking as the material was athematic. Even the available versions of 1974 and 1975, while wider in their range of material and more evolved structurally, did not aim at the sort of dramatic curve embraced by the later performances; the methods by which even such thematic material as exists is articulated and elaborated remain fundamentally minimalist. To that extent, Young's development of *The Well-Tuned Piano* to the mid-1970s runs in parallel with that of his colleagues.

In his commitment to just intonation, however, Young is unparalleled. As Gann puts it:

> This is a very original twelve-pitch tuning, quite unlike the keyboard tunings of any other composer. . . . What [Young] gains from limiting his scale steps is, not only an exotic abundance of tiny intervals, but a flexibility in harmonic modulation potential that few just intonation tunings possess. Harmonic flexibility is given precedence over filling out the melodic space. The tuning grew from the harmonic structure, and melodic considerations came afterward.[106]

In this respect, *The Well-Tuned Piano* stands as the greatest testament to its composer's belief that '[e]qual temperament reminds one of the truth; just intonation *is* the truth'.

Conclusion

Despite the distance he has travelled since *Trio for Strings* and *Composition 1960 #7*, Young's output of the late 1950s and early 1960s remains an enduring legacy to other composers. Terry Jennings was the first composer to imitate his long-note approach, and other close associates in the late 1950s – such as Dennis Johnson, whose work remains almost totally unknown, and Pauline Oliveros, whose work as composer, improviser and teacher is highly regarded, particularly in the USA – were also strongly affected by Young's early compositions. The swift loss – largely deliberate – of his position as New York's leading avant-garde figurehead, combined with his move away from conceptualism and performance art, served to reduce Young's significance for non-musicians in the New York avant-garde community after 1961. Yet many artists associated with Fluxus were influenced by his conceptual output of 1960–61, which – not least on account of its shock value and susceptibility to cheap imitation – still passes for Young's main achievement in the history of music as well as that of avant-garde art.

Young's influence on John Cage in the 1960s has already been discussed. His influence on already established composers who were themselves his student mentors is not, however, confined to Cage. Karlheinz Stockhausen's exploration of the harmonic series, notably in *Stimmung* (1968), has often been linked to Young's example. Less noted is his possible impact on *Klavierstück IX*, the piano piece by Stockhausen which is similarly dominated by a dissonant chord, repeated in sequences governed by the Fibonacci series. Cardew once described *Klavierstück IX* as a 'weak, aesthetic version'[107] of *Arabic Numeral (any integer) to H. F*, composed and first circulated in 1960. The original version of Stockhausen's piece is dated 1954, but he revised it in 1961, and surely heard, or at least heard about, Young's notoriously repetitive work in the meantime. The German composer seems to have visited Young and Zazeela when in New York, in 1964 or 1965, and listened to a rehearsal of The Theatre of Eternal Music. He requested tapes of the group's performances which, perhaps surprisingly, Young gave him. Stockhausen's own musicians visited Young and Zazeela's Dream House installation in Antwerp in 1969.

Well known from quite early on in parts of Europe, and in Japan, Young has influenced many non-American composers. Some became close colleagues: for example, the Swede Christer Hennix, who has also lent her talents in mathematics and acoustic theory to Young's investigation of intervals based on prime number ratios.[108] The list of non-Americans influenced by Young's early works and ideas includes Werner Durand, Takehisa Kosugi, Yuji Takahashi and Michael von Biel.

In Britain, which he did not visit for a public concert of his work until 1989, the composer became known chiefly through the advocacy of Cornelius Cardew, who met him in Stockhausen's Darmstadt class in 1959 and was involved in some of the early European performances of *Poem*. Cardew also subsequently visited Young in New York, and his own incorporation of improvisation into an 'experimental' approach to composition was inspired not only by the early pieces but also by the work of The Theatre of Eternal Music. Many English 'experimental' composers first learnt about Young through Cardew's correspondence and visits in the 1960s. Young first visited Britain professionally when he lectured during a Tape Concert in London's Place Theatre on 20 July 1970, organised by the Scratch Orchestra, at which a recording of The Theatre of Eternal Music was played. On 22 June 1989, an Almeida Festival programme, for which the composer came to London, was devoted entirely to his early output, including *Trio for Strings*.

Young's obsessive work since the early 1960s – and especially the conclusions from his work into tuning – has produced a creative cauldron from which many others have extracted ideas and inspiration. Though the extent of his influence has been limited by lack of access both to the music itself and to the theoretical work which helped fuel it, both musicians and non-musicians have been affected by Young's example. In this respect, the structural complexity and sophistication of *The Well-Tuned Piano* must be accounted as being of perhaps even greater significance than his work with The Theatre of Eternal Music. Drones, clusters and sheer volume are all too easily imitated. But a number of composers have seized his ideas about the potential of these things for exploring the innards of sound through the harmonic series and developed them along individual lines.

The influence of the Young of the Theatre of Eternal Music as opposed to that of the Theatre of the Singular Event can be measured partly via the group's own performers, who now cover several different generations of composers and other musicians. After the early years detailed above – involving John Cale, Tony Conrad, Terry Riley and others – The Theatre of Eternal Music's later incarnations from 1969 onwards involved musicians who went on to explore a variety of approaches: some venturing far away from Young's own style but all owing a debt to him for his approach to sustained sounds and their tuning. Jon Hassell, who first heard tapes of Young's saxophone improvisations when a composition pupil of Stockhausen, was a member of the group from 1971 to 1975; his own studies with Pran Nath encouraged him to invent a 'vocal' style for his trumpet playing. David Rosenboom, an important music theorist as well as composer, was a viola player in the group at this time. Younger generations of composer-performers involved with The Theatre of Eternal Music include another trumpet player, Ben Neill, and the cellist Charles Curtis, and many others who have more recently played in the various incarnations of The Theatre of Eternal Music Big Band and the composer's Forever Bad Blues Band.

In the USA, many composers have acknowledged Young's influence, and some have also studied as well as worked with him. These names include Glenn Branca, Jon Catler, Rhys Chatham, Alex Dea, Arnold Dreyblatt, David Hykes, Donald Miller and Raphael Mostel, several of them important members of the downtown Manhattan music scene from the 1970s onwards. Others particularly attracted by Young's concern with just intonation include Kyle Gann, Michael Harrison – the only other musician besides Young to be permitted to perform *The Well-Tuned Piano* – Michael Schumacher and Daniel Wolf.

Some of the above musicians – including Branca, Chatham and Hassell – have taken Young's ideas further than he has done himself into areas beyond the musical avant-garde, and from early on, the composer's influence has been felt in a variety of other arenas. The second half of the 1962 programme which saw the New York première of *Trio for Strings* saw an hour-long performance of *Composition 1960 #7* – the sustained B and F♯ piece – which was seemingly attended by Andy Warhol; his static films – for some of which Young was asked to provide music – were perhaps influenced by the composer's static sounds.[109] The Velvet Underground, the group popularised by Warhol, and its predecessor, The Primitives, are but two examples of the influence Young has had on 'alternative' rock and other musics related to it. Cale and MacLise, who formed The Primitives with Sterling Morrison and Lou Reed, had worked with Young; Walter de Maria and Henry Flynt, other associates of the composer, played in both groups at various times. Reed – who, according to Conrad,[110] was already tuning his guitar to a single pitch when in The Primitives – acknowledges Young as an inspiration behind his own *Metal Machine Music* in that double album's accompanying notes.[111] Musicians subsequently influenced by Young include Brian Eno – who says that *Arabic Numeral* was 'the first piece of music I ever performed publicly',[112] as early as 1967, and who once proposed that 'La Monte Young is the daddy of us all'[113] – and, more recently, the English rock group Spiritualized.[114]

It was, however, Terry Riley who responded with the greatest individuality to his student colleague's startling radicalism. And it is Riley who produced, as a direct result of Young's example and encouragement, the music which ultimately proved of greatest consequence to the furtherance of 'mainstream' musical minimalism, as we shall see in the next chapter.

2 Terry Riley

True to his hippie image, Terry Riley is a natural wanderer: happy anywhere, at home nowhere, except perhaps in the forests of the Sierra
Nevada foothills where he was born. But his career can be divided geographically into three broad parts: his childhood and student years
chiefly in northern California; a time spent largely away from the West
Coast – mainly in France and New York, but also in Scandinavia,
Morocco and Mexico; and the period of his return to the rural California
of his birth, where he has lived since 1974. Though largely absent from
the West Coast for about eight years – he was twenty-six when he left for
Europe – Riley returned to San Francisco before moving to New York; it
was during these eighteen months that the première of *In C* took place. In
terms of his output as a minimalist, the story conventionally starts there,
when the composer was twenty-nine; but it should really begin some
three years earlier, with the innovative tape pieces that helped prepare the
way for the work that represents not only Riley's personal breakthrough,
but also what is perhaps the key moment in the development of musical
minimalism.

Despite this early interest in the medium of tape, improvisation is as
central to Riley's development as it is to Young's. His approach to improvisation also tends to be more intuitive than that of his colleague; and this
lack of theoretical baggage has implications not only for the difficulties of
separating 'composition' from 'improvisation' already observed with
Young, but also for the continuity of Riley's career as a minimalist composer. It is, for instance, possible to argue that this career not only begins
but ends with *In C* and the *Keyboard Studies* (composed and begun,
respectively, in 1964), if we confine the term to notated music using
modular repetition which is available for others besides the composer
himself to perform. Between these pieces and the works composed for
the Kronos Quartet in the 1980s, Riley concerned himself mainly with
the invention of material, very little of it committed to notation, to use as
the basis for solo improvisations.

It could also be argued that *Shri Camel* (1975 onwards; the commercial
recording was made in 1977, though not issued until 1980) marks the
end of Riley's interest in minimalism, as previously defined in this book,
more clearly than the 1974 version of Young's *The Well-Tuned Piano* does
for his. The consequences of its new approach to harmony and counter-

point could only be fully exploited later, in both the composed and the improvised musics of the 1980s and 1990s, which have rather different goals.

As suggested above, even Riley's output between *c.* 1962 and *c.* 1971 may be further subdivided: not only into the genres of tape compositions, notated pieces and solo improvisations – each of which to some extent have different concerns and functions – but also according to the degrees of structural freedom and stylistic variety Riley wished to encompass at this time. The handful of notated compositions after *In C* reflect this seminal work's influence more directly than do either the tape pieces or the solo improvisations. After *In C* and the *Keyboard Studies* which immediately followed it, however, Riley's music already begins to change.

Though Young and Riley come from somewhat similar backgrounds, have been friends for nearly forty years, have often worked closely together and retain a considerable admiration for each other, they are, both as musicians and as people, extremely different. Riley is ultimately interested only in what he is currently doing. He has little energy or inclination for keeping scores or tapes, a poor memory for detail and scant sympathy for anyone who regards the keeping of the historical record – even a purely musical one, let alone biography – as important and meaningful. Several tape pieces and quite a lot of notated compositions by Riley have been lost, due in part to the fact that the composer moved around a lot during the 1960s. Some years ago – significantly, he cannot remember when – he decided to turn out a lot of old tapes and scores of his work; many of these had only survived because his mother had kept them while her son and family were so much on the road. He had already packed them into his pick-up truck to take them to the dump when his wife, on discovering what he was doing, persuaded him not to destroy them. 'There are wrong dates on all my compositions', he says; 'there are always two dates on each score'.[1] Like his music, Riley lives for the moment, to an extent which is unusual for a man aged over sixty. The consequences for any attempt to provide a complete and accurate account of his development will be obvious.

Early years

Terry Mitchell Riley was born on 24 June 1935 in Colfax, California, in the Sierra Nevada foothills not far from where he still lives. As his name suggests, Riley's father was of Irish ancestry, probably American immigrants due to the potato famine of the late 1840s. His mother was from

Italian stock; both parents were born in the USA. Riley's maternal grand-
father ended up in Colfax largely because it was a railroad town on the
main New York to San Francisco route.

When Riley was about five, the family moved to nearby Redding, but
during the Second World War became rather mobile. The composer's
father was in the Marine Corps and took part in the Pacific Campaign;
the young Riley was brought up by the composer's Italian immigrant
maternal grandparents, speaking Italian and imbibing Italian culture.
For a while, the family lived in Los Angeles. His parents were quite keen
music lovers, but did not play; a maternal uncle, though, played the bass
in several bands. Riley has said he was 'always doing music; almost before
I could talk I could sing all the songs on the radio'.[2] His first musical
experiences seem to have come via the 'standards' of Cole Porter, George
Gershwin and Richard Rogers, and the 'cowboy' traditions of country
and western music, as was the case with La Monte Young. But later there
were the popular classics as well. Violin lessons began when he was five or
six, piano lessons a little later. He first learned the piano by ear, even
picking up the practice of improvising on themes from the Classical and
Romantic repertoire – such as Tchaikovsky's First Piano Concerto – from
an older cousin; it was not until the age of eleven or twelve that he began
to learn music from scores. In 1945 he recalls Dizzie Gillespie and Charlie
Parker being the subject of a cover feature in *Life* magazine; he read the
article over and over again, but couldn't actually get to hear any of their
music at that stage. The record store in Redding almost exclusively
stocked cowboy music.

Back in Redding after the War, Riley went to high school, where his
music teacher, Ralph Wadsworth, introduced him to Bartók, Stravinsky
and other modern composers. Between December 1952 and June 1953 –
in his final year in high school – Riley accompanied his parents to
Beaufort, South Carolina, which gave him the chance to experience the
American South. Then, back home between 1953 and 1955, he attended
Shasta Junior College. Besides the financial advantages of staying at
home, Duane Hampton, a piano teacher with an excellent reputation
from his days at the prestigious Curtis Institute in Philadelphia, had
come to Redding, and Riley had lessons with him for about two years. For
a while, with Hampton's encouragement, he contemplated a career as a
concert pianist, and took part in a performance of Poulenc's Concerto for
Two Pianos.

Riley finally reached San Francisco in September 1955, enrolling at San
Francisco State University for two years. He also had piano lessons at San
Francisco Conservatory with Adolf Baller, Hampton's own teacher,

playing Poulenc's Piano Concerto, with a second piano, for his senior recital. At university, he took up composition, merely to see if he had any talent for it. He had lessons with Wendall Otey; student colleagues included Ken Benshoof, Pauline Oliveros and Loren Rush. In his senior year, Riley decided that his late start to serious piano studies, erratic practising and nerves precluded a career as a concert pianist. Encouraged by the reactions to his composing, he started to write more music. Some time during his last months at San Francisco State, from where he graduated in June 1957, Riley wrote the earliest piece to exist on his present worklist: a *Trio* for violin, clarinet and piano. Now lost, it is described by its composer as 'neo-classic'; some songs – a couple from 1957 survive – are a little more chromatic.

Riley married Anne Smith, an elementary schoolteacher, in January 1958; they had a daughter, Colleen, the following September. (Two sons – Shahn and Gyan – were born much later, in 1973 and 1977, respectively.) He took various jobs – in a grocery store and, in particular, with an airline company – to support his new family, but managed to find some time for composing, studying privately with Robert Erickson, to whom he had been introduced by Oliveros and Rush. Riley was especially impressed by Erickson's ability to suggest new ways of developing one's material without imposing his own compositional personality on his students. Even after he went to Berkeley, he continued to go to Erickson, regarding him as 'a beacon of sanity in the midst of the Berkeley scene which I didn't like at all'.

From this period – around 1958 – we have two surviving piano pieces which Riley describes as being written 'in a free chromatic style' influenced by Schoenberg's piano pieces, opp. 11 and 19. Curiously, in view of his later development, Riley was attracted by Schoenberg's rhythmic fluidity, which contrasted sharply with the motoric rhythms of much neo-classical music. Far from being the enforced product of a repressive academic environment, this idiom was something he excitedly explored with Erickson's help at this time. Twelve-note music, on the other hand, 'didn't feel good. It was too full of anxiety, too dark; it had such a narrow range'.

Some time during 1958 or 1959, he formed an improvising trio with Oliveros and Rush, initially to record music for a film entitled *Polyester Moon*, based on polyester sculptures by Claire Falkenstein. The group performed what seem to have been free improvisations in a non-jazz style at a time when such activities were still rare. Riley played piano, Oliveros the French horn and probably the accordion, and Rush an assortment of instruments including the bassoon and the koto. This experience was important in suggesting to Riley that improvisation, which he already felt to be his natural mode of expression, could be creatively explored quite independently of any jazz idiom; though jazz, too, has been crucial to his development.

Berkeley: Young, Stockhausen and Cage; Maxfield and tape composition

In the spring of 1959, as soon as his wife was able to teach, and was therefore able to support the family, Riley enrolled at Berkeley. Despite already auditing classes, and having had some piano pieces played in class by Rush, the twenty-three-year-old composer initially failed the graduate entry examinations in harmony and counterpoint (he had never even done species counterpoint) and had to take remedial classes. First joining Seymour Shifrin's composition class, he subsequently moved on to William Denny; his other teachers included Arnold Elston. But unlike Erickson, Shifrin and the others seemed to embody a notion of academic composition which he felt to be superficial; besides, Riley has never felt at ease in any academic situation. Though he says that none of his teachers at Berkeley was themself a serialist, it appears that serial compositional projects were more acceptable to them than the work he really wanted to do. Accordingly, he submitted exercises in a kind of integral serialism for his degree – work he has not kept – while engaging privately on compositions and related activities that he mostly never showed his teachers at all.

Chief among Riley's student encounters was the close relationship he established with Young, whom he met through Shifrin's class. Young's experience as a jazz musician and knowledge of developments in contemporary art music far exceeded Riley's own at this time. Yet he needed a collaborator in his new avant-garde activities, and Riley was extremely willing, sympathetic and highly talented. A major problem Riley's teachers at Berkeley seem to have had with him was that they felt the talented composer of those earlier piano pieces influenced by Schoenberg 'was being corrupted by La Monte'.

With Young's help, Riley now quite methodically worked his way through the more progressive developments in contemporary music. He became fascinated by the rhythmic complexity that Stockhausen was generating; *Zeitmasze*, in particular, became important for him, for its simultaneous presentation of different tempi. Riley's *Spectra* for a sextet of flute, clarinet, bassoon, violin, viola and cello (dated 28 December 1959) asks for just two speeds at once, but also incorporates sustained sounds longer than those in Stockhausen's work; again, suggestive of the influence of Young, despite the fact that Riley had missed the student playthrough of *Trio for Strings* in September 1958.

His interest in sustained sounds was explored further in a single-movement String Quartet (dated 31 May 1960), lasting some ten or twelve minutes. After their marriage, the Rileys moved to Potrero Hill in Bernal Heights, then a blue-collar suburb of San Francisco; the sounds of multiple foghorns going off in the Bay were a permanent fixture of the soundscape of this community. The constant permutations of the pitches of these foghorns fascinated him; though they recurred at the same register, they seemed to have no pattern. Without the example of Young's *Trio for Strings*, however, Riley admits he would never have thought of writing a piece based on foghorn pitches; the Quartet is influenced by Young's interest in repeating and returning to a pitch at the same register. He wrote the piece on a practice-room organ at Berkeley, which allowed him to experiment with sustaining pitches for long periods, entirely intuitively, and to 'get a feeling for what the effect would be on a string quartet'. *Pace* Edward Strickland, the work is not a diatonic composition in C major, but rather an atonal one without a key signature.[3] Dynamically, though, the Quartet offers a radical approach: soft throughout, all the markings are *piano* or lower, going down to *pppp*. Within this context, the piece concentrates on single notes in constantly and unsystematically overlapping and changing pitch permutations, rather than anything resembling melody; texturally and tonally, as well as dynamically, it offers a flat landscape with minimum contrasts.

The Quartet and the later piece which is in certain respects its companion – the String Trio of 1961 – both suggest moves in the direction of the kind of minimalism already being explored by Young. Between the two works, however, come several demonstrating a less clear line of development. *Envelope*, dated July 1960, has no score, but totally independent parts for four instruments – alto saxophone, French horn, violin and piano – each of which, according to the materials, 'may be played as a solo or in any combination with the other parts'; its flexible and unsynchronised movement through the notated material points towards *In C*. For Ann Halprin's dance workshop, another collaborative venture with Young, Riley produced *Concert Piece for Two Pianists and Tape Recorder* (probably March or April 1960). As published in *An Anthology*,[4] this consists of two pages of graphic indications for two performers playing on two pianos. Some of the graphics are meaningful, though not explained in the score itself: one turns out to be an ashtray placed on the piano strings; another, a picture of Young lying inside the piano. Otherwise though, Riley says, 'it's bullshit'. The score only existed in order to qualify the performance for inclusion in a symposium concert of student compositions at Brigham Young University in Provo, Utah, on 30 April 1960, at which Young's *Poem* was also performed. In addition, Riley made five mono tapes at Halprin's studio which he describes as '*musique concrète* sounds . . . rolling steel marbles and stuff across the piano sounding board, using that as an echo device'. A surviving, and delightfully amusing, tape of the performance bears out the anarchic manner typical of such experiments in sound.

Both friends obtained a Berkeley scholarship. While Young used his to travel to New York in September 1960, Riley remained in the Bay Area to complete his M.A. Two failed attempts at a language examination, however, caused his graduation to be delayed until the summer of 1961. His remaining semesters were far less productive.

Riley's early efforts with tape technology were assisted by Richard Maxfield – yet another consequence of Young's friendship. The first of these pieces originated as music for another dance by Halprin, variously called *The Three-Legged Stool*, *The Four-Legged Stool* and *The Five-Legged Stool*. His contributions, assembled between late 1960 and the spring of 1961, included both instrumental and tape material, varying in content and assembly from performance to performance; he sometimes played piano amidst the dancers on stage. Using cheap, mono, reel-to-reel, Wollensak tape recorders, Riley now made tape loops for the first time, recording piano playing, speech, laughter and several found sounds. His Potrero Hill home gave him a 'beautiful view of the bay. It was a very romantic little spot, a very old cottage (which has since been torn down) which had a very small garden and a lot of wine bottles outside, and all the tape loops would go out the window of the studio, around the wine bottles, and back into the studio'.[5]

Late in 1961, Riley took the tapes he had made for *The Three-Legged Stool* as the basis of a tape composition called *Mescalin Mix*, or *M . . . Mix*, after the name of the psychedelic drug, discussed below. With help from Ramon Sender, he made use of an echoplex, a primitive electronic contraption allowing a sound to be repeated in an ever-accumulating counterpoint against itself. In *Mescalin Mix* – the only tape piece Riley composed before 1963 to survive – the multiple echo effect was applied to selected material from *The Three-Legged Stool* and, perhaps, some of the tapes for *Concert Piece*. While the sources of some of this material – vocal moanings, perhaps laughter, and what sounds like a popular song on a 'honky-tonk' piano – can be identified, much of it is so distorted

Example 2.1 *String Trio*, bars 1–8

that even the composer no longer recognises it. Frequencies could be altered by changing the speed of the tape, either gradually or suddenly, as well as accumulated and distorted by the echo device. Riley himself says that the results 'sounded just like an acid trip';[6] a lurid climax involving echo effects shortly before the end of this thirteen-and-a-half-minute piece helps bear this out. The repetition of short fragments of sound made possible by this technology suggested that repetition itself, rather than Young's concept of sustained sounds, could be made the chief means of musical organisation; repetition seemed, to Riley, endemic to working with tape.

Riley soon began to realise the potential that tape loops and echo devices held for his work without tape as well. The other work from this period is a String Trio which seems to have been the composer's belated final submission for graduation; the score is dated 2 May 1961. It is here that Riley first explores the modal pitch domain and regular rhythmic repetition which were to become central to his mature output. This single movement piece, lasting around fifteen minutes, is bounded by a kind of A-major tonality suggested at the outset by a constantly reiterated A C♯ quaver pulse on the viola (see Ex. 2.1). This modality is immediately challenged by the more chromatic and fragmented material which surrounds it, in music which is both rhythmically and texturally more varied than that of the earlier Quartet. But the pitches of the A-major triad, and to a certain extent a modality based on A – with some emphasis on the dominant E and a prominent place for C♮ as well as C♯ – retain their significance throughout: returning in a clearer form when the opening material is recapitulated, and maintaining a hold right to the ambiguous ending. Though less significant than Young's *Trio for Strings* of three years earlier, Riley's work, charting out a more diatonic territory in the context of repetition, is a tentative move towards *In C* of three years later.

Example 2.2 *Ear Piece*, complete text

> **THE PERFORMER TAKES ANY OBJECT(S) SUCH AS A PIECE OF PAPER CARDBOARD PLASTIC ETC AND PLACES IT ON HIS EAR(S) HE THEN PRODUCES THE SOUND BY RUBBING SCRATCHING TAPPING OR TEARING IT OR SIMPLY DRAGGING IT ACROSS HIS EAR HE ALSO MAY JUST HOLD IT THERE IT MAY BE PLAYED IN COUNTERPOINT WITH ANY OTHER PIECE OR SOUND SOURCE IF THE PERFORMER WEARS A HEARING AID IT WOULD BE BEST TO MAKE THE SOUNDS CLOSE TO THE MICROPHONE (OF THE HEARING AID) THE DURATION OF THE PERFORMANCE IS UP TO THE PERFORMER CHILDREN PERFORMING EARPIECE SHOULD BE WARNED NOT TO STICK THEIR FINGERS TOO FAR INTO THEIR EARS AS THEY MAY SERIOUSLY DAMAGE THE INNER EAR**

Though tentative and far from all-pervading, this exploration of repetition in a modal context was to prove prescient. The discovery of a new approach to repetition in the electronic studio now combined with his earlier experiences to provide the true beginnings of his own style. The way now seemed clear for Riley to develop his own minimalist approach: based not on the sustained sounds which formed the starting point for Young's music, but on the creation of short patterns and their elaboration through constant repetition.

The two pieces he produced between graduating from Berkeley in the summer of 1961 and going to Europe in February 1962 reflect, however, like *Concert Piece*, Riley's involvement with performance art. *Ear Piece*, a text composition (reproduced as Ex. 2.2), arose from the correspondence Riley had begun with the artists with whom Young was working in New York; it also appeared in *An Anthology*. *Grab Bag* is a 'hanging sculpture' for 'a little theatre piece': underneath a poster board, with drawings on it and holes in it, hangs a bag containing a large number of verbal instructions for performers. Each player takes it in turn to reach into the bag for an instruction and perform such activities as playing without the mouthpiece and putting one's instrument back in its case and taking it out again. Riley eventually gave it to Young. 'I went through the history of Western music pretty much', the composer says, 'and Fluxus was the last stop on the road. . . . After that, I decided I had to do something. I'd gone through this whole thing, and I didn't know who I was'. The String Trio and his work with tape, however, were to provide the chief clues to Riley's subsequent development.

Europe: the search for the mystical experience

Feeling more than usually restless, Riley now determined to go to Europe: 'for reasons of health', states his biography in the programme note for the concert in which *In C* was premièred nearly three years later. On their way there in early 1962, he and his family stopped briefly in New York to see Young, leaving for France some time in February 1962. In the next two years, the Rileys spent a good deal of time there, particularly in Paris; at first, in the spring of 1962, they lived for several months in Algeciras in Spain. But they also travelled extensively, including more than one trip to Morocco, and a visit to what was then Leningrad, during which Riley worked with the Leningrad Jazz Quartet. During this period, Riley was to soak himself in cultures very different from those fully available to him as a Berkeley student.

Some of his activities in Europe continued avant-garde involvements already established back home. Riley took the opportunities offered by the sudden eruption of Fluxus activities at that time – in West Germany, in particular – to explore further the work of such artists as Erik Andersen, Jed Curtis, George Maciunas, Nam June Paik and Emmett Williams. Riley's *Concert Piece* was performed in Wiesbaden on 1 September 1962 in the opening concert of the large-scale Fluxus festival that year.[7] On the same programme was a performance of Philip Corner's *Piano Activities* by Maciunas, Williams and others, in the course of which a piano was destroyed; as a result of this experience, Riley decided that he wanted no more to do with the Fluxus movement. His *Ear Piece* was performed in the same festival on 14 September.

As dismaying to Riley was a visit to the Darmstadt Summer School the following year. The only soul-mates he could find were the Dutch composer Louis Andriessen and, despite his earlier resolve, several people – including Andersen and Curtis – involved with Fluxus. Another of this group was the Danish composer Henning Christiansen. As a result of meeting him, Riley participated soon afterwards in a happening on Christiansen's farm outside Copenhagen. On the same trip, he also visited Stockholm and worked in Finland on *Street Piece Helsinki*, an outdoor theatrical extravaganza conceived by the American writer and director Ken Dewey in collaboration with the Finnish composer and jazz and pop musician Otto Donner. In France shortly before this, Riley became involved in another alternative theatre project with Dewey, described below.

Three experiences conclusively turned Riley away from the models Darmstadt and Fluxus offered him. The first was a much greater immersion in ragtime, jazz and other so-called 'popular' Western musical forms. While at Berkeley, Riley had begun to study ragtime piano with Wally Rose. Being unsuccessful in his applications for grants and prizes, including the Prix de Rome, he had already put his skills to good use by playing ragtime piano in the Gold Street Saloon, on San Francisco's Barbary Coast, earning sufficient money during his final year in college and after to allow him and his family to travel to France. Now, he spent much of his time as pianist for a variety of club and cabaret work, including a spell at Fred Payne's Artists' Bar on the Place Pigalle in Paris. Elsewhere, he played for floor shows with circus acts (also driving the variety show agent's bus), and for dances in the officers' clubs of NATO bases in France. The circus acts proved especially entertaining, since they required Riley to provide musical accompaniment for everything from men shooting cigars out of women's mouths with a bow-and-arrow to contortionists. Almost thirty years later, one of these experiences provided the basis for 'Rubberlady's Theme Music', the foxtrot that forms the third movement of *The Sands*, a work for string quartet and orchestra in four movements composed in 1991. The officers' clubs proved especially lucrative, since they paid at American rates. Among others, Riley worked with a saxophonist named Sonny Lewis, who was to become a frequent collaborator.

Unlike Young, Riley enjoyed the social atmosphere which comes with such musical experiences, finding it more suited to his personality and outlook. Playing ragtime, blues and improvising on jazz 'standards', he began to see the potential tonality held both expressively and structurally, and to consider how he might best develop his own approach outwards from this, rather than from his university training. As Young had taught him, the reason one never tires of listening to the blues, which makes extensive use of the Dorian mode, is that its pitches 'are in perfect agreement with the overtone series of the fundamental pitch. You can keep singing the blues for ever because it's one of the few scales that are built absolutely on a chord of nature'.[8] To this day, he feels that his own music 'abstract[s] this love that I have for "standards" into another form'.

The second important aspect of Riley's European experiences arose from finding himself close to sources of non-Western musics largely new to him. In the 1950s, he had scarcely been aware of the existence of non-Western musics, even after he moved to San Francisco and despite his experiences with Rush and Young. Riley recalls that he failed to get to Ravi Shankar's first concert in San Francisco some time in the late 1950s. The first non-Western musics which seriously influenced him were the Moroccan and other North African musics he heard on the radio while living in Algeciras, only some twenty miles from the Straits of Gibraltar. Riley became obsessed by the way in which this music subjected small amounts of material to extensive repetition, including the use of cyclic techniques, and its ability to sustain interest over long periods through melodic improvisation over static harmony. One of the only two records he carried with him on his travels was a French BAM disc of Moroccan music. The other – *Cookin' With The Miles Davis Quintet* (1961), with its explorations of the different ways in which repetition and modality could refocus the relationship between a melody and the rhythmic basis familiar from earlier jazz – invited Riley to explore the links between Moroccan music and jazz, and to see more clearly the potential of both for his own work. He was helped to these conclusions by the discoveries made around this time by John Coltrane, to whose music Young had introduced him in Berkeley. Coltrane's modal and free-jazz innovations of the early 1960s – from the popularity of 'My Favorite Things' (various recorded versions from 1961 onwards) to the more esoteric *Impressions* and *Ascension* albums (1961–3 and 1965, respectively) – were much influenced by non-Western musics, not least by Moroccan Maqamat. The combination of modality and repetition was crucial to both, and the similarities were enhanced by the extent to which Coltrane's reedy soprano saxophone sounded like the double-reed instruments of the Middle East – and also of India, which was subsequently to be important for both men too. A further loop is thus created in a cycle of influences that all seemed to point in the same direction. Riley was later inspired by Coltrane's playing to take up the soprano saxophone. Jazz, Moroccan music and the example of Young all helped point the way to Riley at this time, not least through what they all had most importantly in common: 'a daily process of learning to improvise, and what all that meant', as the composer has said.

But the main reason for Riley's move towards modal improvisation, he has said, 'was that my own spirit felt happy with it. I could do it for a long time and still feel good, still feel balanced and centered'.[9] Although his knowledge of Moroccan music was derived largely from radio and recordings, the composer also visited Morocco on several occasions. While he was fascinated musically both by the lively street music he encountered and by the Islamic calls to prayer to be heard issuing from the minarets, a major reason for his visits was the search for the hallucinogenic drugs readily available there. Like Young, Riley now finds it difficult to talk about this aspect of his life. Like Young, too, he is concerned both to stress the spiritual and creative possibilities it opens up, and to make clear that, despite the much wider availability of various drugs today, he no longer takes anything besides alcohol. It is evident, however, that Riley's hallucinogenic experiences were as crucial to both his spiritual and musical development as Young's were for him.

In the late 1950s, indeed, Young seems to have been responsible for Riley's first experiences of marijuana; they also had peyote together for the first time. 'When I took peyote', Riley relates, 'then I really saw the sacredness of music'. In the late 1950s and early 1960s, various mind-opening drugs were important to the Beat poets, many of whom settled in the North Beach area of San Francisco. It was via this flourishing counter-culture that Riley had his first experiences of mescaline, one of the earliest 'psychedelic' drugs to achieve wide distribution in the 1960s. When passing through New York in 1962 on his way to Europe, Riley had been given his first psilocybin mushrooms by Maxfield, whom he had already met through Young in Berkeley. In the 1960s, LSD was, he felt, 'the element of the consciousness-raising movement . . . and marijuana as a sister drug. . . . It had a lot to do with those times, you know. There was something emerging then that people were hungry for: almost as a public at large, especially young people. I know we weren't interested in making money; we were really only interested in having these mystical experiences'.

While it is possible to overplay these drug experiences *per se*, it is probably impossible to overemphasise the changes they helped to bring about in Riley's spiritual as well as musical development in the early 1960s. 'Besides just the ordinary music that was going on', the composer has said, 'music was also able to transport us suddenly out of one reality into another. Transport us so that we would almost be having visions as we were playing. So that's what I was thinking about before I wrote *In C*. I believe music, shamanism, and magic are all connected, and when it's used that way it creates the most beautiful use of music'.[10] He has also spoken of using drugs 'to remove certain filters that we have in our brain to make our lives more ordinary. These filters filter out the extra perceptions of angels and all the other things that would make our lives a little bit wild . . . .'[11] It was during this period that Riley firmly established for himself a real purpose and direction for his music, which was, in essence, to lend his work to the search for what the mystics would call enlightenment.

In this search, the taking of drugs was intimately linked to Riley's decision to explore a modal, rather than a chromatic, music. 'It wasn't just tied up with getting high', he recalls, 'it was tied up with trying to find this deeply spiritual quality of music, which modal music had'. Smoking marijuana, in particular, 'was probably the most influential thing that happened in my life. . . . And if the music had too much angularity in it, it would pull me out of this mood which it induces'. Such experiences were also connected to the ways in which repetition led to changing perceptions of what was being repeated. 'I think I was noticing', the composer has said, 'that things didn't sound the same when you heard them more than once. And the more you heard them, the more different they did sound. Even though something was staying the same, it was changing. I became fascinated with that'. It also had more specifically technical consequences, notably for the development of his keyboard playing, discussed below. These discoveries were eventually to lead Riley to find the musical 'real me' for whom he had been searching since the mid-1950s.

While in Europe, Riley says, 'the idea of the [tape] loops, the repetition and the different cycles all came together, staying in my mind'. Through the intervention of Dewey, Riley gained access to the ORTF radio studios in Paris. Here, he explained the looping technique with the echoplex he had used in San Francisco to a French technician, who proceeded to set up a tape-delay arrangement with two Ampex tape recorders to create what the composer calls 'the first time-lag accumulator'. This offered a more sophisticated application of delay devices than were possible with the echoplex used in *Mescalin Mix*, permitting a much cleaner and more vibrant-sounding build-up of layers of the same material repeated against itself. During 1962–3, however, this new opportunity was not pursued in compositions for live performance, but in a pair of pieces – one including live material for theatrical use, one for tape alone.

She Moves She *and* Music for 'The Gift'

The tape piece is entitled *She Moves She*, composed some time during the first half of 1963. The words 'she moves she', spoken by the actor John Graham, are accompanied by a percussive sound like that of a bolt being shot. The time-lag accumulator swiftly piles speech and sound up against each other to produce an increasingly blurred textural wash. While the words 'she moves she' always remain discernible amidst their multiple reiterations, the sonic impact of individual fragments soon seems more important than any conventional semantic hold they may retain: the 'sh' of the word 'she', for instance, quickly becomes detached to form a purely percussive counterpart to the original percussive sound – a 'resulting pattern', to use Steve Reich's terminology. Though *She Moves She* was originally conceived as a separate piece, it is also a part of the music Riley composed for a theatrical extravaganza called *The Gift*.

The mastermind behind this was Ken Dewey, who both wrote the play and directed its production, under the auspices of a festival in Paris, in which members of Living Theater and Halprin's company took part. Dewey had first presented *The Gift* in San Francisco in 1962. Described by Richard Kostelanetz as 'his first public quasi-mixed-means performance',[12] this involved the reinterpretation – the playwright/director's own word is 'resurfacing'[13] – of Dewey's original text in terms of movement and 'movement-dialogue with the environment' by John Graham and Lynn Palmer. The production was mounted in some half-dozen venues, including a church, the deck of a boat Halprin owned and the streets of San Francisco. The following year, Dewey rented an old chateau outside Paris, where a more lavish version of *The Gift* was devised in the summer of 1963. Jerry Walters, a sculptor, constructed a huge mobile, which looked like a kind of aeroplane. The actors had to swing on this, a rather dangerous activity which included the need to avoid hitting the jazz musicians playing beneath. As a text, *The Gift* was what Riley describes as 'very minimal', with very few lines. The show itself changed quite substantially every night, and was sufficiently outrageous to provoke fights among the audience so boisterous that the musicians had to play very loudly to drown out the noise.

Chet Baker – the previously very popular jazz trumpeter who had recently been released from jail in Lucca, where he spent some time on a heroin charge – and his band supplied the main musical forces for *The Gift*, and acted as well as played; one night, Baker didn't show up and Riley had to take his place. Riley added tape material, including *She Moves She* as well as what came to be known as *Music for 'The Gift'*. On the last evening, an actor who had the line 'This is an incredible experience', followed this by destroying the tape recorder, as a result of which some tapes were also lost. *She Moves She* turns out to be based on a line from Dewey's play – 'She moves, she follows' – from which Riley cut the final word.

Most of the half-dozen sections of the surviving twenty-three-minute tape now called *Music for 'The Gift'* seem merely fragments. They are mainly based on a recording of Baker's band playing Miles Davis's 'So What', from his 1959 album *Kind of Blue*; Riley recorded all the instruments individually, which then allowed him to cut up and reassemble the lines as he chose. Davis's abandonment of traditional chord changes in favour of a modal approach involving a much smaller number of harmonic shifts – an approach made famous by 'So What' – was in itself a gift to someone exploring the possibilities of using the time-lag accumulator on such instrumental material for the first time. While allowing Riley to obtain rich cumulative effects, it avoided the sort of clashes inevitable when subjecting to such processes any music with a faster rate of harmonic change. The distinctive bass riff of the original was piled on top of itself to produce 'six layers of bass',[14] which were then subjected to further looping and other modifications. The result was a complex counterpoint, involving multiples of various instruments, in which Davis's original is for the most part undetectable. *She Moves She* itself also makes appearances from time to time.

While the constantly repeated 'answer' to the bass riff of Davis's 'So What' can still be perceived, contrapuntal detail is largely inaudible, since once the time-lag accumulator has really begun to do its work, the interaction of long loops in multiple pile-ups produces an essentially textural effect. Though some passages – especially those built from double bass riffs – exhibit a regular rhythm, the repetitive figures of *Music for 'The Gift'* are not played out against any pulsing grid; Riley has said that the work 'didn't have anything to do with pulse. It was much more dreamlike'.[15]

Music for 'The Gift' is, however, far from devoid of musical subtlety or significance. According to Riley, the decision – apparently Baker's – to use Davis's 'So What' was 'a masterstroke', since the bridge of the original is a semitone higher than the main section: sixteen bars of Dorian on D, followed by eight bars of Dorian on E♭. When what the composer calls the 'fields of loops' based on the Dorian mode on E♭ were mixed with those on the Dorian on D, 'it would be like a wash of colour. And then I'd gradually take away the D, and you'd have this modulation that was half a tone apart. . . . It's one of the most beautiful tonal effects I've ever heard, because it's just a half step taking over from another – a whole mode taking over from another'.

Music for 'The Gift' is the most significant work of Riley's before *In C*, marking the point when he 'really started understanding what repetition could do for musical form'.[16] It proved that it was possible to apply the principles of delay and accumulation to pitched material, as well as to speech and other 'non-musical' sounds, to make a sophisticated composition. *Music for 'The Gift'* paved the way for the more important instrumental works from *In C* itself onwards.

On 23 November 1963, President John Kennedy was assassinated, and the clubs in which the composer earned his living were closed for a lengthy period as a mark of respect. With no savings to support his wife and daughter, and already owed a considerable sum of money by his agent, Riley decided they must return to America. Before that, though, they paid a further visit to Morocco during the Ramadan celebrations of that year.

Return to San Francisco

Riley and his family returned to San Francisco, probably in early 1964, and he resumed piano playing in bars and cabaret. At first, they lodged at his mother's house; later they eked out a bohemian existence in their own apartment on Boccana Street, at the top of Potrero Hill, near where they had lived when the composer was at Berkeley. It was in one of these two places – he cannot recall which – that Riley wrote *In C* some time during that spring. The piece, he has said, came to him one night on a bus, after months of failed attempts to follow up the ideas used in *Music for 'The Gift,'* when he 'started hearing the whole first line of *In C*. It just sort of came into my ear and I wrote it down and then started working it out from there, using the techniques I'd developed in Paris'.[17] The work lay around for several months, until either Sender or Morton Subotnick invited him to share a programme with James Tenney at the San Francisco Tape Music Center the following January. Plans were subsequently changed, and Riley presented a one-man show – called 'oneyoungamerican' – at the Center two months earlier, on 4 and 6 November 1964. In addition to the première performances of *In C* (the composition of which the programme erroneously dated October 1964), these concerts included five other works: *Music for 'The Gift'*, *Coule* (a version of the first *Keyboard Study*), and three tape compositions, *Shoeshine, I* and *In A♭ or is it B♭?*

Between the composition and the première of *In C*, Riley met Steve Reich. That May Reich had mounted four evenings including his own works at the San Francisco Mime Troupe Theater on Boccana Street at one of which, the story goes, Riley (who by then was living in the same street) had been present but left at the interval. The following day, Reich, who also lived close by, sought him out; with his natural impetuosity, he demanded to know why Riley had walked out of his concert. Despite this unpromising beginning, and the considerable differences of temperament between them, the two discovered they had a lot in common and became, for a while, close friends. On learning that Riley had an ensemble piece ready but no ensemble to perform it, Reich offered to help get some players together.

The thirteen-piece ensemble which finally premièred *In C* consisted largely of players Riley brought in: Werner Jepson (Wurlitzer electric piano), Sonny Lewis (the tenor saxophonist who had played with Riley in Europe), James Lowe (electric piano), who in turn was introduced by Lewis, Pauline Oliveros (accordion), Ramon Sender (who played a Chamberlain organ relayed from an upstairs studio), Stan Shaff (trumpet), Morton Subotnick (clarinet), Mel Weitsman (recorder), and Phil Windsor (trumpet), plus the composer himself on electric piano. With Reich, who also played electric piano, came two other performers: Jon Gibson (soprano saxophone) and Jeannie Brechan (electric piano), Reich's girlfriend at the time. In addition, an artist called Anthony Martin, also onstage, projected 'a rhythmic/melodic light composition' of various shapes and colours simultaneously with the music.

The composition of the group varied from rehearsal to rehearsal, with a hard core provided by Riley and Reich, Brechan and Gibson: 'whoever I could get to come and play for nothing', says the composer. Some of those who played at the première had never played the piece before. With such a radical work, allowing much room for improvisation, *In C* was assembled with a high degree of collective input. 'The room was full of composers', says Riley, 'and there were always people making suggestions'. Reich is correct, Riley thinks, in claiming that the pulse was his idea, but he has no clear memory of when this was introduced. The original intention had been to perform the work without a time-keeper of any kind, but this proved impossible. Reich, himself a percussionist, may have at first suggested a drum pulse; finally, though, *In C* was co-ordinated by the constant reiteration of two high Cs on the piano, played by Brechan.

In C

The score of *In C* consists of a single page containing fifty-three modules, presented in its entirety as Example 2.3. Reproduced on the sleeve of the LP disc issued by Columbia in 1968,[18] included in several published anthologies, widely photocopied and even, in former times, hand-copied, *In C* has been more readily available via these means than from its original source.[19] Though Riley produced a list of performance instructions to accompany the score some years after the première, these have never been widely disseminated. The initial San Francisco performances evolved 'by consensus, almost', without any written instructions, and the composer has himself done much over the ensuing years to encourage performances of *In C* to be conceived more as contributions to an ongoing exploration of its potential than as merely a faithful reproduction of the score. Performance practice has consequently evolved quite freely with respect to the written source, making *In C* begin to resemble a kind of urban folk music rather than a 'composition' in a more conventional sense. Some of the salient features of this evolution are described below. Several mistakes have also crept into some of the available versions.

Example 2.3 *In C*, complete score

In C is scored for '[a]ny number of any kind of instruments'. Its 'ensemble can be aided', according to Riley's instructions, by the already mentioned pulse, which can be performed 'on the high c's of the piano or on a mallet instrument'. This has become accepted as a practical necessity, though a few performances under the composer's own direction have managed to dispense with it. Instrumentation is unspecified. The pitch range is basically the octave above middle C, with occasional excursions outside this. Since transposition at the octave is permitted, the potential line-up is almost limitless, though Riley discourages anything which would draw attention to itself. Even the modules themselves have developed variants which have Riley's own approval. For example, any module may be subject to any augmentation or diminution, though in practice few performances, even those under the composer's direction, take much advantage of this. (The interpretation of modules 22–6 at double speed on the commercial recording of a performance in celebration of *In C*'s twenty-fifth anniversary is thus not, as some might think, a mistake.) This proves especially useful in making fast modules available to bass-register instruments in forms which allow clear articulation; they can even, as the composer says, 'become almost like little drones'.

Besides, not all performers need to play all the modules; in their original forms, many of the faster patterns are best suited to keyboard instruments and tuned percussion, while others – notably the major part of no. 35, the only real melody in the entire piece – will sound particularly well on wind instruments. While most performances have followed the première in using only instruments, Riley's subsequent and deep involvement with Indian vocal traditions has encouraged the inclusion of singing as well; the twenty-fifth-anniversary New Albion recording includes three male voices, one the composer's own, and one female voice. The instructions allow vocalists to 'use any vowel and consonant sounds they like'. They also permit 'improvised percussion in strict rhythm (drum set, cymbals, bells etc.)'.

These instructions suggest that '[a] group of about 35 is desired if possible but smaller or larger groups will work'. While a half-dozen performers could produce a very interesting realisation, emphasising contrapuntal clarity, most successful performances known to the present author have used between ten and twenty musicians. Anything much larger risks degenerating into a free-for-all, discouraging the performers from attempting the kinds of close counterpoint characterising the most successful versions. (The twenty-fifth-anniversary performance, however – supervised by Riley – has thirty-one musicians. A revelatory twentieth-anniversary performance in Hartford, Connecticut, in 1984 –

also supervised by the composer, and heard by the present author – used twenty-eight top American new-music performers, including six singers. Additionally, and unusually, this performance abandoned the pulse, achieving a more lyrical interpretation in which slower modules became more tuneful: the triadic overlappings of module 29, for instance, sounded uncommonly like Bruckner.) Dynamics and articulation, too, are unspecified, offering scope for improvisation modified only by prevailing tendencies in any ensemble not subject to the sort of authoritarian direction which seems inappropriate to the spirit of such a piece.

After the pulse has commenced, each performer may enter with module 1 in his or her own time, repeating it as often as wished before moving on to the next one. While performers may move freely from module to module, omitting any along the way, it has become accepted that they should not leap ahead of the majority of the ensemble. While the musicians in many performances pause only between modules, not between repetitions of the same module, Riley permits the latter. In these cases, though, he encourages what he calls 'periodic' repetition: for example, eight repetitions of a module plus another eight, separated by a pause equivalent to four repetitions (especially useful for wind players). The composer's instructions suggest that no more than three or four modules should be in play at any one time; this avoids the joint pitfalls of excessive spareness (risking insufficient musical interest) and of an aural jamboree (in which musicianship is abandoned). They also suggest that '[t]he group should aim to merge into a unison at least once or twice during the performance'; in addition, once a performer reaches the final module, he or she should continue to repeat it until all the others have reached it too, during which Riley encourages crescendi and diminuendi to signal the work's close, the musicians eventually fading out one by one.

The notion, all too frequent, of *In C* as a kind of glorious, hippie free-for-all – the more the merrier, appreciated all the better if you're on certain substances – has tended to encourage performers to 'do their own thing', to use the terminology of the period, and not to attempt to relate much to what other musicians were doing. Yet as the Hartford performance demonstrated, the simultaneous deployment of a maximum of three or four modules encourages performers to work closely together, even to the point of exploiting the potential of playing or singing the same module in unison. The result, in the hands of sensitive musicians, is a rather different sort of *In C*: more focused, more interestingly contrapuntal, encouraging close listening on the part of its audience as well as its performers. While Riley gives his musicians a degree of leeway many would consider unusual, even in such a piece, he is adamant about the need for the development of a true ensemble style in which no performer draws attention to his own part at the expense of others; this would, in his view, 'collapse the structure of the piece'.

According to the composer's instructions, 'performances normally average between 45 minutes and an hour and a half'. Length of performance is clearly determined by the decisions of individual musicians, but also, to a degree, by the size of the ensemble. A large group will usually take longer to get through the modules than a small one, due partly to the former's capacity to sustain interest for longer with its wider range of combinations, both of timbres and modular patterns. Most good performances last over half an hour, some a good deal longer than this; the twenty-fifth-anniversary realisation – not perfect, but among the most varied and exciting – runs to 76′20″.

As will already be clear, the impact of *In C* inevitably varies a good deal, due to the extent to which an essentially improvisational ethos governs even a composition in which all the notes are written down. Yet only in realisations which deploy a large number of modules at once to effect a merely generalised exhilaration will Riley's carefully devised tonal scheme fail to register on its listeners. For *In C* is not really 'in C' at all, even if one accepts a loosely 'modal' rather than strictly tonal understanding of the term. One might even suggest that Riley's concern for modulation – inspired though it was by the example of Davis and first explored in an overtly jazz context – now takes on a more 'classical profile': the sort of description evoked by several commentators to denote the clearer cast of the rhythms and phrasing employed in the individual modules themselves.[20]

The introduction, first of F♯ (module 14), then B♭ (module 35 and, more consistently, from module 49) contributes important modifications to the C-major modality. In tandem with these alterations of accidental come more subtle changes of emphasis. While the opening modules duly stress C as the central pitch, module 8 introduces a sequence of patterns in which G is emphasised by constant reference to the pitches of the dominant-seventh chord. After F♯ replaces F♮ in module 14, introducing a somewhat Indonesian flavour to the proceedings, modules 14 and 15, in particular (the latter consisting solely of an emphatic G), suggest that we have moved into the dominant key. Interpretations retaining the primacy of C are, however, also available here and after the subsequent introduction of B♭ in module 35. Modules 14–17 suggest the Lydian mode on C; the integration of F♯ into a C-based modality is, after all, recognised theoretically both in musics of the 'cultivated' tradition (in Olivier Messiaen, for instance)[21] and in jazz (notably in the Lydian-based theories of George Russell).[22] Module 18, however, begins a long passage in which E minor can be felt as the real focus: the constantly repeated ascents up the first five notes of this key's scale occupy a significant proportion of the work's central portion, before a dramatic change of rhythmic pattern signals a return to C major (module 29) and, with the restoration of F♯, C major's dominant seventh (module 31). (It should be noted that the scalic ascents in quavers of modules 22–6 were originally conceived largely as dotted crotchets: an alternative more difficult to perform than the subdivision into repeated quavers common in versions subsequently disseminated.)

Module 35 alternates a semiquaver passage on the dominant seventh of C with the work's most extended lyrical utterance: a melody which manages to incorporate not only B♭ and F♯, but also B♮ and F♮. The former pair suggests what jazz musicians know as the 'Lydian dominant'. The presence of the natural as well as the flattened seventh, and the natural as well as the sharpened fourth, however, creates the most ambiguous modal moment in the entire work. It comes as no surprise to realise that *In C*'s single real melody comes not only at the point of maximum modal conflict, but also at almost the exact point of the Golden Section (module 35 being as close to two-thirds of the way through the work's fifty-three modules as it is possible to come).

After this, the way seems clear for the return of an Ionian C major via, once again, its dominant seventh. The pitches of the G[7] chord duly arrive (module 36 onwards). But C itself is approached more ambiguously: suggested, briefly, in module 39 and then, much more firmly, in module 42 (though, with the only A♮s in the whole piece outside the E-minor central sequences plus module 35, this could also be the relative minor); apparently confirmed in modules 43–4, but then shifted back on to a dominant focus (modules 45–8). At the point at which one might have expected a gloriously unambiguous return to C major, however, B♭ is reintroduced (module 49), leaving *In C* hanging deliciously in the air: not even on a C[7] chord, consistent with the B♭s, but on a G[7] chord in which the third has now been flattened; though when combined with the C, D or E which the immediately preceding modules 43–7 variously incorporate, the three pitches of the closing modules also suggest a Mixolydian modality on C.

Even the more carefully contrived and conscientiously contrapuntal performances of *In C* will, of course, blur the moves between these modal centres, which are thus more likely in practice to contribute to a polymodality as suggestive of jazz traditions as of any more 'exotic' ones. Like the modulation from the Dorian mode on D to that on E♭ in *Music for 'The Gift'*, *In C*'s shifts of tonal emphasis are accomplished gradually, in effect a moving and merging 'sweep of colour' rather than creating the dramatic shift of perspective characteristic of a conventional 'classical' modulation. The work's 'fields of loops' are subjected to a process at once more controlled and more comprehensive than that found in Riley's earlier use of Davis's 'So What'. While 'on C' might be a better description of the work's tonality than 'in C', even this scarcely does justice to the work's subtle changes of tonal emphasis, cunningly deployed to make structurally satisfying sense, whether a performance lasts fifteen minutes or several hours.

Mexico and New York

While feeling 'very satisfied that that message [of *In C*] had come through',[23] Riley was curiously disinclined to follow where it may have led in any clear, certainly in any careerist, terms. 'I responded', he says, 'by dropping out and going to Mexico for three months'. Riley did not, in fact, travel down to Mexico immediately, but stayed in San Francisco until the spring of 1965. His most notable musical activities during that time were with a jazz group, several members of which had played in *In C*, and for which he wrote two further works, discussed below. The performers included the already mentioned Gibson, Lewis and Weitsman, the trombonist Al Bent, the drummer Pete Magadini and Riley himself on piano. Though the group rehearsed every week for a period, it gave just one fully public concert – probably in April that year, at the San Francisco Tape Music Center – of Coltrane, Ornette Coleman, and *Tread on the Trail*, the work Riley had written specially for the occasion.

After the première of *In C*, its composer had really wanted to go back to Morocco. He heard that it was possible to get a passage on a Polish freight ship for a hundred dollars, leaving from Mexico, and was intending to take the family's Volkswagen bus to Tangier, then live in Morocco on the bus. But when the family arrived in Vera Cruz, probably in April or May 1965, the existence of any cheap passage across the Atlantic – at least one including transporting the bus – turned out to be a misunderstanding. The Rileys accordingly spent about three months in Mexico, having sold most of their possessions in order to pay for their intended trip. They then moved on to New York City where, though at first retaining some notion of sailing to Europe, Riley found himself trading in the bus, on which they had travelled across America, for a downtown loft on Grand Street – near the Bowery and Sara Roosevelt Park – previously rented by a friend of the sculptor Walter de Maria. The temptation to stay was heightened by the fact that the city's cultural scene in general, and its musical scene in particular, were much more dynamic than those of San Francisco.

Basing himself in New York for about the next four years, Riley travelled around the USA, continuing the rootless existence that reflected the emerging 'alternative' lifestyles of the period. 'I guess in those days I was a beatnik, and then I turned into a hippie', he says.[24] 'I enjoyed being in the company of poets and storytellers and other travelers. That was the life of the times. It was very exciting. Compared to the fifties, which was so dishwater dull, I thought things were really happening. And I was hoping the world would always stay like that!' Riley's wife and small daughter accompanied him; Anne found temporary teaching jobs whenever they settled anywhere for a while. In New York, she taught in Harlem, supporting the family until the Columbia recording of *In C* started to bring in some money.

Riley quickly renewed his close friendships with two men who were now established in the downtown artists community. Dewey, though a fairly recent arrival himself, mounted *Sames*, another of his theatrical extravaganzas, at the Film-Makers' Cinémathèque in November 1965. In this work, six women in bridal dress remained immobile on stage throughout, while films were projected on the theatre's walls and ceiling. Riley's music – using both tape loops and the time-lag accumulator system – incorporated three tape pieces, two of them still in progress: *I, It's Me* and *That's Not You*, discussed below.

More important in the long term was the re-establishment of his association with Young, now a close neighbour. In the Theatre of Eternal Music, Riley began to sing for the first time, initially just sitting in on rehearsals. John Cale was still playing with the group, and gave his last concert with it in December 1965. Riley's first concert with the Theatre of Eternal Music came the following February. He sang with the group for the next year or so, carefully keeping his own instrumental improvisations quite separate from his collaborations with the strong-willed and charismatic Young. He also started to study just intonation with Young's colleague Tony Conrad, which had an important, if delayed, effect on his own work.

Tape compositions, 1964–7

Though increasingly occupied with attempting to realise the potential that tape loops and the time-lag accumulator offered in live music-making, Riley continued to compose in the medium which had drawn him to modular repetition in the first place: music for tape alone. He regarded it as his own territory, and his faith in the medium of tape as a solution to his search for a personal style received a blow when Reich produced *It's Gonna Rain*. Riley's brief, intense relationship with Reich in 1964 had been based on more than merely the preparations for the première of *In C*. The two composers had also been showing each other their recent work which, in both cases, consisted largely of tape compositions. Reich recalls hearing *She Moves She*; Riley remembers showing his new friend 'two tape-recorder pieces of mine, loops of mine that I was working with'. Riley's insecurity over his friend's adoption of modular repetition using speech material on tape was compounded when, after returning to New York, 'people would say, "Oh, you're doing the kind of stuff Reich does!" And that hurts, you know'.

Riley continued, however, to compose tape pieces for some three years after the première of *In C*. While Reich built his early aesthetic on the rigour with which his compositions are constructed, Riley was uninterested in applying such structural severities to his material. His fascination was with the found sounds themselves and the process of what we would today call sampling. Riley would tape long stretches of material and loop them live, hoping for 'strange things that would happen' which would later be edited into a piece. He would even cut up pieces of tape without knowing what they were, splice them together and observe the results. While avoiding any systematic structuring of his materials, he nevertheless wanted to produce an 'abstract experience' from them, in which initially identifiable sounds would more often be extensively transformed than retained in a form readily recognisable by the listener.

Between the spring of 1964 and late 1967, Riley produced at least nine pieces, six of which can presently be reckoned to have survived; he also made a lot of other experiments in the medium.[25] Five pieces date from his period in San Francisco around the time of the composition and première of *In C*; a further four were composed later in New York. As so often, it is difficult to date many of these with any precision.

Shoeshine – the earliest of the four San Francisco pieces, composed in June 1964 – was composed for the Dancers Workshop of Marin (County). Here, a blues solo played on the Hammond organ by Jimmy Smith – its identity now forgotten by Riley, who taped the music by chance from the radio – was cut up into loops and extensively reassembled, alternating passages in which the original material is clearly audible, if highly fragmented, with others in which it is only vaguely and intermittently discernible. The programme sheet for the première performances of *In C* suggests that this tape piece received its first performances on the same occasion, but it now seems that it had already been performed with dancers in the previous August. *Shoeshine*'s twenty-one minutes take incessant repetition to curious and, at least from time to time, effective ends. *I* (July 1964) uses the voice of John Graham again, and the time-lag system developed in Paris. This is based entirely on the single word 'I', spoken by Graham using a variety of inflections and subjected to feedback processes which accumulate quite powerfully to produce a continuous drone. In late 1965 or early 1966, in New York, two further pieces (both presently lost) using only a single voice and the time-lag accumulator were completed to make a set of three. *It's Me* uses the composer's own voice, and *That's Not You* that of his daughter. This material provided the basis for the music Riley provided for *Sames*, the theatre piece by Dewey mentioned above.

The Bird of Paradise, the third San Francisco tape piece, was probably composed in the late summer of 1964. Based entirely on a rhythm-and-blues number entitled 'Shotgun', sung by Junior Walker and his All-Stars, this was one of the pieces Riley derived by using chance in his sampling method. While some sounds had been specially chosen, others were arrived at randomly, from loops constructed arbitrarily, without knowing their contents. The latter were 'like wild cards; if I didn't like them, I wouldn't use them'. One loop of Walker's group, played backwards and with the speed manipulated by hand, had what Riley calls a regular rhythmic 'choom, chucka choom' sound that reminded him 'of a huge Pterodactyl flying. . . . That was the reason for the title'. Like many of the sounds used in the piece, this is so transformed that it can barely be identified: a typical Riley technique that allows *The Bird of Paradise* to soar majestically above its sources in an exhilarating three-minute mixture of the metaphorical and the abstract.

The fourth San Francisco tape composition is the six-minute *In A♭ or is it B♭?* (dated October 1964 in the programme for the *In C* première concert). This submitted Lewis's tenor saxophone playing to distortion through immediate processing on tape, circumventing the need to make separate loops first; the material varies from long sustained sounds to a few wild riffs. The accumulating layers of playback, as well as sometimes instant distortions of single lines, call the key of the piece itself into question: hence the title, which can also be interpreted as a (probably ironic) follow-up to that of *In C*. 'Strange things would happen', says Riley, who deliberately exploited such surprising timbral or modal moments in the final mix. Its extension of the 'wash-of-colour', modal-modulation techniques explored in *Music for 'The Gift'* and *In C* was to prove significant, as discussed below. A fifth tape piece, entitled *R & R*, is listed in the programme for a concert at Cabrillo College in 1965 (see below). The programme note describes it as '[a]n electronic piece built from sound sources based on various excerpts from rock and roll stations'; it remained incomplete at the time of the concert and is now presumed lost.

The only two other tape pieces Riley recalls from his New York years are *I Can't Stop No* and *You're Nogood*. The former, probably composed in 1967, was reckoned to have been lost until it turned up quite recently; its composer retains a particular affection for the piece. Though Riley cannot remember exactly what material he used, the source of *I Can't Stop No* is, again, taped from the radio: a voice singing the words 'I just can't stop no' in a high, rising scale. He then separated each word and scrambled them in helter-skelter combinations. Combined with an obsessively repeated strummed open fifth, the spoken words audibly retain their origins in the manic rising figure, producing some interestingly bizarre pitch distortions in the process. Lasting over an hour, it uses, the composer says, 'as much tape as I could possibly fit on a reel', the idea being that the piece itself could not stop. A Long Island club called The World seems to have been interested in using *I Can't Stop No* for dancing, but closed before the piece was finished.

You're Nogood (probably late 1967, after the composition of *Poppy Nogood and the Phantom Band*, see below) is what its composer calls 'a set of variations' on a tune of this name by a New York rhythm-and-blues group called the Harvey Arverne Dozen. Riley was attracted to this source partly because by this time he had started calling himself 'Poppy Nogood'. *You're Nogood* exposes its borrowed material much more directly, and at greater length while remaining untransformed, than do the other tape pieces. By this time, its composer had acquired a sine-wave generator from Young and also, on loan from him, a small Moog synthesizer; Riley had never had access to a synthesizer before. The result was what he calls 'a combination of a synthesizer piece and a cut-up tape-loop piece', adding synthesizer sounds and their transformations to the basic techniques of tape-splicing, etc. Additionally, he now had two decent Revox tape recorders, giving him much better sound reproduction than before; Riley wanted to give his new piece, intended for replay in a discotheque, a cleaner sound.

'My idea was to make an arrangement', he says. 'So you'd have the tune, a set of improvisations, different loops of the tune: an abstract arrangement of the tune, almost like a jazz chorus. And then at some point, this tone generator which has sweeping and pulsing sounds'. A pulsing figure, taking the rhythm of the tune as its basis, starts with a very low pitch, then sweeps right upwards, at which point the tune itself enters. At the end of the piece, there are some very fast, double-speed loops, also supported by the pulses. Commissioned by a Philadelphia discotheque, *You're Nogood* apparently made a curious impact on the dance floor. Initially, the unusual effects seemed to mesh with the strobe lights and the general atmosphere. When the loops started to get out of phase with each other, however, the dancers were forced to stop and attempt to adjust to the constantly shifting metre, with apparently entertaining results.

Riley's tape pieces have both a historical and a musical importance that has been undermined by their composer's *laissez-faire* approach to his own achievements. At the very least, they provide a missing link in the story of Riley's influence on Reich and in the prehistory of sampling.

Composition or improvisation?

Riley has said that he 'never wrote any more music after [*In C*]; I started improvising'.[26] But this is not true. In addition to the tape pieces, he continued to explore the potential of single-page, module-based scores as the basis for group improvisation in two further works. Both were composed for the already mentioned jazz group of which Riley was then a member. The first piece, *Autumn Leaves*, included a tape part as well. The work strips away the chord changes, as well as the tune, of this jazz 'standard', by Johnnie Mercer, replacing them with a series of modules, based on a Mixolydian scale in B♭ with some chromatic extensions, designed to imply the original harmony. Riley did not consider it successful, and the piece was only performed once, in a private concert at Cabrillo College, Santa Cruz, on 13 March 1965, shortly after its composition.

The second piece, *Tread on the Trail*, was written soon afterwards for performance at the previously mentioned concert the jazz group gave at the San Francisco Tape Music Center in the following month. Instrumentation is free, as are dynamics and performance duration; octave transposition is permitted. The material – jaunty, somewhat fragmented melodies, the movement through which is governed by rules similar to those of *In C* – seems best suited to wind instruments; according to the performing instructions, the forces 'can include an ad lib drum set or hand drums or other percussion'. Gibson – who performed a multi-tracked version of *Tread on the Trail* for his 1992 CD as well as playing in the 1965 première – describes the score as 'five different sets of melodies of equal length, each one constructed as a mirror image of itself'.[27] Essentially modal, the five lines use eight, five, eight, eight and seven notes respectively, encompassing all pitches except B♭ and D♭.

Example 2.4 *Olson III*, modules 1–5

Though based on characterful material and in some respects more tightly controlled, *Tread on the Trail* lacks the individuality and expressive range of *In C*.

For Riley, notation itself increasingly seemed an attempt to fix something whose essence is to float freely, intuitively, spontaneously. Improvisation has always seemed central to his approach, even when composing; he delights in the immediacy of interaction with the material and in incorporating the player's own creativity in whatever he does. It therefore seems especially surprising that Riley remains the only one of the four main subjects of the present book who has never formed his own regular ensemble. He once explained this with the suggestion that he is 'not good at telling people what to do'. The fact that the single-page, module-based score proved to have less potential as a basis for group improvisation than the enormous success of *In C* had suggested it should must have played its part in Riley's wariness of regular ensembles. Within two or three years, notation itself had become such an encumbrance for him that he abandoned it altogether for more than a decade.

In 1967, Riley was invited to spend several weeks during March and April in Stockholm and commissioned to write a work for the students in the choir and orchestra of the city's Nacka School of Music. The result, premièred on 27 April, was *Olson III*, his third attempt at a piece for these forces; 'Olson's Rough-cut' was apparently the name by which marijuana was often obliquely referred to in Sweden at that time. The text for *Olson III*, by the composer himself, reads: 'Begin to think about how we are to be'. The piece is clearly modelled on the principles of *In C*: notated on a single sheet, it consists of thirty short modules, beginning in F major and ending in F minor. (See Ex. 2.4 for the first five modules.) Unlike *In C*, *Olson III* uses only equal rhythms – notated as stemless crotchets – thus effectively doing away with the need for a separate pulse. The text is set entirely syllabically throughout. A performance, Riley says, need not start at the beginning, though a complete cycle through all the notated material should be made, probably ending with the module with which it began. While benefiting from a more subtle approach to modality than *Tread on the Trail*, lack of rhythmic variety prevents *Olson III* from achieving the same sort of expressive impact as *In C*, though the piece evidently aroused the students to petition their school to dismiss its orchestral director, who had been less than sympathetic to such radical endeavours.

From keyboards to saxophone and back again

Riley's attempts to stake out some new, independent and solo ground in the years immediately following *In C* took the form of building an individual keyboard style on the basis of his skills in blues, ragtime and jazz piano, interspersed with a temporary preoccupation with the saxophone: the scenario acted out by Young himself in the early 1960s. Both in California and immediately after his move to New York, Riley made considerable efforts to extend his style of piano improvisation. Since surviving recordings are rare, the chief evidence of this essentially improvised activity is, ironically, the two *Keyboard Studies* – out of at least some half a dozen – which Riley bothered to notate. Considerable confusion surrounds the identification and dating of these. Michael Nyman argues that *In C* is 'more developed in many respects'[28] than the *Keyboard Studies*, implying that the latter predate Riley's most famous composition. The project in fact originated around the same time; but even *Keyboard Study no. 1* was first written down, perhaps even first improvised, after *In C*, and the other studies almost certainly date from rather later. The composer gives the date 1965 to the *Studies* as a whole in his own worklist.

Since several of them remain untranscribed, *Keyboard Studies* can best be viewed as a collection of ideas – some eventually notated, some not – assembled over a period of perhaps three years or more as the basis for improvisation. While intended largely for multi-tracked performance by Riley alone, the *Studies* could also be played by a keyboard ensemble, still providing opportunities for working with others and even for musicians to play without the composer present. *Keyboard Study no. 2*, the best-known of the set, in fact originated as an ensemble piece, as discussed below. But whether elaborated by a single musician or by a group, these studies are, as their name suggests, really exercises rather than fully fledged compositions. Riley describes the *Keyboard Studies* as 'a real hard-core minimalist piece'.

Example 2.5 *Keyboard Study no. 1*: (a) modules 1–2; and (b) modules 7–10

Keyboard Study no. 1

Keyboard Study no. 1 was also called *Coule*; the title is a pun on the French word for 'flowing' or 'gliding' (or, in musical terminology, the 'slur' as a phrase marking), and Riley pronounces it, as though without its acute accent, 'Cool', a term of colloquial approbation still new when the piece was first conceived. *Coule* received its first performance in the same November 1964 concerts as the première of *In C*. The first *Study* remains unpublished and little-known; indeed, the only currently extant copies of it are of what its composer calls a 're-creation' of the piece, with some of the original patterns and some new ones added, made in about 1994 for the British pianist John Tilbury.

A series of sixteen short modules, divided into three sections played without a break, *Keyboard Study no. 1* is rooted in a Dorian mode on E♭, including the sharpened leading note D♮ as well as D♭, with octave transposition permitted. The opening module of each section is played immediately with the second, interlocking with the initial module (which is notated off the beat) to produce a continuous flow of semi-quavers. (Ex. 2.5a gives these two modules.) This opening module is subsequently retained as an ostinato against which all the others in that section are fitted, all to be repeated an unspecified number of times. Underneath the constant patter of semiquavers, some contrapuntal consistencies can be detected in the apparently chaotic kaleidoscope of the contrapuntal combinations; Example 2.5b gives one illustration of this. While Riley typically fails to pursue with much rigour any of the canonic structures he sets up, their complexity evolves in tandem with an overall form controlled by the gradual expansion of patterns. The result is already more than merely the setting in motion of what Nyman calls 'tiny eddies in the onflowing continuum from which any other sort of stress, or edge, is excluded'.[29]

Keyboard Study no. 2/Untitled Organ

Over eighteen months after Riley's jazz group had begun improvising on its opening modules in early 1965, Riley recorded a solo improvisation on this material, entitled *Untitled Organ*, as the A side of his first LP, *Reed Streams*. Someone had given the composer an old harmonium with several malfunctioning keys and powered by a vacuum cleaner motor; not having any money to buy anything else, he decided to try and work with it. His mother had helped with the acquisition of two Revox tape recorders, and suddenly he had a viable system to experiment with multi-tracking for solo keyboard performances. *Reed Streams* was made with this equipment on 4 and 5 November 1966, at the request of Mass Art Records, a small company based on Canal Street, with an issue of just one thousand copies.

What became known as *Keyboard Study no. 2* was not notated, at least in its most widely disseminated form, until Riley wrote it out as a response to a request from Cage for a contribution to the book *Notations*, published in 1969.[30] Consultation of the source of this reveals 'NYC/Nov 29, 1966', omitted from all published versions: soon after the *Reed Streams* recording was made. As with the first study, though, *Keyboard Study no. 2* exists in variant forms. Due mainly to the fact that its score became available just as the recording of *In C* began making Riley's music well known, *Keyboard Study no. 2* has been widely performed, especially as an ensemble piece.

Keyboard Study no. 2 (reproduced in its entirety as Ex. 2.6) is notated as a series of fifteen modules, each similarly to 'be repeated in a continuous manner, for a long period of time, so that it turns into a stream of notes, moving steadily, without accent'; these fast and even rhythms provide an implied pulse as firm as that to be found in *Keyboard Study no. 1*. Notes

Example 2.6 *Keyboard Study no. 2*, complete score

are now notated as pitches without stems; once again, octave transposition of modules is permitted. A choice of two ostinato modules of four notes – one a permutation of the other – is offered, one of which 'must be present at all times'. All the other modules – notated two, occasionally three, to a line – are played against these, preserving the 'sequential order of left to right, top to bottom'. Returning to an earlier module is permissible, but jumping ahead is not. Each figure of *Keyboard Study no. 2* 'may start on any note of its group'. In addition, several pitches are required to be sustained once the piece gets under way, providing a drone accompaniment to the constant repetition of the modules themselves.

Rooted in a modal, basically Dorian, scale on F, the pitch range of *Keyboard Study no. 2* gradually expands. The opening pair of four-note modules forms the basis for all the succeeding ones, which alter the

Example 2.7 *Keyboard Study no. 2*, circular version, page 7

original pattern's basic shape through extension, transposition, inversion, permutation and repetition within a pattern, creating a free but often essentially canonic counterpoint with the initial modules. The fourth module additionally turns its penultimate note into a dominant drone, C: the first of five modules to create pedal points around which the music can swirl and eddy. The most commonly available version of the score adds drones on D and F; another version adds F, G and B♭.

Other notated versions of *Keyboard Study no. 2* reflect its free-wheeling, open-form aspect by transcribing the piece's pitch modules in concentric circles. A largely unpublished, eight-page manuscript – its first four pages dated 1966, the remainder 1967 – builds, respectively, four, five, six (twice), eight, seven (twice) and eight circles; mostly in the treble clef, though pages 2 and 5 are notated entirely in the bass clef, and pages 3 and 4 employ both. As Example 2.7 – page 7 of this circular version[31] – shows, Riley exerts some control on his patterns by deploying multiples of 4, 7 and 8 to give a total of fifty-six notes in each circle, since multiples of these numbers can be summed to fifty-six. But while the close connections of pitch and rhythm between the circles allows the unravelling of interesting contrapuntal combinations, no attempt is made to fill all the links in the canonic chain; the third and sixth circles (working outwards), for instance, simply duplicate each other.

Untitled Organ lasts 20′10″ and was performed live in a single take. Riley remains for long periods on a single pattern, alternating this with the polyphony of a pair of patterns. In other performances around this time, unfettered by the constraints of recording, the composer says he would stay on the same pattern for around twenty minutes. For all its limitations, this 1966 version allows the listener more opportunities than might have been expected to experience the shifting downbeats and other psycho-acoustic phenomena. Even the constant clatter of the close-miked harmonium's mechanism contributes to the effect.

Dorian Reeds *and* Poppy Nogood and the Phantom Band

To explore these new dimensions further, Riley now took up the soprano saxophone. Having taught Lewis the tenor saxophone material of *In A♭ or is it B♭?*, Riley concluded that he was perfectly capable of playing the saxophone himself. His immediate example was, of course, Young, who had been inspired to take up the sopranino by hearing Coltrane. It was Coltrane who now also provided a natural model for Riley who, like many others, had first been attracted by his playing some five years earlier. Through Young, too, Riley had come to know the work of the Indian shenai player Bismillah Khan. Gibson – himself a fine saxophonist, and a further influence on this new move – helped him buy a cheap soprano instrument and gave him a few lessons on fingering. After teaching himself to play *In A♭ or is it B♭?*, Riley was ready to deploy the saxophone in developing new improvisational methods for himself. The B side of his 1966 album *Reed Streams* was devoted to *Dorian Reeds*, the earliest surviving example of Riley's soprano saxophone playing. Shortly after this recording was made, Riley made his New York concert debut in his own loft, playing both *Untitled Organ* and *Dorian Reeds*.

Dorian Reeds, probably first worked out in 1965, was just one of Riley's many improvisations using his new equipment. Some time in 1966, he made a 'score' including diagrammatic representation of the equipment and the techniques he had devised for it, which he titled 'Solo Time-Lag Music'. The diagram demonstrates how signals coming from both the microphone (live sound) and Tape Recorder II (tape-delayed sound) can

Example 2.8 Motif used in *In A♭ or is it B♭?*, *Dorian Reeds*, *Poppy Nogood and the Phantom Band* and *Sunrise of the Planetary Dream Collector*

be controlled by separate potentiometers to produce a time-delay of about three seconds; pre-recorded, as well as live, materials can be incorporated into the system. 'Solo Time-Lag Music' offers nine scales on E, C and F♯ – including various gapped scales, such as the one identical to Messiaen's Mode 4, as well as the more familiar Dorian, Aeolian, etc. – plus some further notes regarding their elaboration. Three types of improvisation are identified. The first is slow and melodic, developing into cyclical canons over drones on the first, fourth and fifth degrees of the scale. The second is fast, consisting of chains of repeated figures of between one and nine beats' duration, assembling several alignments of what Riley's accompanying notes call 'a rotational series' both against each other and against 'sub-groups articulating the delay period or groups which may set up an opposing cylic [*sic*] period'. The third involves 'sections containing evenly spaced pulses fashioned into frequency grids which glide across one another by means of a graduall [*sic*] expansion or contraction of the gap (between pulses) over the fixed time-lag period'.

Though this composition appears in worklists under the multiple headings *Dorian Reeds/Dorian Winds/Dorian Brass*, etc., Riley has no memory of any performances by any instrument other than the saxophone. *Dorian Reeds*, meanwhile, turned out to be merely 'the first version'[32] of *Poppy Nogood and the Phantom Band*. The most important of Riley's saxophone improvisations, this uses electric organ as well as soprano saxophone, subjecting both to the multiple delays of the time-lag accumulator. He first seems to have performed this in early 1967, and has said that he 'used to play [it] in various forms at concerts for four or five years'. Riley recorded the work in 1969, when it was issued by Columbia as the B side of *A Rainbow in Curved Air*. The title is often said to be an allusion to drugs, but it actually arose from the fact that the composer was jokingly calling himself 'Poppy Nogood' at this time. His small daughter used to call him 'Poppy', and 'Poppy Nogood' when she was angry with him. Riley then developed this family joke, saying 'if you were "no good", then you could only go up! . . . So it was an attempt to start at the bottom'. The notion of the 'Phantom Band' derives from the time-lag accumulator: the composer's 'multiple, other persona that's being recycled in electronics'.

Riley's own improvised patterns for both works frequently drew on a motif which, though not written down until around 1980, can also be found in the tape piece *In Ab or is it Bb?*, and the 1980–81 string quartet composition entitled *Sunrise of the Planetary Dream Collector* (see Ex. 2.8). In addition, *Sunrise* itself originated as a keyboard improvisation in 1976, before being reworked for the Kronos Quartet. This motif uses only the first four pitches of the D-minor scale. The sixth note is E in some versions, D in others; the group G E (D) F, marked 'x' in Example 2.8, becomes significant both melodically and as an identifiable harmonic unit. This eight-note pattern is a frequent presence on the surface of the music of the LP version of *Dorian Reeds*, also giving rise to several variants. Curiously, though, despite its apparently extensive inclusion in all the concert performances of *Poppy Nogood* which Riley now recalls, this motif is less prominent on the work's commercial recording.

The 1966 recording of *Dorian Reeds* lasts 14′55″; it was made in a single take, without editing. Moving quickly between the three musical types described in 'Solo Time-Lag Music', this improvisation is centred around the Dorian scale on D. As with *Keyboard Study no. 2*, the continuous quavers provide their own pulse. New figures and variants of old ones come thick and fast against the continuum of Example 2.8. The slower music that first occurs about four minutes in is the beginning of a sequence in which slow, fast and staccato materials alternate, and frequently overlap. Bb and later Eb, notes foreign to the basic mode, are introduced, the former creating an uncharacteristically jarring note, reminiscent of the foghorns which inspired the String Quartet. The close canonic treatment of the original motif which appears in conjunction with the latter pitch produces a quite different texture from before, resembling an insistent buzzing around the small group of pitches involved, enhanced by sudden crescendi and diminuendi and producing, as a resulting pattern, repeated Ds. Motivic extension of the original eight-note pattern's second half, subjected to the third type of treatment described in 'Solo Time-Lag Music,' leads to contracting pulses on the dominant, A, taking the improvisation to its conclusion. In a longer performance, all these patterns would accumulate and fade more slowly, and the foreign pitches would probably insinuate themselves into the proceedings with greater subtlety. Whatever its length, however, *Dorian Reeds* effects a curious and delicate balance: neither clear enough to register every contrapuntal relationship, nor sufficiently dense and complex to cause the listener to abandon the attempt.

In *Poppy Nogood and the Phantom Band*, melodic material is immediately subjected to the dense canonic overlays made possible by more extensive applications of the time-lag accumulator. Though some of these are clearly intended to be appreciated more texturally than as audible counterpoint, what the sleeve-note to the 21′15″ LP version calls the 'spatially separated mirror images . . . adapted for studio recording by Glen Kolotkin' to 'resemble the sound Terry gets in his all-night concerts'[33] provide a stereo sound-space which permits the detailed contrapuntal unfolding of some phrases to be readily heard. The saxophone melodies of *Poppy Nogood* are also embedded from the outset in drones supplied by the electric organ, contributing significantly to the textural density and richness of this more 'orchestral' realisation of 'Solo Time-Lag Music'.

The mode is now Aeolian, once again centred on D, emphasised by the prominence of the flattened sixth falling to the fifth of the scale, and underpinned by drones including a prominent dominant, A. Short motifs are common: one based around B♭ A is immediately audible at the outset. Any feeling of regular metre is essentially local. In a slow second section of greater transparency, beginning just after six minutes in, more extended melodies are counterpointed against one another by the accumulator, and the original mode is expanded, at least briefly, by the introduction of E♭, the flattened supertonic, and later by more elaborate pitch bending. The faster, skirling melodic material of the third section – suggesting comparisons with Indian music as well as a variety of world folk musics – now evolves as a series of waves, each focusing on different groups of pitches, some much more extended – both scalic and arpeggiated – than the first.

Like Young, Riley continued to play the saxophone regularly for some two or three years, for which the ideas behind *Poppy Nogood* proved sufficiently rich. With this, he exhausted what he had to say about – and what he could actually play on – the saxophone. Tied closely to the technique of the time-lag accumulator, the saxophone improvisations were governed, and shackled, by it, especially in the area of rhythm. And though he devised various ways of overcoming the restrictions – for instance, through the use of different tape-recorder channels – the kinds of counterpoint possible with such means remained limited.

A Rainbow in Curved Air

From 1967 onwards, as the keyboard gradually returned to the centre of his concerns, Riley's music developed new dimensions. Two particular influences on his keyboard improvisations from this period onwards should be noted. First, the gradual availability of more sophisticated

Example 2.9 *A Rainbow in Curved Air*, two extracts from notated version

types of instrument enhanced the range of contrapuntal and structural possibilities which the continued use of tape delay permitted, as well as timbral quality and variety. Concerned to develop greater structural, and especially rhythmic, control, Riley now abandoned the time-lag accumulator. Secondly, Indian classical music soon became a major force in his life, and specifically his association with Pandit Pran Nath, discussed below.

A Rainbow in Curved Air – its title, Riley says, just an expression of 'the way the music felt', and lacking any specific allusion to drugs – marks an early stage of these developments. The electric organ, electric harpsichord and 'rocksichord', plus a dumbec (a one-sided Persian drum) and a tambourine, to be found on the Columbia recording, offer a wide timbral range. This 18′39″ improvisation mixes several contrasting musical elements in a kaleidoscope underpinned by an almost constant quaver pulse grouped into fourteen-beat cycles and a pentatonic mode centred on A: A C♯ D E G. Most idiosyncratic of the shower of ideas that erupts just after the beginning, and on which the whole improvisation is based, are the shimmering, ornamented melodic lines in quickly moving, ascending and descending shapes which are clearly modelled on the melismatic characteristics of Indian music, and in particular its employment of diminution. While the full impact of Indian classical music did not manifest itself until after he had begun studying with Pran Nath, Riley had heard a good deal both in live performance and, especially, on record by the time he began improvising *A Rainbow in Curved Air*. Its influence already plays a significant part in the work: not only in these imitative elaborations of Indian mannerisms but also in the ways in which the fourteen-beat pattern is deployed cyclically, other material manoeuvring around it in ever-changing, sometimes syncopated-sounding, patterns in relationships too fast-moving, and no doubt too unsystematic, to establish any scheme the ear can readily pick up.

Other material in *A Rainbow in Curved Air* includes a rocking motif, with its own delay already built in, which adds new pitches to the mode, introducing C♮ and G♯ but mainly orientated around E, A, G♯ and D, with the rattle of dumbec and tambourine as accompaniment. A joyous chordal and thematic outburst around halfway through proves a natural development of the earlier material. The final one-third of the improvisation introduces a tabla-like accompaniment on the dumbec, which will underpin the whole section, and a new melody, descending from the dominant and back to the tonic, inflecting the mode with C♮ and F♮.

Several manuscript pages (dated 1968) outlining the basic material and exploring some of its cyclical and contrapuntal possibilities suggest something of the potential which Riley was trying to develop in his improvisations on *A Rainbow in Curved Air*, which are often much more extended than the one on the Columbia recording. It is characteristic that these written-out versions attempt to transcend what Riley saw as the inevitable limits of musical notation by means of some modest graphic departures from convention. Example 2.9 gives two extracts from these pages.

Example 2.9a demonstrates the basic fourteen-beat cyclic pattern in gradually unfolding canon on the five basic pitches of the mode: the right hand remaining fixed while, after beginning in unison with it, the left adds an extra quaver A to the end of each repetition; Riley's original notates the complete canonic cycle resulting from this progressive misalignment. Example 2.9b illustrates the decorative, melismatic right-hand style, unfolding three- and four-note patterns against the same fourteen-beat cycle in the left hand (starting on the second note of the original one), using decorated beams which (more or less) articulate the cycle into seven-note groupings.

Though *A Rainbow in Curved Air* demonstrates greater structural control and flexibility, as well as timbral ingenuity and the beginnings of a melodic style influenced by Indian classical music, Riley's improvisations remained confined to working with variations of the same pattern. Material from *A Rainbow in Curved Air* continued, however, to prove a potent inspiration for subsequent work: it found its way into *Jaipur Local*, a duo piece for voice and tabla for the composer and Krishna Bhatt, originally composed in 1983–4 and performed in various versions by them until 1991, when their CD *No-Man's Land* was issued.

The expansion of Riley's reputation and his changing aesthetic to 1976

Crucial in Riley's development from relatively obscure innovator to guru of late-1960s counter-culture was the much wider availability of recordings. The Columbia recording of *In C* was issued in late 1968, as a consequence of David Behrman's engagement by the company as a producer. Behrman, himself a composer, was sympathetic to new music; the twenty-five or thirty discs he put out during his brief period of influence at Columbia included three works by Reich. *In C* was released at the same time as Walter Carlos's famous *Switched-On Bach* and another, soon forgotten, album entitled *Rock and Other Four-Letter Words*; all three were designed 'to capture the imagination of the young audience', as Riley puts it.

The recording of *In C* resulted from the composer's period as a 'Creative Associate' of the Center for Creative and Performing Arts at the State University of New York at Buffalo during the early part of 1968, and a performance of the work by this group at the Carnegie Recital Hall in March that year. The forty-three-minute recording was made in the same month; it involved experienced and sympathetic musicians, including Stuart Dempster (trombone), Jon Hassell (trumpet), David Rosenboom (viola), Jan Williams (marimbaphone) and Riley himself on soprano saxophone. Though its superimposition of three complete 'takes' creates a muddy sound-perspective, this recording's wide circulation, in Europe as well as in the USA, even encouraged many to play *In C* themselves – the score being reproduced in its entirety on the record sleeve, though with some errors – and to imitate its infectious tonal and rhythmic vitality in their own compositions. Riley's second Columbia recording, issued in 1969, was devoted to *Poppy Nogood and the Phantom Band* and *A Rainbow in Curved Air*. As with *In C*, the accompanying sleeve notes – this time a poem by the composer – were very much of their time, promoting sentiments of peace, especially appropriate considering that the Vietnam War was then in progress, and utopian, and in particular ecological, concerns. In addition, Riley recorded a joint album, *Church of Anthrax*, with John Cale in 1968, at the suggestion of John McClure, now the producer at Columbia for both musicians. While this manages to integrate at least a little of the contrapuntal thinking characteristic of Riley's other output of this period with something of the energy of rock, this recording – released in 1970 – leans too far towards the blandness often characteristic of such 'fusion' projects.

Also in tune with the *Zeitgeist* were the installations, multimedia presentations, all-night concerts, experimental video projects and music for films with which Riley was involved. The first three of these categories are impossible to separate, since it seems that some events involved a variety of visual as well as aural elements, and Riley performed concerts in the installation spaces. Details of such events, too, are rather confused. All-night concerts, both solo and with *ad hoc* ensembles, became an occasional feature of Riley's career in the late 1960s and early 1970s. The first solo all-night event seems to have occurred in Philadelphia, through the agency of Jim Williams: a friend of the composer and an art teacher in the city, whose communal vision of whole families eating and drinking, then sleeping in hammocks and sleeping bags while Riley played appears to have been successfully realised.

In 1968, Riley participated in 'Intermedia '68', a series of late-night concerts in various colleges in New York State, including Albany and SUNY Buffalo (while the composer was in residence there), and ending at the Brooklyn Academy of Music. 'Environments' for these, provided by Bob Benson, consisted of a 'tiny maze of sound chambers and mirrored rooms which contained microphones to capture fragments of conversation and automatically arrange them into sound collages of repeated patterns'. A group of dancers and acrobats – recruited at each college, and known as 'The Daughters of Destruction' – also took part. Other, probably similar, installations included one in Amagansett, on Long Island, and, in the summer of 1969, an event commissioned by the Kansas City Performing Arts Foundation, which took place in the Nelson Atkins Gallery in Kansas City, as part of the Magic Theater Festival; this was repeated in New York in March 1970, at Automation House on East 68th Street.

Other notable landmarks in the development of Riley's reputation included the last two concerts, in June 1968, in the 'January through June' Festival at the Barbizon Plaza Theater (where Young had performed four months before). On 14 April 1969, he appeared at The Electric Circus: a psychedelic rock club – situated on St Mark's Place in New York's East Village, just north of SoHo – which was a crucial venue in the evolution of the late 1960s 'alternative' scene. Here, he and Rosenboom, on violin, performed both *Poppy Nogood and the Phantom Band* and *A Rainbow in Curved Air*, among the audience was Philip Glass. In the early 1970s, too, Riley began returning to Europe, performing not only *Poppy Nogood* and *Rainbow* but also the already mentioned solo keyboard improvisations entitled *Persian Surgery Dervishes* which formed their sequel. France, West Germany and Italy, in particular, were visited quite frequently, though he did not perform in Britain until 1986.

When Riley played with other musicians, the group sometimes called itself Poppy Nogood and the Persian Surgery Band; those with whom he worked at this time included several fellow Creative Associates from Buffalo, such as Edward Burnham (vibraphone), and the already mentioned Hassell and Williams. As a soloist, Riley sometimes appeared under the guise of 'Poppy Nogood's Phantom Band'. The ensemble as well as solo music for these occasions seems to have been drawn from the *Poppy Nogood*, *Rainbow in Curved Air* and, later, the *Dervish* material, elaborated into improvisations not only far more extended but also far more freewheeling and exploratory than those to be found on the commercial recordings.

Riley was also in demand as a provider of music for experimental video projects and both experimental and more commercial films. *Music with Balls*, for instance – a half-hour video by the sculptor Arlo Acton and the producer John Coney – was made by KQED TV in San Francisco in 1969. The composer's worklist for the years 1972–6 gives the impression that he spent at least two years composing, or improvising, nothing but the film scores which came his way as a result of contacts made in the aftermath of his period of fame, though in fact most of these were done quickly and, like the music for many of his other projects of this period, based on earlier material or elaborated much more fully only later. Two examples must suffice. As released on LP by Warner Brothers in 1972, the year of its composition, *Les yeux fermés* – the English title of Joel Santini's film is 'Happy Ending' – parallels the forces, as well as developing the musical materials, of the *Rainbow in Curved Air/Poppy Nogood* album, with one side devoted to keyboard music, the other to the saxophone. *Le secret de la vie* (or 'Lifespan') – a mystery movie in French by the American director Alexander Whitelaw – was made in Holland in 1973. The two short pieces from it – released on the Stip label two years later – again feature both saxophone and organ; the second one, *G-Song*, became the second composition Riley worked up for the Kronos Quartet some five years afterwards.

Having established himself as a significant member of New York's downtown community, Riley made the decision to move back to California in 1969, at first to live once more in San Francisco. While his return to California did not mean he was entirely forgotten there – as a solo performance of 'Music from the *Persian Surgery Dervishes*' at a packed Whitney Museum on 5 April 1973 proved – he now lacked the special career base New York could have continued to provide, as it was beginning to do for Reich and Glass. The desire to return to his West-coast roots was an important part of his reason to forsake the city which he had, in any case, never originally intended to settle in at all. Strongly connected to this powerful feeling of spiritual connection to California – and to the ideals, often misleadingly labelled as 'hippie', which had their wellsprings in a West-coast culture very different from that to be found in the Eastern seaboard's mecca of commerce – was an increasing commitment to Indian classical music.

Indian classical music

Riley now found himself consumed by other matters besides his own creative work, whether composed or entirely improvised. Since 1967 or 1968, his attention had been seized by tapes which Young played him of Pandit Pran Nath, whose singing in the Kirana tradition was becoming a strong influence on Riley's old friend, himself long steeped in the musics of the East. When Young first brought Pran Nath to the USA in January 1970, he also arranged for him to travel to California, where he visited Riley. On being told by Pran Nath that he should at once become his disciple, Riley consulted Young, who advised that he should join him in this adventure. Though uncertain as to what this would involve, Riley had the confidence which came with the feeling that his 'karmic connection' with Pran Nath 'just locked in, and I realized it was meant to be'.[34] In September 1970, his family accordingly embarked on a six-month pilgrimage to the Kailash Colony in New Delhi, to be joined three months later by Young and Marian Zazeela.

Riley initially began studying tabla, on which he took lessons for about two years, learning a great deal about rhythm and the experience of time. Then, like Young, he took up singing in the Kirana style. It had been Pran Nath's particular vocal qualities that had attracted Riley from the start. 'For a while', he has said, 'you thought you were hearing everything you've ever wanted to hear out of music just out of a solo voice'. The impact of Pran Nath, and in particular the experience of attempting to sing ragas in India, caused Riley to doubt the value of his own music. He told his teacher that he wanted to give up composing and improvising in his own style, stay in India and devote his life to its music. Pran Nath, however, said he should go back, telling him it was his role to compose as well as to practise Indian music. As a result, Riley, like Young and Zazeela, continued to devote himself totally to Pran Nath for certain parts of his teacher's regular visits to the USA, as well as during further trips of his own to India; another extended visit to New Delhi was made later in 1971. He still goes regularly to India to teach. As with all relationships between an Indian disciple and his guru, this involved much more than performing with Pran Nath on a regular basis. When, in the autumn of 1971, Riley took a teaching position at Mills College – in Oakland, across the bay from San Francisco – he initiated an Indian Music programme to which Pran Nath regularly contributed. Riley taught at Mills for some ten years, taking the classes in North Indian music in each Fall semester, devoted chiefly to singing with the aid of the tamboura. Pran Nath usually came for the Spring semester.

Such close proximity to Pran Nath pulled Riley even further away from Western ways. From 1974, he and his family have lived on a remote ranch in the Sierra Nevada foothills, close to the composer's birthplace. Like Young, Riley frequently dresses in the Indian manner, adopting some Indian customs in public: for instance, in the way he acknowledges an audience's applause. More importantly, he will begin each day with the spiritual as well as musical exercise of raga singing. As with the earlier influences of jazz, Moroccan music and the example of Young, Indian music encouraged 'a daily process of learning to improvise, and what all that meant'. The discipline and context which Indian music and its intimately integrated philosophy and way of life brought could now be used to refine and focus the purpose and direction for his own spiritual development, and his own musical direction, already discovered almost a decade earlier. Riley's intimate identification with Indian musical culture played a special role in assisting his life-long quest for 'the real me'. Everything he has done since 1970 must be viewed in relation to his consuming involvement – spiritual as well as musical – with Pran Nath's teachings.

Riley's aesthetic and technical development in the 1970s

Through the first half of the 1970s, Riley moved away from 'hard-core' minimalism due to his greater concern with aspects of music which minimalism tended to avoid. Influenced by Indian music, the melodic interest in his work now increased. Lines not only themselves became more elaborate, but also combined to form new kinds of counterpoint which could only, he argues, be created through the immediacy and inspiration of improvisation. 'What could I write?' he asks. 'I could write the patterns, and I did: and got a simple-minded looking sheet of patterns, which doesn't tell the story of what was going on in the music. When I'm really on, when I'm really open, both hands seem to think independently. I can almost think two melodies at once. . . . That's really exciting, because I don't know where it's coming from'. These developments must, of course, be viewed in tandem with the continued search for ways in which repetition and modality could between them refocus the relationships between a melody, its contrapuntal elaboration and its harmonic underpinning. The more of these elements he introduced into his already established universe of repeating modules, the more Riley found that this new approach encouraged stylistic as well as technical diversity. Finally, he says, he got to the point 'where I could do anything I wanted'.

Riley's keyboard playing now also developed new dimensions as a result of his continuing experiments with drugs. Among the new kinds of counterpoint he explored were those which derived from attempting to exploit the potential for two hands on the keyboard to operate simultaneously with greater than usual independence. The practising stages of this would often evolve from a decision to explore a particular relationship: for instance, groups of seven in one hand against groups of eight in another, whether employing the same unit or, in this case, say, seven in the time of eight. But Riley was actually more interested in what could happen if such relationships were then explored freely. This was where hallucinogens could benefit his playing, opening up possibilities not available to him simply through practice and careful co-ordination. 'It had to do with not thinking technically', as he puts it, 'but conceiving something that's sort of impossible, and just watching it happen'.

As he immersed himself in his studies of singing in the Kirana style with Pran Nath, Riley found himself more and more drawn to the voice as the supreme instrument for expressing this awareness. Though it was not until 1980 – in *Remember This Oh Mind* for improvising voice and electronic keyboards – that he felt prepared to employ his own voice in his own compositions, Riley's extensive practice of Indian singing in the 1970s already took the place in his musical concerns previously occupied by the saxophone. This reinforced his increasing appreciation of the melodic potential in the more malleable context now offered not only by the more open stylistic situation in which he found himself but also by tuning systems going beyond the restrictions of equal temperament.

No dimension of Riley's work since the early 1970s illustrates better his pragmatism in balancing old and new, Eastern and Western, than his attitude to just intonation. His reasons for beginning his investigations into non-equal-tempered tuning systems are similar to those of Young, by whose example he was, once again, influenced: essentially, that he came to feel that the whole experience of music is heightened by making it more 'in tune'. Following his induction into some of the mysteries of just intonation through his association with Conrad, as well as Young, Riley began to tune his Vox electronic organ according to just intonation, with the aid of Chet Wood. From about 1972 or 1973, both Riley's new compositions and further improvisations based on older material were often explored with the aid of a variety of tuning systems. At the end of the 1970s, state-of-the-art electronic keyboards began to permit his involvement with Indian music more easily to influence the content and expressive effect, as well as the structure, of his own improvisations. In 1980 he bought the Yamaha computer-controlled piano which has been his main studio instrument for composition ever since.

The great power of just intonation arises from the resonances that build up out of simple intervallic relationships. The unequal sizes of intervals which in an equal-tempered tuning would be identical, enhance the contours of melodies played in just-tuned systems, and Riley is particularly attracted by this distinction. With equal temperament, melodic colours tend, he feels, to blandness: what he calls 'a raw, oatmeal sound'. Just intonation, on the other hand, produces 'gorgeous contours which are dependent on these unequally shaped intervals'.

Any decision in favour of such tunings, however, automatically limits what one is able to do harmonically, and thus runs counter to Riley's contemporaneous interest in more goal-directed structures driven by harmonic motion. His solutions to this contradiction are typically various and undogmatic. He has explored the possibilities of introducing chord changes into the context of improvisations for keyboards tuned to just intonation, discovering that 'you can get harmonic possibilities, they're very unusual ones'. But Riley accepts that the promotion of greater harmonic movement is essentially incompatible with the decision to get involved with just intonation, asserting that he knows of no successful pieces which combine just intonation with a high harmonic complexity. While just intonation became of major concern to him in the early 1970s, he has accordingly also been happy to explore the potential of chord changes in equal temperament. Riley has never been as consumed as Young by the notion that just intonation represents a spiritual force which must be pursued through a moral crusade. Once again, consistency is not his concern.

The Dervish improvisations

Persian Surgery Dervishes, Rising Moonshine Dervishes and *Descending Moonshine Dervishes*, all for solo electronic keyboard, are the only concert compositions dating from the first half of the 1970s in Riley's worklist. Falling between the still hardline-minimalist *A Rainbow in Curved Air* and the more 'post-modernist' *Shri Camel*, they form a large-scale link in the chain comparable, in certain respects at least, to Young's

The Well-Tuned Piano. Work on the series was begun in about 1970. Two public performances of *Persian Surgery Dervishes* were issued on the French label Shanti in 1972: one made on 18 April 1971 at the Californian Institute of Technology in Los Angeles, the other on 24 May 1972 at the Théâtre de la Musique in Paris. A concert performance of *Descending Moonshine Dervishes* was recorded on 29 November 1975 at the Metamusik Festival in West Berlin, but only issued, on the West German Kuckuck label, in 1982.

With these works, Riley's habit of returning to earlier material may once again be observed. *Keyboard Study no. 2* forms the basis for all three. As was by now his habit, however, Riley wrote down no material for any of the *Dervish* improvisations. No notated elaboration of this material came into being until 1994, with *Dervish in the Nursery.* This piano piece's addition of a jazz tune to the original repetitive material constitutes an apt illustration of the ultimate fate of minimalism in a postmodernist age: recycling its pattern-making into the accompanimental figures some had argued were its inevitable consequence.

Starting with the basic modules of the earlier work, Riley began to develop a much more dynamic structure, far removed from the static concerns of the original *Keyboard Study.* Continuing to use tape delay, he was able to achieve a greater flexibility with the aid of a Vox Supercontinental Combo organ. Stereo separation with a very short delay time between the two channels adds an extra dimension to the textures of *Persian Surgery Dervishes.* Three further features contributed to the more sophisticated structural approach to be found in these improvisations. Firstly, melody began to be important in its own right, rather than merely a by-product of the repeating patterns. As with *A Rainbow in Curved Air,* the influence of Indian music was becoming evident: more clearly, indeed, due to the increased role now played by melodic lines with a defined profile of their own.

With this greater concern for melodic development comes the second feature: a greater interest in quite complex contrapuntal imitation – of the kinds discussed above – as opposed to the simple, overlapping repetition of a short musical pattern against itself. Experimentation with cyclic structures, also owing an increasing amount to Riley's study of Indian music, takes a step further in the unravelling of such counterpoint. At the outset of the Paris version of *Persian Surgery Dervishes,* for instance, he immediately transforms one of the basic four-note patterns from *Keyboard Study no. 2* into a five-note pattern (see Ex. 2.10.) This allows him to unfold a cyclic structure of forty beats by multiplying the new five-note pattern by eight. While this forty-beat cycle circulates in the left

Example 2.10 Motif and drones used in *Keyboard Study no. 2* and *Persian Surgery Dervishes*

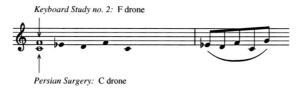

hand, the right hand evolves against it polymetrically. Due to the five-note basis of the left-hand pattern, even simple triplets played against it (three quavers in the right hand against two in the left) will quickly produce more than one layer of new alignment. Later sections see the evolution of the left-hand cyclic pattern as well. The independence of the player's hands, discussed above, can, of course, be exploited to produce many different combinations, allowing the natural expansion of extended and constantly evolving polymetric structures of a complexity difficult, or even impossible, to notate with complete accuracy.

Thirdly, a firmer sense of the evolution of an improvisation is given by the balancing and pacing of distinct sections making a contribution to a continuous whole. In particular, Riley now developed a new, slower style of playing: not so slow as to engender further stasis, but sufficiently reduced in speed to create clearer contrasts with the faster sections, and to balance with them on a more equal basis than had the slower music in, say, *A Rainbow in Curved Air*. In the *Keyboard Studies*, of course, there had been no contrast of tempo at all; even the long-held drones were only ever a background to the *perpetuum mobile* of continuous quavers at a single speed. Drone tones, too, continue to play a part in the *Dervish* improvisations. While in *Keyboard Study no. 2*, the main drone is the mode's tonic, F, *Persian Surgery Dervishes* focuses on the dominant, C (see again Ex. 2.10). Both works employ the Dorian, as well as the Aeolian, mode on F.[35]

The commercial recording of *Descending Moonshine Dervishes* uses Riley's Yamaha YC 45 D electronic organ, modified for tuning in just intonation. The whole performance – 28′18″ on Side A of the LP, 24′14″ on Side B – is, again, relayed with stereo separation of identical channels 'a fraction of a second' apart, '[permitting] a live performance in stereo and an interplay between the two parts'.[36] Once more, the contrapuntal elaboration of themes and figuration is deployed polymetrically over a fixed rhythmic cycle.

Shri Camel

Riley's first American solo album to be released since 1969, *Shri Camel*, came out on CBS in 1980. He began the music during 1975, in response to a commission from Radio Bremen, in West Germany. The main work on the piece occupied some two years; an early version was premièred in Bremen in May 1976. The performance for CBS was recorded in 1977, in the CBS Studios in San Francisco, using the already mentioned Yamaha YC 45 D organ, which offered a computerised digital delay system quite sophisticated by the standards of the day. This permitted exploration of as many as sixteen discrete contrapuntal voices, assembling textures investigating the potential of various degrees of complexity, both within a single performance and from one performance to another. Whether in concert or on the commercial recording, digital delays constitute the only electronic manipulation used; all the playing is 'live'. Different performances vary considerably in harmonic, as well as in contrapuntal, complexity. Though during the mid- and late 1970s – the most active period of engagement with the piece – he tended towards increasing elaboration of his material, Riley today still plays versions of *Shri Camel* on the piano without any delay facilities at all.

The work's title means simply 'Mr. Camel': 'shri' is an Indian title of respect. *Shri Camel* is divided into four movements: 'Anthem of the Trinity', 'Celestial Valley', 'Across the Lake of the Ancient World' and 'Desert of Ice'. The music examples used to illustrate this brief analysis (see Ex. 2.11) draw to some degree on the composer's own notation, provided for the purpose; these extracts make no attempt to reproduce the full range of contrapuntal complexities resulting from the delay systems employed, either on the CBS recording or in live performances. Riley wrote nothing down during the period in which *Shri Camel* was devised and first elaborated, and the kind of performances he plays today have, as he expresses it, put the material 'through metamorphosis'. A version of the complete score for the British group Piano Circus is currently in progress.

All four movements of *Shri Camel* are based on a C-Dorian scale subject to modification. The employment of just intonation enhances the ambiguity surrounding the leading note of the scale, extending this to the submediant which, though perfectly able to help form subdominant harmonies from time to time, is also drawn into the web of dissonances that is conjured from the upper tetrachord of the scale, rendering the harmonic focus much less certain. The combination of such a tuning with the occasional surprise of a sudden rise in dissonance level – the

Example 2.11 *Shri Camel*: (a) two bass patterns; (b) two bars from 'Anthem of the Trinity', Part One; (c) opening six bars from 'Anthem of the Trinity', Part Two; (d) two bars from 'Across the Lake of the Ancient World'; (e) two further bars from 'Across the Lake of the Ancient World'.

(*a*)

(*b*)

clash of the natural-sixth and flat-seventh degrees of the scale, for instance – allows Riley to establish a more individual harmonic idiom: one which, while still relying on a vocabulary of simple scalic and triadic elaborations around the tonic, subdominant and dominant, is crucially spiced by the fresh colours that just intonation brings. Such more adventurous chromatic advances are, however, tempered (as it were) by the incompatibility between the use of just intonation and the exploration of any real harmonic movement.

Some idea of Riley's basic harmonic approach here can be given by looking at the two bass patterns which underpin the whole of *Shri Camel* (see Ex. 2.11a (i) and (ii)). Pattern A outlines i–v–vi–♭vii, suggesting a static seventh chord, while Pattern B articulates a more active i–♭iii–iv–v–i. Neither employs any pitch outside the modified C-Dorian established as the work's basic mode, yet Pattern B lends itself more readily to harmonic motion than does Pattern A. While just intonation precludes the exploration of any real harmonic movement, not all

Example 2.11 (*cont.*)

(*c*)

(*d*)

Example 2.11 (*cont.*)

(*e*)

performances use just intonation. Riley's more recent revisitings of *Shri Camel*, on a piano lacking the delay facilities of his original Yamaha organ, have permitted a combination of the different kinds of chromatic colouring possible with equal temperament and a harmonic language that is more chordally progressive, and even modulatory, in outlook.

In *Shri Camel* Riley investigates ways of dealing with repetition somewhat different from those to be found in his previous output. The work's major innovation is the development of a changing and movable, rather than merely a strictly repeating, pattern. Riley likens the results of using such an evolving pattern to 'having a crochet stitch that you were moving from one level to another all the time'. While its identity remains essentially intact, the original pattern is thus subject not only to continuous alterations in its relationship with its context – notably with the bass line – but also to constant mutation of its own shape. The more melodic profile that emerges as a natural consequence of this malleable technique is inspired by Indian music. *Shri Camel* spins expanding lines of different lengths and complexity over a repeated bass pattern in ways which recall the cyclic principles of Indian musical structure. The schemes, in particular, by which a melodic pattern varies according to its speed – changing its relationship to its surroundings – derives from Indian practice. The bass line, too, has greater independence and flexibility than is exhibited in Riley's earlier works.

The first movement, 'Anthem of the Trinity', is in two parts, both in a slow $\frac{12}{8}$ time; the version on the CBS recording lasts around ten minutes. The first part functions in something like the manner of the ametrical *alap* of a classical Indian improvisation. The ostinato patterns which form the basis of the whole of *Shri Camel* are introduced here (see again

Ex. 2.11a (i) and (ii)). In Pattern A, used in Part One, a single-bar, rocking motif is formed from the notes i, v, vi and ♭vii over a tonic drone. This initially appears some two minutes into the piece, emerging from the more amorphous, scale-based material which provides the context out of which the main ideas and their development can proceed. After a further two minutes, the tonic drone that accompanies this is replaced by an oscillating i–iv bass line; at this point, too, the texture becomes generally thicker. More continuous melodic lines now begin to weave around each other, developing gradually into unbroken semiquavers; the first, i–v–vi–♭vii rocking pattern, meanwhile, carries on functioning as the bass over which this melody can proliferate. As the line unfolds in the right hand, its relationship to the bass pattern evolves in a constant state of flux; an extract from the early stages of this process is given as Example 2.11b.

This demonstrates the work's main innovation, to be found in all movements. While small repeated patterns remain Riley's basic building blocks, he now starts to move them around: both on different degrees of the scale, and in terms of their rhythmic relationships. Patterns can either retain their original length or be subject to augmentation or diminution. Their composer calls the result 'a kind of figuration process going on that would change the motif'. The melody of the first bar of Example 2.11b, beginning just after the initial tonic of the bass pattern, could be moved back a semiquaver on each repetition, 'phasing' right back to its opening position; it could also retain the same pitches throughout. The result – just one of many developments of this kind to be explored – is in this case groups of three semiquavers in cascading sequences occasionally enlivened by grace notes. The evolving relationships which these right-hand patterns form with the bass line are, however, by no means always as strict even as that illustrated here. Riley's improvised, entirely un-notated practice is, typically, much more flexible: not only with regard to rhythmic relationship but also in content. Thus the pattern at the beginning of Example 2.11b is soon varied and expanded, both in pitch and rhythm, in ways which appear largely unsystematic.

Part Two of 'Anthem of the Trinity' subjects Pattern B to mutation via small rhythmic changes, against which a restless, irregular figure behaves, as Riley puts it, 'like a combination of tamboura and tabla', moving quickly from a rhythmic emphasis on the tonic and dominant to expansive, almost continuous semiquaver runs involving a fairly swift expansion up the scale. (The opening six bars of Part Two in Riley's notated fragment are presented in Ex. 2.11c.) 'Celestial Valley', the second movement, turns Pattern A into a faster, two-bar ostinato in $\frac{4}{4}$, with B♮ replacing B♭. Over this, some highly lyrical intertwining melodies owing something to classical Indian practice build a counterpoint exploring new levels of complexity and a wider timbral range.

In the third movement, 'Across the Lake of the Ancient World', Pattern B is likewise speeded up, forming a new ostinato, again subject to metamorphosis. A series of variations is then constructed upon the unbroken revolutions of this pattern, forming two arcs of increased complexity to conclude with a brief, slow, chordal coda. In Example 2.11d, the continuous semiquavers in the right hand begin in groups of seven (G C D F G D F), against the grain of the beat, but quickly add new pitches and spiral away into freer pattern-making incorporating all notes of the mode. In Example 2.11e, various triplet subdivisions dominate the right hand, providing variations on the same idea against the unvarying tread of the bass part. Riley calls the results of combining such duple and triple groupings in the two hands 'a kind of ragtime'. The final movement, 'Desert of Ice', is a kind of rondo, in which Pattern B becomes the basis for an exuberant fantasy where brilliant figuration and more sustained material alternate, and sometimes collide, in a counterpoint coloured by an even brighter range of instrumental timbres. This concluding movement draws together several threads from the previous movements to provide a fitting close to the whole work.

The greater complexity of *Shri Camel* contributed to a quite new way of 'combining inner tranquillity and mental adventure', helping Riley further towards the achievement of the spiritual goals he set himself more than ten years earlier. It represents the culmination of his work with electronic keyboards in the decade after 1966. After the mid-1970s, the seeds which the work had sown for his future development were cultivated in different ground: with the aid of the new kinds of keyboard which then became available – notably the Yamaha computer-controlled piano he acquired in 1980; with the confidence to begin applying his years of training in the Kirana style of singing to his own compositions; and with the arrival of the Kronos Quartet to encourage him to re-explore the potential of notated composition.

Conclusion

Any assessment of Riley's influence must begin – some would say end – with *In C*. For those involved with its première, notably Reich, the work's impact was crucial and immediate, suggesting the potential inherent in the combination of modality and repetition. Riley himself acknowledges that, while 'it wasn't the first minimalist piece, [*In C*] was the first piece that showed people how to do it'. While Young's early exploration of sustained sounds had provided Riley, and others, with the main inspiration to develop other forms of minimalism, it was the repetition of small patterns or modules, not the drone, which was to prove capable of wide application. Young's work with sustained sounds remained little imitated, especially in the early years, due not least to its being very difficult to bring off successfully. Riley's instrumental output from 1964 onwards, on the other hand, had, as he puts it, 'an immediate effect on the audience. Steve noticed that . . . And I think it really made an impact on him: that here was a music that could be avant-garde and get an audience too'.

The rhythmic directness and essential simplicity of this approach also quickly proved captivating to audiences for many different kinds of music. These attitudes to both pitch and rhythm made the work more readily relatable to musics with which its listeners were already familiar, thus rendering it accessible to those coming from jazz or rock, in particular, as well as at least some of the audience for 'serious' music disenchanted by its more rebarbative recent developments. As William Duckworth has written, 'in the late sixties, no one could remember the last experimental composer who had used a key signature, much less written anything in C major'.[37]

In C also proved accessible because it set modality and repetition in an especially effective context in which structural evolution is controlled partly by the composer, partly by the improvisatory interaction of the performers. The notation is sufficiently precise to permit the development of real discipline among performers committed to the music's intentions, yet also sufficiently free to encourage individual expression. Crucially, however, the self-expression of each performer characteristic of all improvisation is here channelled through a collective vehicle that yields expressive results which go beyond individual tastes and intentions, 'transport[ing] us suddenly out of one reality into another', as Riley has described the experience.[38] It is here, as in all Riley's music, that the spiritual dimension of his output has also been important, challenging other composers, and particularly improvisers, to work with modal materials to achieve a contemplative music with higher purposes than mere self-expression.

For the listener, *In C* offers not merely hypnotic repetition but melodic, rhythmic and harmonic changes that not only retain moment-to-moment interest but also contribute to the evolution of the work's structure. This was immediately understood by at least a few outside the composer's own 'alternative' downtown San Francisco circle. Alfred Frankenstein, the *San Francisco Chronicle* music critic, wrote a perceptive review of one of the première performances.[39] He clearly appreciated some of the subtleties of *In C*, observing that 'climaxes of great sonority appear and are dissolved in the endlessness. At times you feel you have never done anything all your life long but listen to this music and as if that is all there is or ever will be, but it is altogether absorbing, exciting, and moving, too'. He also noted the element of ritual in the composition and its realisation, comparing it to Carlos Chavez' reworking of pre-Colombian ceremonial music.

The form in which most musicians and other listeners have experienced *In C* – an LP packaged in a style redolent of the period when the idea of a rock album with integral aspirations was still new – is of itself important. Like the *Rainbow in Curved Air* album, *In C* proclaimed itself as what came to be called a 'crossover' phenomenon. In the parlance of rock, Riley is 'a composer . . . writing pieces which had grooves and improvised around modes'.[40] For many, it is this, and the fact that the creator of such music identified closely with the emerging new technology in producing it, which is more significant than any more specific influence Riley may have had on Brian Eno or on music students.

Riley's influence on rock musicians, especially those interested in challenging the commercial status quo, has, however, perhaps been greater than that of any of the other main subjects of this book, and certainly during the period with which the book largely deals. British groups, in particular, have been affected. Pete Townshend's song 'Baba O'Riley', on The Who's *Who's Next* album of 1971, was apparently written partly in the composer's honour; it begins with a synthesizer sequence in a brilliant C major, evidently inspired by both *In C* itself and by the *Rainbow in Curved Air* album, as well as by the taking of psychedelic drugs. Curved Air took its own name from the latter disc; the band's keyboard player, Francis Monkman, was especially attracted to the *Keyboard Studies*.

David Allen, of The Soft Machine, became friendly with Riley. On the group's *Third* album (another product of Columbia, issued in 1970), the modular keyboard approach, coupled with Coltrane-inspired saxophone, of Mike Ratledge's 'Out-Bloody-Rageous' is clearly affected by Riley's work, which is also one of many influences on the eclecticism – as well as the sheer length (a complete LP side) – of Robert Wyatt's 'Moon in June'; the multiple repetitions of the piano riff in 'The Soft Weed Factor', on the group's *Six* album (1973), provide a further instance. The Third Ear Band made use of modal patterns in a rhythmically repetitive context that evidently owes much to his example. Riley's influence was, however, by no means confined to Britain, or to the USA. Other instances from rock music included the Berlin band Agitation Free, which even included

In C in its own concerts; and the Swedish group International Harvester, in particular the guitarist and keyboard player Bo Anders Persson, who played *In C* with its composer at Swedish Radio in 1967 and subsequently played Riley's music around Scandinavia.

Riley's output has also affected more than one generation of classically trained Western music students. As the concern to develop 'alternative' cultures and lifestyles spread out from California to make an international impact, his music found its way to musicians all over the world as an important musical emblem of the demand for new freedoms and outlooks, social and spiritual as well as musical. *In C* 'has proved to be the single most influential post-1960 composition by an American', suggested Robert Palmer in 1974, listing Glass, Reich, Frederic Rzewski, The Soft Machine, John Cale, Brian Eno and 'some contemporary jazz' among its progeny.[41] One might add composers and improvisers to such a list – the British composer Lawrence Ball is just one example – whose work has little to do with rock and much to do with the search for a new, or perhaps a very old, spirituality through the medium of musical experience. Other works by Riley – perhaps particularly *Poppy Nogood and the Phantom Band* and *A Rainbow in Curved Air* – have been influential too; and the composer's early tape pieces should find a place in history as wild and inventive early examples of sampling to rival Reich's achievement in this field. As Duckworth put it, however, it was *In C* that 'gave voice to the minimalist movement in America. In some ways, it became its anthem'.[42]

3   Steve Reich

Steve Reich's career divides geographically into three parts: his childhood and student years on the USA's East Coast; his further years of study in California; and the period that saw his full establishment as a professional composer based in New York. Reich was just short of his twenty-fifth birthday when he 'went West', almost twenty-nine when he returned to New York. In terms of his output as a minimalist, the story only begins towards the end of the second period, but is already substantial soon after the beginning of the third.

Reich is a slow, painstaking and fastidious worker; since *Music for Eighteen Musicians* (first performed in 1976), he has completed just sixteen unwithdrawn compositions (excluding arrangements of earlier pieces). As he is scarcely ever content to use the same approach, material and structure in a subsequent piece without stylistic or technical modification, almost all these can be claimed to represent an advance of some kind, some half-a-dozen of them importantly so. Yet it still makes stylistic and aesthetic sense to divide his complete output into two, with 1976 as the watershed.

Reich himself has argued that the point of maximum change did not come until around 1979. There is a close link between the instrumentation of *Eight Lines* (written in that year, and formerly known as *Octet*) – the work which its composer singles out as representing possibly *the* major point of change – and the modifications to his thinking about structure; its recuperation of melody and harmonic motion seems all of a piece with the new importance it gives to instruments of the standard Western classical orchestra and to variety of timbral resource. But it is in *Music for Eighteen Musicians* (1974–6) that we find regular instruments of the orchestra used in an ensemble context in Reich's output for the first time. In *Tehillim* (1980–81) the composer's tendencies towards more sustained and clear-cut melodic writing are set into even sharper relief by Reich's return to the task of setting a text, the first time he had done so since his student days; but the seeds of this were sown by his studies in Jewish cantillation in 1976–7.

The stylistic advances made in the immediate aftermath of *Music for Eighteen Musicians* may be seen, in part, as a response to the commissions the composer was now receiving for works for forces other than those of his own ensemble. The uniqueness of these compositions in the composer's total output can be overestimated; after all, he has continued to rely on keyboards and tuned percussion as a central force – both compositional and purely practically – in later works: both those for large forces (*The Desert Music*, 1982–4) and those for smaller ones (*Sextet*, 1984–5). *The Cave* (1989–93) and *Three Tales* (1996 onwards) demonstrate Reich's continuing rejection of aspects of the Western classical heritage (the operatic voice) and the revival of his interest in new technologies which has been a strong feature of his output since *Different Trains* (1988). For the composer himself, the latter work, with its sampling of both speech and other sounds in a live instrumental context, now marks a watershed as significant as that of *c.* 1979. But his rapprochement with the aims and intentions, as well as the forces, of Western classical music is arguably as significant for everything Reich wrote after 1976 as are the repeating structures which remain its 'structure and basis, the main dish of what I do'.[1]

Music for Eighteen Musicians offers, indeed, the best case of all for concluding the present book in that year, marking as it does the end of Reich's interest in minimalism as previously defined herein. Completed in March 1976, its increased debt to Western classical music in general, and its approach to harmony in particular, represent important new departures for its composer. The arrival of a kind of harmonic motion, in *Eighteen Musicians* and, to a lesser extent, in its predecessor, *Music for Mallet Instruments, Voices and Organ* (1973), does not, however, require the complete abandonment of the rhythmic techniques and concern for structural process that characterise Reich's music of the previous decade. *Eighteen Musicians* is crucially 'on-the-edge' aesthetically, and technically, speaking; that its composer was unable to remain in that interesting position now seems an important part of the work's achievement as well as of its historical significance. Harmonic motion – or at least the investigation of it in the surviving context of repetition – and all that came with it led both to works for symphony orchestra more 'symphonic' than we might have thought possible and to approaches to word-setting of considerable variety and imagination – even, in *The Cave* and *Three Tales*, to Reich's own brand of music-theatre.

Surprisingly, however, the achievements of *Music for Eighteen Musicians* proved troublesome for him to follow up. In fact, Reich completed nothing after this for more than two years, and only wrote himself out of what appears to have been a major crisis with a piece which, for him (though not for all his listeners), is at best problematic: *Music for a Large Ensemble* (1978). That, however, belongs to a later part of the story. In the meantime, the onset of the only hiatus of this magnitude in Reich's career creates a natural break in the narrative.

The earlier music may be further divided into two. Reich has himself advanced the notion that *Drumming* (1970–71) embodies the true transition between the phase-structured works of his early years and the more stylistically adventurous and technically varied compositions of his full maturity. The concerns which culminated in *Music for Eighteen Musicians* surfaced in *Six Pianos* and, more importantly, in *Music for Mallet Instruments, Voices and Organ* (both 1973) more clearly than they did in *Drumming*, making it possible to view all four works as a natural development away from minimalist concerns.

But while the works preceding *Drumming* constitute a viable 'early minimalist' period, the division of Reich's output between 1965 and 1976 that may first occur to his listeners is that between the handful of tape pieces composed in 1965–6 – such as *It's Gonna Rain*, with which he established the technique of phasing – and the instrumental works of 1966–7 onwards – such as *Piano Phase*, that first explored phasing in live performance and then extended its implications by incorporating a wider range both technically and stylistically. Reich's surviving interest in the possibilities of electronic technology, culminating in the phase-shifting pulse-gate pieces of 1969, forms a kind of bridge between these; this hybrid area could take in several other works of 1966–8 which combined live players with tape or other technology: notably *Violin Phase* (1967), a precursor of the later 'Counterpoint' series (which begins with *Vermont Counterpoint* of 1982). Another kind of bridge is formed by *Four Organs* (1970), a piece which succeeds in being the earliest work to transcend phasing by taking another idea generated by its composer's immersion in electronics and making live music from it. What follows here attempts an estimation of 'early' and 'mature' even within what is officially the 'early period'.

Early years

Stephen Michael Reich was born in New York City on 3 October 1936. His parents both came from wealthy, upper-middle-class Jewish families; his father was a New York lawyer, his mother born in Detroit. Reich's parents separated when the composer was only a year old and, remaining with his father, he was raised, in considerable part, by a governess, Virginia Mitchell. Until 1942, Reich frequently travelled from his father's home in New York to visit his mother, who had moved to Los Angeles, later inspiring the already mentioned *Different Trains* for string quartet and tape, in which documentary material in the form of interviews is used to contrast the young American Jewish boy's four-day rail trips across the USA with the sort of train journeys he might have been forced to take at the time if he had been a European Jew. In the 1950s, Reich's real mother became best known as the Broadway singer and lyricist June Carroll, under which name she wrote the lyrics of the song 'Love is a simple thing' (set to music by Arthur Siegel), still remembered today.

Reich was brought up Reform Jewish but received little encouragement to take the faith seriously. Leonard Reich hoped that his son would follow him into one of the established professions – law or medicine – or into industrial labour relations, for which Cornell, which the composer later attended, had a school. By opting for music, Reich junior was – from his father's point of view – reverting to his mother's sphere of influence, and father and son became estranged for many years. Only when Leonard Reich saw his son's picture in a Sunday edition of the *New York Times* in 1972 did the two re-establish contact.

Reich has frequently stressed his expansion away from the 'classical' music he heard at home towards rather more immediately exciting concerns for a teenager in the early 1950s:

> As a child I took what I would call middle-class piano lessons, and up to the age of 14 the only music that I was aware of was what I would call middle-class favourites: Beethoven's *Fifth*, Schubert's *Unfinished*, the overture to *The Mastersingers* and so on; I also heard Broadway shows and a lot of popular music. It wasn't until the age of 14 that I heard the music that would end up motivating me to become a composer and informing what I did: that was jazz, Bach and Stravinsky . . .[2]

Crucial encounters with both twentieth-century and older music new to him – including *The Rite of Spring* – thus came in about 1950–51. Jazz, in particular, was to engage him for some time and became very important to his musical development. At the age of fourteen, he took up drumming, studying with Roland Kohloff (later principal timpanist with the New York Philhestra Orchestra). Reich was able to help form a jazz ensemble, in which he was the drummer, thereby laying the foundations for his later obsessions with rhythm and percussion instruments; his approach to pitch was also informed by his jazz experiences. Meanwhile, he began to make pocket-money by spending weekend evenings playing trap drums in dance bands: for church and synagogue dances when still in high school; and later, at university, for fraternity parties and Elks Clubs.

Reich went to Cornell University, not far up the East Coast from New York, in September 1953, just before his seventeenth birthday – unusually young even for the times. Though music was by now crucial to him, he felt he was already too old to pursue music professionally. As a student he therefore majored in philosophy. Reich developed a particular interest in

Ludwig Wittgenstein, who had himself been at Cornell until 1950, the year before he died. While Wittgenstein's ideas were of great importance to Reich at this time, any relationship with the composer's subsequent thinking is somewhat tangential and tends to be greeted with scepticism by the composer himself.[3]

While at Cornell, Reich also took some music courses. Though already mistrustful of 'musical academe', he began a friendship with his chief music professor, the musicologist William Austin, showing him some songs that are probably Reich's first efforts at composition. Austin's musical sympathies included Stravinsky, American music, jazz and non-Western musics (all unusual for an Ivy League musicologist in the 1950s).[4] Reich became increasingly interested not only in Debussy, Stravinsky and jazz but also in medieval music, especially the work of the French composer Perotin, whose use of strict structures such as cantus firmus, isorhythm and, especially, canon and augmentation has remained an influence. (*Proverb*, composed in 1995, demonstrates his continuing debt to Perotin; its setting of Wittgenstein's sentence 'How small a thought it takes to fill a whole life!'[5] also provides evidence of the philosopher's continuing influence in the form of a motto eminently suited to Reich's output as a whole.)

Reich graduated from Cornell in the summer of 1957, and went back to New York. Encouraged by Austin, he had decided to reject the option of postgraduate philosophy studies at Harvard University. Having by now a clear notion that he wanted to compose, he studied privately, from 1957–8, with Hall Overton: an apt choice, since he had both a Western classical compositional pedigree (he had studied at the Juilliard School with Vincent Persichetti) and experience in jazz (he had been a colleague of Thelonius Monk). Little of Reich's efforts at composition of this period have survived, but he says that a song he wrote for Overton in 1957 contains an example of a chord structure which would become characteristic of his mature music: a chord of 'stacked' fifths.

Then, as a student at the Juilliard School between 1958 and 1961, Reich himself studied with Persichetti. His Juilliard colleagues included Philip Glass, though Reich says they had nothing in common at that time, either musically or socially, and the two were never really friends. Arthur Murphy – who had previously studied in Oberlin, Ohio with Richard Hoffmann, Schoenberg's protégé and one-time secretary, later studied mathematics and afterwards became a member of the composer's group – was another contemporary; so were Peter Schickele (later best known as P. D. Q. Bach) and Conrad Sousa. As a whole, the school seemed conservative to Reich – 'the last stronghold of the dying Americana, the end of the Aaron Copland tradition' – and he felt little better about the contemporary music scene in New York generally.

The composer describes the style of his Juilliard output, of which several scores survive, as 'somewhere between the Third, Fourth and Fifth Quartets [of Bartók and] the Webern of Opus 5 [the Five Pieces for String Quartet]'; he has even traced the chord of 'stacked' fifths he had used in his 1957 song to the opening of the second movement of Bartók's Second Piano Concerto. Jazz, too, had a significant influence on this highly chromatic, rather than atonal, approach, with its altered and often ambiguous dominant chords. 'I never wrote a piece where I didn't feel a harmonic centre', he says. During this time, he also attempted to set some of the poetry of William Carlos Williams. Reich responded to Williams' use of American vernacular speech, but found that traditional notions of 'setting' poetry rooted in American speech rhythms to music destroyed its essence. As with his efforts to set Robert Creeley and Charles Olsen, he 'got nowhere'. A wholly original approach to 'text setting' – discovered in the tape pieces of the mid-1960s, and inspired in part by Williams' response to the vernacular – became necessary before he could turn back to poetry in English, which he did by setting Williams himself in *The Desert Music*.

Reich felt an increasing need to experience a different cultural climate. On leaving Juilliard in the summer of 1961, not long before his twenty-fifth birthday, he decided to head West. California seemed to offer not merely a different musical scene but a different social milieu, away from his father's sphere of influence. For the real reason for his move was 'the classic reason that Americans go to California: I was running away from home'.

California

Reich arrived in San Francisco in September 1961 with the intention of going to graduate school. He had recently married in New York, and his wife, Joyce Barkett, had just had a baby. Moving to California ahead of his new family in order to make arrangements for them, he took a job as a stock clerk on Fisherman's Wharf. The child, however – born with intestinal complications – died; when his wife arrived in California she brought his corpse. Stunned, and for the moment totally unclear about his own direction, the would-be composer took various jobs for a while. The couple subsequently had another child, Michael Reich; the marriage ended in divorce in 1963.

Reich had originally intended to go to Mills College in nearby Oakland to study with Leon Kirchner, but it turned out that this purveyor of 'the great Bartók tradition', as Reich thought of him, had just left. He briefly considered going to the University of California at Berkeley to work with Seymour Shifrin, as Young and Riley had done earlier. But on learning that Luciano Berio was to take Kirchner's place, he quickly enrolled at Mills after all, at the beginning of 1962; the college additionally offered the faster programme. It also offered Darius Milhaud, who was teaching alternating semesters with Berio, though by then this venerable former member of the 1920s avant-garde was old and ill. While one or two interesting students turned out to be among his contemporaries – notably Phil Lesh, later bass guitarist of The Grateful Dead – to his dismay Reich found the situation at Mills to be even more stultifying, and certainly more limiting, than that of New York.

Reich's most frequently told anecdote about Mills concerns his attempt to simplify – or subvert – serialism by composing twelve-note music which entirely avoided inversions, retrogrades and transpositions:

> I would just repeat the row over and over. By doing this you can create a kind of static harmony not entirely dissimilar to the Webern orchestral Variations, which are very static and intervallically constant and which suggest this kind of world.[6]

This approach has clear parallels with Young's compositions of 1957–8, though Reich's experience of these had been confined to joining in the general derision when some account of *Trio for Strings*, perhaps even a tape, circulated around Juilliard. The first piece in which he adopted the twelve-note procedure was *Music for String Orchestra*, dated 5/61 on the score and actually the last composition Reich wrote while in New York. His approach to a technique more commonly construed as an ideal way to avoid pitch repetition and create a constant state of flux met with a predictable response from Berio, to whom he showed the score after his enrolment at Mills. 'He liked it', says Reich, 'but he began to realise that those tones weren't going to do anything but repeat'. 'If you want to write tonal music', he apparently said, 'then write tonal music'.

The manuscript reveals a twelve-note set subjected to constant repetition. The set on which *Music for String Orchestra* is based (see Ex. 3.1) concerns itself chiefly with semitones and minor thirds, making it possible to segment it into small groups of notes along the lines Webern used, though Reich is less rigorous in his construction. The composer argues that the close-position voicing of some of the clusters formed from these segments creates 'a static and somewhat tonal situation: ambiguous, odd, but nevertheless not what was intended by the use of twelve-tone technique', and relates it to the kinds of harmonic vocabulary he still uses today; the notion of 'stacking' the same interval, or two intervals, makes a somewhat

Example 3.1 *Music for String Orchestra*, twelve-note set

tenuous connection with his subsequent practice. The set of *Music for String Orchestra* is far less triadic, or in any other sense 'tonal', than that of, say, Berg's Violin Concerto; and the music to which it gives rise is actually as secundally dissonant as most post-Webernian serial compositions, making Berio's observation a little hard to understand. Yet the interest displayed here in static harmony and repetition is the earliest indication in his pre-minimalist output of the direction Reich's mature music would take.

According to his own account, all Reich's pieces composed while he was a student at Mills College follow *Music for String Orchestra*'s approach to static harmony via row repetition. Unfortunately, on his return to New York, many of his scores (in a 'big black book') and tapes were stolen when thieves broke into his car. His description of the three semesters at Mills as 'a very unproductive time', does not, however, suggest that his investigations of twelve-note static harmony and repetition proved at all successful.

The only Mills work which survives is the last composition he wrote there, which reflects, much more directly than any of the others appear to have done, his continuing interest in jazz. Reich had already spent much of his time in New York listening, in particular, to John Coltrane; at the Jazz Workshop in San Francisco, he had even better opportunities to hear Coltrane live. As with Young and Riley during the same period, he was drawn to the startlingly innovative modal jazz that Coltrane was then evolving: a new music bringing together many of the concerns – modality, a regular pulse, influences from earlier jazz and from non-Western sources – closest to Reich's own heart. 'John Coltrane's music between 1961 and 1964 made a tremendous impression on me', the composer has said.

Four Pieces, composed in 1963 as Reich's graduation exercise, reflect a move in the direction of a clearer modality. As their instrumentation – trumpet, alto saxophone, piano, bass and drums – suggests, these are heavily indebted to the resources and idioms of jazz, which Reich attempts to combine with more 'cultivated' materials and procedures somewhat in the then currently still fashionable manner of the 'Third-Stream' jazz-fusion approach of Gunther Schuller and others. Twelve-note procedures still govern the details of their note-to-note structure, subjected to the same technique of 'repeating and repeating the row over and over again'. Here, though, the harmonic organisation owes as much to the application of an altered-dominant chordal vocabulary to a jazz context (from which this

Example 3.2 *Four Pieces*, no. 2, final two bars

vocabulary itself partly derives) as to the set itself. 'How', Reich asks, 'could I group the row into some way to make progressions that seemed to work?' One answer was to use oblique motion: keeping one or more parts at the same pitch while moving the others. (Example 3.2, concluding the second piece, is the last in a sequence in which the chord assembled in the piano is also reflected in the moving parts around it, the already characteristically 'stacked' harmony underpinned by the bass line.) Its composer describes the results as 'twelve-tone jazz licks trying to become tonal . . . somewhere between Steve Reich, Bill Evans and [Schoenberg's] Opus Eleven'. Both the altered-dominant and the oblique-motion aspects of these pieces foreshadow its composer's subsequent approach to pitch organisation. Their incorporation of improvised passages – the second piece includes improvisation on the same twelve-note set used in the written-out sections – prefigures the approach of Reich's next composition, *Pitch Charts*.

Four Pieces' only performance was given by a group of young players conversant with both jazz and fully notated musics: Einer Anderson on trumpet, Paul Breslin on bass, John Chowning (later to become famous in the field of electro-acoustic music) on drums and Jon Gibson (later to work with all four leading minimalists) who played alto saxophone. The pianist was the composer himself, who was by now coming to the conclusion that 'a healthy musical situation would only result when the functions of composer and performer were united',[7] as they so frequently are in jazz. From now on, he decided, 'despite my limitations as a performer I had to play in all my compositions'. *Four Pieces* thus in a sense mark, their composer has said, 'the birth of my ensemble'. The desire to write only what he could play must also have helped Reich towards a much simpler, reductive style.

Theatre and film; improvisation and composition; music for tape

After graduating, Reich remained in the Bay Area for the next two years. Having decided against university teaching as a career path in composition, he worked in the US Post Office for some while, did some taxi driving and taught at the Community Music School on San Francisco's Capp Street. Meanwhile, he involved himself with four main areas of musical activity: composing music for the San Francisco Mime Troupe, playing with an improvisation group and – working at his home-based studio – composing both independent tape pieces and some music for underground films and theatre.

The music Reich composed in California in the two years between leaving Mills College in the summer of 1963 and returning to New York in September 1965 may be divided into three categories: concert compositions involving live performers; music for theatre and film; and works for tape. While nothing he wrote before *It's Gonna Rain* may be much more than a historical curiosity, all the pieces involved – even *Four Pieces* and *Pitch Charts* (discussed below) – illustrate Reich's quest for a more overtly experimental approach to composition which did not deny the validity of tonality.

Before he graduated from Mills, Reich and some of his colleagues formed an improvisation group. Gibson, George Rey (a violinist), a cellist called Gwendoline Watson and others, including Reich on piano, 'met at least once a week for about six months' to play 'free, and sometimes controlled, improvisation'. Soon dissatisfied with the results, Reich concluded that the problem lay in the reliance on purely 'spur of the moment reactions', and decided to compose some material to help provide some 'musical growth'.

The result was *Pitch Charts*, the score of which is dated 11/63. Its three movements are written in open score, but including transpositions for clarinet or trumpet, alto and tenor saxophones, and double bass. The same pitches are allocated in groups, or occasionally singly, to these instruments simultaneously, though not all instruments have all pitches; rhythm remains free. While the tendency to unfold the complete chromatic gamut remains, pitches are now repeated in small units, rather than in twelve-note cycles. (Ex. 3.3 shows the opening of the first 'chart'.) The actual

Example 3.3 *Pitch Charts*, first movement, opening

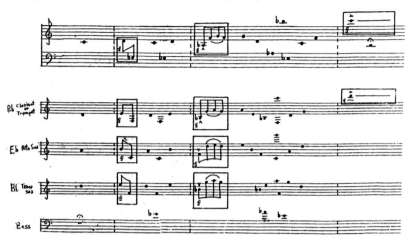

vocabulary, too, is more modal, emphasising particular centres by repetition and piling up intervals to produce chords of the type already used in *Four Pieces*. *Pitch Charts* was performed by students and friends at the Capp Street Community Music School. There also seem to be some other pieces from around this time which explore unconventional notations of various kinds, including two graphically notated compositions entitled *Proportional Pieces #1* and *#2*.

While still at Mills, Reich had admired the work of the San Francisco Mime Troupe, which was then mounting less overtly politicised productions than those for which the company subsequently became famous. About the time he graduated from Mills, Reich met R. G. Davis, the Mime Troupe's head, and at his suggestion wrote music for its production of Alfred Jarry's *Ubu Roi*, staged in the deconsecrated church in the Mission District used by the company on 10 December 1963 (the sixty-seventh anniversary of the play's Paris première). Billed as a '5 Act surrealist farce', its approach made it something of a *cause célèbre*. Reich describes the production as 'very broad slapstick'; the flyer advertised the performance as being 'In Cooperation with the College of Pataphysique . . . West' and promised 'Reception and Disembrainning [*sic*] Following Performance'. The artist William T. Wiley, who designed the sets and costumes, and the composer became friends. Reich's music, presently unlocatable, was apparently scored for clarinet and kazoo, playing a tune in unison, with a strummed violin accompaniment consisting of a single chord; the kazoo was amplified by means of a large Pacific Gas and Electric plastic traffic cone used as a megaphone. The musicians played this tune several times, then turned about face and left. It was, as the composer says, 'very much a thumbing-your-nose kind of thing': at his former teacher, Berio, among others.

Reich's only concert work involving live performance during this period besides *Pitch Charts* is *Music for Two or More Pianos*. Dated 2/64, the score consists simply of a sequence of nine five-, six- and seven-note chords (see Ex. 3.4). Using the kind of vocabulary familiar from *Four Pieces* and *Pitch Charts*, these chords are, as the score says, to 'be repeated as many times as performers feel appropriate'. A tape part may be made of a reading of this repeated sequence, again on piano, which may stand in for one, or more than one, of the live performers, in which case the piece is called *Music for Two Pianos and Tape*. While '[c]hords may be arpeggiated or broken in any way', performers do not have the same freedom as they do in Morton Feldman's somewhat similar *Piece for Four Pianos* (1958); Reich requires his players to 'remain with any chord for as long as desired, but as soon as any performer moves from one chord to the next, all performers should move on similarly, as soon as possible'. The result is a kind of close canonic phasing of the chord sequence. Though the composer had not heard Feldman's piece at the time, he acknowledges the influence of Stockhausen's *Refrain* (1959), a work which similarly exploits repetition of the same material by several performers, and which in turn was probably influenced by Feldman. *Music for Two or More Pianos* thus clearly antici-pates the phasing technique discovered almost a year later in *It's Gonna Rain*.

While many of the composers who were members of the avant-garde community working at the San Francisco Tape Music Center on Divisidero Street favoured synthesized sounds, Reich was more interested in working with the natural sounds of *musique concrète* in undisguised form, pre-serving the 'added emotional layer' which comes with the recognition of familiar sounds. His first finished electronic composition was also his first tape collage: a piece, dating from early in 1964, to accompany a short film called *Plastic Haircut* by the film-maker Robert Nelson, which involved some of the Mime Troupe team. Constructions of paper and wood made by Wiley and the sculptor Robert Hudson were manipulated by Davis, the Mime Troupe's head, to make a kind of 'black-and-white animation'; these were then filmed by Nelson, who sometimes included Davis himself in the shots. Reich's tape, not synchronised with the film, used crowd noises from an LP issued by Columbia Records called *The Greatest Moments in Sports*. The result was 'rather like a surrealist rondo with all kinds of elements recurring', in which loops of individual sounds were first played alone and 'then overlaid just to make noise'. Reich considers that, in his music for *Plastic Haircut*, 'the seeds were there'; at the time, he was especially enthu-

Example 3.4 *Music for Two or More Pianos*, complete score

siastic about the ambiguous residual meanings preserved by this approach.

Like Glass after him, Reich drove a taxi cab for a living, though only in San Francisco, not following his return to New York. *Livelihood* (also 1964) is a three-minute *collage* assembled from sounds collected on these duties: conversations, 'slamming doors, meters being thrown, grunts and groans, people hitting their head . . . the noises that one hears inside of a taxi' were used, often in only tiny fragments. Reich destroyed the mastertape of this piece, along with some other material, in the mid-1980s. The present author has nevertheless heard *Livelihood*, which turns out to be a witty evocation of a taxi-driver's daily life, carefully constructed to evoke all the basic stages of a taxi ride: from stating the destination to casual conversation in the cab, ending with paying the fare and saying 'Thank you' and 'Goodnight'.

In the spring of 1964, Reich and his associates played at the San Francisco Mime Troupe Theater. Presented on no fewer than four nights – 21, 23, 29 and 30 May – 'Koncert I' began with three pieces by Reich: *Proportional Piece #1* and two improvisations on the *Pitch Charts* material ('tape and live version'), performed by a sextet including Gibson ('reeds'), Lesh (trumpet) and Reich (piano). A quintet by Lesh – and, surprisingly, Bach's Third Cello Suite, played by Watson, who also participated in all the ensemble items – closed the first half. In the second, Tom Constanten (subsequently keyboard player with The Grateful Dead) played his own *Piano Piece #3*, and the programme concluded with free improvisations performed by all six musicians, who also included the violinist Rey and the bass player Breslin once more.

It was after one of these nights that Reich first encountered Terry Riley. The story of their meeting has already been told in the previous chapter, including the participation of Reich and other members of his improvisation group in the première of *In C* on 4 November 1964. Riley's influence on his new colleague was crucial. Like so many others, Reich considers *In C* to be a seminal work, and acknowledges it as a major influence on his own development. While Reich had already used repetition to construct everything from twelve-note compositions to *collage*, the modularity of *In C* pointed the way towards a more organised and consistent kind of pattern-making with highly reductive means. Riley's method quickly proved to have greater potential than Young's static approach. It was easier to vary and develop, and it soon became apparent that it could lead to musical results which were more immediately accessible, especially when modular processes were harnessed to modal materials.

It's Gonna Rain

Though himself having had some hand in establishing *In C*'s insistent pulse, Reich did not at first employ one in his own compositions, preferring to imply this through rhythmic continuity. The modality of Riley's composition was a clearer confirmation of Reich's earlier instincts, despite his initial decision to make tape pieces manipulating speech material; speech, after all, has a melodic profile of its own, which may be exploited in the act of composition. Like *In C*, *It's Gonna Rain* begins with a pattern based on a rising major third, which becomes important to the way the work unfolds. Reich's close involvement in the première of *In C* during his

preliminary work on *It's Gonna Rain* suggests more than mere coin-
cidence, though Reich himself considers it of little significance. Later,
modality of a more thorough-going kind became central to his output.

Reich's discovery of phasing in *It's Gonna Rain* was in fact influenced at
least as much by the tape compositions Riley had been composing over the
previous two or three years as by the more evidently seminal *In C*. Reich
says he heard *She Moves She* from *The Gift*, *Shoeshine* and *I* late in 1964 or
early in 1965. His new friend's manipulation of shifting patterns constructed from spoken material with the aid of the time-lag accumulator
and his use of tape loops to effect the transformation of speech through
repetition, overlay and slow changes of speed are clearly influences on
Reich, suggesting effects to him that *In C* itself did not. Riley remembers a
first attempt at what became *It's Gonna Rain* as 'more of a sound-text
piece'[8] like *Livelihood* – which he had enormously enjoyed – and suggests
that his tape compositions were as important to Reich's move away from
collage as was *In C*.

Reich acknowledges a debt to his colleague's innovations, though he
stresses *In C* rather than the tape compositions. At least as late as 14
January 1968 – in the notes for an Arts Now 'afternoon of live and electronic music by Steve Reich' at the Philips Exeter Academy, a preparatory
school in Massachusetts – his first mature tape composition was being
listed as 'It's Gonna Rain, or meet Brother Walter in Union Square after listening to Terry Riley'. 'It was Riley's work that put it all together' for him,
he says, though he sees no relevance in any of his music since *In C*. But
while Riley always allowed his patterns to accumulate into a psychedelic
wash of sound, Reich generally stressed the audibility of his 'gradually
shifting phase relations'. Riley worked by intuition; Reich attempted to
bring rigour to bear in his attempt to 'find some *new* way of working with
repetition as a musical technique'. With *It's Gonna Rain* and *Come Out*,
Reich suggests, 'you're watching the minute hand on the watch. That's not
the effect of Riley's pieces at all: there, you're taking a bath'. Reich's notes
for the concert mentioned above proudly state that '[t]he use of the phase
shift as a basic structure applied to a single figure against itself is, as far as I
know, unique to the music on this program'.

Another, earlier, interest also helped Reich to find his own approach to
the use of everyday sounds and to a method by which 'the authenticity of
American speech' could be captured and turned to fresh account: the
poetry of William Carlos Williams. *It's Gonna Rain* and *Come Out* were
composed, Reich says, 'against the background of having failed to set text
that I would have liked to have set'. Though previously unable to find a
solution to the problem of setting Williams' poetry itself, Reich now

learned an important lesson from this master of modern American poetry for whom he has a special admiration. He noted that Williams, refusing the blandishments of any International Style of modernism, derived his inspiration from his local roots. As a practising doctor in New Jersey, Williams had observed the speech and other sounds around him and made these the basis of his style. As a composer working in an urban environment with the new tape technology, Reich felt that the poet was 'looking over your shoulder and saying, "Go record the street! Go listen to your countrymen and get your music from the way they speak"'. Williams' example helped Reich to find a solution to the problems of writing vocal music and setting texts by turning to the tape recorder.

It's Gonna Rain is the composer's first important composition to use minimalist techniques. In the course of constructing a further *collage*-style piece, Reich failed to achieve the perfect synchronisation of tape loops which he was actually seeking. In his *Writings*, the composer states that '[i]n the process of trying to line up two identical tape loops in some particular relationship, I discovered that the most interesting music of all was made by simply lining the loops up in unison, and letting them slowly shift out of phase with each other'.[9] The two Wollensack machines, plus one borrowed Ampex, on which Reich composed *It's Gonna Rain* were the cheapest he could find, exacerbating the extent of the drift which revealed this effect to him. But as Riley had already discovered, he found that 'it was inevitable with the technology of that day that there would have been drift': a phenomenon which occurred even on the better Sony 770 and Uher portable machines he subsequently acquired, the latter pair bought on hire-purchase with Lesh. Reich now proceeded to alter the speed of one loop against the other by holding the supply reel of the tape providing the second channel with his thumb. The imperceptible slowing down of this second channel against the first produced the phasing he desired. After this, it was simply – though laboriously – a question of making a new loop of each new relationship, feeding it back into the first channel and then continually repeating the process.

The origins and purpose of *It's Gonna Rain* are at least as interesting as its significance in the evolution of musical minimalist techniques. The tale is frequently told of how, following the advice of a friend, Reich went down to San Francisco's Union Square one day in November 1964 to record a sermon by Brother Walter, a young black preacher whose occasional, very fiery, Sunday appearances there had become quite famous. The friend had expressed some intention of making a film, but this never materialised. Reich, meanwhile, had started to see the musical potential of Brother

Walter's heightened form of Black American English, and transcribed the sermon on three large manuscript pages in an attempt to analyse its material. The independent piece he eventually produced lasts 17'31" and divides clearly into two parts, or movements, with a sizeable pause between them. Both open with untreated recordings from the sermon, from which extracts are then taken to provide the basic material for each part. (The complete text as used in *It's Gonna Rain* is reproduced as Ex. 3.5.) Part One uses only the words 'It's gonna rain'. Part Two draws on a longer passage, continuing from where the extract used in the first part left off: as Reich puts it, a 'long description of people trying to get into the Ark and finding that God had sealed the door and that they couldn't get into the Ark, and they were going to die'.

In early 1965, Brother Walter's sermon suggested something more immediate than the fire-and-brimstone message typical of its type. The Cuban missile crisis of October 1962 had created the feeling that 'nuclear disaster was a finger on the button away', and even more than two years later, this gave the story of Noah's Flood a fresh, and urgent, dimension, enhanced by the repetition characteristic of this Evangelical style of preaching. The words of *It's Gonna Rain* thus offer a metaphor for impending nuclear holocaust. While the short Part One treats its material fairly lightly, the 'controlled chaos' of Part Two is a quite different matter. When he presented *It's Gonna Rain* at the Tape Music Center in January 1965, Reich felt that Part Two was too bleak and disturbing to include at all. Part Two also reflects Reich's personal circumstances at the time, which were far from happy: 'I was not', he says, 'in a good psychic way in San Francisco'. His disinclination to 'inflict [his] neuroses on the listening public' was a further reason to stop the tape at the end of Part One. After he returned to New York, he decided the piece should henceforth be played complete.

Part Two uses complex, far less pitch-specific material than that found in Part One. In structural terms, though, this section is fairly straightforward. Firstly, the new loop is gradually phased against itself; then this two-voiced relationship is presented on channel 1, against which a duplicate is phased on channel 2. The resulting four-voiced texture is eventually further doubled, by the same process, to eight voices. The deconstruction of the original into mere noise – a development of the *Plastic Haircut*'s 'surrealist rondo' – reflects in structure and emotional effect the words selected from the sermon.

It's Gonna Rain also has a pitch dimension deriving from the tendency of the sort of declamation used here to enhance the residual pitch patterns of 'normal' speech with the more focused, and retained, melodic

Example 3.5 *It's Gonna Rain*, spoken material

STEVE REICH

It's Gonna Rain

Spoken material used in *It's Gonna Rain* (spelling according to Reich's transcription, punctuation added for ease of reference; words used for musical development presented in bold).

Part One

> He be'gan to warn the people. He said: after a while, **it's**
> **gonna rain** after a while. For forty days an fo forty nites.
> And the people didn't believe him. And they began to laugh at
> him. And they begin to mock him, and they begin to say: It
> ain't gonna RAIN!

Part Two

> They didn't believe that it was gonna rain. But - glory to God,
> haleluya, bless God's wonderful name dis evenin, Ah say this
> evenin, after a while. They didn't believe that it was gonna
> rain. **But, shorenuf,** it begin ta rain - haleluya.

> They begin to knock upon the door. But it was too late.
> Whooo! The Bible tell me they knock upon a door, until the
> skin came off their hand. Whooo! My laud, my laud.
> Ah said until a skin came off der hand. They cried - Ah can
> just hear **der cry**, how! Ah could hear em say: ohh, Noah,
> would you just open the door. **But Noah couldn't open a**
> **door. It had been sealed by the hand of God!**

Example 3.6 *It's Gonna Rain*, Part One, Basic Unit

It's gon-na rain

utterances of real song. Pitch most clearly becomes an issue in Part One, which uses only the single fragment of three pitches that gives *It's Gonna Rain* its title (reproduced in Ex. 3.6), suggesting the key of D major. (From here on, such a pattern will be called the Basic Unit.) In the main section of Part One, a simple phasing process takes these words from unison through a complete cycle and back to unison.

Before this, however, a rather different technique is employed. After the initial extract, the fragment 'It's gonna rain' is subjected to what Reich calls 'a kind of monophonic sampling'. The loop is stereophonically separated 'exactly 180 degrees out of phase, so that the word "it's" falls on top of "rain", more or less', he says. 'Sampling each channel in synchronisation with the voice rhythm will give you "It's gonna, it's gonna . . ." over and over again. Speed up the sampling rate, however, and the result will move from "it's gonna", inching into the "r" of "rain", then into "ain", "nnn", and finally back into "It's gonna"'. Reich achieved this by performing the process with a preamplifier switch, judging the results purely intuitively and submitting the final mix to tape. It should, in addition, be noted that the original tape of the words 'It's gonna rain' also included the sound of a pigeon flapping its wings; the composer was delighted with this extra dimension which, through constant repetition, makes a significant contribution to the overall effect.

The piece with which Reich made the technical discovery which opened the door to the whole of his mature work does not confine itself to a simple, purely mechanical operation of that technique. The monophonic sampling described above is 'phasing' of a kind, and brief at that, while the majority of Part One, like Part Two, is a 'literal embodiment' of the process of phasing itself. But the variety of procedures and the sophistication of the resulting structures make it clear from the outset that Reich is interested in note-to-note composing and in the effect of his final product, not merely in experimentation with a mechanistic process regardless of artistic result. In addition, the difficulties of identifying the musical process at work in the early stages of *It's Gonna Rain* – to which the extraneous sound of the pigeon's wings flapping adds an extra layer of confusion – make an important statement at the outset of a career sometimes interpreted as built merely on the mechanistic application of simplistic procedures to mindless material. While its composer considers that this is 'the purest process piece that I ever did', *It's Gonna Rain* already demonstrates in embryo the compositional control Reich would exert with greater force in subsequent works.

Before his departure from San Francisco, Reich completed only one other piece: *Oh dem Watermelons!*, another score for the San Francisco Mime Troupe, written for a kind of ironic, 'post-modernist' minstrel show, premièred in May 1965, which incorporated another short film by Nelson. The film uses images of watermelons as an analogy for the oppression of Black Americans. Reich's contribution combined two extracts from songs by Stephen Foster – 'Massa's in the cold, cold ground' and 'Oh dem Watermelons': both in D major, the chosen extracts stuck on an endlessly revolving II–V^7 progression on the piano that produces the effect of a dominant pedal. Around this, he constructed a kind of five-part canon for voices on the single word 'watermelon'. *Oh dem Watermelons!* extends Reich's work with tape into the territory of the more straightforward canon – of which phasing is really but a special case, as the composer has noted from the beginning.[10] Its synthesis of tonic and dominant harmonies both reflects the modal approach of Riley's *In C* and foreshadows the unresolved, elongated half cadences of the later *Four Organs* and Part Four of *Drumming*. Reich later performed 'hand-over-hand piano variations' on its material with Arthur Murphy, and sometimes Gibson, in several of his early New York concerts – and even much later on social occasions, usually under the title *Improvisations on a Watermelon*, offering 'a simple shift of accent in a repeating figure, and a gradual expansion of a two-note figure into a five-note one'.

Return to New York

In September 1965, Reich returned to New York, no longer easy with the cultural situation in California. The transformation of the Beat era into the Hippie period was showing itself in many ways, including the emergence of a heavier drug scene. While these manifestations were hardly confined to San Francisco, the city was already on the way to becoming an emblematic centre for the counter-culture of the late 1960s. 'In the group of people I seemed to form a contact with, I did not feel on solid psychic footing', Reich says; he does not, though, find the question of the influence of drugs on his music to be 'a profitable line of discussion'. He also felt that New York offered much better opportunities for the young composer. Within a few weeks, Reich had taken a loft at Duane Street, in the downtown area now known as TriBeCa, in or near which he has lived ever since. He found employment wherever he could: as a sound-man for films, as a social worker for New York University. In 1967, after he had re-established contact with Glass, Reich had a brief involvement with Chelsea Light Moving, a removals company formed by his colleague. In slowly establishing himself among the downtown arts community, Reich found he had more in common with those working in sculpture or painting, theatre or film, than with most musicians. Though he has never held a conventional, still less a full-time, teaching position, between 1969 and 1971 he was a member of the faculty of New York's radical New School for Social Research, where he taught electronic music.

Connections with Minimalist artists and Pendulum Music

When questioned in 1986 about links between his thinking and the aesthetic behind Minimalist painting and sculpture, Reich was derisive about the use of the term 'minimalist'. Interviewed in 1972 by Emily Wasserman for *Artforum*, however, he had been prepared to acknowledge that '[t]here is some relationship between my music and any Minimal art'.[11] The composer's contacts with artists have, in fact, been extensive and by no means confined to sculptors or painters conventionally labelled 'Minimalist' or 'conceptual'. He is insistent that any closeness to Minimalism they may have was of no concern to him: they have simply been artists he has admired.

Among the New York based artists with whom Reich now became acquainted was Robert Rauschenberg, whose involvement with Experiments in Art and Technology (otherwise known as EAT), a project designed to bring artists into contact with scientists and engineers, led to Reich's work with new technologies at Bell Laboratories, discussed below. Rauschenberg was also responsible for mounting a series of performances at New York's School of Visual Arts late in 1967, which included the première of *Violin Phase* (a year before Paul Zukofsky's performance listed in *Writings*) and *My Name Is* (see below).

Asked about the artists with whom he had most contact in the late 1960s and early 1970s, Reich mentions Sol Le Witt, Richard Serra and Michael Snow, the last two of whom lived very near him in the late 1960s. He acknowledges that 'there certainly was an attitude' these artists shared – 'Le Witt's work was very geometric, and *is* very geometric'; Serra's early work in lead had a consistency and objectivity – and that 'a metaphoric connection' is possible between the work of such painters or sculptors and his own. But Reich does not think Le Witt and Serra had any direct influence on him: 'we were just swimming in the same soup'. Reich and Le Witt, says the composer, 'spent a lot of time together' between 1967 and

1970. Le Witt was older and already a fairly well-established artist; in late 1970 or early 1971, he bought the original score of *Four Organs*, and some sections of *Drumming* in manuscript, so that the impecunious composer could buy glockenspiels for *Drumming*. The close contact between composer and artist during the year or so before Reich wrote the 'Music as a Gradual Process' essay in the summer of 1968 clearly has some bearing on the similarities between this and Le Witt's 'Paragraphs on Conceptual Art', as mentioned in the Introduction. Though best known from its publication in the composer's *Writings about Music* collection in 1974 (from which source all the quotations from it in the present book are taken), 'Music as a Gradual Process' first appeared in print just a year after it was written. It was included in the catalogue to 'Anti-Illusion: Procedures/ Materials', an exhibition of the work of Nauman, Serra, Snow and others at the Whitney Museum of American Art in the spring of 1969.[12] While this exhibition was in progress, both Reich and Glass gave concerts at the Whitney, of which further details follow below.

Serra also acquired Reich's original score for Part One of *Piano Phase*, though in this case he exchanged it for a sculpture entitled *Candle Rack*, which the composer later sold. More importantly, it was partly through him, not Le Witt, that 'Music as a Gradual Process' came to be written. Serra, relates the composer, 'was the kind of guy who would call up and say, not "Hello" but "Now look: four by six on the wall, big plate, and then, rolled up, another, maybe six by eight, leaning up against it. You got it?" I'd say, "Yeah." He'd say, "What do you think?" I'd say, "It sounds great."' For Serra, 'the idea of matter-of-factness taken to its absolute extreme' was crucial, regardless of the metaphors that can be read into the work. Reich valued that attitude very much at the time.

But for a closer analogy with music, one must go to other time-based art forms. In this sense, the films of Michael Snow offer a much more fruitful link. The meeting between composer and film-maker arose from Reich's encounter with Snow's film *Wavelength* in 1967. Snow, whom Reich then saw regularly until the artist's move to Toronto in the mid-1970s, worked variously as a sculptor and film-maker at this period. He is also a good pianist; Reich believes that his achievements in film owe a lot to a 'musical intelligence at work organising the time'. In an article he wrote on *Wavelength* in 1968 – his only effort at art criticism – the composer comments on how Snow is '[c]ompletely taken up with the filmic variations possible on one image',[13] and how he avoids spelling out the implications of the narrative, so that 'you complete it in your head'. Snow's films, according to Reich, 'are about drastic time-lengths in the sense in which *Four Organs* is about drastic time-lengths. In one sense, *Wavelength* is a zoom in a room for an hour, but it's also a lot more than that. And what I learned from Snow, that I think probably later surfaced in *Music for Eighteen Musicians*, [is] ... the playing back between the regular and the irregular, if you like; the purely process orientated and the various human imperfections that interrupt such a process'. While Serra stressed the mechanics of his work and the formal problems to be solved, Snow 'saw all the space in between'.

Reich also developed some connection with the Park Place Gallery, an artists' co-operative run by Paula Cooper who later set up her own, more prestigious, outlet at 542 West Broadway. Reich considers that the artists associated with the gallery, most of whom formed one of the chief clusters of hard-core Minimalists, 'were actually terrible . . . . There was only one who was important – Mark De Suvero – and he wasn't a Minimal artist'. But Park Place also showed non-members, including Le Witt, Robert Morris and Robert Smithson. The première performances of *Piano Phase*, discussed below, took place at this gallery in March 1967.

In the spring of the same year, the art patroness Audrey Sable mounted an exhibition in Philadelphia consisting of small editions of prints and reproducible sculptures, which were then offered for sale at a reasonable price. For this, Reich made a piece using cheap cartridge cassette machines. This was based on a tape of the voices of various artist contributors to the show saying 'Buy art!' or 'Buy art, buy art!'; Andy Warhol was among those whom he persuaded to record for him. He then made three identical copies of a cartridge containing an ordered version of these snippets, and let them run simultaneously. The cassette machines soon ran wildly out of synchronisation, and the result – entitled, rather inevitably, *Buy Art, Buy Art* – was an uncontrolled phasing process, producing 'a tacky overlay on the whole show'.

Also in 1967, Reich composed a somewhat similar piece entitled *My Name Is* which, unlike *Buy Art, Buy Art*, he notated as a score. In this, members of the audience are invited to speak their own first names into a microphone, preceded by the words 'My name is'; the resulting recordings are made into loops and phased against each other in a more rigorous fashion than in *Buy Art, Buy Art*. At the première, in November 1967 at the School of Visual Arts in New York, one of the obliging members of the public was Marcel Duchamp. A version of the piece, using the names of the performers in Steve Reich and Musicians instead of members of the audience, was premièred under the title *My Name Is: Ensemble Portrait* at the Whitney Museum on 6 January 1981; this demonstrates the composer's continuing search for ways of using recorded speech material in live performance situations, which led eventually to *Different Trains* and *The Cave*.

Despite his disclaimers, Reich's early mature compositions were conceived in a context in which both Minimalist art and performance art of various kinds set many aspects of the agenda for both their performance and reception. His ideas about gradual processes, their manipulation and perception received a crucial stimulus from his contacts with artists. The personal, as well as aesthetic, connections he made with the art world in the 1960s allowed Reich access to art galleries as performance spaces long before he became accepted in Western classical music circles, and audiences for his work who were often well-informed about its intentions.

Reich's enthusiasm for direct participation in the 'counter-culture' of performance art remained strong into the late 1960s. A particularly good example of this is *Pendulum Music*. According to the score (dated August 1968 but revised in May 1973), 'Three, four, or more microphones are suspended from the ceiling or from microphone boom stands by their cables so that they all hang the same distance from the floor and are all free to swing with a pendular motion'. Loudspeakers are then placed face upwards under the microphones, each connected to the microphone immediately above it. With the volume turned up, each loudspeaker will produce feedback when the microphone is directly above it. When the microphones are pulled back and released, their pendulum motion over the loudspeakers produces 'a series of feedback pulses . . . which will either be all in unison or not depending on the gradually changing phase relations of the different mike pendulums'. 'Performers', the score instructs, 'then sit down to watch and listen to this process along with the rest of the audience'. As the momentum of the microphones' swinging decreases, so the phase relation of the feedback pulses constantly changes. The piece finishes 'sometime shortly after all mikes have come to rest and are feeding back a continuous tone by performers pulling out the power cords of the amplifiers'.

Why would Reich suddenly produce such an uncharacteristically reductive, unmanipulated specimen of phasing after several much more sophisticated applications of this technique? The answer lies in the piece's context. The composer spent much of the summer of 1968 in New Mexico; he has always fled New York during the hot weather. Bill Wiley – the artist whom Reich had encountered through working on *Ubu Roi* and who had remained in the Bay Area – was teaching a summer school not very far away, at the University of Colorado at Boulder. He suggested that the two of them devise a multimedia piece, which was eventually entitled *Over Evident Falls*: a 'very hastily put-together happening in the spirit of the times'. Bruce Nauman, a former pupil of Wiley likewise based on the West Coast, had meanwhile also stopped off in Boulder. 'And while the two of them were in the room and I was sort of feeling Western', says Reich, ' . . . I had [a] microphone and was . . . dangling it like a lasso'. His tape recorder happened to be on, and the passing of the microphone in front of its loud-speaker produced feedback. This accidental discovery led to the creation of *Pendulum Music*, which was immediately incorporated into *Over Evident Falls*.

The whole piece was performed in black light, then very fashionable. A big plastic sack of Ivory Snow soapflakes emptied over the performance space looked like luminescent snow under this light. The soapflakes fell on to a swing, which had two microphones attached to either side of it. The motion of the swing over the tape recorder speakers underneath it pro-duced a 'quasi-unison version' of *Pendulum Music*. The title of the whole event, *Over Evident Falls*, arose from Wiley's somewhat surrealist and punning humour: the soapflakes evidently resembled a waterfall to him. For ease and speed, Reich had insisted on using some pre-existent music. Part of *Piano Phase* – probably just the opening section, Reich recalls – was performed by the composer himself against a tape. *My Name Is* also proved perfect for the situation; during this, Wiley threaded cards with words or syllables taken from the work's source material on a clothes-line across the stage. *Pendulum Music* itself was, both then and subsequently, often mounted using artists as the 'performers'. *Writings about Music* includes a photograph (much reproduced elsewhere) of a performance in the already mentioned Whitney Museum of American Art programme on 27 May 1969, in which the composer (controlling the amplification) and Nauman – who spent 1968–9 in New York – are joined by Serra and Snow, as well as the composer James Tenney.[14] In 1968, Wiley himself – usually described as part of the 'funk' school, not as a Minimalist – painted the watercolour design for the cover of the 1969 Columbia Records disc of *It's Gonna Rain* and *Violin Phase*.[15]

Concerned, musically speaking, purely with unmanipulated rhythm, *Pendulum Music* is the most direct fulfilment of the aesthetic creed pro-pounded in the 'Music as a Gradual Process' essay; it is, in particular, the perfect illustration of the first of this essay's three examples of what '[p]erforming and listening to a gradual musical process resembles: pulling back a swing, releasing it, and observing it gradually come to rest'.[16] In demonstrating this, rather than merely using the idea as a meta-phor, the piece remains the only work by Reich to adhere unambiguously to the slogan 'once the process is set up and loaded it runs by itself', in the overtly mechanistic sense in which this is often understood.

Among those in the art world with whom Reich has had professional and personal dealings since the early 1970s, the most important one to mention is Beryl Korot, who became the composer's second wife on 30 May 1976; they have one son, Ezra, born in 1978. From the early 1970s, Korot worked as a pioneer in multi-channel video, most famously in *Dachau 1974*, and edited *Radical Software*, the first magazine on alternative video. In the 1980s, she painted. A weaving notation – part of a five-channel video installation, text and commentary with five word pieces and five notations – adorns the cover of the 1978 ECM LP recording of *Music for Eighteen Musicians*, appropriately reflective of Reich's concerns with pattern and system. Since the late 1980s, however, when she and her husband began to assemble the footage for their large-scale 'documentary music video theatre' work *The Cave*, Korot has returned to video, adding the computer as a significant tool in her work. At the time of writing, the Reichs are working on their second video opera, *Three Tales*.

Early minimalist compositions

The fifteen works Reich composed between *It's Gonna Rain* and *Oh dem Watermelons!*, in 1964–5, and *Drumming*, in 1970–71, may be divided into four categories: the tape compositions of 1966; the instrumental works of 1966–7; a group of compositions and projects, dating from 1967–70, which continue the composer's preoccupation with electronics; and the instrumental works of 1970. Nine of these are included by their composer in the list of works given as an appendix to *Writings about Music*. The ten compositions from this total of fifteen not already discussed form the subject matter of this section.

Come Out *and* Melodica

Returning to New York shortly before his twenty-ninth birthday, Reich continued to explore the technique of phasing in two further tape pieces: *Come Out* and *Melodica*. *Come Out* was composed in March and/or April 1966; *Melodica* in a single day a month after *Come Out*'s première. The gap of a year between these works and those from San Francisco is due primarily to practical factors involving the composer's move back East; Reich had no studio space in which to work for several months after his return to New York. A follow-up to the breakthrough of *It's Gonna Rain* was now overdue.

Come Out was premièred on 17 April 1966 in New York Town Hall at a benefit concert for the retrial of the 'Harlem Six', a group of black teenagers arrested, and convicted, for the murder of a white shop-owner during the riots of 1964. Truman Nelson, a civil-rights activist, gave Reich some ten hours of taped interviews with the young men involved, and

Example 3.7
(a) *Come Out*, Basic Unit

Come out   to   show them

(b) *Melodica*, Basic Unit

asked him to produce a piece based on these for the benefit. As in *It's Gonna Rain*, the composer took advantage of the potential urban Black speech offers for the rich interaction of musical and semantic levels. Played as it was amidst more familiar and more popular types of 'protest music', while contributions were being collected, the piece was more or less ignored on this occasion; for the considerable impact its release on record made in the following year, see below.

Reich describes *Come Out* as 'essentially a refinement' of *It's Gonna Rain*. Once again, the piece begins with a section of unaltered text, introducing the speech material and setting its context. It was Daniel Hamm who provided the voice that Reich tape-looped to produce his basic material. Maintaining that the six boys had been beaten up when in police custody in Harlem 28th Precinct, Hamm described how he was required to prove visibly bleeding injuries in order to get transferred to hospital: 'I had to, like, open the bruise up, and let some of the bruise blood come out to show them'. By selecting, however, only five words from this as the basis for the whole of what follows – a thirteen-minute piece in a single section – Reich achieves a more purely musical focus than he had managed in *It's Gonna Rain* with the aid of a more melodic phrase demonstrating greater pitch stability: its character determined by the interval of a minor third, suggesting C minor, and enhanced by clearer vowel sounds. (Ex. 3.7a gives the Basic Unit of *Come Out*.) Phasing of the two words 'come out' itself produces identifiable motivic developments: 'co-ma-ma', 'co-ma-ma-ma', and 'co-ma-ma-ma-ma', for instance, each change in rhythm and emphasis resulting from the gradual process of canonic realignment. Even more interestingly, the 'sh' of the word 'show' contains a percussive element – many have compared it to maracas – which allows not merely timbral variety but also provides a starting point for more subtle manipulation of the material, as the 'sh' sound swoops the whole spectrum. In other words, the sounds themselves have become more divorced from their meaning, the 'sh' sound thereby producing the first example of what Reich calls 'resulting patterns'.

Additionally, the phasing process applied to *Come Out*'s Basic Unit does not simply move away from and back to unison, but from two to four to eight voices according to a pattern controlled by predetermined points of arrival. When the phasing process applied to 'Come out to show them' reaches 'Come a', come a'/show them, show them' (a more accurate transcription of the spoken words), around three minutes into the piece, the two-voice canon in quavers, previously on separate channels, splits into four voices, with two on each channel. At the point when 'Come a', come a', come a', come a'/show them, show them, show them, show them' is reached, just after eight minutes in, the four-voice canon in quavers then splits, quite dramatically, into eight voices in semiquavers. This produces a kind of shimmer or blur lasting some five minutes, in which the words have become completely inaudible. The words 'come out' now yield a kind of soft, rounded burr, while 'to show them' has been transformed into alternating pulses of machine-like ferocity. Further panning across the stereo space adds another dimension to this wall of sound before the whole thing is eventually faded out. The procedures of Part Two of *It's Gonna Rain* have thus been expanded with the aid of a much more composerly control of the work's basic material.

Come Out's combination of more purely musical quality of material and its more consistently audible manipulation has been viewed as a move towards a 'phonic' approach, governed by the musical grammar it establishes for itself, as opposed to the 'phonemic' tendencies of *It's Gonna Rain*, in which factors 'outside the music' – the emotional content of the words and their tendency to retain extra-musical meanings – impose on the way the work is perceived.[17] Part Two of *It's Gonna Rain*, as we have seen, exploits the full spectrum between verbal audibility and inaudibility by moving from clear comprehension to the chaos of sheer noise.

Come Out, it could be argued, not only focuses more firmly on the 'phonic', but does so with a mixture of systematic rigour and intuitive control which can be readily appreciated via the clarity – both textural and textual – with which the structure is articulated. One should not, however, ignore the continuing part played in the later work by the 'added emotional layer' provided by the words and their cultural resonances, which themselves help to make the musical results correspondingly richer. While still audible, the words of *Come Out*, already suggestive of social protest, achieve added weight through sheer repetition. The eventual move from 'text' to 'texture' yields, not purity of sound, but a dense complexity charged with the frustration and danger of pent-up repression, enhanced by the grim transmutation of a human outcry against injustice into the relentless machinations of a force beyond human control. And while *It's*

Gonna Rain responded to widespread concern about the escalation of the Cold War, *Come Out* not only reflected the immediate circumstances of its composition but could be interpreted as a warning against the racial strife that itself escalated in the USA shortly after its première. With both works, the acoustic, psycho-acoustic and psychological consequences of using speech sounds to make music become interestingly confused.

Melodica uses a structure almost identical to that of *Come Out*, applying to it a melodic pattern the composer dreamed. Reich 'woke up on May 22nd, 1966, and realized the piece with the melodica (a toy instrument) and tape loops, in one day'.[18] He chose this simple, basically children's, instrument because its sound approximated most closely to that which he heard in his dream. *Melodica*'s Basic Unit (see Ex. 3.7b) consists of just four pitches divided into two pairs covering an octave span – B E and B A – revolving around the central E, supported by its dominant and sub-dominant. The process of phasing gradually turns this into a continuous melodic line, after which, at about three minutes in, the texture expands to four voices. With this canon, the separation of the higher and lower pairs of notes seems even more pronounced than before, encouraging the listener to hear the music in terms of a lower dominant/tonic drone above which a skirling modal melody is spun; unlike *Come Out*, there is no move to an eight-voice canon. The tonal ambiguities offered by such pitch material would subsequently be explored by the composer. The fresh rhythmic perspectives thrown up by the phasing process and the complex overtone structure of each note add further dimensions. But *Melodica*'s reliance on a four-voice texture for almost eight minutes (it lasts 10′45″) ultimately offers too little to sustain musical interest. The piece has remained largely unplayed and almost entirely unknown.

The hint of the gimmick in *Melodica* may suggest that Reich was already finding the technique of phasing with tape to have its limitations. Despite the advances made in *Come Out*, he had, indeed, begun to question the potential of phasing if it could not be somehow extended beyond its use with tape. '1966 was a very depressing year', the composer has said. 'I began to feel like a mad scientist trapped in a lab'.[19] The use of musical pitches, rather than speech patterns, in *Melodica* – 'which turned out to be the last tape piece I ever made' – suggested, however, the application of phasing techniques to instrumental music. Initially, it seemed impossible to perform live a process which was, as the composer has written, 'indigenous to machines. On the other hand I could think of nothing else to do with live musicians that would be as interesting as the phasing process'.[20] 'Aching to do something instrumental', he began to search for a way to put the process of phasing into live practice. The crucial contribution made by tape technology to Reich's development in the late 1960s and beyond remains one of the most important instances in musical history of the influence of electronic music on music for instruments alone.

The early instrumental phase compositions of 1966–7

The three instrumental works composed in the year-and-a-half after *Melodica* – *Reed Phase*, *Piano Phase* and *Violin Phase* – form a natural sequence, exploring the technique of phasing in music designed either for a single player plus tape or, in the case of *Piano Phase*, for just two players. These established the model for a whole series of pieces in Reich's output in which multiples of the same instrument are chosen in order to permit audibility of structure. Despite their economy of instrumental means, the three 'Phase' pieces demonstrate increasing textural and contrapuntal elaboration.

Several principles also hold good for the larger series of phase compositions – including *Phase Patterns* and *Drumming* – of which they form part. Each is constructed from a small pattern (the Basic Unit), from which further patterns may be abstracted for independent development. The scores themselves present the different stages through which this Basic Unit goes in the process of being phased against itself. While phasing in the tape pieces had been achieved by slowing down one tape loop against the other, in the instrumental compositions one player speeds up against the other's fixed tempo, since this proved much easier. (The difference should not be overemphasised, however, since the false impression of one channel accelerating, rather than slowing down, against a fixed speed is as strong in the tape pieces for many listeners as is the true impression in the instrumental ones.) The actual phasing is notated by using dotted lines to indicate the increases in tempo that a player must make against the fixed part, each 'notch' in the sequence then being conventionally notated by showing the new alignment. (The first attempt to notate *Piano Phase* – the single-page score exchanged with Serra dated 1/67, which consists of what became Part One – can be seen in Cage's book *Notations*, published in 1969.[21]) Regularity of metre is crucial during the locked figures, but notable for its absence in what we will call the 'fuzzy transitions'. Each of these figures is to be repeated a number of times (specified but flexible), forming a seamless flow both between repetitions of each figure and between these and the 'fuzzy transitions' themselves.

While it would be perfectly possible to fix the number of repetitions of each figure in advance, in practice there is really no need, since only a

Example 3.8 *Reed Phase*, Basic Unit

single player has to move at any one time. Dynamic markings are given but, with the exception of crescendi for the second player fading in to join the first player with the same pattern, these markings encourage a consistent, 'flat' level, at a medium volume.

Reed Phase *and* Piano Phase

At first, Reich tried the obvious transitional solution to the application of phasing techniques 'indigenous to machines' to instrumental music: a combination of live instrumental performance and accompanying tape. While *Piano Phase* and *Violin Phase* have become two of his most familiar early works, *Reed Phase*, the composer's first attempt at live phasing, has remained almost unavailable and essentially rejected, performed only by Gibson, for whom it was written. Originally intended for soprano saxophone with two pre-recorded saxophone tracks on tape, the work is dated 12/66, and given the title 'Saxophone Phase', in the programmes for its première in the art gallery of Fairleigh Dickinson University on 5 January 1967, and subsequent New York City performances in the 1967 Park Place concerts.

The programme note for the latter says that '[i]n *Saxophone Phase* a performer moves gradually ahead and out of phase with a fixed tape loop'. As published in *Source* magazine,[22] *Reed Phase* consists of three sections: a complete cycle of phasing based on a five-note, five-beat Basic Unit (see Ex. 3.8); a middle section adding a second tape voice a beat ahead of the first, against both of which the live saxophone again phases; and a repeat of the opening section. The five-beat rhythmic scheme fails, its composer himself feels, to create the sort of ambiguities essential to the success of any piece using repetition as a basic tool; the contour, probably more than the size, of its pitch content – outlining a i–v–iv–vii–v pattern on D, using just four pitch classes – similarly produces phasing which 'doesn't seem to make that much difference'. As a result, Reich finds the piece 'repetitious and boring'. Not only is it not included in his 1974 list of 'those compositions which I feel are worth keeping' in *Writings*,[23] but it is not even mentioned in passing in the main text. Gibson suggests that *Reed Phase* is not only the first piece to use live phasing, but also that it is 'probably the first formal western composition to require circular breathing . . . as a performance practice'.[24]

Early stages of work on *Piano Phase*, undertaken late in 1966, turn out to be part of the same transitional process of combining live performance and tape. 'I used tape to get away from tape', its composer says, 'because I didn't have two pianos, nor did Arthur Murphy'. Reich 'recorded a short repeating melodic pattern played on the piano, made a tape loop of that pattern, and then tried to play against the loop myself, exactly as if I were a second tape recorder'.[25] This led to the discovery not only that live phasing was possible, but also that it was highly pleasurable: 'a new and extremely satisfying way of playing that was both completely worked out beforehand . . . and yet free of actually reading notation, allowing me to become completely absorbed in listening while I played'. Reich and Murphy now rehearsed separately against tape loops, allowing each to judge his own accuracy as a performer, and thus also to estimate the potential of live phasing. Instead of simply writing a piece for piano and tape, however – which he says was never his intention – Reich took advantage of his eventual access to two pianos to press on to the next stage. When – at a try-out of *Piano Phase* in the same Fairleigh Dickinson programme that saw the première of *Reed Phase* – the two friends finally got together on two pianos, they 'found, to our delight, that we could perform this process without mechanical aid of any kind'.

Piano Phase apparently went through several versions – including one for four electric pianos with headphones, entitled 'Four Pianos', premièred in March 1967 (see below) – before Reich settled on the published three-part composition for two pianos. Four discoveries Reich made during the period of experimentation that led to this final version establish the main outlines of his future approach to such material and its manipulation. Firstly, it marked the discovery of a viable, and pliable, modal material which would give the vital extra dimension necessary to allow the composition of instrumental music based on rhythmic processes but lacking the added emotional layer of speech and everyday sounds offered by tape. The six-pitch modal fragment Reich devised for his breakthrough into instrumental music proved consistently interesting when phased against itself, as well as against altered versions, due in part to its own ambiguity and malleability. These in turn interact with the second discovery made through work on *Piano Phase*: the potential behind patterns based on units of twelve beats.

This is combined with his third discovery: the further metric ambiguities inherent in the multiple downbeats generated by the phasing process. Contrapuntal presentations of the same pattern against itself, and of related patterns with their own fresh metric emphases, proved especially fulfilling, generating a rich variety of metric resources with the simplest of

Example 3.9 *Piano Phase*: (a) Basic Unit of Part One; (b) Basic Unit of Part Two; (c) Basic Unit of Part Three.

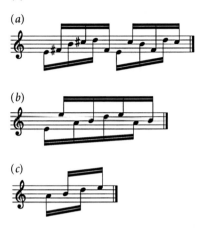

(a)

(b)

(c)

means. Fourthly, Reich began to discover more sophisticated structural ways to complement what was still an essentially schematic deployment of rhythm and extremely limited modal vocabulary.

In *Piano Phase*, the pitch material evolves to create a three-part structure in which modulation (using the pitch centres B, E and A, respectively) plays a significant role. As its clear opposition of white notes in the left hand (E B D) and black notes in the right (F♯ C♯) suggests, the Basic Unit – a melodic pattern of twelve semiquavers, divided into two groups of six, using only five pitches – was devised at the keyboard (see Ex. 3.9a). More obvious to the ear is the division between an upper voice (B C♯ D) and a lower one (E F♯), separated by a perfect fourth. The composer exploits both voices in what is arguably a first step towards the deployment of resulting patterns using instruments rather than tape: their registral separation, for instance, is used homophonically as well as polyphonically. The richness Reich discovers in such simple material relies to a considerable extent on the ways in which white-note/black-note opposition and voice division interact.

The first of the piece's three parts performs a complete phasing operation on this twelve-semiquaver pattern. A modified version of this, eight semiquavers in length, then begins the second part (at Figure 16). Instead of being phased against itself, however, this pattern is joined by a new one, also of eight semiquavers, which in turn forms the basis for the four-semiquaver pattern on which the final part is constructed (beginning at Figure 27); see Examples 3.9b and c. The new pattern in Part Two introduces one extra pitch class (A), plus the E an octave above the already present lower tonic. After this has been pared down briefly to repeated octave Es, the central four semiquavers of the new eight-semiquaver pattern of the second part form the sole material of the third and final one. As a whole, the number of pitch classes used in *Piano Phase* moves from five up to six and finally reduces to just four.

Though its composer states that *Piano Phase* 'is as process-oriented as the tape pieces', it is already clear that Reich manipulates his material here in a quite subtle manner. All three parts perform complete cycles of phase-shifting; but while the first and third phase a pattern against itself, the middle part, as we have seen, phases one pattern against a different one. As Paul Epstein has pointed out (in an article, confined mainly to the first part of *Piano Phase*, which is among the most detailed analyses to be published of any minimalist composition), the second half of Part One's cycle of phasing 'is a retrograde of the first, with the relationship between the two players reversed'.[26] Thus Figures 3 and 13, 4 and 12, etc. present identical combinations of the Basic Unit, but with different starting points (see Ex. 3.10a and b). Figure 8 (see Ex. 3.10c) – in which the second group of six semiquavers is phased exactly against the first six, and then vice versa – marks the midpoint of the cycle, which appears only once. Any complete and strict phasing cycle of this kind will, of course, move into retrograde at the halfway stage. But this is unlikely to be noticed by the listener: an illustration of how even such a purely mechanical process hides 'secrets of structure'.

Another notable feature of Part One's phasing cycle is the alternation of patterns which form dyads of white or black notes alone, and those which combine them. Half the dyads of the patterns in the latter category, occupying the even-numbered figures (starting at Figure 3, see again Ex. 3.10a), are major or minor seconds – E F♯, B C♯, C♯ D, a pair of each – and thus emphasise dissonance; a condition that reaches its point of maximum tension in Figures 7 and 9, in which sequences of repeating seconds alternate with sequences of repeating sixths and fourths. Patterns separating white and black notes, to be found in the even-numbered figures (starting at Figure 4, see again Ex. 3.10b), alternately emphasise the perfect fifth, F♯ C♯, and a collection of unisons, minor thirds, perfect fifths and minor sevenths assembled from the pitches E, B and D, thus emphasising consonance; a condition that reaches its point of maximum repose in Figure 8 (see again Ex. 3.10c), in which white-note unisons (E B D repeated) alternate with black-note fifths (F♯ C♯).

The more consonant patterns do not necessarily lead to greater structural audibility. The relationship between the opposition of consonance and dissonance and the extent to which the 'canons' of *Piano Phase* are audible is at its richest when voice division makes a telling contribution at the same time. In Figure 4, for instance – the first consonant configuration

Example 3.10 *Piano Phase*: (a) Figures 3 and 13; (b) Figures 4 and 12; (c) Figure 8; (d) Figure 6.

following the unison (see again Ex. 3.10b) – F♯ and C♯ always occur together as a 'static' perfect fifth, and the division into two separate voices is clear because it is consistently homophonic; furthermore, the two halves of Figure 4 are identical. Yet it is the very simplicity of this texture – the syncopations of the lower voice supporting the upper voice's close-position rocking motion – which obscures both the Basic Unit and the canon upon it by establishing a clear identity of its own. In Figure 6, by contrast – the following consonant configuration (see Ex. 3.10d) – F♯ and C♯ occur in unison, and the interval between the two voices – reduced as a consequence to zero for half the time – is clear because it is consistently polyphonic (the E F♯ E semiquavers constantly alternate with the rising or falling groups based on B C♯ D). Here, the constant reduction to unison allows the Basic Unit, and perhaps even the canon itself, to be heard. In the more dissonant patterns, the repeating dyads glue the two parts together to create the effect of something texturally, even 'motivically', quite different from what surrounds it. The result is a refocusing of attention sufficient to obscure the canon itself.

This separation into consonant patterns and dissonant ones is also reflected to some degree in the treatment of metre. The absence of a clear, functional downbeat in such music leads to all kinds of interesting ambiguities. Downbeats may, for instance, be felt quite unambiguously in individual parts; when these are combined, however, the consequent multiple downbeats interact with each other to create a more complex metrical situation in which the 'acoustic' and the 'psycho-acoustic' become hard to separate. Metric ambiguities are already a feature of the tape pieces, made all the more musically interesting by the arrival of what came to be called resulting patterns in *Come Out*. But with *Piano Phase*, Reich really begins to capitalise on the metric potential of phasing. The experience of *Reed Phase* had taught him that unusual numbers of beats or notes offered less than they initially suggested. By choosing a pattern of twelve semiquavers for the first part of *Piano Phase* – in this case broken down into two clear groups of six – he began to discover the possibilities of metric reorientation which lay behind the potential subdivisions of a twelve-beat pattern; even where, as here, many (though not all) of these reorientations preserve the basic subdivision into 2×6. The metrical ambiguity between the possible sub-groupings of twelve, of which 3×4 and 4×3 are only the most obvious, is something the composer continues to explore to this day.

The 'fuzzy transitions' also create interesting metrical situations, particularly psycho-acoustically. As Epstein notes – checking his own observations with the aid of a computer realisation, as well as a live performance, of the piece to avoid any conclusions based on performer inaccuracy – several distinct stages may be perceived in the movement from one 'locked' phase structure to the next; furthermore, differences may be observed between the stages involved at different points in the phasing cycle. In the initial 'fuzzy transition' away from the unison, for example, an impression of increasing resonance precedes the effect of actual separation, followed by the replacement of any sense of a beat by what Epstein calls 'a dizzying rhythmic complexity'.[27] At the mid-point, the speed appears to double, producing a brief sensation of stability; after which the previous psycho-acoustic stage obtains until the new phase relationship is established. With the next 'fuzzy transition', on the other hand, there seem to be only three stages: gradual separation, a chaotic kind of swirling and the coalescing of the new configuration. These differences reflect the strong contrast between the dissonance of Figure 3 and the consonance of Figure 4. As Epstein wisely points out, however, such delicate psycho-acoustic situations can lead to variations between even an individual's listening experiences on different occasions.

As a whole, *Piano Phase* explores the modal territory set out by the initial five pitch classes. B, the somewhat ambiguous tonality of Part One, is established by two factors: the formation of iv–v–i in this key by the first three notes of the Basic Unit, and the rise and fall from B to D and back of the upper voice. E and F♯, constituting the lower voice, vie for a superiority probably claimed ultimately by the former: E is the first note in each group of six semiquavers as well as the lowest pitch of all, though it occurs only twice in the basic pattern, while F♯ occurs three times.

It is therefore no surprise to find E assuming an important position in Part Two, though the tonality of this is even more ambiguous than that of Part One. The new pitch, A, oscillates with B in the new pattern, contributing iv–v to the i of an E now strengthened by its representation in two registers. This A B can, however, also be interpreted as downward neighbour oscillation emphasising B: maybe the dominant rather than the tonic of Piano 2's pattern, but simultaneously the tonic of the original Basic Unit, which continues in Piano 1. With A now introduced, and *its* dominant established as the only pitch class to occur in two registers, the move to a tonal centre of A in Part Three seems the logical outcome. All the previous determinants – iv–v–i progression, neighbour-note oscillation, primacy of position as lowest note – help to establish A as tonic. While reducing the range of potential relationships and challenges to any single pitch as central, the reduction from six pitch classes to four draws attention to how much is missing – in the piece as a whole – of the framework normally supporting a more conventionally tonal composition.

Even here, then, room remains for uncertainty. Harmonic motion is more suggested than achieved in *Piano Phase*'s progression from B to E to A; any aural interpretation of its neat progression of perfect fourths in terms of ii–v–i in A is heavily qualified by modal ambiguity. Such a delicate balance – previously tipped in favour of a modal manner made more evasive by an approach to pitch which, in the tape pieces, is inherently more evanescent – is firmly established as a central feature of Reich's music from here on. The roles of rhythm and metre are also enhanced in the instrumental compositions by the precision with which they are deployed and by the extent to which the results of this precision are audible. The establishment of modal diatonicism as a norm seems to have been accepted quite naturally. 'It wasn't discussed', he says, 'it was practised'. But analysis of what were probably largely intuitive decisions on the composer's part demonstrates the role played by tonal prolongation in such music's construction. The resulting structures were to become more complex and sophisticated as time went on. The expressive focus of this music is, however, fundamentally changed by the abandonment of the necessarily less pitch-determinate sounds of speech and the substitution of equally tempered instrumental pitches. Emotionally cooler and more stable, Reich's music from *Piano Phase* onwards is more about pitches and patterns than *Come Out* could ever have been.

From now on, the considerable majority of Reich's compositions would begin with the establishment of a musical idea with a modal pitch profile. The implications of this then determine both the structure and the expressive qualities of the subsequent work. With the background and beliefs already described, the character of Reich's new modality comes as no surprise. There was at this time, indeed, he says, 'an assumption that was pretty much the case with all of us' that diatonicism of some kind would form the basis for such music.

Already very telling is the absence of the bass in Reich's output of this period: not only of a bass line but of any notes in the lower range at all. No mature work composed before *Music for Mallet Instruments, Voices and Organ* with the exception of *Four Organs* – that is, between 1965 and 1972–3 – makes any use of the bass clef. *Piano Phase* has no note lower than the E♮ above middle C; *Violin Phase* no note lower than middle C♯; *Phase Patterns* no note lower than middle C; *Drumming* has nothing lower than the G♯ below middle C; *Six Pianos* nothing below F♯. 'People used to kid me and say, your piano's all dusty on both ends, it's only used in the middle', says Reich. As he explains, 'I didn't know what to do except to have a drone bass. And I didn't want to have a drone bass; that was too boring. I didn't want to do what La Monte and Terry [were] doing with drones. . . . I didn't want any bass that would say, "this is where we are". I knew there were certain ambiguities, and I wanted to keep those ambiguities. But I didn't know how to keep them and still say what they were. So I simply shut up, I didn't say anything! Of what you can't speak, you must keep silent'.

Despite the new importance of pitch, Reich still describes rhythmic structure as 'my *sine qua non*' in 1966–7, and even beyond. 'In those early pieces', he insists, 'the focus was on rhythm, and rhythm, and then again rhythm. The pitches were chosen, and they were chosen quite carefully, believe me, but once they were chosen – *finished* with that decision. You load the machine – and it runs'. Yet the finished products of this process are never mechanistic, even in purely rhythmic or metric terms. This is due to Reich's ingenuity in the exploitation both of the metrical ambiguities inherent in a single pattern, especially in canonic counterpoint, and of the potential of employing more than one pattern.

Violin Phase

In *Violin Phase* (the score of which is dated October 1967), the exploration of live performance and tape in combination is taken up once more. The piece requires either a solo violin plus three more violins on tape or – 'preferably', the composer states in *Writings*[28] – four violins. The resulting increase in the density of texture and counterpoint marks a significant advance, though we should remember that *Piano Phase* in one of its earlier incarnations also had four lines. Reich has described *Violin Phase* as 'basically an expansion and refinement of *Piano Phase*'.

Again, the musical material Reich chooses is devised with the nature of the instrument in question in mind, here stressing the open A and E strings of the violin. The result is a Basic Unit featuring dyads as well as single pitches (see Ex. 3.11a). A and E function more as the mediant and flattened leading note of F♯ in the ambiguous modality created here. The centrality of F♯ is confirmed by its dominant: C♯ and F♯, forming the lower voice, occur as the first two notes and are repeated on beats 8 and 9, and the Basic Unit readily incorporates C♯–minor[7] as well. Since B – the seventh of this chord – as well as C♯ are emphasised as the work progresses, one could describe the modality of *Violin Phase* in terms of a tonic supported symmetrically by the perfect fourth on either side of it. Such is the ambiguity of this material, however, that one could also interpret F♯ as a modal dominant above C♯; the potential of the sort of pitch configuration Reich had first stumbled on in *Melodica* was now beginning to be understood and exploited. As in *Piano Phase*, a twelve-beat pattern forms the basis for the entire composition; here, though, a single longer note-value (in effect, a dotted crotchet) amidst the prevailing quavers introduces an extra dimension to the rhythmic/metric mix.

More important, however, is the exploitation of a new discovery. Even with only two violins playing the same pattern in such now characteristic 'staggered', close-knit counterpoint, it becomes possible to hear new groupings of pitches based, usually, on their registral proximity rather than the 'structural' separation of each line. 'As one listens to the repetition of the several violins', Reich has written, 'one may hear first the lower tones forming one or several patterns, then the higher notes are noticed forming another, then the notes in the middle may attach themselves to the lower tones to form still another'.[29] What the composer now began to call 'resulting patterns' have already been observed in embryo in the spectrum-swooping 'sh' sounds of *Come Out* and the voice divisions of *Piano Phase*. *Violin Phase* is, however, the first composition in which Reich clarifies and really begins to exploit this phenomenon.

Example 3.11 *Violin Phase*: (a) Figure 1; (b) Figure 16; (c) Figure 10; (d) Figure 20; (e) Figure 19a; (f) Figures 22f and 22g. (Ex. (c), (d), (e), and (f), Live Violin only.)

Though, as the composer points out, '[a]ll these patterns are really there',[30] listeners' response to them will differ; to some degree one can choose the patterns on which to concentrate. As a consequence, resulting patterns can be called 'psycho-acoustic by-products', a term which the composer himself uses. 'In listening' – as David Behrman, producer of the first recording of *Violin Phase*, puts it – 'one can bring out these and other combination figures by concentrating on them – a little like those puzzle drawings of geometric three-dimensional figures that can be flipped back and forth in space by an effort of will'.[31]

Reich does not, however, limit himself to allowing the listener to hear these patterns as they emerge naturally in the course of the contrapuntal elaboration. In a performance using a single live violinist and tape, the soloist phases against the static tape part until beat 5 in the process is reached at Figure 6 (about five minutes into the piece). Here, the cycle of phasing is arrested, the tape now assuming the position taken by the soloist (Figure 7). While this 'notch' in the phasing process is retained, the soloist is then required to play specific, notated resulting patterns (Figures 9–11) – some more harmonic, others more melodic – fading them in and out of the total texture. Provision is also made for the player to choose his own resulting patterns, assisted by the notation on a single staff of the complete counterpoint produced by the other parts. These possibilities add a further dimension to the process of phasing. With just two violins on tape, the introduction of a third voice already enhances textural and structural depth.

After around three more minutes, the phasing process is resumed at the point of its arrest, the soloist initially synchronising with the tape (Figure 12). This time, however, the counterpoint resulting from this 'notch' in the process is retained while further phasing takes place, taking the number of voices to three. At beat 9 (Figures 16–17), the phasing freezes again, the tape once more freeing the soloist to play further resulting patterns (Figure 18 onwards). (Ex. 3.11b shows the three voices in the fixed positions they will now occupy for the remainder of the piece.) With three voices now turning to four, the scope of both the resulting patterns themselves and the total contrapuntal fabric is greatly enriched. In addition, Reich quickly subjects the resulting patterns themselves to phasing against the already canonically presented Basic Unit (Figures 19–21). Finally, a markedly more melodic pattern is thrown up that ignores the basic metrical division (Figure 22). With the other three parts still fixed at the 'notches' in the phasing process on which they came to rest much earlier, the work ends with the soloist returning, in a single bound, to the Basic Unit in alignment with the tape, allowing the listener to hear whatever resulting patterns he likes in his head.

In addition to textural and structural depth, resulting patterns may also reinforce, and sometimes clarify, a particular tonal emphasis. While some of the composer's suggested resulting patterns hint at the prevailing F♯ modality and its dominant (Ex. 3.11c and d), others emphasise B and E, by sheer force of repetition (Ex. 3.11e), the latter being interpretable not only as the flattened leading note but also as an extension of the 'stacked'-fourths symmetry of C♯ F♯ B. These resulting patterns move from simple dyads – stressing B and E, as before – to a single repeated C♯ (the dominant of the tonic F♯ and central pitch of the dominant seventh outlined by the Basic Pattern) and a staccato pattern in continuous quavers. Part of the more melodic pattern at Figure 22 is shown in Ex. 3.11f.

Psycho-acoustic by-products and even resulting patterns have been noted in Reich's immediately preceding works, and the compositional control he exerted on these has been argued back as far as *It's Gonna Rain*. Yet the articulation, as well as identification, of resulting patterns in *Violin Phase* integrates such psycho-acoustic phenomena into the fabric of the music in a more detailed and composed-out manner than Reich had previously achieved. Arising naturally from the combinations produced by the phasing process itself, such resulting patterns allow him to transcend more easily and comprehensively the limitations of a single structural process, permitting greater flexibility in shaping the work as a whole as well as bringing an extra textural dimension. The contrapuntal and structural variety achievable through the articulation of resulting patterns already moves *Violin Phase* in the direction of Reich's mature compositions.

The discoveries and achievements of *Piano Phase* and *Violin Phase* established the path he was to pursue for the next few years. While *Violin Phase* is the more advanced musically, *Piano Phase* had already suggested the abandonment of tape altogether in favour of a live music capitalising on the musical richness to be obtained from human fallibility while supposedly attempting to imitate a machine. As it turned out, however, Reich's fascination with the potential of electronic technology was by no means yet satisfied.

The electronic projects and compositions of 1967–9

In addition to concert compositions, music composed with electronic means continued to be an important part of Reich's work at this time. Even before *Violin Phase* was completed, his interest in the compositional possibilities of the fast-developing new technologies surfaced again. This was partly due to the considerable excitement then being generated by Experiments in Art and Technology, a project designed 'to develop effective means of stimulating collaborations between artists and engineers'. A prime mover in this was the artist Robert Rauschenberg, and with him the whole circle around Cage; another important protagonist was the engineer Billy Kluver. Though already disillusioned with tape as a medium, Reich now became so impressed by the potential of technologies already beginning to offer other opportunities to composers that he set about attempting to realise two ideas, both of which emerged out of the concept of phasing.

The first of these, expressed in the form of a piece he called *Slow Motion Sound* (September 1967), was 'to take a tape loop, probably of speech, and

Example 3.12 *Pulse Music* and *Four Log Drums*, pitch material

ever so gradually slow it down to enormous length *without lowering its pitch*'.[32] It remained unrealised due to the technical limitations of the period. Though eventually able to achieve it in 1981 with the aid of the much more sophisticated, computer-based technology of IRCAM in Paris, Reich found the results musically uninteresting, and at the time took it no further. Surprisingly, however, he has returned to this 'slow motion sound' in his most recent work, *Three Tales* (1996 onwards).

The other idea was the transformation of a single pulsing chord into a series of melodic patterns by means of gradual phase shifting. Since the demands this placed on performers seemed unrealistic, Reich set about attempting to construct a device which would allow the process to be achieved mechanically, while still permitting the results to be performed live, not on tape. The EAT project enabled him to work with Larry Owens and David Flooke, technicians at Bell Laboratories in New Jersey, where the composer appears to have spent, or attempted to spend, much of his time between February 1968 and the early part of the following year. The result was the Phase Shifting Pulse Gate, which he proudly unveiled at the New School for Social Research in New York in April 1969, and subsequently in a concert at the Whitney Museum of American Art on 27 May. The score he composed for the Gate was entitled *Pulse Music* (dated 5/69). This gradually transforms an eight-note chord into melodies which finally blur into a fast pulsing chord. In the same month (that of the concert itself), he also wrote *Four Log Drums*, which uses the Gate 'as a programming device for 4 performers each playing a two-note wooden log drum'.[33] Employing the same tempo as *Pulse Music*, and immediately preceding it in the Whitney Museum programme, this changes the eight pitches of the original piece from a rhythmically spread-out version to a single chord, from which point *Pulse Music* went on to unravel it again. The basic pitch material of both pieces (see Ex. 3.12) has the same modal ambiguities – here the alternative tonics made possible by a 'stacked'-fifths structure based on A – which characterised *Melodica* and, more importantly, *Violin Phase*, and which would return later in *Four Organs*, *Phase Patterns* and *Drumming*.

While the basic idea behind these two pieces had at least been realisable – if with technology which 'could easily have ceased functioning at any time'[34] – Reich was dissatisfied with the 'stiff and un-musical' electronic realisation of the sounds and the artificiality of the performance element involved (just twisting dials). Five years later, he wrote that '[t]he Phase Shifting Pulse Gate is still in its fibre case on top of the closet in my bedroom. I haven't unpacked it yet'.[35] His efforts to harness new technologies to the principle of phasing had met only with dead ends. The single 'technology-driven' piece to survive from this period is *Pendulum Music,* itself little more than an exercise in basic physics.

Such continued reliance on electronics seems curious in the light of the course Reich's development was to take over the next twenty years; only in 1988, with *Different Trains,* was he to return with any consistency to such technology and produce a finished composition with its resources, though the *Counterpoint* series of works (starting with *Vermont Counterpoint* for flute(s) in 1982) requires multi-tracking of parts for its solo realisations. His persistence with the much more primitive electronic technology of the late 1960s is, however, certainly characteristic both of his restless concern to experiment with new ideas and of the tenacity with which he pursues them. Surprisingly, perhaps, it took him more than four years – from the beginning of 1965 to the summer of 1969 – to decide conclusively not only that he needed to move beyond music for tape alone, but also that the element of performance as conventionally understood – 'using my hands and body to actively create the music'[36] – was required to turn his technical discoveries into really interesting music.

Musical connections and the evolution of Reich's own ensemble

Reich's obsession with the Phase Shifting Pulse Gate coincides with the period when he and Glass were comparing notes on each other's attempts to discover a technique and style for themselves. While the available evidence suggests that the latter was the main beneficiary in these exchanges, it is also possible that Reich was learning, for instance, from his friend's decision to limit his involvement with electronics to amplification and the newly emerging electronic keyboards. This raises the question of the influence any of the so-called minimalist composers had on Reich, which in his case can most usefully be dealt with in conjunction with the evolution of the composer's own ensemble.

Reich acknowledges the influence of Young and, in particular, of Riley, viewing himself as, at least to a certain degree, a link in the chain of influences that passed from Young to Riley to himself and on to Glass. As we saw in Chapter 2, however, Reich's own dealings with Riley, after their brief period of friendship in 1964 which had led to the première of the latter's *In C*, were far from easy. Following their move – in Reich's case, back – to New York, where Young had by now firmly established himself, all three composers had to decide how compatible they were both personally and musically, and the extent to which their evolving careers should interact.

According to Young,[37] Reich called him some time after the latter returned to New York and asked to join the Theatre of Eternal Music. Reich denies this, and Riley – a member of Young's group at the time – considers it may have simply been a misunderstanding.[38] Whatever happened, Reich's sensibilities and mode of working are so different from those of Young and Riley that it would seem much more appropriate that he should have set up his own ensemble, just as he had in California.

Reich's New York performing group began operations in late 1966 when, as we have already seen, he began playing regularly with two other musicians, Jon Gibson and Arthur Murphy. While Murphy and Reich were mainly keyboard players, Gibson – who had already performed in Reich's improvisation group in San Francisco and was now also working with Young and Riley – used his versatility as a wind player to allow the new trio further instrumental scope. On occasion, he played other instruments too: the maracas, for example, in the early performances of *Four Organs*. Gibson and Murphy were composers as well as players; while Gibson is today better known as a saxophonist, Murphy has disappeared from the professional music scene altogether.

These three soon began to play the music of its members in SoHo galleries and other 'alternative' spaces, meshing with Reich's performance-art activities described above. Of especial significance to his own establishment as a composer were the 'Three Evenings of Music by Steve Reich', presented at the Park Place Gallery on 17, 18 and 19 March 1967; each evening offered the same programme, including, as seen earlier, the first performances of a version of *Piano Phase* for four pianos. In these, Murphy and Reich were joined by Philip Corner and James Tenney, all playing clavinets: rudimentary electronic keyboards that were more or less state-of-the-art for the day. Three of them appear to have performed a multiple phasing process against the fixed fourth part; it isn't clear whether the tripartite structure now familiar from the final version had yet evolved.

Since the gallery was currently exhibiting sculptures by Charles Ross, described by Reich as 'plexiglass prisms filled with mineral oil', these became part of the event, as did an environmental installation called *Bi-product*. The latter was the responsibility of the sound artist Max Neuhaus who, the flyer for the concerts promised, would be 'performing and distributing' his creation nightly. Reich says that Neuhaus 'recorded people's movements and recorded them on tape loops which he gave away at the end of the evening'. The musicians played behind Ross's prisms; the audience accordingly saw not only the players, but also multiple reflections of each of them. This clearly contributed to the 'psychedelic' aspect of the occasion, which should be borne in mind when reading Carman Moore's review of the first night. 'So strong was the effect of "Four Pianos"', he writes, 'that one of the listeners, who were all sprawled on the floor, fell into a howling kind of fit from which he emerged, shaken but otherwise (I think) undamaged after the piece concluded.'[39] Curiously, *Melodica* is the only piece listed in Reich's *Writings* as having a performance at Park Place.[40] In fact, as the original programme notes confirm, three other works of his were played in addition to 'Four Pianos'. *Improvisations on a Watermelon* was performed by Murphy and the composer on clavinetes. And *Come Out*, as well as *Melodica*, represented Reich's work with tape; as did 'Saxophone Phase', the original title of *Reed Phase*.

The audiences for these three evenings consisted largely of artists and their friends, including Rauschenberg. After the second performance, a member of the audience came up to the composer and reintroduced himself as a student colleague from their Juilliard-School days. It was in this manner that Glass and Reich became reacquainted. Both attempting to establish careers in New York with a compositional approach very different from that which each had been following five years before, the two composers quickly recognised what they now had in common, and cemented a working relationship that took two symbiotic forms. Both became the prime movers in the ensemble that constituted the main outlet for their own works over the next three years or so. And as compositional associates, they naturally showed each other their pieces as they developed individual approaches along related lines. According to Glass, Reich was 'very, very pleased'[41] to see someone else working in the same territory. According to Gibson, Reich was impressed by *Strung Out*, the first piece Glass seems to have written after his re-encounter with his former Juilliard colleague; Gibson says that 'there was a lot of interaction'[42] between Glass and Reich during this period. Glass turned out to offer not only support but also a kind of legitimation of Reich's own activities: a spur to activity very different from Riley's suspicious attitude to anyone treading on ground he considered rightfully his.

On the matter of actual influence, Reich maintains the view that, just as Riley, in particular, had been important in helping him to find his own way forward, so he himself now assisted Glass in his search for a technique and a style of his own. Having discovered his basic technique of phasing more than two years before his re-encounter with Glass, Reich viewed their sharing of ideas as basically one-way traffic, the more experienced composer giving to the relative novice the benefit of his advice concerning, for instance, the need to find a systematic technical procedure to compare with his own discovery of phasing. As one piece of evidence for this, or at least as some indication of the grateful respect Glass showed him at the time, he points to the first manuscript copies of his colleague's first substantial exploration of additive process, the technical breakthrough which made Glass's later work possible. The title page of this score, dated February 1969, reveals that this piece's original title was *Two Pages for Steve Reich*; only later did it become known simply as *Two Pages*.

The trio formed by Gibson, Murphy and Reich now expanded further to include not only Glass but several other musicians brought in by one or another of the already existing members of the group, usually Reich or Glass themselves. This rather loose association of composer-performers spawned two groups – Steve Reich and Musicians, and The Philip Glass Ensemble – which exist to this day. But though Reich has dated the former from 1966, and Glass the latter from 1968, this pool of performers – meeting, sometimes, as much as two or three nights a week – had neither fixed membership nor, at first, strongly separate allegiances; as so often happens, all its members initially worked on a more equal footing than subsequently became the case. Significantly for any notion of the evolution of separate ensembles attached to Reich or Glass, no composition requiring more than three players – the early version of *Piano Phase* aside – was produced by any of its members until Glass wrote *600 Lines* in the summer of 1968.

Reich himself produced no further ensemble pieces besides *Four Log Drums* and *Pendulum Music* until *Four Organs* some eighteen months later. In the interim, Gibson had gone to Los Angeles for around eight months to work for a Brazilian musician, Marcie Santos. He says that Reich and Glass 'were close'[43] when he left New York in the summer of 1968, and were still so when he got back, probably in March 1969, one month after *Two Pages* was completed. Some time after this, however, there appears to have been something of a falling out between the two composers, leading ultimately to a complete break between them.

The group run, in the main, by Reich and Glass nevertheless jointly gave several important New York concerts in 1969–70; the two composers performed in a few of each other's pieces, but the programming of their own music was kept separate. These concerts included the two already mentioned programmes at the Whitney Museum on 20 and 27 May 1969. An important programme at the Guggenheim Museum a year later, on 7 May 1970, saw the premières of *Four Organs* and *Phase Patterns*. After the Guggenheim programme, there was an important four-night series at the

Walker Art Center, Minneapolis, a week later, with two evenings devoted to each composer. The two made no further appearances together on the platform, with the exception of the concerts on a jointly arranged tour of Germany, France and England in March 1971; playing their ensemble works in Europe for the first time, the two found it expedient to fix a combined visit.

Reich used contacts he had made with Michael Nyman in London and, through Gibson, with Chantelle D'Arcy at the record company Disques Shandar in Paris to make his first European tour. Both his concerts – at the Institute of Contemporary Arts in London on 7 March, and at the Théâtre de la Musique in Paris on 16 March – consisted of the same programme: *Four Organs, Piano Phase, Pendulum Music, Phase Patterns* and Part One of *Drumming*, the last described in the list for the programme as 'in progress'. The personnel for most of these was the same as before; for *Pendulum Music*, local musicians assisted the composer. The Paris concert, mounted by Shandar, led to the record company's release the following year of a disc coupling *Four Organs* and *Phase Patterns*. The London programme resulted in a closer association with Nyman: the man behind the Hayward Gallery performance of *Drumming* almost a year later and one of the composer's most receptive commentators.

Several musicians were involved specifically with Reich from early on. In addition to Gibson and Murphy, Paul Zukofsky was among the first to work with the composer, giving the first performances of *Violin Phase*, as we have seen. While Corner and Tenney were only occasional members, the keyboard player Steve Chambers joined Reich for the Guggenheim programme in May 1970 and remained until the early performances (including the first recording, made in 1976 though not issued until 1978) of *Music for Eighteen Musicians*.

It was *Drumming* (1970–71) which caused the largest single expansion in the history of the group, which now became known for the first time as Steve Reich and Musicians. The work was put together via painstaking rehearsals, allowing for 'many small compositional changes while the work is in progress and at the same time [building] a kind of ensemble solidarity that makes playing together a joy'. This included the devising of the extensive resulting patterns, in which several performers assisted the composer. With *Six Pianos*, too, in which extensive use is also made of resulting patterns, both the choice and the ordering of these were made in rehearsal.

After various 'in progress' performances, *Drumming* was finally given complete at three different venues in New York City in December 1971: the Museum of Modern Art on the 3rd, Brooklyn Academy of Music on the

11th, and New York Town Hall on the 16th. The last of these performances was issued on record in April 1972 by (a completely different) John Gibson and Multiples Inc. (an art gallery press), in a limited edition of 500 complete with full score; meanwhile, the work was also toured. In the process of its assembly, two percussionists joined the hard-core group of Chambers, Gibson, Murphy and Reich himself: Russ Hartenberger and James Preiss now became mainstays of Reich's ensemble. *Drumming* also led to the engagement of three female singers: Jay Clayton, Joan LaBarbara and Judy Sherman. With Sherman replaced by Janice Jarrett, this trio also featured in *Music for Mallet Instruments, Voices and Organ*. Bob Becker, Tim Ferchen and Glen Velez, all three of them subsequently core percussionists of Steve Reich and Musicians, did not join until 1973, by which time Murphy had left. Other members of the group stayed for shorter periods; and, since Reich could not afford to take all the performers in his newly enlarged group out of New York, the early European performances of *Drumming*, *Six Pianos* and *Mallet* were augmented by local musicians. After these performances, Gibson left Reich's ensemble to work only with Glass and on projects of his own.

Though the eighteen (originally twenty-one) musicians required for *Music for Eighteen Musicians* enlarged Reich's ensemble to near-orchestral proportions, this was conceived and assembled under the same intimate, intensive and exploratory conditions that had characterised all Reich's ensemble efforts. This work increases the line-up of female vocalists to four, one of whom may also take a piano part in Section IIIa; other doublings involve the vibraphonist, who plays piano in Sections II and IX, and one other percussionist, who also plays piano in Section IX. The first commercial recording of *Music for Eighteen Musicians* retains only Clayton among the composer's original singers, adding Rebecca Armstrong, Elizabeth Arnold and Pamela Fraley. The four orchestral instruments new to Reich's ensemble music were played by Shem Guibbory (violin), Ken Ishii (cello), Virgil Blackwell and Richard Cohen (clarinets doubling bass clarinets). The core team of keyboard and mallet instruments added Larry Karush, Gary Schall, Nurit Tilles and David Van Tieghem to six regulars: Becker, Chambers, Hartenberger, Preiss, Velez and the composer himself.

Rehearsals for *Music for Eighteen Musicians* were held over a long period between April or May 1974 and the work's première on 24 April 1976. Structurally, the work is so complex that no attempt was made to notate repeats or achieve synchronisation in what was written down. No complete score authenticated by the composer existed until 1996, when Marc Mellits completed what is basically a transcription of the 1978 recording.[44] *Music for Eighteen Musicians* nevertheless precipitated its creator's move into writing for larger forces not gathered together and rehearsed over long periods under the composer's own control.

The instrumental compositions of 1969–70

Four Organs

One of Reich's technology-based notions, at least, proved adaptable to more conventional instruments; he is not, after all, a composer to waste ideas. The transformation of a single pulsing chord into a series of melodic patterns could still be achieved with live musicians if the notes of the chord were simply lengthened very slowly, one by one. The result of this discovery, made in August 1969, was *Four Organs*, completed the following January. Here, four electronic organs repeat the pitches of a single chord, gradually extending them so that, while the pulse remains intact, the music gives the impression of slowing down. The piece is thus additionally a kind of realisation of *Slow Motion Sound*; it was also influenced by the augmentation techniques found in the organum of the twelfth-century composer Perotin. All that was required to keep the players together was some kind of percussive pulse. Reich decided on maracas: breaking, for the first time in more than five years, his self-imposed rule about employing only identical instruments in any single piece.

Four Organs takes as its entire pitch material a dominant-eleventh chord based on a low E (see Ex. 3.13a). It is thus Reich's first significant composition to have a real bass part; the first in which he found a solution to the problem of handling the lower register in suitably ambiguous terms. Its six pitches – E G♯ B D F♯ A – are spread over the four instruments (basically a lower and upper pair), producing a total of nine notes spanning three-and-a-half octaves. A central cluster of mainly major seconds – D E F♯ G♯ A B – gives this chord a strongly dissonant edge; yet, as its distribution among the players partly demonstrates, this can readily be interpreted as a conglomerate of 'stacked' fifths, following the example of *Four Log Drums*. At the same time, as this suggests, such a dominant-eleventh chord is a relative of the material Reich had already explored in, among other works, *Violin Phase*.

This chord occurs at first in quavers on beats 1 and 4 of a repeated figure of $\frac{11}{8}$ (see again Ex. 3.13a). Constituting Reich's first use of a pulsing chord as a basic structural component, this is something he was to explore extensively in future works, often with a more regular pulse than that provided by the three + eight-beat unit to be found here. As it repeats – as a consequence establishing, of course, its own kind of regularity – single notes are progressively augmented beyond the quaver length of the chord as a

Example 3.13 *Four Organs*: (a) Figures 1–4; (b) Figure 8 (treble only).

whole: at first extending forwards, on the beats already established (G♯, Figure 2; E, Figure 3), then backwards, suggesting an anticipatory upbeat (E, Figure 4). The inevitable result of this process is the filling up of the whole figure with continuous organ sound; or, putting this another way, the substitution of notes for rests – what Reich later called 'rhythmic construction'. In temporarily abandoning phasing altogether, *Four Organs* already pointed the way towards approaches which would prove fertile in years to come.

   Once the original pairs of irregularly pulsing chords have silted up into a continuous sound (at Figure 10, about 3′15″ into the work's first recording, which as a whole lasts 15′35″), the figures themselves start to lengthen (some twenty seconds later). Beginning with the basic eleven quavers, this gradually expands to an enormous 265 quavers-worth of continuous sound. *Four Organs* thus divides into two sections: the first highly rhythmic, the second focusing on the harmony that has been present all along. Both subject highly reductive material to quite systematic scrutiny. Both, however, give a powerful impression of the ground shifting uneasily and unpredictably beyond the listener's grasp, since it is only possible to follow the general trend of their unfolding, not their detailed structure.

Though transcending the technique of phasing for the first time in Reich's output since 1965, *Four Organs* is even more restrictive and reductive than *Piano Phase* or *Violin Phase*. It is the first of only three pieces in Reich's output up to 1976 that began life as an abstract idea, that 'didn't have notes right away'. (*Drumming* and *Clapping Music* are the others.) Though its two sections audibly contrast the beginning of a process with its consequences, the piece is really a single process performed, without deviation, on a single harmonic unit. Yet *Four Organs* is by no means as one-dimensional as it may at first seem. The process has several by-products: chordal subdivisions and melodic cells assembled note-by-note as the basic chord gradually unravels, for instance (some of the latter ordered in pairs of perfect fifths); and sustained notes played out of phase on two or more organs (a new purchase on phasing). Since these by-products accumulate as the work proceeds, their impact is structural, not merely incidental. Yet such contrapuntal and textural variety as exists is still overwhelmed by the relentless reductiveness. *Four Organs* is in some respects Reich's most 'difficult' score.

Tonally, however, the piece takes a significant step in line with some of the above advances. The dominant implications enhanced through the chord's constant repetition are pursued in the pitches chosen for extension into sub-chords as the work proceeds: Figure 8, for instance (see Ex. 3.13b), reveals an E^7 chord, subsequently opposed by the emergence of a triad on D. Or reinforced by it, if you take the view that this V–IV in A major (or perhaps it should be I–VII in an E modality) represents neighbour-chord oscillation prolonging E.

Reich takes advantage of the fact that the eleventh of this dominant chord is also its tonic to play some interesting games with the listener's perception of harmony. Since the dominant is the bottom note (E) and the eleventh/tonic the top (A), 'all you have to do is release the bass, and all its doublings, and pretty soon you've resolved your chord'. While on the face of it suggesting a return to the bass-less ambiguities of the immediately preceding compositions, the progressive abandonment of the bass E in *Four Organs*' closing stages implies, in context, a closure of a kind previously unknown in Reich's post-student pieces. The result is a new approach to the traditional materials of harmony: a basic V–I cadence articulated by subjecting a seemingly static object to an inspection so intense that it threatens to turn into something else. One might point out that any tonic chord takes on dominant suggestions through relentless

Example 3.14 *Phase Patterns*: (a) Figure 7; (b) Figure 8.

(*a*)

(*b*)

repetition. Reich's dominant eleventh is much more interesting, however, and his structural ingenuity in developing its potential for a kind of harmonic motion in such protracted circumstances far greater. For all its radical rigour and harmonic reductiveness, *Four Organs* marks the beginning of Reich's serious interest in harmonic motion.

Phase Patterns

Though written for the same combination of four electric organs, his next composition, *Phase Patterns* (the score of which is dated 2/70), returns, as its title tells us, to phasing. It treats these keyboard instruments as tuned drums, constructing a phasing cycle on that most elementary of percussive figures, a simple alternation of the left and right hands called the paradiddle: L–R–L–L–R–L–R–R. Players 1 and 2 phase a pitched version of this Basic Unit against itself (see top line of Ex. 3.14a), while Players 3 and 4 build resulting patterns into the mix. A complete cycle of phasing is avoided: Player 2 moves ahead of Player 1 just four times out of a possible total of eight, to beat 5 (Figure 7). This is not only exactly halfway through the sequence, but also the point at which rhythmic unison – not exact unison, but still perceptible – is reached: the right hand of the moving player synchronises with the left hand of the stationary player, and vice versa (see again Ex. 3.14a). It occurs towards the end of the piece at 11′32″ in the 16′10″-long performance on the Shandar recording. This is the cue for Players 3 and 4 to bring in, unfaded, a second pattern, at 12′20″ (Figure 8). Like the first, it is based on the paradiddle model (see Ex. 3.14b) and, again, is phased only as far as its fifth beat (Figure 12). It is not, though, accompanied by resulting patterns. Instead, in the manner of *Violin Phase*, the first two players continue with the phased version of the first pattern they had already reached as a background against which the second pattern moves forward.

The spacing and modality of Part One (see again Ex. 3.14a) recall those of the first part of *Piano Phase*. Yet its five pitch classes – with E doubled at the octave and a top G extending the span to a tenth – contain a secundal dissonance, F♯ G, all the sharper for being a minor ninth rather than a semitone. They not only reinforce the tonic E triadically, but its dominant too, combining tonic and dominant, just as *Four Organs* had, in a single chord rich in potential; a chord which makes *Phase Patterns* just the latest in the list of pieces, starting with *Melodica*, which are based on such pitch material. In the work as a whole, triadic emphasis, neighbour-note oscillation, secundal dissonance and ultimate shift to an area of more ambiguous modality all come together, however, to allow the tonality of *Phase Patterns* to condition, and underpin, its resulting patterns with an energy of its own, and to provide a 'coda' which some may indeed hear as a kind of resolution all the more effective for the surprise of its proposed new key of C major.

The trip to Africa (and his later study of Indonesian gamelan)

Reich's treatment of the organ as a percussion instrument is surprising only in the immediate context of an apparently growing interest in harmony. Pulse-dominated percussion-based music had in fact fascinated him since he was a child, as we have seen. And as a student, he had become particularly excited by African drumming, with its complex counterpoint generated with the aid of multiple downbeats in an essentially ensemble context. As a member of Berio's composition class, he had gone to a composers' conference in Ojai, California, in the summer of 1962, where he encountered the composer, conductor and musicologist Gunther Schuller, then already contemplating his authoritative history of early jazz.[45] Schuller recommended A. M. Jones's then fairly recently published, now classic, *Studies in African Music*,[46] and the following year Reich derived more of his first knowledge of African musical structures from reading this book, and its accompanying volume of transcriptions, than from actual listening. He later corresponded with Jones and had two lessons in New York from Alfred Ladzepko, a master drummer of the Ewe tribe.

Reich now determined to spend a period studying African drumming in Ghana, feeling that, as he wrote three years later, 'non-Western music is presently the single most important source of new ideas for Western composers and musicians'.[47] In the summer of 1970, he arrived in Accra, the capital of Ghana, for what was intended to be a stay of several months, supported by a travel grant from the Special Projects division of the Institute of International Education. Contracting malaria after only five weeks, his visit was cut drastically short. But this brief experience of daily

Example 3.15 Ewe tribe – Ghana, *Agbadza*

lessons with Gideon Alorworye, another Ewe master drummer, gave him just as much as he needed. Alorworye was in residence with the Ghana Dance Ensemble in the Institute of African Studies at the University of Ghana. Reich recorded each lesson with him, and later transcribed the bell, rattle and drum patterns he had learned. These experiences allowed him to find out a good deal about the structure of African ensemble music, its texture characteristically consisting of an unchanging bell (gong-gong) pattern, a related rattle pattern and the drum patterns which overlay these. It is the relationship of each drum pattern to the gong-gong that is most important, and in particular, the polyrhythmic counterpoint of patterns of different lengths and different downbeats which results.

Example 3.15, one of three transcriptions of Reich's own reproduced in the *Writings* volume,[48] demonstrates the essence of this type of musical structure. Though the other two are, he claims, the first attempts to reproduce the basic drumming of Gahu and the Hatsyiatsya patterns on which it is based, Example 3.15 is the only one of the three to have a gong-gong pattern in $\frac{12}{8}$ (top line): not only the most common in West Africa, but also the time signature which Reich had, as we have seen, come to value most for its polyrhythmic potential. Though the downstrokes of the rattle part (second line) double the gong-gong, the upper notes filling in the rests, this pattern, while of the same $\frac{12}{8}$ length, begins on the second crotchet (the third quaver beat) of the gong-gong pattern. Against these, the three drum parts illustrate different relationships. The kagan (third line) plays short, unchanging $\frac{3}{8}$ patterns with downbeats on the third, sixth, ninth and twelfth quaver beats of the gong-gong. The sogo master drummer (fifth line) begins with a four-quaver pattern dividing $\frac{12}{8}$ into three groups of four (itself subject to improvised variations); then – after continuous quavers signalling the impending change of pattern – continues with a six-quaver pattern, similarly commencing on the gong-gong's main downbeat but this time incorporating syncopations. The kidi (fourth line), meanwhile, responds to the master drummer by providing quaver beats in sogo's rests, also doubling sogo's beats with muted ones of its own, likewise in $\frac{4}{8}$

groupings but two quaver beats' distant from sogo – which means its downbeats are on the third, seventh and eleventh quavers of the gong-gong.

Wishing to penetrate beneath the 'exotic' surface of such music – thus helping to avoid the temptation, surrendered to, in his view, by earlier generations of Western composers fascinated by non-Western musics, merely to re-create its sounds – Reich was committed to learning as much as possible about its structure and essence. He was especially attracted by the polymetric ingenuities to be found in African ensemble music such as the example just described. But as a composer, rather than an ethnomusicologist, he was concerned to retain his Western individuality and not get too involved. That illness may have been a blessing in disguise.

Regarding the effect his visit to Africa had on his work, and *Drumming* in particular, Reich wrote that '[t]he answer is *confirmation*. It confirmed my intuition that acoustic instruments could be used to produce music that was genuinely richer in sound than that produced by electronic instruments, as well as confirming my natural inclination towards percussion'.[49] The trip to Accra served as a 'green light' for him to place percussion at the centre of his ensemble. It also alerted him to the potential of voices as a part of such an ensemble: not for articulating texts in any conventional Western, or for that matter African, sense – something Reich would continue to reject for another ten years – but to sing nonsense syllables tied closely to the music's rhythmic structure and to imitate the sound of instruments themselves. While this fitted in well with the expansion of timbres that was one of the main characteristics of his compositional development, African music also encouraged Reich to see new dimensions in the virtues of simplicity. The hand clapping that so often underpins an African ensemble, for instance, was surely one inspiration for his own *Clapping Music*.

Reich's aesthetic approach to non-Western music was thus governed by his already familiar constructivist attitude. Though in the course of the early 1970s he became less obsessed by the need to make the structural details of his own compositions as audible as possible, the expressive concerns behind his own work remained in marked contrast to those of Western Classical and Romantic music. Though West African music has an important improvisatory element to it, he was fascinated by the control exerted on individual expression by the limitations within which that improvisation must be conducted. 'The pleasure I get from playing', the composer wrote in 1974, 'is not the pleasure of expressing myself, but of subjugating myself to the music and experiencing the ecstasy that comes from being a part of it'.[50] That subjugation of the individual in the controlled activities of an ensemble in which each musician knows the precise nature of his contribution to the whole is, he discovered, as typical – if not more typical – of the Indonesian gamelan. In addition, Reich was attracted by the integration of dance and music in both African and Indonesian cultures. His relationship with the dancer and choreographer Laura Dean in 1970–73 led to several of his own compositions being used for dance purposes: something taken up by many other choreographers since that time.

In the summers of 1973 and 1974, Reich took advantage of Bob Brown's establishment of the American Society for Eastern Arts to travel West and take lessons, from native musicians, in Balinese gamelan. In the first year, he went to Seattle, Washington, where his main teacher was Nyo Man Sumandi; the year after to the Center for World Music in Berkeley, California, where he was taught by Pak Sinti. In both cases, he taught his own music as well. Balinese music has certain similarities to that of Ghana: its individual parts are usually simple to play, and the chief interest derives from an ensemble producing multiple downbeats. 'Not being a virtuoso', he writes, 'not being interested in improvisation, and being thoroughly committed to my own ensemble that performs music I have composed with repetitive patterns combined so that their downbeats do not always coincide, it may be natural for my interests to run strongly towards Balinese and African music'.[51] Furthermore, what Mantle Hood describes as the 'stratification'[52] of the Indonesian gamelan's complex layering of pitch as well as rhythmic material is also an apt term for Reich's music.

The gamelan, with its typical texture of fast interlocking patterns underpinned by slower, more harmonic material performed by an ensemble dominated by metallophones, seems an inevitable influence on *Music for Mallet Instruments, Voices and Organ*. Its composer, however, only undertook his formal studies in Balinese music after completing this work. The use of a percussion instrument (in Reich's case the vibraphone) as an aural cue to mark section and other changes in the later *Music for Eighteen Musicians* was inspired by the use both West African and Indonesian ensembles make of the drummer for similar purposes.

The expansion of Reich's reputation and his changing aesthetic to 1976

From his SoHo base, Reich's reputation slowly spread, fuelled in considerable part by recordings. The composer may be the first to have an important record company behind the release of every significant piece he has written. *Come Out* was issued on Columbia Records in 1967 as part of an album entitled *New Sounds in Electronic Music*. One of some two-dozen or more releases of new music produced by David Behrman at this time, including Riley's *In C*, the record received reviews and press coverage – including articles in *Time* and *New York* magazines – which 'put me on the map', says Reich. The same company's issue of *It's Gonna Rain* and *Violin Phase* (performed by Zukofsky), on the album *Steve Reich: Live/Electric Music*, furthered this process two years later. The already mentioned Whitney and Guggenheim Museum concerts in 1969 and 1970 did a good deal to further Reich's career, as did the European tour with Glass in the spring of 1971. Even before the première of the complete *Drumming* in New York at the end of that year, Reich had moved from being known largely by the downtown artistic community to national and even international attention.

Important in this development were two performances of *Four Organs* in concerts by the Boston Symphony Orchestra, mounted through the advocacy of the conductor Michael Tilson Thomas: in Boston on 8 October 1971 and New York's Carnegie Hall on 18 January 1973. Reich's first performances by musicians besides those of his own group – and his first to be given in major Western classical concerts halls – still took place, however, at his own insistence, with himself as both rehearsal supervisor and performer (and Tilson Thomas as one of the other organists). Some members of these largely very conservative audiences, including most critics, were hostile; accounts of the Carnegie Hall performance – their variations on the theme of concert as riot are a textbook case of uncorroborated, sometimes conflicting details – include the brandishing of umbrellas and a woman walking down to the front, perhaps banging her head on the platform and crying, among several alternatives, '[a]ll right – I'll confess!'[53] Despite, or just possibly because of, such notoriety, Reich could probably at this point have obtained an orchestral commission through Tilson Thomas if he had really pressed for it. Surprisingly, too, Pierre Boulez chose *Phase Patterns* for a New York Philharmonic 'Prospective Encounter' programme on 29 October 1971, just three weeks after the Boston performance of *Four Organs*; in this case, though, Reich's own musicians were the performers.

Only in the late 1970s, however – when the increasing size of Steve Reich and Musicians not only led him naturally towards the real orchestra but also posed increasing practical problems for a composer still undertaking many of the responsibilities of management – did he first attempt a work for forces other than those of his own group: *Music for a Large Ensemble*. Though a few performances by others took place in the 1970s – with the aid of manuscript copies passed on by Cornelius Cardew in Britain, for instance, and a student performance of *Drumming*, Part Two, in Seattle in the summer of 1973, in which different singers came up with new resulting patterns subsequently incorporated into performances by Steve Reich and Musicians – it was not until 1980 that any substantial number of the composer's early scores was commercially published;[54] and not until the mid-1980s, and then only slowly, that more recent scores started to become widely available.[55]

For some time, art galleries and museums, particularly those sympathetic to Minimalist art, remained the most hospitable. Following the attention his early recordings received, music critics began to write more consistently about Reich in the early 1970s. Daniel Caux's enthusiastic review of the composer's 1971 Paris concert assisted the already mentioned issue that year, by Shandar, of the LP devoted to *Four Organs* and *Phase Patterns* which helped raise his music's profile, in Europe as well as in the USA. Michael Nyman championed his cause in Britain.[56] Major exposure later that year at West German festivals in Bremen and Berlin helped consolidate Reich's position, at least on the avant-garde music scene, despite the hostility his works still sometimes created, including the psychological and social, as well as purely musical, difficulties some in Germany had with music so devoted to a regular pulse. 1973 saw the release, on the Angel label, of a second recording of *Four Organs*, involving Tilson Thomas. And in 1974, through the intervention of Rudolph Werner, the prestigious classical label Deutsche Grammophon released *Drumming* as part of a three-disc set with *Six Pianos* and *Music for Mallet Instruments, Voices and Organ*.

Back home, while critics such as Donal Henahan of the *New York Times* often continued to be scathing,[57] others more sympathetic to Reich's work were gradually emerging. As mentioned in the Introduction, Tom Johnson – himself a minimalist composer – marked the beginning of his tenure at the *Village Voice* with a review of *Drumming*'s première.[58] Soon after this, John Rockwell also began regular coverage of Reich's music, and the downtown music scene in general, for the *New York Times*.[59]

It was to be another few years, however, before the première of *Music for Eighteen Musicians*, and a further two before the commercial recording of this made Reich's music widely known internationally. Deutsche Grammophon recorded the work, but were uncertain as to whether they could successfully market it. Eventually, Roland Kommerall – in charge of the PolyGram group of which Deutsche Grammophon was part – took the unusual step of letting the recording go to Manfred Eicher's ECM label, which had a track record in the promotion of experimental jazz and other more 'difficult' musics to largely non-classical audiences. Robert Hurwitz – who worked for ECM at the time, and who later moved to the Nonesuch company, taking Reich with him in 1984 – has written that the release of *Music for Eighteen Musicians* was 'a genuine breakthrough for new music, and it proved to many of us that contemporary music could appeal to more than just a small, specialized audience'.[60]

Reich's aesthetic development in the early 1970s

It is clear that Reich's main preoccupation from 1965 to at least 1970 was with structure and, in particular, with the purity and clarity of that structure. In order to achieve structural audibility, the music had to be extremely simple, with 'all the cards . . . on the table'.[61] The rate of change, too, had to be slow: 'everyone hears what is gradually happening in a musical process'. Everything depended on how the small changes in this music were perceived. Early on, too – as we have seen – Reich had realised the joy of being free of reading notation. Yet such objective, 'experimental' absorption in pure process had, in reality, seldom been the whole story, and it had recently taken a few further knocks. As Nyman perceptively pointed out in an extended interview with the composer in 1976, the articulation of resulting patterns by instruments imposes one performer's view of them on others, and thus promotes subjectivity as much as it encourages structural clarity. Now, as Reich began to deploy resulting patterns performed by forces different from those which instigated them – as when, according to the original plan, voices produce resulting patterns from the original bongo and marimba material in, respectively, Parts One and Two of *Drumming*, and the glockenspiel material of Part Three is taken up by both vocal whistling and piccolo – the whole approach to sound is changed. '[T]he doubling', as Nyman puts it, 'separates out from what is doubled'.[62] Even before the more complex textures of Part Four are reached, *Drumming* has already accomplished the move from a quintessentially 'experimental', flat texture to something more resembling a melody-plus-accompaniment one.

In the same interview – among the most penetrating he has ever given – Reich suggests that, immediately he had written it, he found *Piano Phase* 'lacking a certain kind of musical excitement and interest that I personally am attracted to', on account of its reliance on phasing without resulting patterns. It would be naïve to suppose that a composer interested in 'a compositional process and a sounding music that are one and the same thing'[63] could ever be somehow uninterested in the actual sound his music made. Reich, however, seems constantly to have questioned whether he was over-preoccupied with structure as such, and to have increasingly felt the limitations of treating sound itself as merely the means by which structure was articulated.

Reich's move from 'structure' as such to greater concern with sound was itself a gradual process. The resulting patterns first used compositionally in *Violin Phase* may be psycho-acoustic in origin, but they arguably serve to reinforce the work's structure as much as they focus on the music's texture. Even as *Four Organs* breaks the 'mould' of phasing, it appears to enforce a new severity of structural purpose, though the process involved is, in fact, not 'pure'. These days, Reich himself views all his compositions before *Drumming* as 'very radical works that . . . have a kind of etude status. They are studies – very rigorous studies, [monomanically] exclusive studies – in a technique that I had discovered and was absolutely pursuing single-mindedly'. The extent to which *Drumming* draws on a wider range of musical techniques, as well as its significantly larger scope, makes it much more than an 'etude'. This expansion beyond phasing seems to demonstrate an impatience not only with the limitations of a technique Reich had mined assiduously for some six years, but also with being tied exclusively to any highly rigorous approach to a single technical procedure, no matter how imaginatively that technique was explored and set in new contexts. It also demonstrated the lessening importance for him of the audibility of any structural process.

Mature minimalist compositions

The year 1971 saw the completion of *Drumming*, begun the previous year and the crowning achievement of this period. *Drumming* is considerably more substantial, in terms both of length and complexity, than any of its composer's previous works, and an important breakthrough both technically and stylistically. Its rigorous reliance on rhythmic processes nevertheless still makes the work sound more like a summing up of his early music than the beginning of something new. The two pieces which followed – *Clapping Music* (1972) and *Music for Pieces of Wood* (1973) – are short, 'etude-status' pieces once again. *Six Pianos* and *Music for Mallet Instruments, Voices and Organ*, on the other hand – both completed in the first months of 1973 for their premières in the same concert on 16 May that year, at New York's John Weber Gallery – are more important statements. But it was not until March 1976 that Reich was able to complete *Music for Eighteen Musicians*, the work which capitalised on these developments and took them forward to an altogether new level.

Drumming

Drumming introduces a greater concern with sound as such: with the sheer sonic impact of timbre and texture made possible by contrasting and ultimately combining different groups of instruments as part of the evolving structure of an extended composition. Reich's ensemble was now expanded to include an extensive range of tuned percussion instruments: bongo drums, marimbas and glockenspiels. Though he chose, he writes, 'instruments that are all now commonly available in Western countries',[64] all are redolent of their various – by no means exclusively African – origins.

And not only instruments: he now also added voices to his ensemble for the first time. Though impressed by his African experiences of voices combined with drumming, it was a long-held admiration for the scat singing of Ella Fitzgerald that now inspired Reich to explore the possibilities of using voices wordlessly – 'to become part of the musical ensemble by imitating the exact sound of the instruments'. He has written that '[w]hile first playing the drums during the process of composition, I found myself sometimes singing with them, using my voice to imitate the sounds they made. I began to understand that this might also be possible with the marimbas and glockenspiels'.[65] The score suggests 'using syllables like "tak", "duk", and so forth'; all voices must be amplified. Despite his own vocal efforts, and though both male and female voices are specified at different points in the scores which have up to now been available,[66] Reich favoured the female voice from early in the work's composition and rehearsal. Men's voices were soon abandoned, though perceptive listeners may be able to detect a single male voice – the composer's – on the Deutsche Grammophon recording. Singers and/or players contribute resulting patterns at various stages of the phasing process in each movement.

The decision to use percussion, and to avoid the keyboard instruments which had dominated his instrumental output in the previous few years, suggests, perhaps surprisingly, the retention of a firm focus on rhythm at the expense of Reich's still new interest in harmony. The basic material of *Drumming* was – furthermore, and unusually for Reich – conceived initially as pure rhythm: patterns inspired, in fact, by the mundane act of strumming his fingers on a table while on the telephone. But while it was his first work to begin life in the form of a rhythmic pattern, this was later 'given a great variety of pitches'.

According to his publisher's catalogue, *Drumming* (composed between the autumn of 1970 and the autumn of 1971) may last between fifty-seven and eighty-six minutes.[67] The original 1974 LP recording takes around eighty minutes: the longest the work ever got, according to Reich himself. The 1987 Nonesuch CD version (the only one currently available, and from which the timings below are taken) takes 56′44″. Though all his works to this date from *Piano Phase* onwards permit of some variability in length, owing to the freedom allowed for the repetition of each 'figure', most performances seem to have lasted between about fifteen and twenty minutes, usually closer to the former. *Drumming* thus represents a substantial change of scope. In 1974, Reich gave the work's length as 'about one and a half hours'[68] and wrote that it had 'turned out to be the longest piece I have ever composed'.

The composer does, however, divide *Drumming* into four parts, each lasting the sort of length an earlier whole piece of his would have done. Though these are continuous in a complete performance, each part is also playable separately. The main reason for this division is the opportunity it affords to exploit, contrast and eventually bring together a timbral palette much larger than any he had previously used. Part One is scored for drums (originally plus male voices, as we have seen), Part Two for marimbas and female voices, Part Three for glockenspiels, whistling and piccolo (substitutes for the previous vocal activity, the pitches now being too high to sing); Part Four combines all the musicians required for the previous three to make a highly original kind of 'orchestra'. Transitions to each new timbre are continuous and gradual: while the previous group fades out, the new one fades in, 'the new instruments doubling the exact pattern of the instruments already playing'.[69]

The way in which these forces are deployed is designed to produce a dramatic curve: rising from Part One (17′30″) to Part Two (18′10″), then falling for the 'scherzo' of Part Three (11′12″), prior to a further rise for the climactic Part Four (9′44″). Simultaneously with this overall emotional trajectory there runs an even simpler one based on register: rising in steps from the G♯ – C♯ (a low version of composer's familiar 'low treble') of Part One through the expansion up to C♯ two octaves higher of Part Two, to the glockenspiels of Part Three, which rise to A♯ almost two octaves above that. Part Four then employs almost the full range: from the drums' low G♯ up to the glockenspiel's high A♯. In *Drumming* Reich takes on, for the first time, the challenge of sustaining the listener's attention over a long time-span, putting to good use his experiences of constructing fifteen- to twenty-minute forms of considerable structural sophistication to produce a large-scale work of cumulative complexity and power.

In *Writings*, the composer says that the work 'is the final expansion and refinement of the phasing process, as well as the first use of four new techniques'.[70] In terms of both rhythm and timbre, *Drumming* breaks important new ground. Of the new techniques, one is the already mentioned use of voices. The second is purely rhythmic: the process Reich calls 'gradually substituting beats for rests (or rests for beats) within a constantly repeating rhythmic cycle', or, respectively, 'rhythmic construction' and 'rhythmic reduction' (the former already explored in *Four Organs*). The third and fourth are, like the first, essentially timbral: 'the gradual changing of timbre while rhythm and pitch remain constant'; and 'the simultaneous combination of instruments of different timbre'.

All four parts of *Drumming* are based on a single pattern, once again of twelve quaver beats, given in Example 3.16a. The Basic Unit changes not only its phase position and timbre, but also its pitch configuration; Reich reveals the pattern's rhythmic origins when he says that 'all the performers play this pattern, or some part of it, throughout the entire piece'.[71] This typically Reichian construct gives rise to a technical *tour de force* as the potential ambiguities of different downbeats resulting from many subdivisions of twelve into twos, threes, fours and sixes are exploited. Since the crotchet, rather than the quaver, becomes the main building block both compositionally and perceptually, 'beats' will from here onwards refer to crotchets, not quavers. Part One of the work will be analysed in some detail to demonstrate how Reich combines already familiar techniques with new ones to create one of his most sophisticated structures while retaining essentially simple means. Shorter discussions of Parts Two, Three and Four will then illustrate a few more of the timbral and modal, as well as rhythmic, ingenuities to be found in the remainder of the work.

Analysis of Drumming, *Part One*

Part One introduces the drums in a small ensemble of eight small tuned drums, or bongos. The bongos are stand-mounted in pairs, divided into two groups (one for each pair of players), and tuned to four pitches: in ascending order, G♯, A♯, B and C♯. They are played with both hard and soft sticks. Since the two performers in each pair face each other, playing the same four drums, neither pitch order nor use of left and right hands will be the same for each, and the latter is left to the musicians' choice.

The second 'new technique' mentioned above – that of 'rhythmic construction' – makes its appearance at the outset, as two drummers assemble the Basic Unit note by note. (The original score suggests 'two, three or four drummers', but the revised score adopts the simple pair of players long since used by the composer's own ensemble.) This process, which takes just over a minute, is later reversed; after Figure 15 (9'36"), the Basic Unit is progressively reduced to a single note, played just once. Within this framework, a series of 'fuzzy transitions' carries the phasing process forward; each of these transitions occupies between about twenty and thirty seconds. There are four such transitions, in which the Basic Unit is twice moved out of phase on a simple crotchet-by-crotchet basis, then subjected to a more complex procedure described below. On three of these stages, resulting patterns are constructed, the patterns entering and leaving in the now familiar crescendo/diminuendo fashion. The score specifies no lengths for these sections; on the 1987 recording, each occupies between about one and three minutes. They provide the main 'meat' of the movement.

When 'rhythmic reduction' has reversed the opening process (10′54″), soft sticks are exchanged for the original hard ones, and a slightly different version of the Basic Unit is now assembled (from Figure 23). A further series of 'fuzzy transitions' of similar length then unfolds. This time, there are five of them, in which the Basic Unit is again twice moved out of phase, then subjected to more complex treatment, once again described below. In this shorter section, though, no resulting patterns are highlighted. Instead (starting at Figure 35), all four players prepare for the timbral change to Part Two by alternating between hard and soft sticks. While Players 1–3 retain the phasing positions they have reached, three marimba players, using soft rubber mallets, fade in with the same patterns (Figure 47), which the drummers now fade out (concluding at 17′30″).

Each figure gradually assembling the Basic Unit, at the opening of Part One, is repeated 'at least six or eight' times; when one drummer moves to the next figure, the other may either join him at once or continue with the same figure and join him after a few more repeats. This initial process of rhythmic construction already offers a subtle range of ambiguities both metrical (it can be heard, for instance, in both $\frac{6}{4}$ and $\frac{3}{2}$) and tonal (G♯ and B establishing positions of primacy in a pitch gamut reductive even by Reich's standards).

Players 1 and 2 then commence the sequence of 'fixed' and 'moving' patterns of the basic phasing process that follows. The other pair (Players 3 and 4) now participates in the resulting patterns against this continuing 'grid'. The score's range of resulting patterns for 'drummers 3 & 4 and/or male voices' rings the changes on a Basic Unit using only four pitches with considerable resourcefulness; both Reich's previous instrumental compositions with separately articulated resulting patterns had employed five pitch classes for their Basic Units (and, in *Phase Patterns*, a second pattern introducing a sixth one). The distribution of phasing patterns and resulting patterns is the most complex combination of the two which Reich ever devised for a single pattern without pitch extensions. Example 3.16b–d demonstrates the nature of these patterns' evolution through the

Example 3.16 *Drumming*, Part One: (a) Figure 9 (Basic Unit); (b) Figure 10;
(c) Figure 11 (Drummers 1 and 2 and composite of resulting patterns only);
(d) Figure 13 (Drummers 1–3 and composite of resulting patterns only); (e)
Figure 28; (f) Figure 42.

Example 3.16 (*cont.*)

(*e*)

Drummers

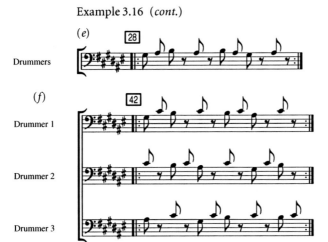

(*f*)

Drummer 1

Drummer 2

Drummer 3

three figures involved; the following notes also make a few observations on what can be heard on the Nonesuch recording.

In Stage One (Figure 10), both resulting patterns notated in the score are four bars in length, each covering four statements of the Basic Unit, itself now written out in two-bar repeating sequences (see Ex. 3.16b). Each resulting pattern outlines a broadly descending sequence in each bar, revolving initially around C♯ and B, the upper pair of pitches; one pattern obligingly picks up all four available C♯s on the first four beats, alternating them with B. More important, however, is the fact that almost every bar articulates the lower pair of pitches, A♯ and G♯, in a kind of extended upbeat to the next bar's main downbeat, implying a ii–i reinforcing G♯ (sometimes accompanied by its mediant, B) as the central pitch. This is further emphasised by a crotchet-based pattern using all four pitches in a descending sequence from C♯ to G♯. It is this which dominates the early moments of Stage One in the 1987 recording; they can, in fact, be heard for some time in every bar, either as the effect of multiple repetitions of the two notated patterns, or as a consequence of newly invented ones. Later, the focus is on A♯G♯. The patterns here suggest $\frac{6}{4}$ rather than the previously dominant $\frac{3}{2}$.

In Stage Two (Figure 11), one notated resulting pattern is eight bars long, the other four bars (see Ex. 3.16c, which gives only the composite of this stage of the phasing process). In the composite itself, C♯ now occurs on the second, fourth and sixth beats, making it suitable for incorporation into a resulting pattern establishing a strong alternative downbeat and a marked contrast to Figure 10. Instead, the eight-bar pattern makes the C♯ on beat 4 the top of the curve of a short sequence in mid-bar that initially alternates with the other pitches' emphasis on beats 1, 3 and 5, suggesting $\frac{3}{2}$.

After repeating this in bar 3, though, this pattern abandons C♯ until the second beat of its penultimate bar. The four-bar pattern offers just a single C♯, on beat 2 of its first bar, being more concerned with stressing the opening G♯B quavers of the Basic Unit in its unphased form. On the 1987 recording, the most obvious elements seem to be, first, the G♯A♯ sequences in $\frac{3}{2}$ and, following these, groups of five quavers on quavers 1–5 and 7–11, which suggest $\frac{6}{4}$. Cross-rhythms feature prominently in the deployment of the resulting patterns in this performance of Stage Two.

After this, at Figure 12, a drummer from the second pair (Player 3) enters with the unphased Basic Unit in unison with Player 1, prior to phasing one beat ahead (beat 2), thus occupying a position midway between Player 1 (beat 1) and Player 2 (still on beat 3). The third section of resulting patterns thus has three simultaneous canonic statements of the Basic Unit from which to draw its material, but only one drummer (Player 4) to perform them.

In Stage Three (Figure 13), the score offers four patterns: one of four bars, plus three each of a single bar to be repeated (see Ex. 3.16d, which gives, again, only the composite). A notable feature of the new contrapuntal composite is that B now occurs on every quaver. One of these single repeated bars is accordingly devoted solely to quaver Bs, which are also taken up by beats 5 and 6 of the four-bar pattern. Additionally, all the other bars of the longer pattern place B at their beginning, and in general they offset the potential metric anarchy of continuous quaver Bs by emphasising the main crotchet beats. On the 1987 recording, the main effect is again of descending sequences, moving quite quickly from C♯ to stress A♯ and G♯.

Following this, at Figure 14, Player 4 moves directly, without phasing, to Stage Four (beat 4). When the consequent four simultaneous statements of the Basic Unit have been held for about a minute, Players 2, 3 and 4 move ahead, without pausing on each 'notch', until all are back in unison with Player 1's 'fixed' version (Figures 15–16). The cycle of phasing has thus been completed in a telescoped manner taking '30–45 seconds', characterised by a tumble of patterns, more chaotic and exciting than usual, moving in 'fuzzy' mode from different positions at slightly different speeds. With the return of all four players to the Basic Unit in unison, 'rhythmic reduction' now proceeds (Figures 16–22) until only a single, unrepeated G♯ remains: the logical conclusion of the tonal focus that this process has itself highlighted. With the switch to soft sticks (Figure 23), the altered version of the Basic Unit, now constructed by at least two players, leaves out C♯ entirely for the moment, but preserves not only the rhythms but also the shape and tonal emphasis of the original (see Ex. 3.16e).

As before, Players 1 and 2 begin the phasing sequence, the latter moving progressively to the third 'notch'. While this combination (on beats 1 and

3) is once again frozen, Player 3 this time joins Player 2, then proceeds from this new position a further two 'notches', to beat 5. With no separately articulated resulting patterns to be performed this time, on these three phasing positions – on beats 1, 3 and 5, the combination itself suggesting $\frac{3}{2}$ – Player 4 briefly replaces each of his colleagues in turn to facilitate the change back to hard sticks. This accomplished, and Players 1–3 all remaining in position, Player 1 exchanges the A♯s on quavers 5 and 8 in the alternative Basic Unit to C♯s, a procedure progressively adopted by Players 2 and 3 (Figures 39–41). Further modification – involving exchange of another A♯ for a C♯, but also the replacement of a G♯ by A♯ itself – allows the emergence, though not the players' own reinforcement, of a resulting pattern of continuous quaver C♯s (see Ex. 3.16f). Also audible as a response to the previously reiterated Bs of Stage Three, this nicely complements the C♯ tonality of the incoming Part Two, allowing the G♯ of Part One to be interpreted as its dominant: another instance in Reich's output of accepting the 'natural forces' inherent in the repetition of a single pitch, while retaining the modal complexities that come with this. A final change back to soft sticks, again with the aid of Player 4, permits the three main drummers of Part One to blend with the emerging three main marimba players of Part Two.

Parts Two, Three *and* Four

Part Two uses only three instruments. But the choice of marimbas and number of performers involved here are crucial: with nine players altogether, the sound is newly rich and strange. To this marimba mini-orchestra are added two female singers ('two, three, or more female singers' in the original score), vocalising wordlessly. These supply a further dimension to the woody percussive timbre, exploiting and enhancing the marimbas' natural tendency to produce a halo of upper partials. Marimbas and voices together provide not only a much fuller texture than any its composer had previously used, but also one in which tonal emphasis can play a particularly well-defined and subtle part in the uncovering of resulting patterns. In the sections for marimbas alone, on the other hand, the nature of these instruments contributes almost as much to the difficulties of hearing the structural details of the basic phasing process as does the increased contrapuntal complexity of that phasing process itself.

Once the marimbas have phase-shifted the drumming pattern of Part One back to unison, they begin to add a sequence of patterns – all derived from the Basic Unit – expanding the register upwards via the gradual addition of new players: first to G♯ (Figure 51), then to F♯ (Figure 58) and finally to high C♯ (Figure 63), adding the pitches on which the glockenspiels of

Part Three can enter, after the marimbas' lower patterns have gradually been faded out. Example 3.17a gives the combined patterns of Part Two, demonstrating their differing responses to the shape of the opening one, and the now expanded modality incorporating all seven pitch classes in the six-sharp key signature. With C♯ occupying a stronger, partly because more regular, position in the pattern than it had in the majority of Part One, Reich is now able to exploit much further the kind of dominant/tonic ambiguities which he favoured earlier. Player 1's left-hand lower voice, for instance – all pitches other than C♯ – simultaneously forms a iii–ii–i cadence emphasising G♯ as a tonal centre.

The progressive expansion is based on the now familiar 'stacked' fourths/fifths scheme, allowing different pitches to emerge as it proceeds. The first new pattern to be added, for instance – starting on D♯, in parallel fifths with the opening one – reinforces G♯, implying an initial modulation from C♯ to G♯. Ambiguities are compounded by the stacking up of patterns itself, eventually producing a complex interaction of multiple tonal centres forming the common pentatonic scale, with G♯, C♯ and F♯ emerging as the strongest pitches. As the patterns fade out at the end, however, D♯, F♯ and finally A♯ emerge in turn in a kind of modulatory process which Reich was to explore again in later works.

Meanwhile, the resulting patterns arising from Part Two's cycle of phasing provide further modifications to the modal mix. These resulting patterns are now performed by a separate group, the singers; the score gives them a much wider range of patterns and offers them considerable flexibility in their use, as well as the option of creating new ones. Released from any responsibility to supply resulting patterns, all nine marimba players are free to pile versions of their proliferating phase patterns on top of each other. Like Part One, Part Two evolves in a two-part sequence. Firstly, a two-stage process offers repeating patterns on the first two, and then the first three beats (Figures 49–55, based on the expansion to G♯). Secondly, after a return to unison, a three-stage process yields repeating patterns up to a combination of beats 1, 2 and 3 (Figures 56–63). With the arrival of top C♯, Player 7's new pattern is immediately supplied, by Players 8 and 9, with 'notches' of its own phasing cycle on beats 2 and 3 without any intervening 'fuzzy transitions'. After the fade-out process described above, it is these three players who are left holding their patterns while three of the erstwhile marimba players transfer to glockenspiels, and Part Three begins.

Part Three, at 11'12", is much shorter. Its move to the high register of three glockenspiels played by four musicians – plus the amplified whistling of resulting patterns by a single performer or a pair of performers, moving

Example 3.17 *Drumming*: (a) Part Two, Figure 63 (Marimbas and composite of resulting patterns only); (b) Part Three, Figure 71; (c) Part Four, Figure 109.

(*a*)

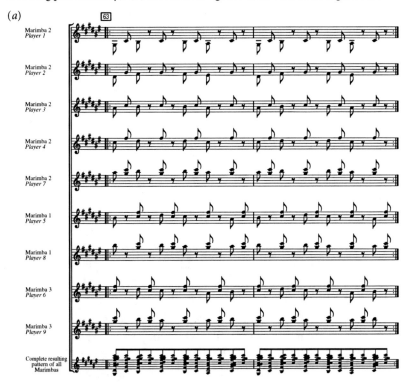

(*b*)

(*c*)

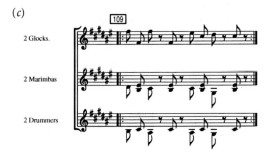

to the piccolo when the register becomes too high to whistle – forms a natural conclusion to the upward registral expansion charted by Parts One and Two. Though it functions as *Drumming*'s scherzo, it is structurally the most complex movement yet encountered.

Part Three preserves the broad outlines and tonal approach of Part Two, while modifying the relationship between the cycle of phasing, articulation of resulting patterns and registral expansion. After a phase-shifting of the final marimba pattern of Part Two back to unison, following the practice adopted earlier, phasing of its own version of the Basic Unit (see Ex. 3.17b) is carried forward two 'notches', involving all four players (Figures 70–77). Registral expansion to its upper limit, E♯, has, though, already occurred with the arrival of Player 2 at Figure 72. And before the expected resulting patterns can occur – on the patterns now formed on the expected beats 1, 2 and 3 of the phasing process – Player 4 modifies his pattern: clarifying the combination then available at Figure 78 for the resulting patterns' Stage One. One dimension of this clarification is the reintroduction of pitches below E♯: in particular, A♯, which now, providing its mediant, underpins a clear tonal focus on F♯. Player 4's modified version is then adopted in turn by Players 1 and 3, Player 2 retaining his original pattern with the high E♯s. Stage Two of the resulting patterns, in which the piccolo takes over from the whistling, now takes place (Figure 80).

Stage Three is formed on a further modification of the pattern, which is assembled and phased by three players – to produce patterns on beats 1, 2 and 3 once more – around the previous version, which Player 1 continues alone (Figures 80–87). Lowering the top pitch to D♯, this modification also includes B♯s for the first time in *Drumming* (Figures 83–90), suggesting a modulation to C♯ major; the resulting patterns themselves, though, tend to emphasise the high D♯ itself. One interpretation of the tonal scheme of Part Three – emboldened partly, it would seem, by the appearance of B♯s – argues for a symmetrical progression from F♯ through C♯ and A♯ to D♯, and back again. The final minutes (Figures 88–101) – in which yet another version of the pattern, revolving around F♯ itself, takes over – certainly emphasise the return to F♯. This is eventually subjected to the substitution of notes by rests, its reduction to a single F♯ mirroring the close of Part One.

While Part Three's F♯ tonality fits nicely into what appears to be an evolving scheme of central pitches – G♯ (Part One), C♯ (Part Two), F♯ – itself derived from Reich's favoured 'stacked' fourths/fifths, it should be noted that the high register of the glockenspiels, and their accompanying whistling, makes the detailed pitch content of Part Three quite difficult to discern; the higher glockenspiel patterns, in particular, are heard more as rhythmic articulations, or even as merely a jumble of overlapping pulses, than as pitch sequences, though the resulting patterns suggest pitch content and direction more readily. In Part Four, however, the previous movement's focus on F♯ contributes to a combination of tonal emphases as rich and complex as are the finale's bringing together of the textural and rhythmic characteristics of all three earlier movements. Part Four represents *Drumming*'s natural, indeed inevitable, culmination, combining the three groups of performers previously deployed separately into a celebratory final ten minutes (9′44″ on the 1987 recording). Its relative brevity can be accounted for not only by the psychological requirements of a composition that has already held its audience for nearly three-quarters of an hour before the movement arrives, but also by the amount of information it packs into its contrapuntal space.

At its start, pairs of glockenspiels, marimbas and drums each assemble their own further new version of the Basic Unit by 'rhythmic construction' (Figures 102–9; Ex. 3.17c gives the completed pattern). This starts with, and centres on, the glockenspiels' F♯. The more prominent first three pitches of the marimba – D♯ C♯ G♯ – give its beginning a temporary focus on C♯, though: simultaneously suggesting the tonalities of Parts One and Two and anticipating Part Four's subsequent tonal development (see below). Phase shifting is then performed on all three patterns, the forward motion of each against its fixed timbral partner being staggered. The marimba is the first to move, followed by drum and glockenspiel (Figures 110–12). This sequence is then repeated, moving each player to beat 3 against his partner (Figures 113–15). At this point, each pair is turned into a trio by the addition of a new player on beat 3, and phasing moves ahead once more, to beat 4 (Figures 116–19) and beat 5 (Figures 120–22). With phasing now established on beats 1, 3 and 5 of each timbral group's independent pattern, a final riot of resulting patterns – which can occupy more than a third of this movement's length – brings the work to its conclusion.

Reich points out that the complexities of both the phase shifting itself and the resulting patterns here are saved from sheer confusion by timbral contrast.[72] The interdependence of the processes involved and their ultimate derivation from a single rhythmic pattern also give Part Four a cohesion amidst its undoubted variety; a cohesion further enhanced by the feeling one gains of the movement as an essentially unitary process, a single unravelling sweep of phasing leading straight into the consequences of its own momentum. That variety is tonal as well as timbral, and again it demonstrates a certain unity. On the one hand, each group's pattern demonstrates the wealth of ambiguities typical of such material, even when, as we saw earlier, one tonal centre may be interpreted as of greater significance than the rest. On the other hand, the progression from G♯ via C♯ to F♯ may now be said to culminate in a gigantic half cadence, implying closure on B♮ (now restored, after the B♯s of Part Three, and the next logical pitch in that 'stacked' sequence), but actually coming to rest on its dominant, F♯ (see Ex. 3.18). As in *Four Organs*, tonic and dominant, tension and

Example 3.18 *Drumming*, Part Four, Figure 122

resolution, are combined, fused into an entity different from that of conventional Western tonality, yet supplying something of that tonality's strength of purpose to modal certainties that are as old as the hills.

In *Drumming*, Reich extends his practice of using groups of identical instruments to develop a fresh approach to his instrumental forces; the blending, as well as the variety, of timbres found here is new in his output.

His abandonment, for the moment, both of any of the usual instruments of the Western 'classical' orchestra in their conventional groupings and of the keyboards which had been central to his music since 1966, suggested that the emerging Steve Reich and Musicians would focus on the tuned percussion inspired by Reich's trip to Africa. With this new array of timbral possibilities, he proved the continuing viability of a music based ultimately on rhythm, even if the details of that music's structures were now less audible than before. Yet *Drumming* also demonstrates an already quite sophisticated concern with harmony and tonality that would increasingly characterise Reich's output during the decade it helped set in motion.

1972–3

Clapping Music *and* Music for Pieces of Wood

In the immediate aftermath of *Drumming*, however, Reich bided his time over its pitch concerns, and wrote a small-scale piece devoted purely to his continuing fascination with rhythm. *Clapping Music* (its score dated April 1972) was written merely for the pairs of hands of two performers. Inspired by experiencing the rhythmic hand-clapping of a Brussels flamenco troupe, this was also a response to the practical complications which accompanied the touring of a work for a van-load of percussion instruments. Since the gradual sliding of phasing's 'fuzzy transitions' would be too difficult in this case, Reich simply subjected a typical twelve-beat Basic Unit (see Ex. 3.19) to a process of jumping directly from 'notch' to 'notch' of an otherwise typical cycle of phasing.

Each 'notch' in the second player's movement away from the fixed position of his partner gives the impression of creating a new pattern: another example of Reich's sleight-of-hand approach to the ambiguities of $\frac{12}{8}$ metre. The Basic Unit of *Clapping Music* throws not only placement within the metre but metre itself into doubt, by including notes on the fifth, eighth and tenth quavers. The listener can thus hear the complete pattern in a variety of ways; when performed in canon, the choice of downbeats is naturally increased. In addition, it can be difficult to hear that both performers are clapping the same pattern, despite the elementary character of the timbre involved. Even in a simple piece such as this, audibility of process is relegated in favour of its broader rhythmic consequences. Reich's fascination with $\frac{12}{8}$, and indeed with this particular pattern, was to be explored further when it became the Basic Unit of many of his later works, including *Music for Eighteen Musicians*.

Example 3.19 *Clapping Music*, Basic Unit

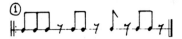

The composer's only other piece since *Drumming* to give primacy to rhythm over pitch is *Music for Pieces of Wood*, which followed *Clapping Music* over a year later, in November 1973. Its five pairs of claves deploy patterns built on the process of rhythmic construction found in *Drumming* as extended by the already composed *Six Pianos* and *Music for Mallet Instruments, Voices and Organ*, for which see below. Though rhythm remains crucial in an elementary percussive situation that rivals *Clapping Music* for audacious simplicity, the claves of *Music for Pieces of Wood* are tuned in seconds, except for the high pulse, thus allowing the contrapuntal consequences of the process to be heard as melodies as well as interlocking rhythmic sequences.

Six Pianos

Drumming's expansion of timbral resources continued to be put on hold while Reich returned to keyboard instruments alone to explore further his passion for using only a group of identical instruments. His initial idea had been to compose a piece for all the pianos in a piano shop: hence its working title, 'Piano Store'. Jack Romann made it possible for Reich and his colleagues to spend many evenings during the autumn and winter of 1972–3 at the Baldwin Piano and Organ Company's New York premises, trying out ideas. The eventual choice of a half-dozen upright 'spinet' pianos for *Six Pianos* (undated on the published score, but completed in March 1973) permitted the rapid articulation of complicated counterpoint without too much resonance, as well as the players' close proximity and the assistance this gave to ensemble precision for such a seemingly unwieldy combination. (*Six Marimbas*, the alternative scoring the composer made in 1986, represents a more practical version.) *Six Pianos*' application of 'drumming on the keyboard' is more sophisticated than that of *Phase Patterns*, but scarcely a new departure. The harmonic potential of half-a-dozen keyboard instruments, on the other hand, was just what Reich needed to renew his exploration of tonality.

Six Pianos presents a more developed form of 'rhythmic construction': the gradual assembly of a rhythmic pattern does not emerge out of silence, as at the beginning of *Drumming*, but unfolds in canon against a fully formed statement of the same rhythmic pattern using the same pitches. At the opening, for instance (see Ex. 3.20), Pianos 1 and 6 present the eight-quaver rhythmic Basic Unit in unison, doubled an octave lower by Piano 3

Example 3.20 *Six Pianos*, Figures 1–8

and a perfect fifth lower by Piano 2. Against this, Pianos 4 and 5, playing in unison, then assemble a further version of the first pattern in canon, at Piano 3's lower octave.

Beginning with the dyad to be found on the fifth quaver beat of the other parts (the half-bar, in other words; the time signature is $\frac{4}{4}$ throughout), the Basic Unit is gradually built up. The complete statement, though, turns out not to be in unison with the original, but starts two quaver beats later, on the third crotchet beat of the $\frac{4}{4}$ bar. Discounting the octave doubling of Piano 3, this means that three pitch patterns are presented simultaneously, all based on the rhythms of the Basic Unit, and all in parallel, though not exactly similar, motion. The resulting patterns accruing from this contrapuntal combination are then themselves doubled by players whose contribution to the basic three-voice texture can be spared. This process of rhythmic construction followed by doubling the resulting patterns is presented a second time, again with three different pitch patterns. After this, a third section performs rhythmic construction on a further three pitch patterns, concluding the work without further resulting patterns. The deployment of resulting patterns in a work not itself based on phasing is typical of Reich in bringing a fresh perspective to an apparently well-worn technique. Again, however, the detailed working out of these patterns is made more difficult to hear by his adherence to the use of identical instruments.

Six Pianos' deployment of three separate modal areas – D major, E-Dorian and B minor, respectively – corresponds to the three-part rhythmic scheme described above, making the overall progression of the work easier to follow. The three patterns in each of the three modal areas may, like those of earlier works, be analysed for their ambiguities both within themselves and via their effect on each other. In Section One, for instance, Example 3.20 contributes to the prime modality of D major, but breaks down into three levels prolonging, in descending order, D, B and F♯. This suggests B minor rather than D major, though it encompasses not only the characteristic relationship of a perfect fourth met earlier, but also the minor third of two keys linked as relative major/minor, and thus incorporates both these. This, too, will become important in Reich's subsequent development of tonality.

The three modal areas of *Six Pianos* share a key signature of two sharps and could even be said, for example, to articulate III–IV–I in B minor. Yet precisely because all three keys use the same seven pitch classes, there is less modulation in *Six Pianos* than there is in *Drumming*, despite the fact that all nine patterns, in the three sections together, prolong at least two different pitch centres in the manner described above; and though *Six Pianos* is admittedly a good deal shorter, and thus changes modal focus at greater speed.

Music for Mallet Instruments, Voices and Organ

The dense textures of *Six Pianos* rival those of *Drumming* while resorting to Reich's tried-and-tested use of a single group of identical instruments. His other composition completed in the early part of 1973 has a sumptuousness – textural, timbral and also harmonic – based on percussion and voices that is new in its composer's output. Reich asked himself 'what if you really have an orchestra of your own, and mix the timbres right from the very beginning?' He began to experiment with wind instruments – a pair each of clarinets and bass clarinets, later a brass group – doubled by voices, male as well as female. Finding these combinations difficult to keep in tune, as well as too heavy, his eventual answer was an ensemble consisting of four marimbas, two glockenspiels, vibraphone without motor, three

Example 3.21 *Music for Mallet Instruments, Voices and Organ*, Figures 1–2

female voices and electric organ: a grouping guaranteed to seduce the ear, while retaining something of the woody crispness of *Drumming*. Important in the composer's approach to what he calls 'the prototype of what was going to become my orchestra' is the doubling of female voices and electric organ. This 'new timbre which is both instrumental and vocal at the same time'[73] articulates identical pitches and rhythms along lines long familiar in Western orchestral music. In Reich's mature output, however, such doubling is new. It makes manifest an extended process of augmentation and diminution of sustained notes which not only forms one of the two rhythmic devices used in the work, but also helps to focus attention on the harmony.

This technique, the first of what the composer calls 'two simultaneous, interrelated rhythmic processes,'[74] derives from *Four Organs*. In *Music for Mallet Instruments, Voices and Organ*, two chords are used (performed on the electric organ, doubled by two female voices), their choice suggesting an ambiguous 'cadential progression',[75] initially in a Dorian F minor (see Ex. 3.21). The ambiguity of this 'progression' is strengthened by its refusal to behave in a 'proper' cadential manner: all four parts move downwards; there is no traditionally functional movement in the bass line; the upper two parts prolong Bb rather than F; and a ninth chord followed by a seventh chord scarcely constitutes a standard cadence. But the oscillation between its two components is in itself sufficient to give a greater sense of motion than anything in Reich's previous output. Cs in the right hand of the vibraphone – first in sustained notes, then in semiquavers – meanwhile follow the same process of augmentation and diminution, adding a dominant to the prevailing F, while the left-hand prolongs Bb. The two glockenspiels play a continuous pattern, in two canonic positions, that further emphasises F.

The functioning of this new feature is triggered by the second of the 'two simultaneous, interrelated rhythmic processes': the rhythmic construction of a pattern against an already existing version of itself, already familiar from *Six Pianos*. In the first of the work's four sections, for instance, three marimbas, doubled by the third female voice, play parallel pitch patterns on the rhythmic Basic Unit, while a fourth assembles the middle one of these against the others in a different canonic position, in the manner of the earlier work. Again, as with *Six Pianos*, a range of central pitches is shared and prolonged, here underpinned by the main tonal centre of the lowest pattern to produce an overall F-Dorian modality. Once the rhythmic construction is under way, the two voices and organ begin augmentation of the 'cadential progression' (see again Ex. 3.21); this naturally also prolongs the F-Dorian modality, though with suggestions of B♭, adding yet another fourths relationship to the list in Reich's output. The lengthening and shortening of this process create what the composer describes as 'a certain richness and a certain power'; this also allows the pair of chords to register in a proto-cadential manner. Set against the rhythmic construction, the potential of these constantly rocking oscillations to create a feeling of tonal motion, however limited, begins to achieve something quite unprecedented in his work. Also essentially new in the composer's acknowledged output is the use of an arch form: inspired, Reich says, by the model of Bartók's Fourth and Fifth String Quartets.

The overall structure of *Music for Mallet Instruments, Voices and Organ* consists of four sections, based on this linked pair of processes and creating four arch forms. The putative tonal motion of the chords within each section is now enhanced by something more akin to real modulation. These sections themselves form two pairs, each articulating a modulation to a different modality centred on A♭. The already mentioned Dorian F of Section One gives way to the Dorian A♭ of Section Two. Though their pitch centres have a relative minor/major relationship, the minor (Dorian), rather than major, version of the scale on A♭ brings about the modulation, making three changes to the key signature, which moves from three to six flats. In $\frac{2}{4}$, Section Two is the only one of the four to employ a duple metre; all the others are in $\frac{3}{4}$. The B♭ minor of Section Three shifts the tonic a tone higher, creating just a single pitch change, the return of C♮. The modulation to the Mixolydian A♭ major/A♭ dominant of the concluding Section Four moves the tonic back again, retaining the five flats.

Music for Eighteen Musicians

It is with *Music for Eighteen Musicians* that we reach the culmination of Reich's achievements in the works composed between 1965 and 1976. A summation of a decade's efforts, this composition also introduces several innovations. The new expressivity of *Music for Eighteen Musicians* is certainly discovered with the aid of procedures which his previous music had neglected. Yet its innovatory aspects should not prevent us from observing the close connections which exist between the techniques and structural processes of the new work and both those of Reich's earlier output in general and those of the compositions immediately preceding it in particular.

Lasting almost an hour, *Music for Eighteen Musicians* is longer than any of its composer's earlier works except *Drumming*. This offers scope not only for structural and other kinds of technical variety, but also for a significant expressive extension of the composer's musical language. The most obvious advance the work makes is in its instrumentation. As a 'Work in Progress for 21 musicians and singers', as it was billed for some try-out performances at The Kitchen in May 1975, it required ten more performers than had *Music for Mallet Instruments, Voices and Organ*, seven more than the maximum forces its composer has deployed in *Drumming*. Though this number had been reduced through some judicious doubling by the time of *Music for Eighteen Musicians'* full première, the group was still significantly larger than Reich had ever employed before. Of especial importance is his use, for the first time in an ensemble context since the early sixties, of regular orchestral instruments – a violin, a cello, and two clarinets doubling bass clarinets – in addition to the now familiar tuned percussion (three marimbas, two xylophones and vibraphone without motor), keyboards (four pianos) and (four) women's voices. While some of these are amplified, the absence of electric organs – an original intention behind *Music for Mallet Instruments, Voices and Organ* – is notable; with the emphasis firmly on acoustic instruments from all sections of the standard orchestra except brass, Reich has here taken a significant step towards working with the conventional, as well as larger, forces of the Western classical tradition. It should be noted, though, that he originally intended the string bass role to be taken by a viola da gamba: a decision influenced by the composer's ongoing interest in 'early music'. The textures produced by this highly individual 'orchestra' have all the allure of those in his previous mixed-ensemble works, plus much greater variety.

One of the work's new techniques is a consequence of Reich's wish to avoid using a conductor for such a large ensemble. Instead, the vibraphone plays aural cues at the end of each section, and at moments of structural change within sections as well. These short melodic patterns in octaves signal transitions not only to the players, of course, but also to listeners, making a long and complex composition easier to follow.

Music for Eighteen Musicians' developments in the fields of harmony and tonality are even more significant. Structures unconnected to the work's basic rhythmic processes play an even more important role than did the augmentation of two-chord 'cadential progressions' in *Music for Mallet Instruments, Voices and Organ*. The basic technique of these 'cadential progressions' is now borrowed in the course of devising a more evolved role for harmony. The work begins and ends with a cycle of eleven chords, each performed twice by the whole ensemble. As a result, in 1978 Reich made the often-quoted remark that '[t]here is more harmonic movement in the first 5 minutes of "Music for 18 Musicians" than in any other complete work of mine to date'.[76] On the two commercial recordings available in 1998, each chord is held for between fifteen and thirty seconds. In between, the bulk of the composition consists essentially of each of these chords held in turn – for between four and six minutes each – while what the composer calls 'a small piece' is constructed on them in turn; two 'pieces' – marked 'IIIa' and 'IIIb' in the score – are constructed on chord iii. Most sections chart an arch form in a clear tripartite structure, another feature borrowed from *Music for Mallet Instruments, Voices and Organ*.

The sense of progression this brings gives harmony a structural force new in Reich's output. The composer himself has, though, pointed out the connection with twelfth-century organum – with its initial statement of a complete cantus firmus followed by a sequence of organum sections taking each note in turn as a harmonic centre – to which he had so long been attracted. Typical, too, is the fast and unvarying quaver pulse (at $\downarrow = 204$); the constant presence of this pulse on the music's surface provides a textural, as well as rhythmic, patina against which the panoply of patterns can unfold. These patterns, in turn, borrow the process of rhythmic construction from a single beat (introduced in *Drumming*) applied to an already existing version of itself (as in *Six Pianos* and, again, *Music for Mallet Instruments, Voices and Organ*).

Other new techniques also affect the way in which tonal grammar operates in *Music for Eighteen Musicians*. Most immediately evident is the use of pulsing notes played or sung for the length of a breath. While mallet instruments and pianos maintain the kind of regular pulse familiar from *Drumming* and its successors, voices and clarinets (expanded, sometimes to dramatic effect, by strings, and other mallet instruments and pianos) offer a different approach: what Reich calls 'the rhythm of the human breath'.[77] Here, the notes of a chord are repeated as an insistent pulse, their duration controlled only by the length for which each performer's breath may comfortably be sustained. These pulsing figures rise and fall in dynamic, from silence to *forte* and back to silence; each swell is slightly staggered between instruments, again following a natural breathing rhythm. The effect is striking: '[t]he combination of one breath after another gradually washing up like waves against the constant rhythm of the pianos and mallet instruments', as the composer himself describes it. They occur throughout the introductory and concluding chord cycles, and at some point – usually the central panel of the characteristic arch-form shape Reich chiefly deploys – during each of the work's main sections.

A new freedom and depth to the articulation of the harmony is thereby also achieved, as the flexibility and naturalness of this ebb and flow contrast with the grid of the fixed tempo. By permitting his performers an expressive input previously denied them even via the articulation of resulting patterns, Reich – thinking once more of Snow's film *Wavelength*, as already noted – brought a new kind of irregularity into productive conflict with the apparently prevailing regularity. Different kinds of periodicity could be combined; stasis was confronted with new possibilities of motion. Previously in Reich's work, too, any departure from a single dynamic level sustained for the length of a whole section, or even a whole work, had been due purely to the mechanics of the rhythmic processes involved and their accompanying resulting patterns. Now, dynamic markings have an expressive, as well as structural, role.

Another technique first explored in *Music for Eighteen Musicians* is that of underpinning a repeated melodic pattern by rhythmically shifting chord changes. While owing something to the link between rhythmic construction and the expansions of the cadential figure in *Music for Mallet Instruments, Voices and Organ*, in *Music for Eighteen Musicians* a two- or four-chord sequence may begin on different beats of a melodic pattern. Though these patterns remain constant against the shifting harmonic rhythm, 'a sense of changing accent in the melody will be heard',[78] as Reich puts it, allowing a new kind of relationship between melody and harmony. As with the combination of regularity and irregularity, '[i]ts effect, the clear distinction between foreground and background that this affords, sets the stage for all the harmonic, thematic and developmental explorations' for which this work is so important.

The cycle of chords

The cycle of eleven chords on which *Music for Eighteen Musicians* is based (see Ex. 3.22) is built on a mode of seven pitches in three sharps. Individual

Example 3.22 *Music for Eighteen Musicians*, cycle of chords

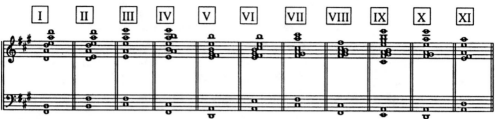

chords are constructed on the now familiar principle of 'stacked' fourths
and fifths. All chords are divided into clearly separate treble and bass
levels, often with an octave or more between them. Even as first tried out in
performances of what the composer calls 'the opening chorale',[79] these
chords originally lacked a bass level entirely, recalling the 'treble-dominated' approach of everything he composed before *Music for Mallet
Instruments, Voices and Organ,* with the exception of *Four Organs.* Despite
his experiments with lower pitches in the former work, Reich was still wary
of spelling out the bass, fearing this would over-define and limit the function of each chord.

   When he came to add lower pitches to the 'chorale' – inspired by the
suggestion from a member of his group that he bring a bass clarinet to the
next rehearsal – these notes were accordingly kept separate from the upper
ones. The independence of treble and bass, and the greater importance of
the former over the latter, is maintained throughout. It is immediately to
be noticed in the Introduction, where each treble crescendo (women's
voices and violin) is audible before the bass one (bass clarinets, pianos and
cellos) that accompanies it. In the main sections of *Music for Eighteen
Musicians,* the pitches of the chord sequence's treble as well as bass register
are in fact subject to change; omission and, in particular, addition of
pitches can be found in both registers, as can occasional pitches foreign to
the basic mode. Reich acknowledges that he treated this cycle of chords
very freely in the main body of the work. The appearance of the treble level
with different bass notes, or no bass notes at all, is nevertheless a fundamental clue to understanding the work. Though its composer says that 'it
was clear to me that what was important in *Music for Eighteen Musicians*
was the introduction of some kind of functional harmony',[80] it is by continuing to be evasive about the role of the bass, in particular, that the work

pointedly avoids any clear fulfilment of such 'functional' expectations as it
sets up.

As a consequence of this, the actual bass line of the chord sequence has
been described as 'no more than decorative'.[81] Some chords in the cycle are
simply inversions or revoicings of the preceding one, further implying a
colouristic approach. Yet it is helpful to regard the pitches of the bass register as offering another level of tonal interpretation to the pitches of the
treble: in other words, as another example of the dualities and other
ambiguities which pervade Reich's approach to tonality. Even though the
bass line proper may indeed be elusive, the dyads of the bass register, with
their consistent suggestions either of root position or of second inversion,
do have some role to play in activating tonal motion. In keeping with this,
the total aggregates themselves can have a true harmonic, as well as a
colouristic, function.

Taken as a whole, indeed, the bass register of Example 3.22 would seem
to offer potential for functionality. It outlines (with an interpretation of
the dyads given in brackets) a i–iv–v–i (iv–iv–i–i) progression in F♯ minor
(the minor key with three sharps), followed by a iv–i–iii–vi–v–iv–i
(iv–i–vi–vi–i–iv–iv) progression in A major (its relative major). It is hard
not to experience something of these progressions in the Introduction and
Epilogue, especially when the two interpretations coincide or suggestively
collude: an initial iv–v–i in F♯ minor, say, followed by vi–iv–i–vi–vi–v–iv–i
in A major. As we shall discover, however, Reich is prepared to depart from
his original chord sequence sufficiently to challenge such conclusions
based on listening to the Introduction and Epilogue alone. Sometimes,
only complete separation of its treble and bass registers can make sense of
the music based on them.

Other progressions may also be noted in Example 3.22: three sequences,
each charting a move to the greater consonance of chords containing only
four pitch classes (chords iii, vii and xi); the fact that, from chord vii
onwards, triadic elements in the treble reinforce, rather than undermine,
the tonality suggested by the bass; the gradual reduction in secundal clusters in the concluding sequence of chords viii–xi. The division into two
types of chord change – smooth (between inversions of the same chord, as
in chords i and ii) and abrupt (between chords of more differing content,
as in chords vi and vii) – is employed in the transitions from section to
section in the main body of *Music for Eighteen Musicians* to make quite
dramatic contrasts between evolution and juxtaposition.

With a single harmonic aggregate as the basis for each arch-form
structure, all the composer's imaginative powers are required to avoid

monotony in constructing this sequence of eleven 'small pieces'. Reich's strategies for ensuring momentum as well as variety may be illustrated by analysing Section I in detail, and then looking, more briefly, at the other ten.

Section I

In Section I, which lasts just four minutes, articulations of the basic chord frame a series of 'length-of-a-breath' pulsings in the typical arch-form structure. Its material and layout are illustrated in Example 3.23. After the A-major close of the introduction, the return to the first chord (Ex. 3.23a) makes it sound even more like D major; E is a now easily assimilable added second or ninth; B is readily accommodated as an added sixth, with the bass F♯, when it is audible, providing a first inversion. To the constant chatter of two marimbas and two pianos familiar from the opening, an additional marimba and piano supply single-bar patterns, built on the Basic Unit of *Clapping Music* and already flavouring the original treble harmony of chord i with C♯s (Ex. 3.23b). (Such single-bar patterns – naturally related to the more prominent ones similarly derived from the Basic Unit, and present throughout the section in which they occur – are also a feature of some of the work's later sections.) As mentioned earlier, the pattern already used in *Clapping Music* constitutes the chief rhythmic material of *Music for Eighteen Musicians*; Reich was attracted to the metric flexibilities offered by its now familiar twelve beats in a bar. Like the various versions of this pattern to be found in subsequent sections, some identical to the first, the one used in Section I is subsumed into the accompaniment to what follows.

Then the main business begins: to an oscillating accompaniment of voice, violin and cello, two clarinets introduce a variant of the third marimba's continuing counterpoint (without the C♯) that becomes the basic melodic material of the whole section. This turns out to be the preliminary stage in assembling the old friend mentioned earlier, and already present in the accompaniment: the Basic Unit of *Clapping Music*, now supplied with the beginnings of a melody. While based on the familiar process of rhythmic construction, this is expanded in a more subtle manner, involving not only the substitution of beats for rests, but also length, changes of doubling, accompaniment and texture, and the shifting of register. Also found frequently in the ensuing sections, this method of generation naturally varies in detail, each version characterised by its particular balance of elements and the way this affects the overall design.

Example 3.23 *Music for Eighteen Musicians*, Section I: (a) basic chord; (b) Figure 97 (versions of *Clapping Music* pattern); (c) Figures 103–04 (melody based on *Clapping Music* pattern); (d) Figures 108–12 (melody and chords only); (e) Figures 124–28 (melody and chords only).

Cued by the vibraphone, the Basic Unit of *Clapping Music* soon develops into its familiar form with an expansion to two bars, now doubled by the second clarinet and two voices, in parallel fourths (see Ex. 3.23c). Increasing to four bars, by adding repetitions of the *Clapping Music* Basic Unit, it proceeds to alter its accompanying line (from parallel fourths to fifths, then thirds; each repeated several times), and to rise in pitch. As it develops, the figure takes exploration of the ambiguities of $\frac{12}{8}$ a stage further. The extension of chord i via augmentation of a two-chord 'cadential progression' results in a two-chord structure of alternating B minor and F#7 chords, subjected to expansion and contraction. Expanding to a total of twenty-two beats, the different lengths of the chords – 3 + 3, 4 + 2, 3 + 3 and 2 + 2 – shift the harmonic rhythm while the melodic pattern remains the same (see Ex. 3.23d). These subtle manoeuvres contribute to the 'sense of changing accent in the melody' referred to above, and feature throughout the work.

The thirds-based version of the clarinet pattern brings harmonic as well as rhythmic changes, replacing B by the extraneous pitch C# in the melodic pattern itself, and altering the 'cadential progression' to G^7 and D^7 (both with sharpened sevenths), now presented in progressive diminution as 6 + 6, 3 + 3 and 2 + 2, to make the same total of twenty-two beats as before (see Ex. 3.23e). Including G♮ – a pitch foreign to the mode of the chord sequence itself, reinforcing D major – this progression underpins everything through the middle panel to the following return of the thirds-based pattern. As the clarinets fade out, the two voices continue the basic pattern over the same shifting accompaniment.

It is at this point that the pulsing figures of the central panel begin, on the two clarinets. Confined to the dyad of D A – first low, then high, each repeated – they emphasise D major against the same ambiguously shifting harmony beneath. The pair of voices continues with the same material throughout this middle section, as do the original chord and its first offshoots in the marimbas and pianos. After this, the material of the first panel returns, reducing back to its opening by presenting the elements described above in reverse order. Thus the overall shape of Section I – as of most other sections of *Music for Eighteen Musicians* – is A B C D C B A, with D representing the pulsing figures at its centre. It is interesting that foreign as well as extra pitches are added so early in the work. No pitches foreign to the basic mode now feature until Section V.

Sections II to XI

Example 3.24 offers some of the material of Sections II–V. Since the pitch content of chords i and ii is identical, Section II might be expected to operate with the same basic tonal centres as its predecessor. The restricted compass of the new melody rhythmically constructed on the Basic Unit of *Clapping Music* (see Ex. 3.24a) suggests F♯ minor. While this continues in the voices, a xylophone-and-piano pair simultaneously assembles two further patterns, both related to the first, in rhythmic unison on the Basic Unit of *Clapping Music* (see Ex. 3.24b). After this is completed, a further xylophone-and-piano pair constructs the same patterns in canon in the manner of *Six Pianos*. This requires the addition of a fifth pianist, made possible by the already mentioned 'doubling'. Length-of-a-breath pulsings arrive just one minute into the section. When the contrapuntal structure has been assembled, these pulsings expand registrally and texturally: adding a pair of xylophones, and subsequently a single piano, to the clarinet and strings. They dissolve barely half a minute before the whole section's close, having taken over a larger proportion of it than is generally the case elsewhere. These pulsings include pitches in the bass register.

The F♯-minor^7 of chord iii – the first, more consonant, four-pitch aggregate – has two contrasting 'small pieces' built on it: Sections IIIa and IIIb. Section IIIa builds its xylophone and marimba patterns on E A alone, but these are filled out – in the treble as well as the bass – not only by C♯ (once again) and F♯ but also by B and (again) G♯, pitches additional to chord iii; the melodic patterns on clarinets and strings are similar to those of Section II. The alternating F♯-minor/C♯^{7} of the outer 'cadential progression' is soon pulsed by two pianos in the lower register, their repeated quavers articulating a fairly slow harmonic rhythm. When the parallel-sixth stage is reached in the unfolding of melodic patterns, the alternating I–V of the pianos' root-position chords gives an unusually dramatic feel to the F♯-minor tonality. The cello's sustained dyads of D A and E A and the vibraphone cues subsequently suggest a move to A major, but the repeated upward curve to C♯ of the expanded melodic patterns seems more ambiguous. This key finds a clearer tonal focus in Section IIIb, which acts as a sweeter, almost placid foil to the energies of IIIa, though the bass of the 'cadential progressions', descending to F♯, reminds us of the key signature's alternative.

A less secure, more evasive A major seems to be the basis of Section IV, with D♮ returning for the first time since Section II to complete the chord sequence's basic mode. The marimba and piano's single-bar pattern is especially prominent here, its dalliances with top A already implying the centrality of that pitch. Clarinets and a single voice take the melodic patterns, all in parallel fourths, circling around C♯ and G♯. The other three voices join the strings in 'cadential progressions' in which C♯ features as a

Example 3.24 *Music for Eighteen Musicians*, Sections II to V: (a) Section II, Figure 175 (first version of *Clapping Music* pattern); (b) Section II, Figure 180/ii (second version of *Clapping Music* pattern); (c) Section IV, Figures 326–30 (melody, chords and drone only); (d) Section V, Figures 372–4 (final canonic position and first resulting pattern only).

drone. The relationship between melody and accompaniment here – based on the latter's expansion to crotchet beats of $3+3+4+2+3+3+2+2$, plus 2 beats rest, against which the four-bar melody creates its own ambiguously shifting metre – is one of the work's most compelling (see Ex. 3.24c). The length-of-a-breath pulsings on the bass clarinets recall F♯ minor again. But the next three pairs of pulsings expand the E A dyads which had alternated with the bass clarinets' F♯ C♯ into rich five-voiced chords emphasising A major. The bass of the first chord then descends to D, and that of the second chord to C♯, to create the C♯-minor[11] chord on which Section V begins.

Section V establishes its place at the work's centre by three new departures. Firstly, the key signature now changes to four sharps, the new pitch, D♯, being incorporated into a C♯-minor tonality. As described above, the bass register of chord v (the source of this section) proposed D major as the IV of a progression leading to the final A major: an interpretation completely undermined, of course, by the new pitch. When the bass register arrives for the length-of-a-breath pulsings, on bass clarinets, two voices and strings, an A[9]–E[7]–C♯-minor[7]–C♯-minor[11], then alternately A[7] and E[7], progression is outlined with typical 'stacked' fourths and fifths, suggesting the possibility of a move to A major.

Before this, however, we find the second of this section's new departures: the first, and only, use in *Music for Eighteen Musicians* of a pattern unrelated to the *Clapping Music* Basic Unit. This is, however, nothing other than the one already used in *Violin Phase*, transposed down a perfect fourth and now deployed in a double exposition of rhythmic construction with canon similar to that of Section II. It is first presented complete on two pianos, taking the place of any less closely related single-bar pattern common as a supplement to the pulsing quavers. A canon on quaver 9 of the twelve beats is then assembled by the two other pianos; this begins with what will turn out to be the second of its two D♯s, on quaver 7 of the original pattern. (In *Violin Phase*, the Basic Unit had also been phased to the ninth quaver, but only after the 'notch' on beat 5 had been held.) Then, while this canonic position is maintained by one pair of pianos, a third one is assembled, by the other pair, on quaver 3 of the original; after which first just a single piano then also two marimbas and two voices perform resulting patterns on the three-stage canonic position (Ex. 3.24d gives the latter, plus the first resulting pattern).

Underpinned at the very beginning by the already mentioned C♯-minor[11] chord and, much more extensively, by the pulsing chords which follow the arrival of the resulting patterns, the C♯-minor tonality of this process reflects the higher dissonance level of chord v's treble register, which itself already included G♯. In its early stages, however, it does so in ways more reminiscent than almost anything else in *Music for Eighteen Musicians* of the structural clarity of Reich's treble-dominated earlier compositions. In doing so, it reinforces its refusal to succumb to any tonal interpretation involving harmonic motion propelled by a bass line.

Example 3.25 offers some of the material of Sections VI–XI. The continuous rattle of maracas decorates Sections VI–VIII, giving them – as did the glockenspiels of *Drumming*, Part Three – something of the feel of a scherzo before the more complex machinations of the finale; they also include an appropriately recapitulatory element. Despite its basis on chord vi (the first chord with A as its root), and the previous section's oscillating chords prolonging E as potential dominant, Section VI uses the return to a three-sharp key signature to revisit the root-position, F♯-minor certainties of Section IIIa. That section's pulsings on the more ambiguous sustained dyads of D A and E A are again included, bringing back D♮ after the aberrant D♯. The elaborations of the melodic pattern themselves, though – a relative of the Basic Unit of *Clapping Music* – are now articulated by pairs of clarinets, marimbas, pianos and voices, plus violin and, occasionally, cello: a texturally more complex combination than before (see Ex. 3.25a).

Sections VI and VII share not only the complete modal gamut of seven pitches – Section VII adding B and E, as well as D, to its official basic chord – but also narrow-range, predominantly thirds-based melodic patterns. Section VII returns, however, to the *Clapping Music* Basic Unit proper. The measured tread of dyads in the bass – related to those of the previous section, though now not only more foursquare but also extending its bass progression to make a clear I–VI–VII–I – helps retain the focus on F♯ minor (see Ex. 3.25b). With the shorter Section VIII, the sun finally comes out on a bright A major; though the single-bar introductory pattern and the process of rhythmic construction built on a further version of the Basic Unit of *Clapping Music* are rather uncertain about their tonality, both are firmly underpinned by tonic and dominant harmonies in A, backed up by dominant-based pulsings and vibraphone cues. The absence of D in this case seems to assist the dominant focus.

In Section IX, D♯ returns in a four-sharp key signature that once again ignores the absence of D in the section's official chordal basis to effect a return to C♯ minor. Built, like Sections II and V (the latter sharing the same key with the present section), on the process of rhythmic construction overlaid with canons, it is clearly designed to function as the final climax of *Music for Eighteen Musicians*, and it is too complex to detail all its delights

Example 3.25 *Music for Eighteen Musicians*, Sections VI, VII and IX: (a) Section VI, Figures 408–11 (melodic pattern only); (b) Section VII, Figures 487–9 (melodic pattern and chords only).

Example 3.25 (*cont.*)

(c) Section IX: (i) Figure 617 (newly completed melodic pattern only); (ii) Figure 622 (newly completed melodic pattern only); (iii) Figure 627 (newly completed melodic pattern only).

here. The basic material is given in Example 3.25c. After a single-bar melodic pattern of more than usual prominence on the piano, another thirds-based version of yet another variant of *Clapping Music*'s Basic Unit is assembled on pairs of clarinets, voices and strings (Ex. 3.25 *c*i). Xylophone and piano then fill this out in parallel motion in the same canonic position, assembling their notes according to a different constructive scheme (Ex. 3.25 *c*ii). The third process of rhythmic construction is then carried out canonically, another xylophone-and-piano pair assembling an altered version in canon on quaver 9 (Ex. 3.25 *c*iii). Overlapping with this, an unusually, and increasingly, rich collection of pulsing chords – joined by two pianos in its latter stages – outlines an extended sequence in C♯ minor.

Section X is little more than a pendant to the preceding activities. Using the first dyad, D A, of the bass register of chord x in oscillation with F♯ C♯, it simply alternates D^{13} and F♯-minor^{11} pulsing chords above these in a stack of pitches ascending high into the treble, with two xylophones joining those which had concluded Section IX. This reminder of earlier bass lines which moved from D to E while themselves only tentatively suggesting F♯ (Sections IIIa and VI) is accompanied by the piano's single-bar melodic pattern from Section IX, now an octave higher. Including all pitches of the basic mode, it adds only B to chord x.

Section XI adds G♮, and further extends chord xi with B and C♯. This makes what is in several respects a return to familiar territory – a simple arch-form structure with 'cadential progression', plus length-of-a-breath pulsings – less conclusive than it might have been, leaving the final say to the chord sequence itself in the Epilogue. The pulsings of the central panel, though – now without pianos – outline E-minor^7 and A^{11}, giving the latter at least some suggestion of a closure on A.

The above analysis demonstrates that the 'tonal motion' of the main sections themselves has a rather different agenda from that of the chord sequence on which they are based. This is surely as it should be, since not only is such a sequence – even one as rich in ambiguous harmonic potential as this is – literally stretched to its limits as the basis for an hour's music, but there is much to be gained from supplying further layers of ambiguity by such 'departures from the text'.

The possibility of a double progression – one in F♯ minor, followed by one in A major – suggested by the chord sequence itself has been replaced by a more complex progression of tonalities. These have incorporated a four-sharp key signature, with strong suggestions of C♯ minor, at what seem critical moments (Sections V and IX) when the arsenal of rhythmic techniques is also replenished. Three sharps have sometimes indicated an F♯ minor which is surprisingly clear, elsewhere a more unstable implication of that key, and A major less than one might have expected, even at the end. D♮ has sometimes been removed altogether, while G♮ – the only pitch foreign to the mode besides D♯ – has been brought in at either end of the work's main body, pushing the modal territory towards two sharps as well. All this has been achieved with the aid of a wealth of rhythmic, melodic, contrapuntal and, by no means least, timbral and textural elaboration, drawing on all Reich's experience during the preceding decade, and on more than one piece of borrowed material from those years too. The result has such an inevitable momentum about it that it comes as no surprise to learn from its composer that the work 'virtually wrote itself, especially the second half'. *Music for Eighteen Musicians* is surely one of the masterpieces of late twentieth-century music.

If the consolidation of sonic impact and putative harmonic motion already redefines the minimalism of *Music for Mallet Instruments, Voices and Organ*, its successor's extensions of these render *Music for Eighteen Musicians* more clearly 'post-minimalist'. Conducted in the context of such a rich display of melodic, rhythmic and timbral techniques – some old, some new – these tonal discoveries were eventually to show its composer the path to fresh and fertile territory. Composing it demonstrated, he says, 'a way of working, which enabled me to continue the kind of work that I've been doing'. Such increased preoccupation with texture and timbre – with what the composer calls 'beautiful music' – as well as with harmony and tonality led inevitably to a further decrease in concern for the old minimalist virtues of 'filling the structure' and audibility of process.

Reich at first, however, found it impossible to capitalise on the advances of *Music for Eighteen Musicians*. The reasons for this seem complex, and their full examination, in any case, beyond the scope of this book. Crucial among them is the composer's absorption in Hebrew cantillation. This already began when the work was on tour; after its British première, in January 1977, he went on a trip to Jerusalem particularly for this purpose. Over the next year or so, Reich became so involved with exploring his Jewish roots that he seriously considered giving up composition to become a rabbi. More purely musical explanations for his difficulties must begin with his realisation that, as he puts it, he 'couldn't stay put in one key as long as I had'. It became clear that the 'on the edge' qualities which make *Music for Eighteen Musicians* what it is could not be sustained: something which the work's imitators have also discovered.

For more than two years, from March 1976 onwards, Reich composed almost nothing. Several tours of *Music for Eighteen Musicians*, for which he was effectively business manager as well as artistic director, left him no time. Besides, as he puts it, 'the faucet was dry'; when he began to find time to write again, he had lost all compositional momentum and, as usual, was determined not to repeat himself. The only piece dating from this period is an aborted one based, surprisingly, purely on pulsing rhythms. Reich describes it as 'all colour and harmony, all skin and no bones'. It was apparently loosely scored for 'whoever was around', and a sizeable group of musicians – between eighteen and twenty-five, the composer remembers – even tried it out in rehearsal before it was abandoned. Determined to honour the commission that he had by now received from the Holland Festival for the Netherlands Wind Ensemble, he borrowed the basic techniques of *Music for Mallet Instruments, Voices and Organ* and *Music for Eighteen Musicians* to assemble *Music for a Large Ensemble*, completed in December 1978: the first work Reich had written for forces besides those of his own group.

Octet – finished in April 1979, on his second commission, from Hessischer Rundfunk in Frankfurt – has become one of his best-loved and most-played pieces, not least for the way it begins to integrate ideas from Hebrew cantillation into a new emphasis on melody. But Reich's first really successful composition for anything more fully resembling Western orchestral forces is *Variations for Winds, Strings, and Keyboards*, completed in December 1979 for the San Francisco Symphony Orchestra. Also the first work after *Music for Eighteen Musicians* in which a harmonic cycle was the clear starting point, this 'mega-chaconne' takes functional, and faster, harmonic motion beyond the stage it had reached in anything he had composed before, thus truly paving the way for Reich's development in the 1980s.

Conclusion

While the tape recorders via which Reich discovered the technique of phasing may have soon been set aside by him in the pursuit of instrumental music, the transferral of phasing from tape to live performance must count among the major influences which electronic music has had on the development of music for players of conventional Western instruments. The composer's use of the sounds of American vernacular speech as a basis for composition has inspired a host of others, whether they wished to explore this territory in similarly experimental ways (Scott Johnson is just one of many examples) or in the more conventional Western contexts of opera and song (for instance, John Adams). The advent of what we now call 'sampling' in the mid-1980s not only gave a new lease of life to the use of tape (and later entirely computer-controlled) sounds (and, also subsequently, visual images too) in the composer's own more recent output (spearheaded by *Different Trains* of 1988), but has also led to the re-evaluation of *It's Gonna Rain* and *Come Out* as pioneering examples of a technique central to late twentieth-century composition.

Since Reich has been uninterested in following Young and Riley into singing and playing non-Western music regularly – including their adoption of a version of Indian lifestyle – his own, more purely technical, example of how to integrate ideas from non-Western musics into Western composition has probably been more widely appreciated, and his influence correspondingly greater. The composer's ensemble, in which he himself continues to perform, has long demonstrated the advantages to composers of direct involvement in playing their own music, whether inspired by non-Western models or not. The Western influences on his work – medieval music, Debussy, Stravinsky, Bartók, Coltrane and the drummer Kenny Clarke – remain potent to him, and no doubt to others too, partly because not one of them is itself purely 'Western classical'.

Of the five 'Optimistic Predictions . . . about the Future of Music' which

Reich offered in 1970, the most significant is the one suggesting that '[t]he pulse and the concept of clear tonal center will re-emerge as basic sources of new music'.[82] Rhythmic repetition underpins everything the composer has done since *It's Gonna Rain*, even those works, or parts of works – such as the first movement of *The Four Sections*, his orchestral composition of 1987 – in which his typically fast audible pulsing all but disappears. The contrapuntal potential of polyrhythmic composition has been explored by Reich with the kind of rigour which brings greater approval from Western classical composers and theorists than does any other so-called minimalist music. Such structural strictness is in itself generally less attractive to improvisers and others outside the Western classical tradition. But its results still possess sufficient 'vernacular' energy to stimulate a wide range of musicians and their listeners in more 'popular' fields too.

Radicalisation of harmony lies at the heart of Reich's present endeavours. While it would be wrong to inflect his present stance on his past output, one does not have to view what Ronald Woodley has called the composer's 'gradual realignment with certain branches of "mainstream" European music'[83] as antithetical to his previous concerns. Reich's interrogation of the Western classical tradition, as Woodley would put it, had to begin with the purging power of rhythm on pitch materials so reduced that little remained of their traditional force. Yet an important part of Reich's achievement has been a specifically harmonic interrogation of that 'tradition' which quickly supplies energies brought in from outside 'the post-Renaissance inheritance of harmony'. This process began in earnest as early as *Piano Phase*, and allowed its composer to question, from then on, the notion of a modal melodic and harmonic language as simply conservative. That Reich soon found himself doing this with the aid of the same engine – harmonic motion – that drove that post-Renaissance inheritance itself is one of the most interesting conundrums of late twentieth-century composition. Though harmonic motion also became a compelling concern to Glass, and even to Young and Riley, no one has impelled it with more vigour, and rigour, than Reich himself.

The development of Reich's reputation outside the downtown Manhattan artistic community can be pinpointed in three quite different musical areas. Firstly, Reich had a particular effect on the development of English 'experimental music', largely through his early friendship with Michael Nyman. There are, as we saw in the Introduction, several aesthetic parallels between minimalism and this sort of 'experimental music'; and for a while, in the early and mid-1970s, Reich's rigorous approach was a strong influence on what composers such as Chris Hobbs, Dave Smith and

John White called 'systems music', despite the wider range of musical references that this kind of composition brought with it.

Secondly, there is the composer's subsequent, and still increasing, impact on the Western classical music scene itself. Though he only really became at all widely known, and appreciated, by the audiences for such music after the period to which this book is primarily devoted, Reich has not only become an important member of its worldwide community, but also an influence on a considerable number of composers brought up in that tradition, including its avant-garde wing. The 'post-minimalism' he represents has more points of contact with the Western tradition than does the music of Young or Riley, and he was at crucial periods an influence on figures such as his compatriot John Adams and the English composers Simon Bainbridge and Colin Matthews.

Lastly, there is the arena of Western popular music. Significant parts of Reich's reputation from the mid-1970s onwards have been made in the world of pop music; a world in which electric guitars and keyboards had arguably already fulfilled the first of Reich's predictions, concerning the integration of electronic and instrumental music, by the early 1970s. A performance of *Music for Eighteen Musicians* sold out the New York nightclub The Bottom Line in the autumn of 1978; the ECM recording of the same work – which sold over 10,000 copies – prompted articles and reviews in *Rolling Stone* and *Billboard* magazines. In Britain, Brian Eno attended the Steve Reich and Musicians concert at London's Queen Elizabeth Hall on 4 February 1974, which included the then recent *Six Pianos* and *Music for Mallet Instruments, Voices and Organ*. Eleven years later, he said that he considered Reich's abandonment of his earlier, more rigorous and minimalist approach 'rather fortunate because that meant I could carry on with it';[84] he describes his own *Music for Airports* as 'one of the products of that'. Eno's one-time associate, David Bowie, once called the composer 'a tonetrack into the future'.[85] And even today, some listeners are introduced to musical minimalism via Mike Oldfield's *Tubular Bells* album, originally issued in 1973, which seems to owe at least as much to Reich as to Riley.

At the end of the 1970s, a younger generation of composers with roots in all three of these musical arenas – English 'experimental music', Western classical music and rock – found *Music for Eighteen Musicians* a particular influence; the English composers Jeremy Peyton Jones and Andrew Poppy are two of them. This is but one illustration of Reich's significance above and beyond the categories listed here. Two generations on, the English group The Orb acknowledged Reich's seminal role in the development of music which thrives on the sampling of musical cultures still thought incompatible by some, when 'Little Fluffy Clouds', the first track on the group's 1991 double album, *The Orb's Adventures Beyond the Ultraworld*, sampled the composer's *Electric Counterpoint* of 1987. The ultimate acts, so far, of sampling the work of this pioneer of the technique himself are the English artist Chris Hughes' *Shift* (1994) – a whole album of reworkings of Reich's early compositions from *Piano Phase* to *Drumming* – and, in particular, *Reich: Remixed* (1999), on which several leading 1990s 'techno' artists (including Coldcut, Ken Ishii and DJ Spooky) remix a whole panoply of the composer's music from the last thirty-five years.

4   Philip Glass

Philip Glass's career divides geographically into three parts: his childhood, student and, briefly, professional years in the USA; his time as student once again in Paris; and the period that saw his full establishment as a professional composer based in New York. Glass was twenty-seven when he went to Paris; just thirty when he moved back to New York. In terms of his output as a minimalist, the story only begins during the second period, and becomes of substance only in the third.

Glass must be among the most prolific of contemporary composers, and the years since the première of *Einstein on the Beach* in 1976 have seen a considerable rise in his rate of production. Yet it still makes stylistic and aesthetic sense to divide his complete output into two, with 1975–6 as the watershed. Some commentators have argued that the album *Glassworks* (1982) marks a significant trend towards the greater commercialism which so often troubles listeners, and critics, from the Western classical music world; but *North Star*, dating from 1977, attempted a similar 'accessibility' and is only infrequently mentioned because it failed to circulate as widely as was intended; Glass's involvement with whatever trends were current in rock music grew much deeper from about 1977, too. Operatically, Glass's first work for the resources of the conventional opera house is *Satyagraha*, premièred in 1980; but this was conceived and composed well before that, and the urge to move from the performance-art approach of *Einstein* towards the conventions of 'proper opera' came as early as 1976.[1]

Most importantly, *Einstein* (composed in 1975) marks the end of Glass's interest in minimalism as previously defined in this book as clearly as *Music for Eighteen Musicians* (1974–6) does for Reich. The arrival of harmonic motion, in *Einstein* and the compositions immediately preceding it, does not yet require the abandonment of the rhythmic techniques and concern for structural process that characterise Glass's music of the previous decade. *Einstein* in particular, dealing with all the concerns of drama as well as music, is crucially 'on the edge' aesthetically, and technically, speaking: that Glass was unable to remain in that interesting position now seems an important part of its achievement as well as of its historical significance. Harmonic motion – or at least the investigation of it in the surviving context of repetition – and all that came with it led both to opera as we more normally understand it and to the composer's more rock-orientated and commercial endeavours. The music he wrote before that had rather different goals.

That earlier music may be further divided into two. The concerns which culminated in *Einstein* first surfaced in 1970, causing everything from *Music with Changing Parts* onwards to be seen as part of a natural development away from previous minimalist concerns. Even Glass's output between 1965 and 1969 may be further subdivided: most sensibly, perhaps, according to the adoption of a rigorous, as opposed to more 'intuitive', approach to Glass's most basic minimalist technique, additive process. Since the works from *1 + 1* (1968), and more particularly *Two Pages* (1969), which use rigorous additive techniques are so much more successful than those which precede them, this also allows a division into 'early' and 'mature' even within what is officially the 'early period'.

Early American years

Philip Glass was born in Baltimore on 31 January 1937; he is thus scarcely four months younger than Reich. His father's parents were Lithuanian Jews, his mother's were Jews from Belorussia; both his own parents were born in the USA. His father owned a small record shop, his mother was a teacher and librarian.[2] Glass grew up surrounded by music: of the vernacular traditions of what was then called 'hillbilly' music from West Virginia and the Appalachians (both nearby), the commercially popular songs of the 1930s and 1940s, a certain amount of jazz; but also music of the European classical tradition – eighteenth- and nineteenth-century chamber music and even the 'modern music' of Bartók, Hindemith and others – via the 78 rpm records that his father brought home from the shop when they didn't sell. He began playing the violin at the age of six, the flute at eight; he attended, part-time, the Peabody Conservatory in Baltimore from 1945 to 1952. From early on, too, he seems to have had composition lessons, paid for by working in his father's shop. Glass also played in school orchestras, marching and theatre bands, and even for some amateur television, while attending Baltimore City College, a selective and competitive boys' high school. There was something of a family tradition in vaudeville and other kinds of popular theatre: Al Jolson was an uncle of Glass's father, and another uncle had played drums for the Marx Brothers. But his parents – 'working-class aspiring to be middle-class people'[3] – discouraged him from entering the music profession.

Glass must have been a precocious youngster, since he gained entrance to the University of Chicago by the age of fifteen. It was at this age, he has said, that he attempted his first composition: a string trio written 'in a strict twelve-tone manner'.[4] He graduated in 1956, aged nineteen, having studied philosophy and maths, as well as music, and obtaining an A.B. liberal arts degree. During the summer of 1955, he had, in addition, studied harmony with Louis Cheslock. In 1957 Glass went to the Juilliard School in New York City, initially as a non-matriculating student in 1957–8. Wishing to specialise in composition, he submitted about a dozen pieces for the entrance examination and began regular composition studies at Juilliard in September 1958. His teachers included William Bergsma and Vincent Persichetti; student colleagues at Juilliard included Peter Schickele and, more importantly to Glass's future development, Steve Reich. Glass obtained a School diploma in 1960 and an M.S. in 1962. Meanwhile, he also attended the Aspen Music Festival summer school in 1960, where he worked with Darius Milhaud. Interviewers are sometimes told that he became fascinated at this time by the new jazz of Ornette Coleman and John Coltrane; though Glass, unlike Reich, hardly ever elaborates on any style of jazz as an influence.

In 1962, on leaving Juilliard at the age of twenty-five, Glass obtained one of the earliest school-based composer-in-residence jobs to be offered in the USA, and for the next two years was based in Pittsburgh, working in the public school system there on a $10,000 Ford Foundation Young Composer's Award. The demands of this job no doubt influenced his output, which may at least partly account for the style of works such as *The Haddock and the Mermaid* (1962 or 1963). This is a choral setting, with piano accompaniment, of words by Gertrude Norman in a modal E♭ major, with occasional chromatic sidesteps; perhaps interestingly, the bass line is confined throughout to an accompanying twenty-bar ground to the word 'doo-doo', which is just beginning its fourth revolution when the upper parts bring the piece to a conventional end (see Ex. 4.1). Joan LaBarbara discovers – in another a cappella choral work, *Haze Gold* (1962) – 'an early indication of Glass's attraction to steady rhythmic foundation: a slow eighth-note ostinato figure, first in the alto and later in the tenor voices, forms the base over which a melody is floated'.[5] But though some accounts suggest the use of twelve-note or even more radical techniques, Glass describes all his output from these six years as 'straight, middle-of-the-road Americana'.[6] All the pieces the present author has seen are rhythmically quite unadventurous, even if some explore a 'wrong-note tonal' manner. Few precise dates of composition can be established.

From the beginning of this period, if not earlier, Glass was prolific and, in circumstances which encouraged immediate performance, in the fortunate position of hearing most of his music played almost as soon as he had written it, as well as winning several awards. By the end of the Pittsburgh

Example 4.1 *The Haddock and the Mermaid*, bars 1–9

period, he had apparently composed over seventy pieces, some twenty of which had been published. 'I was getting things into print as soon as I wrote them. That's what happens when you play the game',[7] he suggested, when his reputation had still to achieve its peak. As editor of Theodore Presser, his teacher Persichetti had been instrumental in getting Glass's music published; other companies, though, including Novello in London, also took pieces at this time.

Europe and the East

At this point – he was now twenty-seven – Glass might have been expected to settle into a university or conservatory post and continue a perhaps unexceptional academic compositional career. Instead, he decided on further study: in Paris with Nadia Boulanger, with whom he worked from the autumn of 1964 to the summer of 1966. Here, Glass was following an already well-trodden path. American composers since Aaron Copland in 1921 had been making the pilgrimage to Paris; and though by the 1960s Boulanger was accustomed to teaching American students with more money than talent, Glass was playing his part in a tradition that also had its honourable, and musically very significant, side. The one-year Fulbright award must have been an incentive, too. He used it to help him stay for a second year, during which he took odd jobs and received lessons on credit, though Boulanger – who had encouraged him to stay on – died before her former pupil was earning sufficient to be able to pay her back.

Glass says that his main motivation for going to Boulanger was his need to return to basic musical principles. He felt that his Juilliard lessons, though extremely practical, had not laid sufficient emphasis on the theoretical aspects of music. Boulanger taught harmony and counterpoint according to strict classical procedures. In addition, he was able to spend two years in Paris free to pursue his own interests. Increasing impatience with current musical modernism led him to dismiss the musical avant-garde he encountered there, centred around Pierre Boulez, whose Domaine Musical concerts he attended. Two other encounters, however, were to become formative in the development of the minimalist style that had at least some of its roots in Glass's Paris period.

Theatre (i)

Glass's interest in experimental theatre was motivated in part by a personal concern. His developing relationship with JoAnne Akalaitis – a theatre director and actress whom he had met in New York while still working in Pittsburgh – had led him to invite her to join him in Paris. The couple married in July 1965, going over to Gibraltar for the ceremony because Gibraltarian law made it easier to wed quickly and cheaply there than in France. Jean-Louis Barrault's Paris company regularly presented new plays by Samuel Beckett and Jean Genet at the Théâtre Odéon which particularly impressed these young Americans. Glass and Akalaitis met Beckett in Paris some time in 1964 or 1965, through the actor David Warrilow. The Irish-born writer's output was to become central to the work of Akalaitis and her fellow actors for some years afterwards. The couple also developed an especial interest in the types of non-narrative performance art that were beginning to evolve around this time. In the summer of 1964, they saw the Living Theater's première production of *Frankenstein* in a small festival outside Marseilles; Glass had already gained some knowledge of the collective's work while at Juilliard. *Frankenstein* particularly impressed him in its extension of theatrical time: the performance lasted some seven hours. He was later to experience a similar scale not only in the work of Robert Wilson but in Khatikali theatre of South India. The following winter, Glass and Akalaitis met Julian Beck and Judith Malina, the prime movers behind the Living Theater, in Berlin; they also saw the Berliner Ensemble in the city's Eastern sector.

The experimental theatre collective with which Glass became involved in Paris at this time consisted largely of American *émigrés*. Of its original four members – Akalaitis, Lee Breuer, Ruth Maleczech and Warrilow – all except the last-named had been involved with the San Francisco-based Actors' Workshop and the San Francisco Tape Music Center. This Parisian group subsequently survived removal to New York to become the nucleus for the theatre company Mabou Mines.

While still in Paris, the collective presented English-language versions of two classics of European modernist theatre, both directed by Breuer. Mabou Mines' archives state that Bertolt Brecht's *Mother Courage*, with Glass as musical director (the original Paul Dessau score was used), was performed at Gordon Heath's Studio Theatre. The performances were probably in the spring of 1966; Jack Kripl – the saxophonist who later recorded the musical material for *Play* (see below) and subsequently became a member of the Philip Glass Ensemble – says that they took place at the American Church.[8]

Mother Courage was preceded by the group's first Beckett production, *Play*. Beckett has been central to Mabou Mines' work throughout its existence; Glass himself, though, had little direct contact with the playwright, who, he says, preferred to work though a 'designated person', in this case Warrilow. *Play*, directed by Breuer, had been mounted at the American Cultural Center on the Rue du Dragon, possibly in late 1965, though it has been impossible to establish precisely when. The three characters in Beckett's *Play* – a man (performed by Warrilow), his wife (played by Akalaitis) and his mistress (performed by Maleczech), all encased in funeral urns – speak in interrupted monologues, each spotlit only when talking and apparently unaware of the other two. The complete text takes some twelve minutes, after which there is a total blackout and the whole thing is repeated. A second repeat, following a further blackout, is abruptly curtailed.

The music Glass provided for this production was his first original theatre score for the company. It was also, as he assesses it, 'the first of the highly reductive and repetitive pieces that occupied me for years afterward'.[9] The music for *Play* was written – somewhat eccentrically but partly, no doubt, with practical considerations in mind – for a soprano saxophone overdubbed on tape. The performer was Kripl, then a Fulbright Scholar also studying with Boulanger. The score, as Glass recalls it, was 'a series of five or six short pieces separated by equal lengths of silence'. It is described by its composer as

> a piece of music based on two lines, each played by soprano saxophone, having only two notes so that each line represented an alternating, pulsing interval. When combined, these two intervals (they were written in two different repeating rhythms) formed a shifting pattern of sounds that stayed within the four pitches of the two intervals. The result was a very static piece that was still full of rhythmic variety.[10]

No score or recording of *Play* seems to survive. The absence of a score is hardly surprising, since this consisted simply of the four pitches Glass wrote down for Kripl to record – which he did separately for each pair of notes – and the tape consisted of loops which could be played, either separately or together, in a variety of ways each night. Kripl remembers the upper saxophone line as a descending major third, but cannot recall the lower one. He says that, as with the stage action itself, there was a lot of silence in the resulting music, which was in any case 'almost inaudible . . . very ghostly'. Kripl felt that Glass's response to Beckett demonstrated 'a great sense of theatre'. It also suggests that the composer's interest in reductive repetition was first awakened by realising the powerful impact repetitive elements were contributing to Beckett's *Play* itself.

Like other new European theatre of the time, Beckett's plays go a lot further than the drama of earlier periods in requiring their audiences to devise interpretative strategies of their own. What Glass calls 'the assumption that the audience itself completed the work'[11] leads to quite different experiences by the same viewer at different performances: including, as the composer himself found, that 'the emotional quickening (or epiphany) of the work seemed to occur in a different place in each performance'. This desire to transcend 'a theatrical mechanism with an interior mechanism designed to evoke a specific response' can readily be connected with the aesthetic behind *Einstein on the Beach*: Glass's first major collaboration, with Wilson, on a theatrical project in which his music becomes manifestly integral, rather than 'incidental'. The composer, however, seems to suggest that its underlying aesthetic also affected his approach to concert works as well, as also discussed below. A developing association with Beckett, meanwhile, subsequently allowed Mabou Mines to continue performing his plays, in adapted as well as original versions, with music (something the writer's estate normally forbade), thus giving Glass several more opportunities to explore these ideas inside, as well as outside, the theatre.

Soon after the Paris production of *Mother Courage*, however, the group temporarily disbanded. Neither of its productions had been a great success in the French capital, due not least to being staged in a foreign language. Besides, Glass and Akalaitis had developed a strong desire to travel and to explore some non-Western, non-narrative theatre traditions at first hand.

Indian classical music

For Glass, an interest in Indian theatre traditions had recently been augmented by his first experience of North Indian classical music, in the winter or spring of 1965–6. A friend of the composer was engaged as a photographer on a film called *Chappaqua*, directed by Conrad Rook, then being made in Paris. Glass himself describes the film as 'a psychedelic fantasy involving such heavies from the New York literary scene as Allen Ginsberg, Peter Orlovsky and William Burroughs';[12] John Rockwell calls *Chappaqua* 'an archetypally sixties hippie film'.[13] The composer was originally hired by Rook to edit soundtrack material already provided by Ornette Coleman, but discouraged the director from meddling with a perfectly acceptable tape by such a major figure.

In the end, the music for this film was composed by Ravi Shankar, already well established as a sitar player in the West as well as in India. Shankar, though, needed an assistant to transcribe his work into Western notation for the French musicians recording the soundtrack, as well as to do a little conducting and translating. Additionally, it turned out, some sections of the score needed what he called 'modern music' – for 'the scary parts of the film . . . psychedelic trips' – and Glass wrote this as well. Kripl, who was a member of the standard jazz quartet line-up of tenor saxophone, bass, drums and piano which performed the 'Western' part of the musical contribution, says that the players spent a wasted jam session attempting to improvise freely to repeating loops of images taken from the film. Since this did not work at all, he himself suggested a melody to use as a basis; Glass then simply wrote this down, and the four musicians improvised on it.

It appears that Glass's understanding of the technicalities of Indian rhythmic practice – and even more those of Indian theory – were somewhat shaky. But the important thing for the composer's future development was that working for at least two months with Shankar – and also with Shankar's tabla player, Alla Rakha – provided his first full exposure to the very different technical methods, as well as style, which lie behind this music. In particular, Glass noted that it is based on the accretion of small units to make larger ones, rather than on the Western method of taking 'a length of time and [slicing] it the way you slice a loaf of bread'.[14] In other words, while Western music worked on the principle of division, Indian music – and, as he soon discovered, many other non-Western musics – worked on the principle of addition. The basic, but crucial, distinction between additive rhythm and 'divisive' rhythm was the epiphany Glass was seeking. The principle of additive rhythm was to revolutionise the way he thought about composition, and it seems that the initial inspiration for this was Shankar. 'That was the closest I'll ever get to a moment when the creative light suddenly kicks on',[15] Glass subsequently said. Yet the rhythmic techniques, discussed below, to which this experience introduced him would not be properly investigated for almost another two years.

Glass and Akalaitis spent the winter of 1966–7 travelling in North

Africa, Central Asia and India. Hitchhiking first from France to Morocco, they finally found their way to India, with various stops in Central Asia; the composer spent his thirtieth birthday – 31 January 1967 – in Darjeeling. '[S]oaking up Eastern music and analyzing its processes'[16] was, of course, important for Glass. But both he and Akalaitis were also concerned to discover the cultures of which these musics formed part. Both developed what amounted to an obsession with India, in particular, later returning in alternate years for trips lasting anything from three weeks to two months. Glass has travelled the whole subcontinent, 'from the Himalayas in the North to Tamil Nadu in the South. I witnessed theater in the South, ashrams (spiritual communities) in the North, dancers and musicians everywhere'.[17] The integration of dance, theatre and music with religious traditions soon began to take on a particular fascination. Glass himself has said that the thing which especially interests him in Khatikali theatre 'is that it's a theatre that joins together music and dance and acting. . . . [T]hat's why I keep coming back and seeing it'. He also points out that Indian theatre is both popular and sophisticated: 'it has no trouble being communicative'. For both his immediate development as a composer of music for the theatre and his longer-term emergence as a composer of opera, these experiences were crucial, both aesthetically and practically.

Soon after his return to New York, Glass learned more about the basic rhythmic principles of Indian classical music. In the winter of 1967–8, Shankar and Rakha came to teach at City College, and Glass took the opportunity to have private tabla lessons with Rakha. A great deal of the inspiration he found in Indian music for his own compositions derived from this experience; his subsequent study of South Indian music taught him yet more about the different ways in which melody can combine with a rhythmic cycle. It was as a consequence of these later experiences that he really began to come to grips with the possibilities of cyclic processes.

While the techniques of Indian classical music became important to Glass in the late 1960s, their significance later faded for him. His interest in Indian culture – and in the cultures of other countries of the Orient, particularly Tibet – has, on the other hand, continued and developed. Glass remains to this day a practising Buddhist; first encountering Tibetan refugees on his first trip to India, he later became associated with several New York groups involved in bringing them and their culture to the USA. Ideas about the transformation of society by non-violent means and 'the power of an idea' permeate the operatic trilogy of which *Einstein on the Beach* forms the first part. (*Satyagraha* – based on the early South African years of Mahatma Gandhi – is the second; *Akhnaten* – premièred in 1984 – the third.) Glass has, however, never adopted the more overt Indian lifestyle embraced by La Monte Young or Terry Riley, and Indian music has affected him in very different ways from them. In 1990 he collaborated again with Shankar on a compact disc entitled *Passages*.[18]

Return to New York

Probably in late February 1967, Glass returned briefly to Paris before embarking for home. He was back in New York by mid-March, certain that this was the best place to set about re-establishing himself as a composer with an approach very different from the one with which he had made his previous reputation. For the next ten years, rejected by those who had formerly championed him, he was to work entirely outside the domain of Western classical music and its support systems: a situation very different to the one he had experienced while at Juilliard and later in Pittsburgh. To earn a living, he took any job offering sufficient flexibility to allow him at least some opportunity for composition. Later, Glass's publicists were able to capitalise on his other 'professions'. His employment as a taxi driver has been turned into the stuff of legend; so, too, via a story involving the art critic Robert Hughes, has his work as a plumber.[19] One of the significant aspects of such occupations is that they were still necessary as late as the beginning of 1978. Glass drove a taxi, on and off, for a living for five years from 1973: the period that saw the completion and complete première of *Music in Twelve Parts* and the creation, first performances and immediate aftermath of *Einstein*. Though the latter was an enormous artistic success, he returned to cab driving after its performances at New York's Metropolitan Opera House in November 1976, partly to help pay the considerable debts the production incurred. In the spring of 1978, soon after his forty-first birthday, he received both the Netherlands Opera commission for *Satyagraha* and a $15,000 Rockefeller Foundation grant, renewable for several years. These sources of income marked the beginning of Glass's wider recognition, and the end of his need to earn money from non-musical employment.

Less well known are some of the earlier occupations he had: from being a crane operator in a steelmill to running a removal business with his cousin, the sculptor Jene Highstein. Chelsea Light Moving provided Glass with his first main employment for at least eighteen months after his return to the city; the company was quite successful once it acquired its more *chic* title, abandoning its original name, Prime Movers. 'No-one got the joke, and we didn't get the work', the composer observes ruefully. Employment was flexible, allowing time for music. According to Glass, he was joined in this job for one weekend only by Reich, though the latter suggests he had a longer-term involvement. Plumbing, also with Highstein, overlapped with the furniture removing, and continued until some time in 1971; it was better paid but too hard on a musician's hands.

At first Glass and Akalaitis lived in a loft on Sixth Avenue, near 25th Street, but soon moved to 23rd Street near Ninth Avenue. Here the couple rented the upper two floors of a house, Highstein occupying the remainder. At 23rd Street, the singer and songwriter Moondog had a room for about a year, during 1969–70, having been invited by Glass to stay when he had nowhere else to live. Private tapes, made on Reich's Revox machine, of some of Moondog's songs were made at the house by Jon Gibson, Glass, Reich and Moondog himself. In late 1970 or early 1971, the family – about to add a son, Wolfe-Zachary, to a two-year-old daughter, Juliet – moved to Second Avenue on 4th Street, in the East Village, retaining the 23rd-Street apartment until 1997.

Developing his contacts in the downtown Manhattan arts scene, Glass continued to find experimental theatre and other newly nascent forms of performance art especially invigorating and open to the possibilities of musical collaboration. Contacts with the sculptors and painters of Minimalist art also offered not only further ground to fertilise his own compositional ideas, but one significant further employment opportunity. Glass gladly gave up plumbing when, some time in late 1971 or early 1972, he secured a position as full-time assistant to Richard Serra. He had first met the sculptor in Paris when the artist and his then partner Nancy Graves, a sculptor and painter, were in Europe on travelling fellowships; Serra settled in New York in late 1966, and after Glass's return the following spring, the two became collaborators, in addition to friends, in the late 1960s as well as the early 1970s. The composer's association with Serra will be discussed below.

Musical connections

Glass considers that the suggestion of any linear development from Young to Riley to Reich and on to himself fails to represent the real situation, stressing instead the 'supportive environment' which he found on his return to New York. In this 'more spontaneous' set of circumstances, a variety of other musicians – those fairly well known today and some less familiar, at least outside what now survives of this community; and both those widely associated with minimalism and others less often contextualised in that way – all operated within the larger orbit of a downtown Manhattan art scene characterised, for Glass, by its concern for 'the reform of language' in a range of sometimes conflicting ways. Any notion of a 'torch' being passed between the members of an elite group now seems a nonsense to him.

The actual question of the influence on Glass of any of these other three composers, however, remains to be addressed. Like Reich, he may have heard about, if not seen a score of, Young's *Trio for Strings* while still at Juilliard; as with Reich, though, this seems to have made little impression on him at the time and he says he has never heard the work. In 1961, Glass saw Young's performance of *Composition 1960 #7* (Draw a straight line and follow it) at Yoko Ono's loft. 'He had a pendulum hung to the ceiling', he says, 'and he would swing the pendulum and wait until it came to a halt. And when it came to a halt, he would draw a long white line. And he did that for about three hours. And I stayed for three hours; it was just a fabulous performance'. But for Glass, this – like the performances by Robert Morris, Claes Oldenburg and others which he saw around that time – was Dada or performance art; 'there was no music content to any of that work'. The first actual music by Young he heard seems to have been one of the performances at the Barbizon Plaza in 1968. Though he knew little of his music, he says that 'La Monte was a part of our life' for downtown artists like himself.

Glass can recall hearing nothing by Riley – whom, like Young, he says he never met until much later – until the Columbia recording of *In C*, which came out in 1968. David Behrman – the producer for *In C* and the Columbia disc of Reich's music released the previous year – apparently told Glass that he would be next, but Behrman then lost his job with the record company and no LP materialised. Glass may have even heard the Columbia recording on tape before its release. In addition, Reich has said he had earlier played Glass a tape of the San Francisco première of *In C*. Glass now agrees he may have heard it, and seen the score, prior to writing *Two Pages* (his first piece to use rigorous additive process with fully composed-out modular patterns) in February 1969. Gibson, who was already working with Glass as well as Reich by this time, says he is sure that Glass heard it.[20] 'Steve', Glass observes, though, 'was very quiet about Terry'. Glass also heard Riley perform at The Electric Circus in April that year. Riley's essentially improvised music is 'too unstructured for me', says Glass, who cannot recall ever hearing a live performance of *In C* itself.

It is unlikely that Glass even knew about the existence of Reich's early tape pieces before his return to the USA in 1967. In 1978, in the course of a probably unique live discussion between the two composers on radio, Glass said that he and Reich 'had been developing our own music in our own distinctive ways'[21] since their Juilliard days. This remark was presumably intended to assert an already existing interest in reductive repetition developed before 1967, entirely independent of Reich. Glass's first experience of his erstwhile student colleague's post-Juilliard output came, as already related in Chapter 3, when he attended one of Reich's Park Place Gallery concerts in March that year. Attending at Serra's suggestion, Glass recalls the occasion as 'a beautiful concert, a very striking concert'. The association the two composers went on to form has already been discussed. On the matter of specific advice being traded by Glass and Reich while works were in progress, Glass says that little went in either direction. 'The pieces were usually done so fast that there wasn't much time to do that. We had rehearsals with finished pieces, basically'. He emphasises that the general sympathy and support – of Gibson and others besides Reich – were the most important things. Agreeing with this view, Gibson nevertheless acknowledges not only that 'Reich was very giving to Glass' at this time, but also that Reich and Glass were both 'much more driven' than their other colleagues in the search for compositional solutions. And Glass today acknowledges that, among the composers working in this community, Reich 'probably had the most commitment and the greatest clarity of vision, the most intelligence and energy'; he was also 'one of the most inspiring'.

It is clear that, as stated in the previous chapter, 'there was a lot of interaction'[22] between Reich and Glass for at least two years. But it is also evident that a mixture of influences was making itself felt on Glass at this time. Such disputes concerning intellectual property can never be fully resolved; it is easier to conclude, as Robert T. Jones does, that '[n]o one composer invented this new music. It was an eruption of the times, an inevitability. It *happened*'.[23] Yet an understanding of the role played in Glass's search for new ideas by compositional developments close to his own need not damage his significance in the emerging story of musical minimalism. Further discussion of the relationship between Glass and Reich may be found below.

Theatre (ii)

For some while, Glass's theatrical involvements in New York helped sustain his compositional efforts. While scarcely providing him with much income, they gave him an outlet for his work and a sympathetic context for it. His closest and most regular theatrical collaborations continued to be made with the company that, from 1970, became known as Mabou Mines, following the regrouping in New York of most of the actors involved in the earlier Paris-based ensemble. The following details attempt to supplement, and where necessary to correct, the information given in the composer's own book.

This group was active soon after Glass and Akalaitis's return to New York. Resuming its connections with Beckett, the company began to make a speciality of devising 'theatre pieces based on texts which Beckett never originally intended to be staged'. It has also operated on the principle that theatre is essentially a collaborative act, working closely with visual artists as well as with Glass, and comfortable with material generated by the group itself, including adaptations of non-theatrical writing by other authors. Beckett's *Play* was eventually revived at La Mama Experimental Theater Club (E.T.C.), on East 4th Street, in June 1971 with a tape of the music made for it in Paris. Several further USA performances of this production helped Mabou Mines survive during the next few years, though not all included Glass's music.

The first major new work to involve Glass was Breuer's *The Red Horse Animation* for three actors: probably composed in the spring or early summer of 1970, though only two years later the composer gave its date as 1969.[24] A two-page extract from the score for *Red Horse Animation*, published in the company's own *A Comic of The Red Horse Animation*, is copyrighted 1971.[25] The summer of 1970 was the first spent completely at the vacation home the Glasses had acquired the previous year, a thousand miles up the coast from New York City, in Nova Scotia; the abandoned summer camp they bought, together with the writer Rudolph Wurlitzer, was near the town of Mabou Mines, which is how the theatre group finally got its name. It was here that the piece was extensively rehearsed.

Devised and directed by Breuer, *Red Horse Animation* is especially significant – both in the development of 'alternative' theatre in general and in Glass's evolution as a composer – for the integration of its different components. The three actors jointly represented the Red Horse which embodied, as Breuer explained it, 'psyches as actual animals, in the sense that you can be in the human world and the animal world – or the world of ghosts – at the same time. [The animations are] sort of choral monologues, each one dealing with a different psychological personality'.[26] Seeing the action from above, at a 45° angle to the stage, the audience could follow the images both vertically and horizontally.

Movement and sound were closely allied by the simple process of deriving both from a single, essentially rhythmic, source. For the piece, a special floor was constructed (with the aid of the painter and sculptor Power Boothe) which, when amplified by contact microphones, became 'the instrument on which the actors performed the music – stamping, tapping, using all manner of percussive effects'.[27] Ruth Maleczech recalls that the piece was divided into three sections, devoted respectively to 'singing, singing and tapping, and tapping'.[28] Such 'text' as exists for the work was not only collectively evolved in close integration with the theatre piece's other elements but also published – as a 'comic book', with drawings by Ann Elizabeth Horton – in a form which makes clear its inseparability from its visual imagery.

Money to pay for the floor, New York rehearsal space and even a basic salary for the five members of the company, including Glass, was provided by Ellen Stewart of La Mama. The completed *Red Horse Animation* was finally mounted at the Guggenheim Museum on 18–21 November 1970; a partial version had earlier been seen at the Paula Cooper Gallery. A surviving videotape formed the basis for a revival of the piece in 1996, in which several children of the original actors took part; here, clapping took the place of the floor-tapping which had been such a feature of the original version.

Another theatre piece from this period with music by Glass – *Music for Voices*, apparently devised in the winter of 1970–71, though possibly later; in 1972 its composer described it as 'a new piece'[29] – also exploited links between sound and gesture. In this work, 'six or eight people, whoever was around' sat in a circle facing inwards, filmed in extreme close-up by cameras whose operators lay on the floor in the circle's centre. While the mouths of individual singers appeared on monitor screens visible to the audience, vocal sounds would be passed across the circle. Its composer actually calls *Music for Voices* a 'concert piece', and as a work of only eight or ten minutes' duration for a theatre group, it was usually performed as a prelude to the main theatrical event of the evening. A 'work-in-progress' performance was given at the Paula Cooper Gallery in June 1972, together with *Arc Welding Piece*, in which performers reacted to the cutting of a seven-foot steel cylinder by Highstein, the composer's former colleague in his removing and plumbing activities. The official première performances of *Music for Voices* took place at The Kitchen on 19 and 20 February 1973. More information on the scores of both *The Red Horse Animation* and *Music for Voices* can be found below. Glass continued his association with Mabou Mines up to the mid-1980s, estimating that he has written 'at least a dozen scores for the company'.[30]

Connections with Minimalist artists

In contrast to his enthusiasm for discussing theatrical connections, Glass has often proved unwilling, in published interviews, to talk about the nature and extent of his relationships with the Minimalist artists. In 1972, he said that

> I don't make a direct connection between my work and visual work. Obviously I'm close to a number of artists that we know, and some I've worked with, but I never consciously make references to their work in a direct way. . . . I know the relations are there, but it bothers me to make those kinds of assertions directly, because it sounds as if I'm trying to define something which I'd rather leave undefined. I feel more comfortable relating to people's work subjectively and indirectly, rather than think of myself as . . . let's say music as a form of sculpture or sculpture as a form of music. . . . I think those ideas can best be developed by other people.[31]

In his own book, there is much more about theatre than about the fine arts, though this can be explained by its operatic focus.

Yet some connections with fine art are not hard to find. As we have seen, Glass had already met the sculptor Richard Serra and the sculptor and painter Nancy Graves in Paris. There, too, he became reacquainted with the art critic Barbara Rose, whom he first came to know when the two were students on a summer school in Paris in 1957. Rose's influential article, 'ABC Art', was published in 1965,[32] around the time of the renewal of her friendship with the composer. Immediately on his return to New York, Glass began to make gallery connections. 'I was basically working in the art world', he says, 'and I knew all those people'. He quickly realised the potential offered by the considerable interest shown in minimal music by sculptors and painters who appreciated the kinship with what they themselves were doing. Various artists helped Glass with money and assisted in setting up contacts with the galleries, museums and arts festivals that proved to be much more interested in his music than were the main concert halls. Among these were Graves and Sol Le Witt; Graves, as already noted, was also involved with Mabou Mines. Glass and his colleagues were also invited to play in the SoHo lofts of artists such as Donald Judd. Graves and Le Witt were among the many artists who designed posters for Glass's concerts; others included Barry Le Va, Brice Marden, James Rosenquist, Joel Shapiro and Keith Sonnier. Chuck Close made the famous Photo-Realist painting of the composer, *Phil*, in 1969. In 1977, several of these artists contributed work for sale when Joe Helman, of the Blum-Helman Gallery, organised an art auction to help pay off the debts incurred in mounting *Einstein on the Beach*.

Notable among Glass's links with such artists is an early association with the Canadian film-maker, and occasional musician, Michael Snow and, in particular, the impact of his already discussed film *Wavelength*, which also made such an impression on Reich. The theatre director Richard Foreman wrote an article about Glass and Snow in 1970,[33] in which he drew attention to the way in which both composer and film-maker were confronting 'the consciousness mechanism of the spectator' – 'encrusted with a web of associational conditioning' – with 'minimal, systemic, primary structure space objects'. 'The light, color and textural variations of the image [of *Wavelength*'s 'single, slow, forty-five minute zoom down the length of Snow's studio']' he observes, 'briefly punctuate, at five- or ten-minute intervals, the unceasing zoom'; such variations are 'filmic events on an equal basis with several events involving people'. Neither creative artist sought 'to re-create the image of an intuited or sensed reality that is normally unavailable to consciousness; rather [they took] the material ([in Snow's case] the view of the room, in Glass's case the musical phrase) and [subjected] it to a series of reiterated manipulations in which its elements are held in unchanging relation. . . . The changes that are slowly introduced respect the integrity of the found image or structure and are specifically designed to show how they sustain themselves under the impact of *time*. Going back and forth over the image or the musical [phrase], time is a heavy truck knocking them a little this way, a little that way . . . repeatedly impressing a bit of dirt from the road'.

The result is an art in which the listener or spectator, wrote Foreman, 'in order simply to *notice* the work itself, *must* replace himself so that he is no longer confronting an object, but putting "himself-as-self" elsewhere, so that naked presence is the mode and matter of the artistic experience'. Not surprisingly, such an analysis fits Glass's output of the late 1960s better than it does his subsequent music. It is, though, tempting to suggest a comparison between the 'textural' approach of Snow's film and Glass's attitude to the psycho-acoustic by-products of his music, of which more later. Foreman's suggestion that his own work – and that of film-makers such as Hollis Frampton and choreographers such as Yvonne Rainer, as well as the music of all four composers featured in the present volume – teaches those who experience it 'to be more attuned to the ontological truths and categories' does, however, add a further dimension to our perspective on the extent to which such downtown creative artists of this period shared aesthetic goals, as well as resources and outlets. Snow, also an occasional improvising pianist, issued a double LP of his group's improvisations on Glass's Chatham Square label in 1971.

But the closest personal relationship Glass established in the late 1960s with any of the Minimalist artists was probably with Serra, some two years his junior. Though Serra says that when he arrived in New York, just a few months ahead of Glass, 'the critic-gallery-museum system was completely closed to me',[34] he became the most helpful of all the composer's Manhattan colleagues in offering financial aid, gallery contacts and so on. Both the artist's support and the composer's manual labour on behalf of his colleague began before their friendship led to Glass's full-time assistantship. Deploying gravity as an essential forming agent, Serra's sculptures often consist of slabs or sheets of metal balanced precariously against each other, gaining an important part of their impact through their threat of imminent collapse. In 1969, Close, Glass, the performance artist Spaulding Gray, Dicky Landry (a member of the composer's ensemble) and others helped the sculptor mount his 'second lead series' of pieces – entitled *1–1–1, 2–1–1, 2–1–2*, somewhat reminiscent of Glass's own recent *1 + 1* (see below) – at the Castelli Warehouse: in itself a 'choreographed' exercise (to use Serra's own word)[35] demanding considerable skill. At least one of Serra's sculptures – *Slow Roll: For Philip Glass* (1968) – is dedicated to the composer.

In March 1969, Glass's first solo tour to Europe was put together by Serra, chiefly to persuade the composer to travel with him to help install a series of his own exhibitions. Fascinated by film at this stage of his career, and himself a film-maker, Serra also showed Snow's *Wavelength* several times on this trip, being as enamoured of it as were Reich and Glass. Playing either electric organ or piano, Glass performed *Two Pages* at the Stedtelijke Museum in Amsterdam on 10 March and at the Galerie Ricke on 14 March, and *How Now* at the Kunsthalle in Bern on 22 March; *Wavelength* was screened on each occasion, and a tape of Reich's *Reed Phase* was played. Audiences became extremely exasperated. At the Amsterdam performance, someone joined in on the keyboard; Glass (who had done some wrestling while a student in Chicago) punched him, knocking him off the stage, and continued playing. In the same venue, Serra says, the audience for *Wavelength* toppled over the projector.[36]

Like *Wavelength* and *Back and Forth*, also by Snow, three of Serra's own films were included two months later as part of the 'Extended Time' works in the Whitney Museum's 'Anti-Illusion: Procedures/Materials' show, mentioned in Chapter 3. Made in early 1969, these 'hand films', as Serra calls them, consist of *Hand Catching Lead*, a three-minute study of the artist's own hand in the repeated attempt to grab constantly falling strips of lead; a seemingly untitled film, in which the same single hand is eventually forced, through sheer exhaustion, to drop the roll of cloth it is holding; and *Hands Scraping*, in which two pairs of hands (those of the sculptor and Glass) attempt to untie the rope which binds them by the wrists and then gather it up.

In addition, Glass and Serra collaborated on several other occasions, both on what the composer calls 'art/music pieces'[37] and on at least one other project without music at all. In June 1969, immediately after the Whitney show, the composer made tape music for an installation at Loveladies, in the New Jersey marshes, by Serra called *Long Beach Island, Word Location*. In this, fifteen-minute tape loops consisting entirely of the word 'is' were relayed on thirty-two loudspeakers positioned around a thirty-acre site so that, wherever a listener stood, he or she could only hear one of them. 'Our inability', states a text jointly credited to Glass and Serra, 'to form a meaningful relationship between the coinciding occurrences, i.e., the word system and the experience of the place, points to the failure of language to comprehend experience'.[38]

For around three years, ending some time in 1974 – a period which largely overlaps with the composition of *Music in Twelve Parts* – Glass then became the artist's regular studio assistant. Serra liked having technical help from a knowledgeable non-professional, since other sculptors in this role had a tendency to claim some rights in the authorship of the finished artworks. The two friends spent even more time together during these years, cementing their personal attachment and also bringing them close as colleagues, even though they were working in different media. Whilst he was as wary as Serra of anything resembling 'one-to-one' connections between different art forms, Glass now acknowledges Serra's influence on his own development as comparable to that of Snow, and today includes Bruce Nauman in this list as well. Serra denies any 'shared stylistic premises',[39] but argues that the two were part of a group 'investigating the logic of material and its potential for personal extension – be it sound, lead, film, body, whatever'.

While the concern of all these artists with process and the unity of form and content affected the composer profoundly, the period of his closest contact with Serra interestingly coincides with the sculptor's further development of 'post-minimalist' processes and his movement towards what has been characterised as the 'expanded field' of post-modernist art. Here, the boundaries between 'sculpture' and 'architecture' were challenged in new ways by continuing to employ sculptural means. Already working in non-sculptural media, and moving towards this position by the time of the important 1969 Whitney show, Serra took these concerns much further in his more public, situation-specific work of the early 1970s onwards. From 1970, Glass began his move away from a hard-line structuralist approach to one involving a more malleable attitude to sound and an increased concern with the sensuous effect of his music on the listener.

Once again, 'one-to-one' comparisons risk misrepresenting both their creators' intentions and their achievements. It can, however, be suggested that Glass's change of approach during this period was affected by his unusually intimate knowledge of Serra's work and the ideas which lay behind it. Both developments, indeed, may be described as critiques of the more evidently constructivist concerns which had triggered these men's first individual creative efforts. It is interesting, however, to discover that when composer and artist conducted the already quoted dialogue in 1986 for publication in a catalogue for a forthcoming collaborative installation in Columbus, Ohio, Glass argued a larger role for what he called 'subjective aesthetics' in the sculptor's choice and manipulation of materials than Serra himself would acknowledge.[40] To understand the trajectory of Glass's move towards post-modernism, however, we must return to its process-orientated origins.

1 + 1: *Additive and cyclic processes*

The first composition to be mentioned in many accounts of Glass's development is *1 + 1*, the piece for amplified tabletop and a single player.[41] Dated 11/68 on the score, it is the obvious work to introduce any technical discussion of his minimalist output, since it pares its material down just about as far as one could go. Despite the improvised looseness of its appearance, it is the earliest example of the composer's rigorous use of additive process. An understanding of how *1 + 1* works will – for all the piece's simplicity, even *naïveté* – be valuable as a key to all Glass's minimalist output. The score is reproduced complete as Example 4.2.

    1 + 1 is concerned purely with rhythm, emphasising immediately that Glass's starting point, like Reich's, was rhythm not pitch. The player taps on a tabletop amplified by means of a contact microphone; though Michael Nyman's account suggests that other surfaces are also permitted, the score itself fails to indicate this. Glass does not give a fully composed score; instead, he offers just two basic 'rythmic units' (*sic*; like many musicians, Glass seemingly cannot spell 'rhythm'), plus examples of the ways in which these may be used as 'building blocks' to construct a performance. While 'length is determined by the player', the score does not indicate whether the music should be improvised – which it conceivably could be – or realised in advance. It is interesting that its improvised character has led the US Copyright Office to refuse to register *1 + 1*, regarding it as a 'theoretical model' rather than a real composition.

    In addition, the score of *1 + 1* specifies only that the two given rhythms should be combined 'in continuous, regular arithmetic progressions'. The music is so simple that it only takes a moment to realise that the composer is referring to 'additive process': numbering the two 'units' as 1 and 2, for instance, the first of Glass's three examples comes out as 1 + 2; 1 + 2 + 2;

Example 4.2 *1 + 1*, complete score

$1 + 2 + 2 + 2; 1 + 2 + 2; 1 + 2$ etc. That is, while the first unit is represented only once in each alternation, the second unit expands and contracts, consistently, so that the last combination is the same as the first.

This rigorous, though not fully composed-out, approach to additive process is the equivalent – conceptually, perceptually, and in terms of style and compositional development as well – to Reich's notion of phasing, and it served Glass well as his main structural technique for the better part of ten years. Yet surprisingly, perhaps, it took him more than two years to conclude that rigour was required to make additive process work really interestingly. The composer himself has described the works composed in 1967–8 before *1 + 1* as coming 'before I had the idea of additive process. It's funny, it's such a simple idea, but believe it or not I just hadn't thought of it then. Actually it was the result of a year or two's work: I looked back and thought of simplifying all the processes I had used into that one idea'.[42] This means that even within the years 1965–9, the period of Glass's most radically minimal compositions, two fairly distinct stages are involved.

In order to understand the function and significance of this, it is necessary to disentangle two confusions. The first is the distinction between rigorous and non-rigorous uses of additive process. In the above quotation, Glass is referring to a *rigorous* use of this technique. Works immediately pre-dating *1 + 1*, such as *Strung Out*, clearly also use a kind of additive process, but this is looser, more intuitive. It may not be sufficiently free to prevent at least one commentator from confusing it with the kind of structures to be found in works from *1 + 1* onwards.[43] Any intelligent listener, however, can readily distinguish this approach from the later, stricter uses of additive process on account of the different challenges these offer to following the progress of the music. In both categories of compositions, notes or groups of notes are added, and subtracted, on the alternating principle outlined above; though even in works employing strict additive processes, the identity and integrity of the sub-units that constitute the basic material for such expansion may be left for the work's structure itself to clarify, not exposed at the outset. (From here on, such initial material will usually be called the Basic Unit, in line with the use of this term in the previous chapter.) Only works from *1 + 1* onwards, however, elaborate this process according to systematic rules of expansion and contraction.

This has the important function of making the unfolding structure clearly audible; the compositional process and the sounding music become one, as it were, just as we have already seen is the case in Reich's works using phasing. Rigorous additive process offers, like phasing, a way into a musical structure which may otherwise seem merely aimless. One does not *have* to concentrate on its machinations, at least *all* the time – free-wheeling, sensuous experience is always available for those who want it. But additive process offers the listener the possibility of combining a thrilling aural experience based on rhythmic and textural immediacy with the opportunity of appreciating the note-to-note details of the music's structure as it unfolds.

The second confusion is between additive process and cyclic structures.

Glass's cornerstone technique of additive process was, as we have seen, inspired by his initial contact with Shankar in Paris and nurtured by his lessons with Rakha two years later in New York. The kind of additive processes which Glass made the basis of his own music are not, however, to be found in Indian practice; even the rigorous application of these is not a direct borrowing but an extrapolation of the composer's own from the Indian approach to rhythm. Cyclic rhythmic structures, on the other hand, are to be found in Indian practice. Cyclic process, as the composer later described it, involves 'something that lasts maybe thirty-five beats and then begins the cycle again. Then you join cycles of different beats, like wheels inside wheels, everything going at the same time and always changing'.[44] The full significance of this in Indian practice can only be understood in relation to the melodic improvisation based on the chosen *raga*: as the composer put it, '[t]he interaction of melodic invention – or improvisation – with the rhythmic cycle (the *Thal*) provides the tension in Indian music, much as that between melody and harmony (rhythm is the poor relation here) provides it in Western music'.[45]

Glass's attempts to incorporate cyclic techniques into his early minimalist approach in fact predate his rigorous use of additive rhythms and even his espousal of the modal approach to pitch organisation which characterises his output after his return to New York. The 1966 String Quartet is an early example, and *In Again Out Again* – a piece for two pianos composed in March 1968 – is of particular importance in this development; both works are discussed below. Such attempts proved problematic, however, when the material was otherwise shaped only by literal repetition or with the casualness of 'intuitive' additive process. Glass's slowness in finding fruitful ways of incorporating cyclic techniques in his own work may also be related to his initial determination to purge his music of genuinely melodic, as well as harmonic, constructs altogether, thus depriving himself of such interaction between dimensions. Yet the stimulus to make rhythm, rather than pitch, the basis for a new kind of Western music itself derived ultimately from Indian practice, suggesting the rich potential offered by the reintegration of melody and harmony. This reintegration could, however, only be explored after rhythmic techniques had been pared down, subjected to rigorous manipulation and turned to new account.

Early minimalist compositions

The twelve works composed in the three or four years before *1 + 1* (that is, before November 1968) may themselves be divided into four categories: three works written in Paris in *c.* 1965–7, all now lost; a string quartet (its score dated August 1966) that is the only surviving Paris piece, and thus also Glass's earliest extant minimal composition; a group of seven works written in 1967–8 for single instruments, duos or trio, before the composer's group had taken on a more permanent form; and *600 Lines*, the single work he wrote, some time during the summer of 1968, for a larger line-up that was clearly the first manifestation of what later became the Philip Glass Ensemble. Following *1 + 1* come the five works of 1969–70 written for that ensemble, which apply additive process in the rigorous and vigorous manner which was to characterise Glass's mature output. Together with *Music with Changing Parts* (which, though also dating from 1970, must be considered separately) and *Music in Twelve Parts* (1971–4), these five compositions are the works by which Glass first became known outside his immediate SoHo circle. They are, though, very much the product of that downtown ethos, and did not become known at all widely until about 1973 or 1974. In addition, the already discussed music for theatrical use also helped to establish Glass's reputation in the early 1970s; *The Red Horse Animation* and *Music for Voices* will be discussed further below. Only one out of all these compositions, *Strung Out*, has been conventionally published; and only one, *Music in Similar Motion*, remains in the regular repertoire of the Philip Glass Ensemble to this day.

The Paris compositions

Most of the pieces Glass composed before *1 + 1* are largely unknown today and differ technically from *1 + 1* and the compositions of 1969. Though perhaps little more than historical curiosities, they illuminate an interesting stage in the development of musical minimalism. Three works surround, probably all actually predate, the Quartet: all, according to Glass's own book,[46] were composed in 1965–6 (though precise dates and even ordering are not clear); all are seemingly lost.

What was possibly the earliest of them – *Play*, the music for the Paris production of Beckett's play of the same name – has already been discussed. In 1974, Joan LaBarbara wrote that all four works written in Paris used cyclic structures,[47] which suggests that Glass may have already been attempting to use some kind of cyclic technique *before* his encounter with Shankar in the winter or spring of 1965–6. *Play* was probably written late in 1965; the other three pieces could all have been composed after this.

The other two lost works from this Paris period are *Music for Woodwind Quartet and Two Actresses* and *Music for Small Ensemble*. Both are part of what Glass calls 'a whole series I wrote at this time'[48] built, it seems, on the basic principles of *Play*. *Music for Woodwind Quartet and Two Actresses* is described by its composer as 'a concert work for JoAnne Akalaitis and Ruth

Maleczech (in which they declaimed a soufflé recipe over my music)'. LaBarbara wrote that the work 'had two movements of serial writing and two movements based on repetitive structures and steady pulse with abrupt starts and stops and no dynamic changes',[49] suggesting a more hybrid, even confused, approach. In 1997, Glass remembered it as 'a one-movement ensemble piece based on tonal modular repetition'. Kripl recalls the composition as 'more traditional', along the lines of the works which Glass wrote during his Juilliard days. What must be *Music for Small Ensemble*, the second piece in question, is described by LaBarbara as 'for winds', having 'parts dropping out and re-entering with new material so that the cycle kept changing'.[50] Its composer's failure to find sympathetic performers for this work in Paris was a factor in his decision to return to New York.

The First String Quartet

The string quartet written in Paris in August 1966 is now known as the First String Quartet, since there are, to date, four more; Glass no longer counts a 1963 quartet from his Pittsburgh period, despite its publication soon after completion. LaBarbara, writing only eight years after the 1966 quartet's composition, stated that 'Glass considers [it] . . . to be the most successful'[51] of the four Paris pieces, which is no doubt why the work – written shortly before he and his wife left Paris for the East – has survived. Its composer says that 'I was 29 and for the first time my music didn't sound like anybody else's'.[52]

The First String Quartet consists of two 'parts', divided into twenty and sixteen sections, respectively. Between the two parts, which the score estimates should take a total of about sixteen minutes, a 'pause of about 2 minutes' is specified. All sections are very short, each containing between seven and ten bars; a 'pause of 1½ to 2 seconds' is indicated between these. Speed relationships between sections are based on a strict system of metronome markings: all seven-bar sections are to be played at ♩=80, and those of eight, nine and ten bars at ♩=88, 92 and 100, respectively. This schematic arrangement, linking speed change incrementally to the number of bars, results in the actual length of each section being exactly the same.

There are, in fact, only eight different sections of material in the quartet as a whole: a pair of sections for each of the four categories listed above. The sustained level of secundal dissonance, both melodic and harmonic, is surprising, in view of the essentially modal approach of everything Glass has written since 1967, though this also seems a characteristic of at least parts of the lost Paris scores.

Example 4.3 First String Quartet, Part One, bars 1–8

The opening eight-bar section – shown in Example 4.3 – should make clear the quartet's approach to a kind of atonality; note that the first violin does not play here. Within a section, each instrument usually has only two or three notes, which rock to and fro and are repeated exactly several times; occasionally an instrument is confined to a single repeated pitch. While other sections employ *pizzicato* as well as *arco*, and occasional hairpin dynamics for some repeated patterns, the surface of the whole work is, like that of Example 4.3, essentially static, with no changes of speed or dynamic within any section.

This extract also serves to illustrate something more typical of the quartet's composer: experimentation with a rather basic cyclic structuring in which the patterns underpinning the 'main' part are simply cut off in mid-stream when the 'main' part finishes. Here, the two-bar (basically eight-crotchet) repeating pattern (rocking F♯s and G♯s) of the second violin has two further patterns cycling underneath it. A six-crotchet-plus-one-crotchet-rest cycle in the viola (C and E) starts one quaver later than the violin and, being one crotchet beat shorter, has begun its fifth statement by the eighth bar. A ten-crotchet pattern (two minims plus a crotchet rest, then the same again, articulated by three octave Fs) in the cello meanwhile completes one full cycle against the violin in five bars, begins again at bar 6, but manages only one note of the second statement of this second cycle before it too is curtailed. While probably akin to the rhythmic structuring Glass had employed in his other Paris compositions, such a cyclic process would not be taken up again with such enthusiasm, and even with this degree of strictness, until *In Again Out Again* a year-and-a-half later.

Glass's subsequent concern with structural rigour is, in addition, foreshadowed by the Quartet's extended deployment of structural repetition, animating such apparently static music into a fairly readily perceptible shape. The material discussed above is assembled to form two alternating sequences characterised by almost completely strict palindromic repetition.

The early New York compositions

Glass composed at least nine works between the summer of 1967 and the end of 1968, including *1 + 1*. These are clearly designed to experiment more fully with his new-found minimalist approach. As near a definitive list of these as possible runs as follows: *Strung Out* for solo amplified violin (dated July/August 1967); *Head-On* for violin, cello and piano (October 1967); *for Jon Gibson*, also known as *Gradus*, for soprano saxophone (dated February 1968, though Gibson thinks it was begun, if not finished, rather earlier); *Two Down* for two saxophones (composed after *Gradus*, say both Glass and Gibson; there is no date on the only score I have been able to obtain); *In Again Out Again* for two pianos (March 1968); *Piece in the Shape of a Square* for two flutes (May 1968); *How Now* for solo piano or, alternatively, ensemble (undated in the score, but probably written in April or early May 1968); and *600 Lines*, officially the first of Glass's 'open' scores (again undated in the score, but seemingly composed in the summer of 1968); as well as *1 + 1* (November 1968).

All eight works prior to *1 + 1* apply 'intuitive' additive procedures to basically modal pitch materials. *Strung Out*, *Gradus* and *Piece in the Shape of a Square* also reflect Glass's continuing concern to build a theatrical dimension into his 'concert' pieces. LaBarbara calls this '[t]rying to alter the traditional staid concert situation . . . scores which made shapes and had performers move around a space to follow a score'.[53] But he was also responding to the conditions in which these works had their first performances: not in conventional concert halls, for the most part, but in art galleries, lofts and other 'alternative' venues. Space permits detailed

Example 4.4 *Strung Out,* first three lines

discussion of *Strung Out* (which, though the earliest, is the only one to have been published), with brief references to the other seven pieces.

Strung Out

Strung Out for solo amplified violin gets its name from the way the original manuscript score of some twenty pages was bound. It unfolded in such a way that it could be 'strung out' around the performing space on music stands, or even pasted on the walls. The violinist's manoeuvres round the space thus became part of the event; a contact microphone was used in order to amplify the sound while giving the player complete freedom of movement. With the exception of two short sections, the work consists of a continuous string of fast quavers, marked 'mechanically'. The published score estimates a playing time of '*c.* 21 minutes';[54] Paul Zukofsky's 1976 LP recording lasts twenty-three minutes.[55] Glass himself says that the title of *Strung Out* related both to the idea of stringing a violin and to the colloquial expression meaning 'at the end of one's tether';[56] it also has drug-related implications, but the composer does not seem to have ever mentioned these.

The opening lines of *Strung Out* may serve as an illustration of the intuitive, non-systematic approach to additive process mentioned above (see Ex. 4.4). The absence of bar lines in this score, the earliest to profit from Glass's studies with Rakha, demonstrates that Glass had already found his own way of conveying his tabla teacher's insistence that '[a]ll the notes are equal'.[57] The initial division of a five-note Basic Unit (E G, E D C) into 2 + 3 notes forms the basis for an additive expansion of these two sub-units independently of one another, as in *1 + 1.* The sub-units are continually grouped and regrouped, in a constant quaver motion, to form repetitive sequences which look at a glance as though they might be rigorously additive. The opening E G immediately returns, played twice, as one might expect. Yet on its next appearance, it not only fails to increase this to the expected three, but also gets tangled up – at what is obviously still so early a stage that the musical building blocks have scarcely had time to register – with a note (C) which the listener has probably already registered as part of the *other* group of pitches. Not until the next line is E G offered three times uninterruptedly; but in the first three lines we hear these two notes as part of a phrase with C almost as many times as we hear them separately. (Clearly, a certain amount depends on phrasing, too, since there is no actual gap between any of the notes.) The original five-note Basic Unit returns quite frequently in the piece's early stages. But no rigorously consistent pattern of additive expansion can be observed.

Yet if it predates Glass's realisation that it is the rigour of additive process that makes it musically interesting, *Strung Out* already demonstrates a certain structural sophistication. The descending group of pitches, E D C, emphasising a C-major modality, proves to be the basis for a downward expansion: first to B (page 2, line 2), then to A (page 2, line 5); and later to G (page 4, line 4), F (page 4, line 10), E (page 5, line 4) and finally D (page 5, line 11). And as this expansion is revealed, the first group of pitches, E G, is progressively abandoned in favour of scalic patterns, using E D C as a point of departure, retaining E as the highest pitch and incorporating each downward expansion as it is introduced, or shortly thereafter, as the departure point for patterns which ascend, especially once A is reached, as well as descend. After A is firmly established, the even patter of quavers is broken by discontinuous fragments stressing A and B (from page 3, line 5). The expanding scalic patterns are then resumed.

When the downward expansion reaches E, the E G sub-unit is reintroduced (from page 5, line 6), but it soon gives way to conjunct movement once more. After D is reached, discontinuous fragments reoccur, this time based on D and E (from page 6, line 1). E is re-established as both top and bottom note (page 7, line 1), suggesting a retrograde of the whole process, but this is soon followed by an unsystematic series of contractions and expansions – involving G, E, D and A as lower notes, and E, D, C and B as the upper pitches – now emphasising ascending scalic patterns.

After the range finally contracts more decisively in favour of the upper notes, high Fs and Gs briefly burst the E–E octave frame (from page 8, line 10), after which the original complete five-note Basic Unit returns and almost the whole piece is repeated. The *Da Capo*'s omission of the last three lines leads to the eventual prominence of the pattern B C D E: as conclusive a resolution as can perhaps be achieved in a work which delights in several kinds of repetition but almost entirely excludes one of the most obvious: repetition of a single note.

For the listener, *Strung Out* is disconcerting. It is hard to get much out of such simple music, and in particular to concentrate on its progress, when what *appears* logical on a note-to-note level cannot be 'read' on a note-to-note level as it unfolds, when rigour is implied but not offered. The sorts of structural properties outlined above – which can be readily followed by any intelligent listener – show that, even at this early stage, Glass is composing with a clear overall and audible design. But analysis in greater detail here risks merely providing evidence to frustrate the listener more than to assist the listening process.

Other compositions of 1967–8

In his next composition, Glass addressed the problem of applying additive processes to music for more than one instrument. *Head-On* (omitted from the worklist in the composer's own book) is scored for violin, cello and piano. According to Glass, the title refers to a basic progression from a sparse texture to a dense one, with 'a collision of music at the end', though the contrast is in practice more a matter of tessitura than of instrumental voices in play. The piece develops rhythmically independent parts for violin, cello and piano at a steady tempo in a rather brittle G major, their unwinding co-ordinated by reverting to bar lines. The piano's initially high-lying interlocking patterns of continuous quavers gradually descend over the course of the piece, loosening and re-establishing their connections and continuity as the 'grid' they provide is notated in bars of slowly decreasing length, from twenty-eight quavers to the bar to just five. But overall, the details of this work's rhythmic processes are even harder to follow than the additive elaborations of *Strung Out*.

Glass assesses *for Jon Gibson*, also known as *Gradus*, for soprano saxophone as 'a better version of *Strung Out*'. Apparently searching for a more systematic approach, he applied a strict scheme of thirty-two-beat lines to the unfolding of his material. The piece is based on a five-pitch Basic Unit, its two sub-units – a 2 + 3 structure like that of the violin piece – almost immediately losing any clear identity. An extended sequence of registral contractions and expansions, beginning with an octave's span, A–A, and concluding with the note at its top, transforms an initially pentatonic gamut into a Mixolydian one. While playing it, Gibson moved along two intersecting lines of music stands which reflected the two-part structure of the piece.

Two Down for two saxophones – described by its composer as 'an elaboration of *Gradus*' – is the second of three pieces from this period written with Gibson in mind; the other player was probably Landry. Both were permitted to choose which type of saxophone to use. Its two lines demonstrate a high degree of similarity, being contrapuntal elaborations of an initial four-note Basic Unit – A B D F – which at first expands upwards, fragmenting unsystematically, then contracts. A thirty-two-beat line scheme is again deployed to bring some further control to this, but, curiously, in a more casual fashion than was the case in *Gradus*. Imitation between the two saxophones remains the broad principle, and for short passages this can be rigorously canonic in terms of pitch and at least consistent in terms of rhythmic relationship. Glass describes the piece's rhythmic scheme, with its tendency towards fragmentation, as a 'count down'; the title of *Two Down* derives from the combination of progressive reduction and its articulation by two musicians.

With *In Again Out Again* for two pianos – intended for its composer and Reich to play – Glass hit on the idea of single figures subjected to unwritten-out repetition. He also attempted to develop the kind of counterpoint first explored in *Head-On* in the context of a more practicable framework, in particular by returning to a more rigorous investigation of cyclic processes in combination with additive structures. The combination of related repeated figures, in an F-minor modality, in close and constantly shifting counterpoint on two pianos suggests the influence of Reich's *Piano Phase*, completed exactly a year before. The relationship between the two players – one continuous, the other moving against it, the latter constantly alternating between entering into a relationship (motivic, contrapuntal and cyclic) with the former and then abandoning it – gives *In Again Out Again* its title. Halfway through the piece, the pianos exchange functions, and their material is presented in retrograde. This whole ingenious structure fits neatly on to just two pages.

Some of the advances of *In Again Out Again* were then pursued in the context of another thirty-two-quavers-per-line structure. *Piece in the Shape of a Square*, the third of these seven compositions to involve Gibson, is for two flutes; its title is a pun on Erik Satie's 1903 *Trois morceaux en forme de poire* for piano duet. Like *Strung Out*, the piece has a theatrical dimension: for it, he said in 1975, the composer constructed 'a big square about twelve feet by twelve feet and pinned up the music around it. There was music on the inside of the square and on the outside, and Jon Gibson and I played it, walking round in opposite directions and coming back to the beginning'.[58] In his own book – where the alternative titles 'Music in the Shape of a Square' and 'Music in the Form of a Square' may be found, and in which he reports the side of the square as being about ten feet – Glass writes that Gibson played inside the square, with himself on the outside; as in *Strung Out*, use was made of the contact microphone.[59]

Each of the piece's 160 lines unravels a disjunct modal melody constantly doubling back on itself, which is subjected to additive rhythmic expansions becoming more scalic as the centre of the piece is reached. The application of additive process to this scheme is somewhat stricter than that to be found in *Strung Out*. The second flute part is basically a line-by-line retrograde of that of the first, with some significant modifications, mirroring the scheme of perambulation described above. *Piece in the Shape of a Square* moves from a pentatonic mode with G as tonic to one on E mixing Phrygian and Lydian tendencies, and back again.

The title of *How Now* is apparently a reference, made by a somewhat self-conscious as well as assertive young composer, to the up-to-date nature of the procedures which he was using. Originally conceived as a piece for solo piano, it was turned into an ensemble work for saxophones (played by Gibson and Landry, using both soprano and alto) and electric organs (played by Murphy, Reich and the composer) as Glass began to employ a more regular group of musicians. Returning to the short figures subjected to unwritten-out repetition that had brought such notational economy to *In Again Out Again*, he constructed a similar series of related patterns to articulate a simple retrograde structure. Beginning in an ambiguous D♭ major, subsequently expanding to a black-note pentatonic modality, *How Now* has a middle section outlining a move from A minor to D minor before returning whence it came.

Eleven figures based on quavers in a steady tempo should each, according to the score, 'be repeated for twenty to thirty seconds before changing to the next figure. A good average length for "How Now" is twenty-five to thirty minutes'. The eleven figures of *How Now* are not, however, played in exactly this order, but according to a fixed sequence given in the score. This advances according to a scheme which is itself essentially additive, allowing the original Basic Unit to be accompanied, additively altered and transposed before the player advances towards and then away from the central figure, no. 8, using the last untransposed figure, no. 4, as a reference point before completing the retrograde sequence to return the piece to the opening right-hand pattern on its own. While lacking the additive sophistication or, necessarily, the contrapuntal ingenuity of *In Again Out Again* or *Piece in the Shape of a Square*, this solo piano piece assembles as many of the ingredients that were to prove fruitful to Glass in the ensuing few years as do any of his other early compositions.

The only work from this period originally intended for more than three performers is *600 Lines*. Omitted from the worklist in Glass's book, it seems unlikely to be successful in performance. Like all his compositions after *1 + 1* and before *Einstein on the Beach*, the score does not actually specify instrumentation; *600 Lines* is in fact the 'training piece' for the

ensemble of assorted electric keyboards and wind instruments that Glass
was shortly to make his own.

The piece consists, as might be expected, of 600 single lines of music,
presumably to be played, as with the composer's later works, by the whole
ensemble throughout, players dropping out to rest as necessary.
Employing again a 'grid' of thirty-two quavers, the composer fits into this
framework – a much more extended one than any he had previously constructed – a varied sequence of additive and subtractive processes using a
mere five notes – C, D, E, G and high C – in a clear modal C major reminiscent of the opening material of *Strung Out*. Several schemes – simple
repetition, a retrograde which is not literal but reverses the order of patterns, additive process, altering the placing of rests as expansions and
contractions occur – operate on this basic material, extending and trans-
forming it in ways familiar from its predecessors. Processes such as these
tend to undermine any establishment of Basic Unit and sub-units which
such simple five-note material inevitably sets up. Neither 'internal' additive process nor line repetition (whether of prime or retrograde) is consistently adhered to as the work unfolds. And though the 'grid' of thirty-two
quavers per line conditions and confines these elaborations, there seems to
be no particularly systematic exploration of the interaction between the
additive processes themselves and the cyclic framework within which they
are contained.

The effect appears likely to offset any musical interest created by such
unpredictability by confounding the listener's chances of following the
work's development with any consistency. Any overall tendencies observable in the deployment of the five pitches – for instance, that individual
notes are abandoned, sometimes for short periods, occasionally for long
ones – are similarly loose in nature. There is, however, a certain logic to the
work's conclusion on the bare fifth C G: though less obvious than the frequent octave Cs that have preceded it, this still represents a reduction of
modality to its primal, 'perfect' essence, as it were.

The combination of Glass's rather casual use of additive process and the
time estimated to play all 600 lines – some two hours – would in all proba-
bility render the work impossible to listen to. Reich has said that it was
through his guidance that his friend abandoned *600 Lines* and began to
concentrate exclusively on a rigorous application of additive process late in
1968.[60] The work also presented, in an extreme form, a practical problem
raised by some of Glass's other pieces of this period. Music based on such
repetitive structures apparently necessitated many pages to notate, and
some of his scores had attempted solutions to this encumbrance. Now that
these compositions were venturing into ensemble territory, though, the

burden was exacerbated. For *600 Lines*, Glass devised a system involving slide projections of the score changed by a foot pedal, but this proved unreliable. Though endlessly rehearsed, *600 Lines* was in fact never performed in concert.

Glass describes all eight of these scores, including *String Out*, as 'rather awkward pieces' and says that he felt he 'had practically reached an impasse' by the time of the sprawling impracticalities of *600 Lines*. He now solved the problem by taking the matter of how a score could be notated to the opposite extreme. The result was the single-page, improvised 'model of a piece', *1 + 1*. 'In order to solve the notational problem, I had to define the structural essence of the idea', says its composer. Rethinking his notation led directly to the realisation that a rigorous, rather than more intuitive, use of additive process offered much greater potential. As we have seen, *1 + 1* 'was the first real additive piece'.

The evolution of the composer's own ensemble

The group that from some time in 1968 was referred to as the Philip Glass Ensemble had its beginnings in the same loose association of composer-performers which produced Steve Reich and Musicians, as we have seen in Chapter 3. *600 Lines* was the first unrevised composition any member of this circle produced to require more than three players.

Several musicians were involved specifically with Glass from early on. The violinist Dorothy Pixley-Rothschild, another ex-Juilliard colleague, gave the première of *Strung Out*, but did not stay long. Gibson, by contrast, now quickly became a permanent member of the ensemble, despite the fact that he went to work in Los Angeles for around eight months at a crucial period for both Glass and Reich. Glass pleaded with him by letter to return, sending him not only a copy of *600 Lines*, but also, on 10 February 1969, the score of a little piece for him entitled *Come Back*: a play on the words of the title in the manner of *1 + 1*.[61]

As Glass's need for wind players, especially saxophonists, grew, both Landry and Richard Peck became regular members, helping to form the nucleus of the Philip Glass Ensemble after the break with Reich in 1971; Anthony Braxton, too, was an occasional member. Kripl, an ally from the time when both were Boulanger pupils in Paris, joined later, in 1979. Kurt Munkacsi, the Ensemble's sound designer and mixer, joined in the autumn of 1970, having been introduced by Gibson, who met him when both were working for Young in France that summer. His contribution became increasingly significant in the early and mid-1970s, as we shall see; he also later became Glass's regular record producer.

Keyboard parts, the other central feature of the group, were initially provided by Glass, Murphy and Reich, as well as several visitors, some quite well known. Frederic Rzewski, Richard Teitelbaum and James Tenney, all important composers as well as players in the emerging downtown scene, were among them. Among the regular performers, Gibson, another composer, played electric keyboard as well as saxophone and, occasionally, flute. Steve Chambers and Robert Telson, the former subsequently more associated with Reich, were other early keyboard players; Michael Riesman – a central figure in the Ensemble and for several years now its music director – only joined in 1974. Like Reich, Glass began to incorporate voices into his group from 1970. As we shall see, this arose more or less accidentally, and at first – notably in *Music with Changing Parts* – vocal sounds were provided by the (predominantly male) instrumentalists. The arrival of a female singer as a formal member of the group dates from 1971, when Glass was approached by Joan LaBarbara. Despite her current involvement with Reich – something of a problem, given the two composers' increasing estrangement – LaBarbara remained a member of the Philip Glass Ensemble until the early performances of *Einstein on the Beach* in Avignon in the summer of 1976; she was unique in managing to perform with both composers in the mid-1970s. The soprano Iris Hiskey, who replaced her, also arrived quite early in the group's history. Further occasional members of the ensemble at this time included David Behrman (viola), Barbara Benary (electric violin and voice) and Beverley Lauridsen (cello). Rusty Gilder and Robert Prado, two unusually versatile musicians from Louisiana with backgrounds largely in more vernacular traditions, joined for a while in 1971–2. Both played trumpet, though Gilder had originally been an electric bass player. Prado performed mainly on keyboard with the group, and occasionally added flute and voice as well; he died in an oil-field accident not long after the ensemble's West Coast and European tours of 1972.

When Glass wanted to organise a concert, he says, he 'went to the Film-Makers' Cinémathèque or the Public Theater. I would never go to a concert hall; they wouldn't have had me anyway'. Early New York performances included one at Queen's College on 13 April 1968 (including *Strung Out, for Jon Gibson* and *In Again Out Again*) and at the New School for Social Research on 9 May (including *Strung Out*). Several of Glass's early compositions – including *Strung Out, for Jon Gibson, In Again Out Again, Piece in the Shape of a Square* and *How Now* – were performed (the last two of these their premières; *How Now* in its original solo piano form, played by the composer) at his first major New York concert: on 19 May 1968 at the Cinémathèque, on 80 Wooster Street. Through Tenney, who was an occasional member of the circle, Glass had met the film-maker and critic

Jonas Mekas, who made the Cinémathèque available to him. Though the space could only hold about 120 people, the event was clearly significant in the development of the composer's reputation: Gibson calls it 'Philip's first NY coming out concert for sure'.[62]

Following Glass's solo European tour with Serra, the ensemble's next important New York concert came on 20 May 1969. The earlier of the pair of concerts that Glass, Reich and their colleagues gave at the Whitney Museum, this included films by Serra, framed by *How Now* and *Two Pages* performed by soprano saxophones and electric keyboards. In January 1970, there were two consecutive nights (the 16th and 17th) at the Guggenheim Museum with a programme that included the first major performances of *Music in Fifths*, *Music in Eight Parts* and *Music in Similar Motion*. Glass's first important American engagement outside New York City was a two-night stand at the Walker Art Center, Minneapolis, on 13 and 14 May 1970, following the two programmes of Reich's compositions. The concert at Fifth Avenue Church on 10 November 1970 that included the première of *Music with Changing Parts* was the last in which Reich performed with Glass, with the exception of the programmes on their European tour in February and March 1971. Glass's concerts in the latter, all of which included *Music with Changing Parts*, included one in Düsseldorf on 3 March, and two rather low-profile events in London, following Reich's programme at the Institute of Contemporary Arts, already mentioned in Chapter 3. The first of these took place at Wimbledon College of Art on 8 March, the second two days later at the Royal College of Art. The latter was held in the entrance hall; in the audience were David Bowie and Brian Eno, both by then former RCA students.

The compositions of 1969

The ensemble works written immediately after *1+1* took swift advantage of the potential offered by its combination of additive process and notational economy. Now able to 'collapse twenty minutes of music into two pages', Glass composed a continuous single line (the 'unison' of Nyman's reference to the piece as '*Music in Unison*'),[63] in which additive expansions and contractions of an initial five-note Basic Unit (see Ex. 4.5a, below), presented complete at the outset, provide the only material and sole process. The fully composed-out modular patterns in open scoring are reminiscent of Riley's *In C*, and *Two Pages* became the first piece in the repertoire of the composer's emerging group. Reich says that Glass originally headed the score '*Two Pages for Steve Reich*' but, when the recording came out in 1974, dropped the homage to his erstwhile friend: in the continuing aftermath of their break-up a few years earlier, Reich felt this to be a further act of denial of his significance for Glass's development.[64] Glass says that Reich liked *Two Pages* so much in rehearsal that he appended the words 'for Steve Reich' to a score and presented it to him, never intending this as anything more than the spontaneous gift of a copy.

The economy of Glass's new notational solution seems in turn to have helped suggest the use of rigorous, as opposed to intuitive, additive process. The composer then embarked on a logical sequence of works in which quite strict application of additive and subtractive processes is explored via increasing textural and contrapuntal elaboration. The titles of these compositions – *Music in Fifths, Music in Contrary Motion, Music in Similar Motion, Music in Eight Parts* – suggest the basis in each case.

Several principles also hold good for the whole series, which may be described as a rationalisation of the explorations and discoveries Glass had made during the previous few years. Each work is constructed from a Basic Unit, which may vary in length from piece to piece and is usually easily divisible into two or more sub-units, which may be worked on independently. The scores simply notate the expansions and contractions of the Basic Unit that form the structure of each work. They do this, though, by grouping sub-units and their expansions and contractions into figures of varying lengths; there is, importantly, no regular metre. Furthermore – and crucially – each of these figures is to be repeated an unspecified number of times, forming a seamless flow both between repetitions of each figure and between each figure and the next.

Instrumentation is never specified in these scores, and register can be flexible; while the earliest of them may – stamina permitting – be attempted by solo performers, Glass's own ensemble soon turned them into quartets, quintets, sextets or beyond, using electric keyboards of various kinds as a basis plus, most often, amplified wind instruments – usually soprano saxophones and flutes. The number of repetitions of each figure may be fixed in advance; whether the latter is the case or not, the composer indicates transfer to the next figure by a necessarily rather exaggerated movement of the head. Also missing from the scores are dynamic markings or any other interpretative indications, though several are headed simply 'fast, steady'. While Glass himself has usually played all these works at a high intensity – loud as well as fast – there is no reason why performances should not explore quieter dynamics, if not slower speeds, thus altering, most notably, the listener's perception of structure and, in particular, the nature and extent of its tensions, their accumulation and any potential they may have for resolution. It would, however, seem to run counter both to the music's natural logic and to the 'experimental' aesthetic to which they subscribe to subject dynamics to frequent change, especially via 'expressive' crescendi or diminuendi.

Two Pages

Two Pages (February 1969) represents Glass's first use of rigorous additive process in a composed-out score. Though octave doubling of a single line – played on the commercial recording by piano (Riesman) and electric organ (the composer) – does little to colour its deliberately barren soundscape, the work's technical procedures quickly proved their potential for deploying a variety of ways of balancing moment-to-moment unfolding of material, holding attention through the rigour of its operations upon it, and the need to provide a satisfying overall formal structure. They were soon taken up in works which were more lasting contributions to the repertoire of the composer's full ensemble.

As Wes York has pointed out (in an article on the piece which is among the most detailed analyses to be published of any minimalist composition),[65] the procedures in operation here are already quite sophisticated. York's transcription of the 1974 Shandar recording, made for his own analysis, is the only currently available published version. The following analysis makes use of surviving copies of the composer's manuscript score (which York was unable to see); the figure numbers employed here follow this definitive version and are accordingly sometimes different from York's. When the latter's 'measure numbers' differ from the manuscript's figure numbers, they are given in square brackets. Since York's interpretation of where a new part begins sometimes contradicts the original manuscript, his measure numbers have been adjusted to fit.

Example 4.5 gives the Basic Unit – G C D E♭ F – and some illustrations of the operations performed upon it in the five parts of *Two Pages*. The contrast between the opening interval of a perfect fourth and the ensuing conjunct motion helps suggest the possibility of two sub-units, while simultaneously permitting the usual sorts of ambiguity: notably that between the 'common-sense' division into G C and D E♭ F (2 + 3) and the 'psycho-acoustic' isolation of G suggested by the larger interval separating it from the other four notes. The five additive (and in two cases also subtractive) processes performed using these five pitches explore these and other sorts of subdivision. York identifies four processes at work: expansion and contraction of whole figures, expansion and contraction of parts of them, and what York terms 'external' and 'internal' repetition (the number of repetitions of each figure actually played, again applied to whole figures ['external'] and to parts of them ['internal']). These pro-

Example 4.5 *Two Pages*: (a) Figures 1–7; (b) Figure 15; (c) Figure 44; (d) Figure 61; (e) Figure 78.

cesses of expansion/contraction and repetition interact in various ways throughout the work, with 'external' repetition, one section excepted, a constant feature.

Part One (Figures 1–7, lasting about three minutes on the commercial recording; see Ex. 4.5a) treats these five notes as a single unit. To complete statements of G C D E♭ F, the first four, three and two notes (what York terms a 'subtractive process') are each added in turn, to give a fourteen-note figure; at this point (Figure 4), the process is reversed. Part Two (Figures 8–41 [mm. 8–39 in York's transcription], lasting some six minutes) again takes off from the original five-note pattern. While a single G C sub-unit begins each figure, the sub-unit D E♭ F is expanded in additively rigorous fashion: adding a note each time, until (at Figure 15) three complete statements of this three-note pattern, plus a 'tail' consisting of the notes D and E♭ alone, have been assembled (see Ex. 4.5b). From Figure 16, the number of repetitions of the whole sub-unit D E♭ F is then gradually enlarged to thirty statements. Following this, contraction occurs, using the same repetitions in reverse order and returning to a single statement of the whole five-note unit, plus the two-note 'tail', at Figure 41 [m. 39].

Part Three (Figures 42–59 [mm. 39–55a], which also takes around six minutes) builds a still more complex additive structure around this seven-note figure by adding a second one to it. The 'new' figure placed in front of it – another seven-note grouping, at first eliding with the previous one (Figure 43 [m. 40]) before achieving full separation (Figure 44 [m. 41]) – has built-in subtraction (1234 123, or G C D Eb, G C D) of the kind first encountered in Figure 3 (see Ex. 4.5c). Figure 45 [m. 42] begins this seven-note pattern's additive expansion, but also treats D Eb F D Eb as a further semi-detached five-note pattern, with its own built-in subtractive tendencies, by repeating this as a sub-unit. These two figures now both proceed by additive expansion to twenty statements each.

Part Four (Figures 60–78 [mm. 55b–71], lasting some two-and-a-half minutes) begins by abandoning G and C altogether; Figure 60 [m. 55b] squeezes a final additive expansion from the five-note pattern of Part Three. Figure 61 [m. 56] then adds C D Eb F in front of this, and it is this four-note pattern which is now additively expanded; the pitch G remains entirely absent from this section (see Ex. 4.5d). Twenty repetitions are assembled in the manner of the previous scheme until, in Figure 78 [m. 71], the five notes with which this section had begun – now themselves assuming the function of a 'tail' – are abandoned altogether, and C D Eb F becomes the kernel for the expansion of Part Five (Figures 78–81 [mm. 72–4], which takes less than two minutes). This begins by placing the original five-note unit in front of C D Eb F, returning G to the mode (see Ex. 4.5e). Finally, two more patterns – D Eb F and Eb F – are added to give a sequence mirroring Part One's 'subtractive' accumulation of $5+4+3+2$ quaver patterns to produce the fourteen-note bar with which the work concludes.

York's analysis demonstrates how the simple arch shape of Part One is first contradicted, then subsumed by the unfolding of *Two Pages* as a whole. While Part One employs whole-figure development and purely 'external' repetition, Part Two dissects its figure and involves 'internal' as well as 'external' repetition. Both, however, involve contraction as well as expansion. The basic shape of Part Three, on the other hand – a rise not followed by a corresponding fall – is a kind of contradiction responding to the essentially expanding characteristic of the additive structure itself. So is its division into two parts: the first (Figures 42–4 [mm. 39–41]) a logical continuation of Part Two; the much longer second part (Figures 45–59 [mm. 42–55a]) superimposing internal repetitions equally logically on to an additively expanding version of what has preceded it. Part Three's pivotal status is further established by its simultaneous use of all four processes deployed on the basic material of *Two Pages*.

Throughout Part One, G appears to function as the dominant of a clear-cut C-minor mode. Due to amplification and repetition, however, G C starts to be heard as a kind of drone, while G maintains a degree of independence by rhythmic means. In Part Two, Figure 8's initial expansion of the basic five-note pattern to six quavers suggests a clarification of the v–i relationship between G and C; it is quite easy to hear the new four-note pattern D E♭ F D and the immediately following G as outlining G^7, which then resolves on to C. The expansion of the sub-unit D E♭ F, however, gradually refocuses attention on these three pitches as an independent entity contrasting with the dominance of Part One's C D E♭, and on the potential of both F and D as a 'tonic'. The impossibility of mentally ordering these D E♭ F repetitions into predictable shapes is highly subversive, their almost inordinate prolongations sending Part Two into a spiral of tension only resolved as these D E♭ F repetitions gradually return to an uneasy equilibrium with those of G C.

The return of C D E♭ enables Part Three to offer a more tonally stable answer to the previously hesitant modality. Here, syncopation reinforcing C as tonic – a characteristic of all patterns in which C, D and E♭ are interrupted by G – is now fully exploited, the constant returns of the seven-note pattern of which all these pitches form part acting as a strong foil to the five-note alternative exclusively derived from D E♭ F. While the single G C isolated by the additive process in operation here forms a pivot point, the reassembling of the opening five-note unit allows G C to be readily subsumed: a constant reminder of the original unit's possible return.

Part Four destroys this equilibrium by abandoning both G and C and reducing matters to a whirling, climactic celebration of the second sub-unit, D E♭ F. C then returns (Figure 61 [m. 56]), as part of an additively expanding C D E♭ F pattern, prising apart the first sub-unit for the first time and suggesting the centrality of C without the help, or hindrance, of any dominant associations at all. Though now assisted by the psycho-acoustic energy associated with the lowest note in any incessantly repeating sequence, underlined by the only example in *Two Pages* of four-note modular repetition, the centrality of C here lacks the dominant dimension which gave to Part Three's syncopated tonic assertions a suggestion of tonal depth. While the D E♭ F D E♭ pattern is confined to single statements amidst the developing, and eventually enveloping, C D E♭ F, its presence remains rhythmically disruptive, allowing the listener to supply a downbeat anywhere, or nowhere. All this continues to feature in what York identifies as the second section of Part Four (Figures 65–78 [mm. 60–71]):

a seamless continuation of the additive process of the first section, but distinguishable from it through its absence, unique in *Two Pages*, of 'external' repetition, as performed on the commercial recording.

With its rhythmic and tonal processes now in gear to drive the work to a critical point in a context which does not imply the existence of convenient and clear resolution, *Two Pages* could have concluded here. The more conventionally conclusive Part Five, however, brings about a different kind of resolution. The reincorporation of G now brings with it the return of many of the characteristics of Part One: the original five-note unit (not heard since Part Three), and a 'wedge'-shaped 'subtractive' accumulation involving patterns of rigorously decreasing size to produce a fourteen-note pattern. The unencumbered recapitulation of these initial components of the work's surprisingly varied scheme brings a strong sense of finality to the last moments of *Two Pages*, despite the absence of a return to the arch-shape structure which had characterised Parts One and Two and then been abandoned. The structural openness of Part Five is mirrored by a degree of tonal ambiguity; its tendency to conclusiveness is, however, enhanced by the focus on purely 'external' repetitions.

Music in Fifths *and* Music in Contrary Motion

For *Music in Fifths* (June 1969), Glass took the same pitch array as he had used in *Two Pages* and simply moved the dominant up an octave, so that it now became part of the stepwise movement of what Nyman calls a 'five-finger exercise'[66] (see Ex. 4.6b). One further pitch decision remained – one that was to become important in subsequent compositions. To create a second line, consistently doubling the other a perfect fifth below, he transposed the C minor of the first into F minor; in Glass's own recording, both lines are doubled an octave below. The combination creates a modal ambiguity in which two lines a fifth apart maintain a certain, rather rigid, independence resolutely focused on the lower five pitches of their respective scales – or even circling around Ab and Eb, the relative major tonics of the two keys involved – yet are simultaneously yoked together to form a composite readily describable as in the F-Dorian mode. While the fast repetition of patterns based entirely on these two parallel sequences of pitches produces an uncertain euphony by creating the suggestion of thirds and sevenths in the resulting 'harmony', the continuous parallel fifths make for a raw and uningratiating sound. The perpetrator of this rough ride in such a relentless machine encourages the notion that its rigorous adherence to the consecutive fifths banned in the conventional training a Western music student receives is 'a sort of teasing homage' to his former teacher Boulanger. Reich apparently once said that *Music in Fifths* was 'like a freight train'.[67]

Example 4.6 *Music in Fifths*: (a) Figure 1; (b) Figure 13.

(*a*)

(*b*)

Rigorous operation of additive process, using two immediately identifiable sub-units, only begins at Figure 13. Figures 1–12 offer an irregular, already deconstructed version of Figure 13's 4 + 4 unit of eight quavers, divided into two sub-units of 6 + 7 (see Example 4.6a). The first, six-quaver sub-unit serves, in unaltered form, to introduce each figure. The second, seven-quaver sub-unit leads, in Figure 2, to a statement of what will prove to be the 'proper' eight-quaver Basic Unit of Figure 13. The latter then gradually takes over, accumulating repetitions in the course of alternately following single statements of the seven-quaver sub-unit and replacing it altogether (in the odd-numbered figures up to 7).

The eight-note 'five-finger' pattern of Example 4.6b is now revealed as the essential kernel of *Music in Fifths*. It is subjected to a purely additive process, expanding the eight-note pattern to a total of 210 quavers in the course of twenty-three figures (Figures 13–35). Changes first occur alternately in the ascending first sub-unit or the descending second one; from Figure 19, they appear in both sub-units at once, consistently turning the expansions of the second sub-unit into inversions of the first. As figures become longer, notes are added in groups of six and seven, recapitulating in the process the patterns of the introduction.

While the additive procedures of *Music in Fifths* obviously modify any rhythmic regularity, its basis in a unit of eight quavers dividing easily into 4 + 4 offers more sense of real metre than does the 2 + 3 unit of *Two Pages*. The advantages of establishing a regular metre – against which other possibilities can then be measured and compared – first seem evident here. The sheer relentlessness of *Music in Fifths*, on the other hand, draws attention to its lack of both structural and harmonic sophistication.

Only a month later, in July 1969, came *Music in Contrary Motion*. This

Example 4.7 *Music in Contrary Motion*, Figure 1

proved tricky as a group piece, and the only commercial recording is of a solo version played on electric organ by the composer himself. Glass's train of thought at this period may also be gathered from the following response to a question about the evolution of his early minimalist methods:

> My reasons for writing pieces were often very strange . . . *Two Pages*, you remember, is in unison. Someone asked me if I was attempting to trace the progress of musical history and if, therefore, my next piece would follow on logically and be fifths. So I wrote *Music in Fifths*. That was all in parallel motion, so I obviously had to do one in contrary motion next. And after *Music in Contrary Motion* came its opposite again, *Music in Similar Motion*. It was a very easy going thing. In 1969 nobody knew me or cared much what I wrote, so I could make any jokes I liked.[68]

Whatever this idea – of building a compositional development in ironic homage to Western musical history's expansion from plainchant to organum and so on to more elaborate contrapuntal forms – tells us about his attitude, it helped to provide Glass with a sense of continuity about his compositional development for the first time.

Music in Contrary Motion is devoted entirely to two-part contrary motion, the lower part being a 'tonal' inversion of the upper one; the five pitch classes used (A B C D E) produce a modal A minor uninflected either by the contrapuntal layout or by any additional pitches (see Ex. 4.7). There are, in fact, really only two sub-units at work in this piece – the four-note scale and the five-note third-based pattern – plus their inversions, giving rise to a notable degree of economy, a highly symbiotic relationship between the parts, and an exact mirror relationship between the first and second half of each figure. Glass's own recorded performance crucially adds a pair of pedal points – one on the tonic, the other on the dominant – to signal each half figure, though these are not indicated in the score.

Once more, additive process governs the structure, here supplemented at the close by a hint that a subtractive process could eventually eat away what the additive one had built. The fluctuating fortunes of scale- and third-based sub-units become the main feature of the structural design. Sudden, subsequently drastic, expansion of third-based sub-units and slower expansion of scalic sub-units give rise to the basic structure of

Music in Contrary Motion. With Figure 20, however, the two kinds of sub-unit offshoots, so far kept pretty much intact, now start to alternate with greater speed, and the third-based sub-unit decreases for the first time as the work reaches its last stages. The additive and (more briefly) subtractive processes of *Music in Contrary Motion* are harder to follow than those of *Two Pages* and *Music in Fifths*, despite the articulation, and suggestion of tonal motion, provided by the pedal points on the commercial recording. The effect, as the composer's description 'open form' suggests, is of music spun out endlessly with no reason for concluding even when it does: like *Music in Fifths*, a more typical model of musical minimalism as often understood.

Music in Similar Motion *and* Music in Eight Parts

In *Music in Similar Motion* (November 1969), Glass returned to the parallel motion explored in *Music in Fifths*, changing and expanding both the number and the consistency of the parallel intervals involved and thus creating a situation in which the ambiguous approach to modality found in the earlier work could be turned to more complex and satisfying account. The work readily divides into four parts according to the progressive accumulation of its lines. Part One (Figures 1–5) consists of a single line doubled at the octave; Part Two (Figures 6–11) supplies a new treble line, basically a perfect fourth higher. Part Three (Figures 12–23) adds a bass line notably less strictly parallel than the new upper line; Part Four (Figures 24–33) completes the textural expansion with a further top line, partly a perfect fourth above the previous treble.

The work begins with an eight-note figure (see Ex. 4.8a), the Basic Unit for the now familiar expansion and contraction across a total of thirty-three figures. On the page, these eight quavers form a rhythmically irregular $2 + 3 + 3$, suggesting three sub-units for the additive process to work on. Yet initial hearings, without access to a score, of the commercial recording suggested that the opening module was $4 + 4$. While this could be due as much as anything to our conditioning as listeners, the ambiguity here is telling. Like Reich, Glass found the potential of twelve beats in a bar especially fruitful. The pairs of figures which provide the transitions between Parts One and Two (Figures 5 and 6) and between Parts Three and Four (Figures 23 and 24; see Ex. 4.8c for the latter) all have twelve quavers subdividable by the ear in ways different from the notated $3 + 2 + 3 + 4$; the same rhythmic structure provides the fixed element in the evolving additive patterns of Part Two and – since the first figure of its successor (Figure 12; see Ex. 4.8b) is also the same as the last figure of Part Two (Figure 11) – the beginning of Part Three as well.

Example 4.8 *Music in Similar Motion*: (a) Figures 1–6; (b) Figure 12; (c) Figure 24.

The additive structure of *Music in Similar Motion* is shown as a whole in Example 4.9, some further details of it in Example 4.8. As Example 4.8a demonstrates, the division into three sub-units is brought into operation straight away. Figure 2 repeats the second sub-unit, suggesting merely a simple additive process involving the expansion of each sub-unit in turn. Figure 3, however, adds on a 'new' pattern which, partly due to its incorporation of the first sub-unit, to which it supplies a small extension, has a strong cadential feel. From here on, every figure will conclude with

Example 4.9 *Music in Similar Motion*, additive structure

Figure No.

```
1     12 123 432
2     12 123 123 432
3     12 123 123 432 12 52
4 .   123 123 43 432 12 52
5     123 43 432 12 52
6*    123 43 432 12 52
7     123 432 123 43 432 12 52
8     123 432 123 43 123 43 432 12 52
9     123 432 123 43 1234 123 43 432 12 52
10    123 432 123 43 1234 123 123 43 432 12 52
11    123 432 123 43 1234 123 12 123 43 432 12 52
12**  123 432 123 43 1234 123 12 123 43 432 12 52
13    123 432 123 43 1234 123 12 123 43 432 432 12 52
14    123 432 123 43 1234 123 12 123 43 432 43 23 432 12 52
15    123 432 123 43 1234 123 12 123 43 432 43 23 43 432 12 52
16    123 43 1234 123 12 123 43 432 43 23 43 432 12 52
17    1234 123 12 123 43 432 43 23 43 432 12 52
18    123 12 123 43 432 43 23 43 432 12 52
19    12 123 43 432 43 23 43 432 12 52
20    123 43 432 43 23 43 432 12 52
21    123 43 432 43 432 12 52
22    123 43 43 432 12 52
23    123 43 432 12 52
24*** 123 43 432 12 52
25    123 43 432 12 52 12 52
26    123 43 432 12 52 12 52 12 52 12 52
27    123 43 432 12 52 12 52 12 52 12 52 12 52 12 52 12 52 12 52
28    123 43 432 12 52 12 52 12 52 12 52 12 52 12 52 12 52 12 52
29    12 52
30    12 12 52
31    12 12 52 52
32    12 52 12 12 52 52
33    12 12 52 12 52 52
34    12 12 12 52 12 12 52 52 12 52 52 52 12 12 52 52
```

	G = 1
* + 4ths	B♭ = 2
	C = 3
** + bass	D = 4
*** = 7ths, etc.	F = 5

this four-note 'tag'. Figure 4 drops the first sub-unit, adds two notes to the third sub-unit and repeats the new pattern, making three changes to the previous figure but preserving its fifteen-quaver length. Figure 5 then subtracts the repetition of the second sub-unit introduced in Figure 2.

While it would be tedious to proceed with such a blow-by-blow account, Example 4.9 demonstrates several further ingenuities which help to mould *Music in Similar Motion* into a more complex and, in its way, evolutionary structure than *Music in Fifths* or *Music in Contrary Motion*: the most sophisticated instance yet of Glass's exploration of additive process. Beginning with the twelve-beat pattern established in Figure 5 (the end of Part One; see again Ex. 4.8a), Part Two expands to thirty-two quavers, progressively prefacing this undeviating pattern with additive expansions of sub-units two and three until, in the last bar (Figure 11), the first sub-unit also appears as a natural outcome of this process itself (another product of 'redundant overlapping').

Beginning with the thirty-two-quaver pattern of Figure 12 (see Ex. 4.8b), Part Three initially takes the expansion to forty-one quavers (at Figure 15) by breaking open the now well-established concluding twelve-beat pattern with logical extensions of the third sub-unit. The bulk of this part is, however, concerned with subtraction. Figures 16–20 drop the first six, five, four, three and two quavers respectively of the six-note pattern that had begun Figures 7–15, until only the twenty-one-quaver concluding pattern of Figure 15 remains. This is the pattern formed by extending the 'transitional' twelve-beat grouping, and Figures 20–23 now progressively subtract the extra notes (43 23 43 432) by four, three and two quavers respectively until only this twelve-beat pattern itself remains again to take matters forward to the final part.

Here, in Part Four, there is a double process of expansion and contraction to match the single one of the previous part. Up to this point, the four-note 'cadential' pattern introduced in Figure 3 has been notable for its occurrence, unrepeated, at the end of each figure. Now this 'tag' itself becomes the focal point, subjected for the first time to additive expansion. Beginning with Figure 24 (see Ex. 4.8c), it grows exponentially, from two statements up to sixteen. After this (from Figure 29) it takes over entirely, the twelve-beat pattern itself finally being jettisoned in favour of repetitions of the four-note 'cadential' pattern, now broken down for the first time into two two-note sub-units. Having swallowed the rest of the work's material, this deconstructed form of what started life as a mere 'tag' accumulates repetitions as it goes along, its two components locked in rivalry in a fairly rigorous additive pattern.

Modally, too, *Music in Similar Motion* extends the territory mapped out by its immediate predecessors. The single line of Part One (Ex. 4.8a) establishes a pentatonic modality which the opposition of conjunct and non-conjunct movement within the G–D frame suggests is centred on G; the absence of As reinforces the centrality of G, since the gap between G and B♭ renders the repetitions of G more prominent. Figures 1 and 2 use only four pitches (G, B♭, C and D), the fifth, F – expanding the original perfect-fifth frame – being added only at Figure 3. B♭, the relative major, had initially suggested itself as an ambiguous alternative to G minor, but the arrival of F seems more to confirm G by providing its flattened leading note than to offer a dominant to B♭.

The new treble line of Part Two (last figure of Ex. 4.8a) reproduces the pattern of the continuing G-minor line a perfect fourth higher, except for the penultimate note of each figure, which falls not to B♭ but to G, thus spanning an octave. Introducing C, the only further new pitch of the work, this line seems to be in C minor. Once again, the two lines taken together create a more ambiguous modal mix, which the G seems to inflect significantly, suggesting E♭ major as much as C minor by allowing the B♭ E♭ dyads on either side of it to be heard as first inversions of the tonic chord in this key, and consequently the preceding G F E♭ descents as 321 in E♭ rather than 543 in C minor. The major second produced by this G with the F of the lower line blurs the harmonic outline, though, creating a fleeting tension amidst the chain of parallel fourths.

The arrival of the bass line at the beginning of Part Three (Ex. 4.8b) provides the most dramatic moment in *Music in Similar Motion*, due partly to the new weight and depth it brings to the texture. But the modality of this line, with the potential it offers to operate as a functional bass for the emerging harmony of the now three-part structure, is also significant. Its emphasis on G, C and D, employing an upper as well as lower tonic, supplies an underlying i–iv–v in G minor which supports and to some extent refocuses the movement above it, reconfirming G minor as the true tonic key.

Part Four (see Ex. 4.8c) blurs the tonal issues once again by adding a further top line centred on F, operating partly in parallel sevenths with the original part and offering another dominant, C, in place of the strictly parallel flattened leading note, E♭. This further transformation of the original material unfolding exultantly over everything that has come before can, of course, be read in the modalities already established, G minor and C minor, as well as filling out the harmony to supply extra weight, for instance, to the C-minor⁷ chords. These latter recur with increasing frequency during the protracted second section of Part Four, in which the former 'cadential' tag takes over from the other, predominantly stepwise, material. C minor is, meanwhile, given a further final boost by becoming the insistently reiterated i in alternation with its own v and iv.

Music in Similar Motion's piling up of lines produces the effect of a much richer, more complex modality than may be found in any of Glass's earlier works. The particular delight in thwarting any expectation of rhythmic regularity is surprising in a work that consists entirely of continuous quavers. As a result of this carefully proportioned and integratedly progressive approach to texture, additive process and modality, *Music in Similar Motion* possesses a subtlety, richness and depth foreign to its predecessors: the main reason why it is the composer's only work before *Einstein on the Beach* both to remain in the repertoire of the Philip Glass Ensemble and to have been frequently performed by others.

Music in Eight Parts is described by Glass as 'an abandoned piece', and for years he thought no manuscript had survived: in itself, some indication of his estimate of its worth. Though a copy recently surfaced, the composer has not released it for inspection. Probably completed at the end of 1969, possibly early 1970, it continues Glass's lighthearted gloss on 'attempting to trace the progress of musical history'. The title of the culminating work in this series, *Music in Twelve Parts*, indicates that this work is in twelve sections; since that work is much better known, it may be thought that the 'parts' of its predecessors also refer to sections or movements. In fact, both *Music in Eight Parts* and *Music with Changing Parts* are single-movement compositions, the titles of which refer to the number or nature of instrumental lines involved. Glass describes *Music in Eight Parts* as

> actually for eight contrapuntal parts. The piece begins in unison and with each successive note the number of parts increases. As it goes on, you get eventually to a twelve-note figure and the piece comes to sound like an accordion: it keeps opening up and closing. That's what I meant by 'parts' there.[69]

Though clearly an advance texturally speaking on its predecessors, and likely to produce an opulence of sound rivalling that of its immediate successors, it seems logical to regard *Music in Eight Parts* as the final work of Glass's 'early minimal' period. Its transitional nature is one reason its composer adduces for its status as a problem piece. 'I think it was a fumbling attempt at something which I did much better when I got to *Music in Twelve Parts*', he says.

The Red Horse Animation *and* Music for Voices

With *1 + 1* and its immediate progeny now examined, it is possible to understand the scores Glass composed at around the same time for the two theatre pieces mentioned earlier. Since the actors of *The Red Horse Animation* (the piece using the specially constructed floor) could not read music, its composer taught them their parts by rote; he agrees that the more rigorous the rhythmic systems used, the easier the music would have been to learn in such circumstances. In his book, Glass recalls that the music was 'organized into a highly logical arithmetic system I later began to call "additive process", a cornerstone technique that has served me well ever since.'[70] In what is evidently a homage to the father figure behind so much of the downtown Manhattan artistic aesthetic, the surviving extracts (two pages, the first headed with the Roman numeral V) reveal that Glass used the pitch sequence C A G E to construct a sequence of short figures for additive expansions to be devised in rehearsal. (Example 4.10 gives the first of these pages).[71] Though employing a five-line staff, the score is a series of simple 'grid' systems in proportional rather than conventional rhythmic notation, assembling figures ranging between four and fourteen beats in length, often in symmetrical patterns. The first stages of each additive process are sometimes shown, in the manner previously employed in the score of $1+1$; 'percussion' is both indicated on the staves and added separately.

The repeating patterns of *Music for Voices* were assembled into an informal score which divided the performers into pairs; each singer's part rose and fell in volume in a regular pattern, and the entry of each voice coincided with the dynamic peak of its partner. The unaccompanied vocal parts used only *solfège* as text; its composer describes it as 'a piece for nine voices in which I define a rhythmic phrase by the use of repeated syllables, building up a continuous rhythmic structure out of this material'. Once again, he conveyed his music to the members of Mabou Mines without recourse to conventional notation, and whatever he used seems not to have survived. Though it apparently explored the psycho-acoustic possibilities of overtone production to which he was concurrently directing his attention in his instrumental works, the piece employed no amplification.

The fact that both these theatre pieces are contemporary with the composer's discovery of the potential that voices had in his instrumental ensemble suggests that the earlier of them, *Red Horse Animation*, was probably an influence on Glass's development of vocal sounds in his concert music. With its use of *solfège* syllables, *Music for Voices* was in turn to be the inspiration for their deployment in *Music in Twelve Parts* and *Einstein on the Beach*.

The *Comic of The Red Horse Animation* also includes a page of graphics consisting of two parts.[72] The first is a representation of the additive process technique of $1=1$ – 'in which I . . . in which I demonstrate my sound' – less specific than the original score. The other is a cartoon sequence entitled 'That's My Sound Now', in which a character (presumably the composer) muses, in an alternating sequence vaguely mimicking the $1+1$ technique, as follows: 'I don't think/I used to sound like much of anything./I think/I'm making things up as I go along./I've come along/. . . I'm in a different place./I/guess that means/this isn't the beginning./If this were/the end/And I were still here making things up/I'd be crazy./I don't think/I'm crazy'. An apt summary of his situation and state of mind in 1970, this suggests that

Example 4.10   *The Red Horse Animation*, V, page 1

having rejected his earlier manner in favour of a 'back-to-basics' approach, Glass now realised he was on the brink of capitalising on these new discoveries. The compositions of the previous year or so were certainly not 'the end', but they may be regarded as 'the end of the beginning'.

The expansion of Glass's reputation and his changing aesthetic to 1976

From its SoHo base, Glass's reputation now slowly spread. From about 1971 to 1974, the composer mounted unadvertised Sunday afternoon concerts in his loft on Bleecker Street. An important stage in his move from local to national, and international, fame was the first complete performance of *Music in Twelve Parts* at the New York Town Hall on 1 June 1974. Even though it had to be organised and promoted by the composer himself, this was Glass's first major mid- or uptown concert. At this time, John Rockwell suggested that 'Glass still plays his music with his own ensemble because he can't get performances – or at least adequate performances – elsewhere'.[73] This may have been true; but the composer's attitude at that time to proposals from performers outside his own immediate circle should also be noted. As Dave Smith wrote in the following year, 'Glass is not interested in publishing his compositions. . . . To make scores easily available would result in a good number of mediocre performances which, apart from anything else, would be detrimental to the music'.[74] Smith tactfully fails to mention that this approach also generated more work for Glass's own ensemble, which effectively retained exclusive rights to his music. This situation was to change at the end of the 1970s, when Glass started writing operas for the forces of the conventional opera house. Even now, however, few of the composer's early scores, in particular, are available to performers, or to others.

Beyond New York, meanwhile, Glass's reputation grew. His first important American engagement outside the city was at the Walker Art Center, Minneapolis, in January 1970, already detailed; in the same year, the composer's first tours were backed by the art departments of American universities, as well as by art schools and museums in Europe. Though already viewed by some of his downtown colleagues as increasingly a businessman rather than an artist – a taunt that has stuck ever since – in the early 1970s Glass was still operating on a very small and independent scale, avoiding commercial distributors. In 1971, he started his own record company, Chatham Square Productions, in collaboration with Klaus Kertess, owner of the Bykert Gallery on East 77th Street, who had previously helped the composer with funds and bookings. Only two recordings of his own music were issued by Chatham Square Productions: a double album of his then latest work, *Music with Changing Parts*, released that year; followed by a single album of *Music in Fifths* and *Music in Similar Motion*, issued in 1973. Munkacsi used his contacts with John Lennon to gain access to a mobile recording studio for a weekend in May 1971 to record *Music with Changing Parts*; this was used again for *Music in Similar Motion*, recorded the following month, and *Music in Fifths* exactly two years later. In 1975, the French label Shandar released an LP devoted to *Two Pages* and *Music in Contrary Motion*. The whole of *Music in Twelve Parts* was also recorded at this time, though only the first two parts were released immediately: on the Caroline label, a subsidiary of Virgin Records. These discs significantly raised the profile of Glass's music, in Europe as well as in the USA.

As was the case with Reich, European interest in Glass not only made his work more widely available, but also promoted a helpful sense of legitimacy back home. The composer became particularly popular in France at this period. In 1973, Michel Guy, director of the Festival d'Automne in Paris, invited the Philip Glass Ensemble to play; by the following year, Guy had been appointed Secretary of State for Culture, and he soon commissioned the work which enhanced Glass's reputation more than any other: *Einstein on the Beach*. Premièred at the Avignon Theatre Festival on 25 July 1976, this immediately toured Europe with great success. Two performances at New York's Metropolitan Opera House later that year – on 21 and 28 November – brought even greater attention. While this collaboration with the American director and designer Robert Wilson triggered its composer's eventual move into opera – and his return to patronage and promotion by the support systems underwriting Western classical music – interest in Glass's music elsewhere was to take his work into the even bigger arena of rock music. The composer's early involvements with such music had as much to do with the British and German rock scenes as with downtown Manhattan developments in popular musics; further reference to this will be found in the conclusion to this chapter.

Glass's aesthetic development in the early 1970s

The common ground between Glass and the Minimalist artists has, as we have seen, been described as 'formalist' or even 'structuralist'. It is clear that the composer's main preoccupation from 1965 to 1969 was with structure and, in particular, with the purity and clarity of that structure. In order to achieve purity and clarity – and especially the audibility which was its most particular manifestation – the resulting music had to exhibit a strong surface simplicity. Everything depended on how that music was perceived. Yet Glass's note-to-note processes arose directly from the basic ideas of additive rhythm and cyclical structuring which – though derived, at least in part, from Indian practice allied to an improvising tradition – were turned into composed-out structures pursued with the aid of notation which limited the expressive input of both composer and performer in a conceptually highly formalist fashion.

Glass himself hints at this in an already quoted 1972 interview which is among the most penetrating that he has ever given. He had, he says, 'to get over my preoccupation with formalism before I began noticing what I was doing'.[75] What he was doing was dealing ultimately with sound, and he started to feel that this had begun to get lost amidst the concern for process which had so crucially defined his development during the previous few years. Foreman has argued that the noticing of process could itself become exhilarating in Glass's music.[76] And this had been borne out by the resilience which that music had already shown in sustaining musical interest with such highly reductive material. The trouble was, however, that by 1970 its creator was already questioning the validity of an approach which ultimately seemed to him to be divorced from aural realities.

Glass came to feel that he had been over-preoccupied with structure as such; the limitations of treating sound itself as merely the means by which structure was to be articulated increasingly concerned him. To some extent, he was responding to what he understood his audiences were actually doing when they listened to his music. They were, he found, despite his efforts to encourage structural listening, less preoccupied than he with such matters. '[W]hen I was still superconscious of structure and purity of form', he said, 'my audiences were already picking up on the sound'.[77] Glass also notes a parallel with the ways in which those involved in other art forms were thinking at the same period. 'In the last two years', he said in that same 1972 interview, 'there's been a real change of sensibility, in the content of the experiences we're interested in'.

One stage in the move to greater concern with sound can be dated unusually precisely in Glass's case, since it was precipitated by an actual experience of *Music in Similar Motion* in rehearsal, in May 1970. As the composer explains,

> We were playing in a theatre-in-the-round made of wood in Minneapolis. It was like playing inside a Stradivarius. It was the most beautiful sound I ever dreamed of.... [W]hen we go [*sic*] into the end of the piece, I thought I heard someone singing. I *did* hear someone singing, in fact, and I stopped, thinking Arthur [Murphy], one of the guys who likes to horse around, was improvising and I said, come on, who's singing, and we looked around because we thought someone was there. It was that real an experience. It

wasn't us playing. But there was no-one in the room; as I said, it was a rehearsal. So we started playing again and the sound came back, and of course then we realized that the sound happened because of the acoustical properties of that room and because of the texture of the music . . . I thought that was the most interesting thing that I had seen in my music up to that point: it was a spontaneous thing, an acoustical phenomenon but it sounded like a human voice. So the next piece I did that summer, *Music with Changing Parts*, had a lot of singing in it.[78]

This experience led the composer to investigate the possibilities of using the female voice wordlessly: instrumentally, one might say. *Red Horse Animation*, the composer's first theatre piece using voices, also dates from around this time, possibly earlier, concurrently with Reich's development of his own approach to the 'instrumental' use of voices. Glass says that his colleague was present at the Minneapolis rehearsal. Reich performed in the première of *Music with Changing Parts* the following December; he actually hated the work and, as we have seen, quit his involvement with Glass's music shortly afterwards. At the time of the Minneapolis incident, Reich's work on *Drumming* had probably not proceeded very far. Though, once again, it is impossible to establish with any security a sequence of events which is open to different interpretations, Glass may have preceded Reich here.

Glass now allowed the instrumentalists of *Music with Changing Parts* to contribute unspecified sustained notes, either played or sung, in certain sections, introducing an element of individual improvisation into his ensemble works. While the number of repetitions of each figure was left unspecified in the original scores, decisions about this were, though, necessarily controlled. And although performers are permitted to drop out from time to time, this is purely to allow them some respite.

But it was, of course, more than simply a question of writing music which 'had a lot of singing in it'. More important was the encouragement that this event gave Glass to take account of the 'psycho-acoustic by-products' of his compositions. These included not only the illusion of voices singing (which continued to function, ambiguously, in conjunction with the use of *real* voices), but also such related phenomena as the hearing of lines in the music which were not in fact composed. That is, the combination of instrumental parts which Glass actually had written, and which were present acoustically in a performance, sometimes turned out to produce other, illusory effects, even of actual counterpoint. These were usually the result of overtones or undertones formed by the combined notated pitches as actually performed.

The reason for the, apparently sudden, occurrence of such phenomena was the increasingly heavy amplification which the composer was beginning to use for his ensemble as his music became more popular and he started to perform in larger halls. Crucial to the changing sound of the Philip Glass Ensemble was the arrival of Munkacsi as sound designer and mixer in the autumn following the Minneapolis incident. His creation of an amplification system for the group to deploy at dynamic levels common in rock music had its own effect on the composer's increasing interest in texture and timbre.

Mature minimalist compositions

1970 saw the completion of just one concert composition, *Music with Changing Parts*. *Music in Twelve Parts*, Glass's crowning achievement of this period, then occupied its composer for some three years, between the spring of 1971 and April 1974. These two works are considerably more substantial, in terms of both length and complexity, than any of Glass's previous compositions. The harmonic and textural advances of *Music with Changing Parts* resulted in a composition which is essentially experimental and transitional. It was only with *Music in Twelve Parts* that Glass was able fully to capitalise on these developments and take them forward to an altogether new level.

Music in Twelve Parts in many respects takes on the function in its composer's output which in Reich's is fulfilled by *Music for Eighteen Musicians*. During the period in which Reich was composing the latter piece, Glass proceeded to explore his own discoveries further in the context of a stage work, *Einstein on the Beach*, completed in 1975. It was with the new language he had forged in a purely concert context that he was then in a position to approach the writing of this ambitious 'opera', much longer and more complex even than *Music in Twelve Parts*.

Music with Changing Parts

Rhythmically, *Music with Changing Parts* breaks no new ground; the first of its two large parts confines itself to units and sub-units of only two or four notes. In pitch and, particularly, timbral terms, however, the work is more adventurous. The deployment of sustained notes allows the emergence, for the first time in Glass's mature music, of harmony as more than merely an accidental by-product of the rhythmic and melodic repetition, their articulation improvised by using a range of timbres unusual in the composer's ensemble. Changes of section are too few to suggest a real ambiguity of meaning in the work's title: though never clarified by the composer, this would seem to be a further case of 'parts' as 'lines' – though possibly too as specifically 'instrumental lines', implying a greater interest in colour and texture, a suggestion borne out by the recorded performance. Even the lean, treble-dominated character of the early Philip Glass Ensemble's sound presents an appropriate background against which the sustained pitches can generate powerful contrasts. Vocal drones are, for example, complemented by others on the trumpet. Deciding whether these sustained sounds act as background or foreground is, in fact, one of the fascinations of listening to the work. So, too, is deciding whether these notes provide a secure harmonic, even structural, focus or, as the pitch-bending on the recording might suggest, that they are more 'experimental', more Young-like.

The indications for the entry point of improvisation in general and the employment of sustained pitches in particular represent the only additions to the sort of modular material by now familiar from Glass's previous scores. The set of eleven 'changing figures' (marked 'C.F. #1', etc.) that help to give *Music with Changing Parts* its title is also to be found on a tabular reduction of the score (similarly dated August 1970, with the added inscription 'Cape Breton, N.S.') that charts its additive schemes. Glass explains that these 'C.F.' signs indicate that 'individual players were permitted to play one note for the length of a breath . . . a note they heard emerging from the pattern of the music'. The employment of purely sustained pitches suggests a comparison with Reich's use of resulting patterns. This is strengthened by the fact that, on the recording of the work, shorter note values are also incorporated. The 1973 performance in fact offers an interpretation which is much more varied than a literal reading of the score might suggest; this is, after all, a work designed to thrive on the improvising skills of the composer's now maturing ensemble.

A simple two-part texture forms the basis of the first four minutes, during which the two sub-units on which the music is built gradually become clarified. (Ex. 4.11 gives the Basic Unit of *Music with Changing Parts*.) Almost immediately, though (Figure 1, C.F. #1), first dominant and then tonic drones, in the key of C minor, are introduced. From Figure 6 (C.F. #2) it is increasingly hard to account for everything one hears in terms of the notated score, or to distinguish between the 'acoustic' and the 'psycho-acoustic'. The psycho-acoustic effect which results in greater emphasis on E♭ and D in what is still the top line in the ensuing section, for instance, is seemingly turned into a resulting pattern on these two pitches played on what sounds like the electric piano (first emerging at 4'40" on the recording), drawing attention to the first two ten-quaver, five-beat figures (Figures 8 and 9) by emphasising each figure's anacrusis and down-

Example 4.11 *Music with Changing Parts*, Figure 1

beat. This seems to be the first example in Glass's music of an actually articulated resulting pattern which is not simply a sustained pitch.

Sustained pitches soon also return, though, heralding the arrival of Figure 11 (C.F. #3). With voices now more prominent, a fresh expansion occurs, involving high Cs which protrude above the texture with considerable force – piccolo and soprano saxophone supplying further treble energy. These arise as part of an extra beat added to the two sub-units in Figure 12. A more familiar additive and subtractive sequence based on this three-beat pattern takes us into a sequence tumbling deliciously through ambiguous metrical territory – each high C sounding more like a downbeat than do the B♭s the notation itself offers – which is further enhanced by resulting patterns. At Figure 19 (C.F. #4), the full six parts enter in the recorded version for the first time, with an additive process having a transitional function, suggested by its emphasis on a further variety of treble textures (including piccolo, flute and saxophones), rather than any dramatic emphasis on bass lines or sustained notes.

It is Figure 23/C.F. #5 which ushers in a more decisive change. Here, electric keyboards lay down a more evenly balanced version of the six-part texture; the bass, so long delayed, outlines F C F E♭ which, while scarcely complemented in any clear fashion by the harmony above it, offers sufficient sense of root movement in the already half-established E♭ major to provide a further, crucial stage in the move from C minor to its relative major. A veritable textural orgy now ensues, unsanctioned by the tabular score, in which the performers are given their head to improvise sustained pitches in profusion around an unravelling sequence of additive schemes. During the second of these (Figures 28–33, with C.F. #6 occurring at Figure 28 and C.F. #7 at Figure 34), this full, rich texture is further developed via pitch expansion upwards and a more concerted, especially telling approach to the dynamic unfolding of sustained pitches. The result of these co-ordinated crescendi and diminuendi is a wave-like rise and fall of fixed pitches against the familiar constant rhythmic repetition akin to that achieved some four or five years later by Reich in *Music for Eighteen Musicians.*

In the main, however, the effect of these sections is less disciplined, not only because such extemporised collaboration encourages spontaneity, but also due to the fact that Glass permits a surprising degree of pitch bending in the improvised sustained notes. In addition, some rather bumpy new resulting patterns break up the flow, increasing the variety of musical energy involved, but disturbing the evolution of any longer-range drama. The third and final additive scheme of Part One (Figures 36–49) underpins a continuation of this development, allowing improvisation to unfold for some time against a low series of readily assimilable six-beat figures before contracting to the two-beat pattern that ushers in Part Two.

After Figure 50/C.F. #10, metre and, later, modality move to new terri- tory. The first ten figures of Part Two (Figures 50–59), which served as an introduction to the main section, have been largely cut on the recording and in the only available manuscript score. From Figure 51, the metre changes to $^6_8$: a fairly seismic shift, considering that more than half an hour has just been devoted to music built largely on crotchet beats. In pitch terms, matters initially remain much the same, though the greater con- junct melodic movement leads to faster harmonic motion. Previous cer- tainties are further undermined by the score's leaner, basically three-part counterpoint in contrary motion. $^6_8$ provides the basis for the ensuing additive expansions. On the recording, sustained notes return at Figure 61, the starting point of these.

Following a further small excision in both score and recording (Figures 71–2), Figure 73 returns to the basic six-quaver figure. The two unseg- mented sub-units of this are performed in reverse order in Figure 75, fol- lowing the juxtaposition of the two versions in Figure 74. Figure 76 rotates all parts to begin, respectively, on the second and fourth notes of the origi- nal pattern, juxtaposing this with its own reverse statement. From Figure 77, these altered versions then form the second part of each figure, alter- nating with the originals. Expanding to fifty-four quavers at Figure 79, these then reduce to forty-two quavers at the close (Figure 81).

After the return to a regular $^6_8$ at Figure 73, the recorded performance elaborates on the above description by making an unscored upward shift during the same figure at 49′23″: maintaining the mode, of course, but heightening the tension by drawing more attention to the dissonances of the contrapuntal lines as well as by registral expansion. The sense of denouement is quickly strengthened by the arrival of sustained E♭s at 50′11″. The final expansion of Figures 76–9 returns the voices to prominence, saxophones and flutes also playing a significant role. The apparently intended final riot of sustained pitches is, admittedly, somewhat spoilt in the recording by a falling away in the texture and some poor co-ordination. The final additive manoeuvres do, however, suggest a flatter landscape after the earlier peaks. The performance retains, moreover, an unpredictable wild streak which seems in character with the work's spirit.

While rhythmically relying mainly on the techniques its composer had already established in his compositions of 1969, *Music with Changing Parts* is much more forward-looking in harmonic and textural terms. For the first time in Glass's output, the rate of textural change rivals that of rhythmic change; as a consequence, the emphasis seems more firmly placed on the shifting sound-world than on the structure beneath it. The sustained notes allow the emergence of harmony as a real issue. Resulting patterns of other kinds, too, bring another new dimension to his output. And the range of timbral combinations available from the composer's newly expanded ensemble suggests a new depth to what is still essentially undeveloped modal harmony. The exploration of drones and improvisation, and the delight in the discovery and exploitation of psycho-acoustic aspects, may seem to categorise *Music with Changing Parts* as an experimental *cul-de-sac*. It is true that Glass never followed up this work's more obviously adventurous aspects; the composer himself has suggested that, even at the time of its composition, the work 'was a little too spacey for my tastes'.[79] On the other hand, *Music with Changing Parts* offers a foretaste of the textural variety, the dramatic flair, and even an interest in creating attention through harmonic emphasis and elaboration, which only came to full fruition later.

Music in Twelve Parts

With *Music in Twelve Parts*, we reach the culmination of Glass's achievements in the works written for his own ensemble between 1968 and 1974. The twelve parts, or movements, of this composition each last between fifteen and twenty minutes, making a total performance time of more than four hours with suitable intervals. A work of such length offers considerable scope not only for structural and other kinds of technical variety but also for a significant, and progressive, extension of Glass's musical language and expression.

The composer's own programme notes of the period record that the function of *Music in Twelve Parts* was to 'describe a vocabulary of tech-niques which have [appeared] and are appearing in my music'.[80] '[I]ndividual parts', Glass wrote, 'feature one or several aspects of a common musical language, presenting and developing them in somewhat unusual ways'. But he also points out that 'the individual parts of *Music in Twelve Parts* tend to be highly divergent from each other, exhibiting a range as wide as I could conceive of at the time of writing'. Additive process continues to be a mainstay, now explored in a variety of new structural as well as harmonic contexts, and pointed up via the use of *solfège* syllables in the female vocal parts.

Building on the ways in which chordal oscillations and hints of root movement in the bass line, already features of his own earlier music, had been developed in the more experimental context of *Music with Changing Parts*, Glass abandoned that work's sustained sounds and other more psycho-acoustically adventurous aspects to focus on his own approach to what, in Reich's music, has already been called the 'cadential progression'. By the time *Music in Twelve Parts* was complete – in April 1974, just a month before Reich began the first sketches for *Music for Eighteen Musicians* – Glass had extended the oscillation of two-chord 'cadential progressions' to the deployment of a whole chord sequence with real root movement in the bass line: a different approach to harmonic motion from that of his former colleague.

The work began as a single-movement piece, itself entitled *Music in Twelve Parts*, completed in April 1971 and first performed at Yale University on 16 April that year. Following the composer's recent practice, the 'parts' of this title referred to the individual instrumental lines. As he related in 1975:

> We played it at a concert in 1971, and afterwards someone in the audience asked me when I was going to write the other 'parts'. I realised that they meant 'parts' in the sense of sections. And that's where I got the idea for the whole piece. At first I tried to keep the idea of twelve contrapuntal parts throughout, but it broke down right away. It seemed like a useless encumberance [*sic*].[81]

In 1994, Glass said that the composer Eliane Radigue had given him the idea after hearing a recording of the piece.

The original twenty-minute composition now became Part One, and the other eleven 'parts', or movements, followed over the next three years. Composed mostly in the order in which they were finally presented, the sequence was supplemented by at least two new movements every year. Each would be tried out in informal concerts at 10 Bleeker Street or in a gallery. At first, the new addition would be performed with all its prede-cessors, but once the work became too long for a single programme, only the preceding two movements would be heard before the new one. Concerts usually consisted of three movements; if four were performed, there was an interval between the two pairs. The completed work was pre-mièred on 1 June 1974 at New York Town Hall.

As Example 4.12 indicates, *Music in Twelve Parts* is constructed to make a complex but coherent tonal statement, in which the key of each individ-ual part finds its place in a cumulative sweep of the whole that is new in Glass's output. Continued advantage is taken of the fact that apparent modal stasis activated by rhythmic repetition readily leads to ambiguity between any key and its relative major or minor, and this is exploited from the outset: hence the alternatives offered in Example 4.12 for the tonalities of Parts One and Two. But until he had discovered a flexible but more con-sistent way of exploring the vertical dimension of his music, and a means to control its horizontal unravelling with more moment-to-moment pre-cision, Glass could not fully explore the sort of richness and variety which allow the full perspective of 'development' to unfold. *Music with Changing Parts* had shown how particular pitches, and even whole chords, could be enhanced by the use of improvised long notes. The short-range source of such flexible consistency, however, lay, as Reich had already discovered, in what both composers called 'cadential progressions'. The long-range source of such consistency was to be found in modulation between one part and its successor, and in the overall tonal planning this necessitated.

As his work was slowly assembled, transitions between movements – at first seen merely as juxtapositions; the composer called them 'joining-places' – were soon considered by Glass in terms of their modulatory potential; at one stage, the work was entitled 'Music with Modulations'. As Example 4.12 shows, key connections between movements are not usually as conventional as the tonic/dominant relationship between Parts One and Two. The tonal centres of Parts Two and Three, for instance, are separated by a tritone: the most distant relationship possible. The dominant/tonic connection between Parts Three and Four is compromised by the latter part's unusually high level of secundal dissonance. Links can, on the other hand, be as simple as the drone of a single pitch. At the end of Part Four, for instance, B♮ – one of only two pitches which this part has in common with its successor – clashes insistently, and consistently, with the rest of Part Four's pitch gamut, and in particular with C, the movement's notional tonal centre. This paves the way for the B-major tonality of Part Five, the modal clarity of which comes as a dramatic release after the tensions of Part Four.

Example 4.12 *Music in Twelve Parts*, tonal structure

Part	Tonality	Pitches used	Number of pitches	Chord/scale type
Date of composition				
1 (April 1971)	F-sharp minor (A major)	F# A B C# D E	6	13th/Aeolian (without 3rd)
2 (March-May 1973)	D-flat major (B-flat minor)	D♭ E♭ F A♭ B♭	5	pentatonic
3 (July 1971)	G major (D minor)	G A C D	4	stacked fourths
4 (August 1971)	C major	C D E F G A B	7	major
5 (August 1971)	B major/Mixolydian	B C# D# E F# G#	6	13th/major or Mixolydian (without 7th)
6 (February-March 1972)	D-flat major (F minor)	D♭ E♭ F A♭ B♭ C	6	major scale/stacked fifths
7 (September 1972)	C minor	C D E♭ E F G A♭ B♭ B		harmonic minor plus E and B
8 (July 1973)	F Mixolydian	F G A B♭ C D E♭	7	13th/Mixolydian
9 (winter 1973-4)	A major	A B C# D E F# G# E♭ G B♭	7 8, 9, 10	major scale plus "tritonic triad"
10 (ditto)	F-sharp minor>A major	A B C# E F#	5	pentatonic
11 (ditto)	A major/E major/F#-minor A-flat major C major	A B C# D# E F# G# A♭ B♭ C D♭ E♭ F C D E F G A B	7 6 7	Lydian/stacked fifths major scale/stacked fifths major scale
12 (April 1974)	A major/ C minor modulating >>>	A C# E F# C E♭ F G >>> +	4	A⁶ C-minor⁴ modulating

Composed in quick succession, the first large-scale statement of climax and resolution formed by these two movements shows its composer getting into his stride, and even beginning to see tonal, rather than rhythmic, processes as the most fruitful constructional tool to deploy in conjunction with his new concern for texture. While the tonal centres of *Music in Twelve Parts* adopt no simple schematic pattern, A and C, each in several tonal guises, become the two focal points of the work's progress towards its conclusion. C major forms one of the three ingredients in the new, more developmental kind of tonality to be found in Part Eleven. The F#/A 'relative' relationship can now be seen as an important cog in the wheel of the overall tonal scheme. Another of the three ingredients in the developing tonality of Part Eleven is an A major/F# minor which develops by acquiring D#s, taking on a strong E-major aspect as it progresses. This, too, will play a role in the final denouement of Part Twelve which, with that of Part Eleven, is detailed below.

Within this scheme, *Music in Twelve Parts* unfolds a sequence of movements demonstrating considerable stylistic, as well as technical, variety. Part One is Glass's first slow minimalist piece, its impression of sustained F# C#s achieved as a resulting pattern derived from the interaction of its shifting counterpoint. Parts Three, Four and Seven also explore resulting patterns, while Parts Two, Five, Six and Eight unfold a process of augmentation and diminution within a fixed rhythmic cycle, extending Glass's early efforts at cyclic process to new levels of sophistication. While most earlier movements operate 'monothematically' with a single process, Parts Seven to Nine are more sectional and complex; Part Two, written at around the same time as these, also falls into this category. While Parts Ten to Twelve are essentially single processes once again, they chart a rising curve, the highly chromatic Part Ten leading to the harmonic motion of the concluding two movements to bring *Music in Twelve Parts* to a dramatic conclusion.

Part Five

The B major of Part Five is clarified by bass movement emphasising iv, iv and i and, more audibly, by the repeated i–ii and v–vi–v–iii in the upper parts and the held D# (iii) near the top of the texture. But the already mentioned feeling of release after the tensions of Part Four is celebrated more by rhythmic than by harmonic ingenuity. The most significant aspect of Part Five is its delineation of a process of augmentation and diminution within a fixed rhythmic cycle.

Example 4.13a gives the opening two figures of Part Five, while Example 4.13b outlines the rhythmic elements involved. A bar-length of six quavers is maintained throughout; characteristically, though, Glass rings the changes on its equal potential for $\frac{6}{8}$ and $\frac{3}{4}$ from the outset. Continuity is provided by the repeated quaver patterns: in both treble and bass, but most clearly in the left hand of Organ 4, its unchanging pitch patterns being notated, like those of the treble, in whichever metre best suits the tendency of those other parts which change. As one would expect, the listener may choose to hear the metre at almost any point as either $\frac{6}{8}$ or $\frac{3}{4}$. The opening texture (Example 4.13a) demonstrates the variety of both metric

Example 4.13 *Music in Twelve Parts*: (a) Part Five, Figures 1–2.

Example 4.13 (cont.) *Music in Twelve Parts*: (b) Part Five, rhythmic structure.

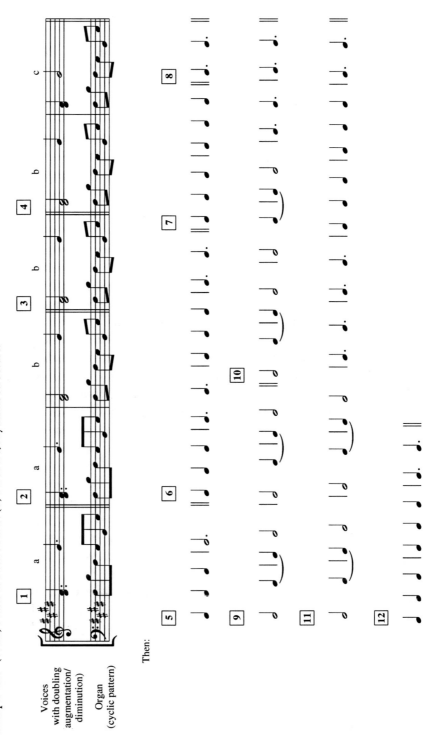

Voices
with doubling
augmentation/
diminution)

Organ
(cyclic pattern)

Then:

emphases and contrapuntal elaboration. The various doublings of the bass include one (Organ 2) which reproduces part of the basic pattern exactly, but also introduces a cross-rhythm. Another bass line (Organ 1) picks up this cross-rhythm in a resulting pattern formed from the E F♯ of the bass and the D♯ drone.

While the clearly audible top instrumental line helps provide the already mentioned v–vi–v–iii, it is the rocking iii/v–vi of the voice parts singing *solfège* syllables, aided by some instrumental doubling, which unfolds the process of augmentation and diminution, oscillating a dyad and a single note over the repeating cycles of six quavers beneath. Example 4.13b shows how this clearly audible augmentation/diminution process unravels against the cyclic underlay. The composer's ensemble would seem to have experimented with different versions of this scheme at different periods; the one given here is that to be found in the only manuscript score which the present author has been able to see. In Figures 1–4, the rhythmic progress of these oscillations unfolds in a strict scheme alternating a single bar with a pair adding a new configuration to the first. As the figures increase in length, they establish four-bar minim groupings (forming cross-rhythms with the six-quaver cycle below) which first alternate with, and are eventually succeeded by, differently ordered sequences of crotchets and dotted crotchets. The effect is of an endlessly shifting metre, always grounded, however, by the underlying cyclic 'grid'. Amidst its greater focus on sheer sonority and harmonic sophistication, *Music in Twelve Parts* still finds room for the rigours of rhythmic process.

Parts Eleven and Twelve

With Parts Eleven and Twelve, Glass infuses harmonic motion with an additive process of its own to create a suitably charged and fulfilling climax to a composition of such length and complexity. Part Eleven consists of twelve basic chords (see Ex. 4.14) defining three tonal areas. In Area A, chords i, iv and vi are constructed on the bass notes A, B and F♯, being built on the principle of 'stacked' fifths (from A upwards) to produce: firstly, five-pitch aggregates of increasing density on A (chords ia, ib and ic); then, with the bass note B, a chord containing all seven pitches of the A-Lydian mode, adding G♯ and D♯ to the previous 'stack' of fifths (chord iv); then, with the bass note moving to F♯, a four-pitch aggregate built on an inner segment (E B F♯ C♯) of the 'stacked'-fifths gamut (chord vi).

Area B – to be found in chords ii, v, ix and xii – is constructed on the bass notes A♭, C and B♭, being built, again, on the principle of 'stacked' fifths (from A♭ upwards) to produce: firstly, a five-pitch aggregate on A♭ (chord ii); then, with the bass note C, a chord adding D♭ to chord ii (in 'stacked'-

Example 4.14 *Music in Twelve Parts*, Part Eleven, twelve basic chords

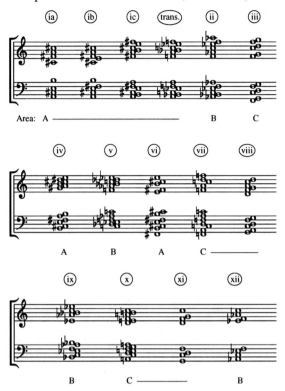

fifths terms, theoretically below A♭) to produce all pitches of the A♭ major scale except G (chord v); then a pentatonic aggregate with the bass note B♭ (chord ix); and finally, returning to a bass note of A♭, two pairs segmented from the original 'stack' of fifths on A♭ (chord xii). A single transitional, thirteenth chord (marked 'trans' in Ex. 4.14) mediates between Areas A and B, transposing all pitches but one of chord ic down a semitone to produce the pitch content of the 'stacked' fifths above A♭ characteristic of Area B, but retaining the bass note A♮ as the fifth pitch.

Area C – to be found in chords iii, vii, viii, x and xi – is constructed on the sequence of bass notes F F G A G, and is also built on 'stacked' fifths (from F upwards) to produce 'white-note' aggregates revealing their 'stacked'-fifths origins to the listener more clearly than do the chords of Areas A and B. The first, four-pitch aggregate on F (chord iii) returns in a different form on G (chord xi) to conclude this group. Chords vii and viii add A to the 'stack' of fifths, the former assembled on the bass note F, the latter on G. Chord x, on the bass note A, adds E and B, expanding the 'stack' of fifths to produce all seven 'white' notes.

Glass cleverly juxtaposes these three tonal areas, leading the listener to perceive a logic to the progression of his chords, yet periodically doubling back to delay its natural consequences in favour of repeating a whole sequence to raise the dramatic temperature by thwarting the listener's expectations. In purely rhythmic terms, Part Eleven is simply an extended sequence of ten-quaver units; except for the opening, whose expansion from six to eight to ten quavers in the bar allows chord i to assemble further doublings. Units of ten, dividing their two subdivisions of five quavers each into 2 + 3, permit an even flow, but compensate for the lack of any expanding rhythmic process by avoiding the metric predictability produced by multiples of 4. The application of additive process to harmonic motion itself is, however, the main thrust behind Part Eleven's unfolding, allowing tonal expansion, and the expectations this brings, to take on a more important role than in anything the composer had previously written.

The twelve chords of Example 4.14 are only performed as a complete sequence after this has been assembled in stages. Following the initial exposition of chord i, the transition chord – still surprising even after the chromatic scales of Part Ten – would be expected to move the harmony from the A♮-based Area A to the A♭-based Area B. At first, however, the return of chord ic (Figure 5) leads to a repeat of ic and the transition chord before the arrival of chords ii and iii. This process of doubling back is then used twice more, taking the sequence first from chords ic to viii (Figures 9–17), and finally to the complete twelve-chord progression (Figures 18–30).

The function of the two female voices in this process is crucial, their oscillating dyads doing as much, sometimes more, to point the path of harmonic movement as do the bass line, the periodic scale passages or any other structural devices to be found in the instrumental parts. For instance, the descending C B♭ in the voice parts of Figure 6 (transition chord) is followed very naturally by the A♭ C of Figure 7 (chord ii), which leads equally smoothly to the G C of Figure 8 (chord iii). The voices thus suggest – more than does the bass line's shifts from A♮ to A♭ to F, though the latter is followed by G in the actual arpeggiation – that the goal of this progression really lies in the C major of Area C, potentially extending the feeling of suspension generated by chord iii to some more permanent resolution. Yet the first time we heard the descending C B♭ in the transition chord (Figure 4), it was followed, in the doubling-back process, by the abruptly juxtaposed A C♯ of Area A's chord ic. In addition, any hints of impending resolution offered by chord iii are in turn thwarted by avoidance of the 'white-note' Area C in the choice of modality all this chord's successors are permitted: the Area A of chord ic again in Figure 9, of chord iv in Figure 13 and, after repetitions of this whole sequence, the Area B of chords ix (Figure 27) and xii (Figure 30).

Though Part Eleven concludes in Area B, both other tonal areas are notable for their expansion during its course. This expansion takes different forms. Area A's addition of D♯s (Figures 13 and 22) pushes its A-major modality towards its dominant, while chord vi – with its bass note F♯ and, again, in particular the voice parts, which oscillate F♯ B – suggests a suspension on the dominant of B major. The chords of Area C also fluctuate in the number of pitches they employ; more significant, though, is the progressive importance of its 'white-note' modality as the complete chord sequence unravels.

Such still ambiguously shifting tonal areas were now to be superseded by chordal progressions articulating harmonic motion with greater direction and consistency, and integrating this more thoroughly with additive process. In Part Twelve, Glass replaces the three areas of Part Eleven with just two. The first, the new Area A – an added-sixth chord on the major triad of A, the key which had already dominated the previous three movements – could not be simpler, and its arpeggiations retain a firm hold on the root position of this chord throughout the whole twenty minutes of the concluding movement. The second, Area B – a chromatic sequence beginning with an added-fourth chord on C minor, the key of Parts Four and Seven, and a strong candidate for the goal of Part Eleven – is quite complex; its ramifications become the determining factor in the work's denouement, despite the fact that A major has the final say.

Example 4.15 gives a harmonic outline of Part Twelve. During the opening three-and-a-half minutes, A^6 and C-minor^4 chords alternate in the kind of expanding then contracting rhythmic process long the stock-in-trade of the composer's output. For a further two minutes, C-minor^4 is joined by what Glass himself seems to regard as an added-fourth chord on B♭, though it is also interpretable as an added-second chord on E♭; this pair of tonally related aggregates now contrasts with the single aggregate of Area A. As Area B continues to expand, however, its starting point on C and tonal focus on a key signature of three flats are dissolved in a sequence of triads juxtaposed with surprising abandon. B major and A♭ major arrive as a linked pair; the other four – major triads on E♭, D♭, D♮ and E♮ – are similarly linked, joining the sequence at about nine-and-a-half minutes into the movement. This constitutes what the performance materials for the work term Part Twelve A.

The sustained tonal expansion of Area B, at first forming such a contrast with that of Area A, makes it seem likely that it will devour the latter and conclude the work in the ambiguous chromatic space which Area B has surprisingly opened up. Part Twelve B initially confirms that suspicion,

Example 4.15 *Music in Twelve Parts*, Part Twelve, harmonic outline

Part 12a

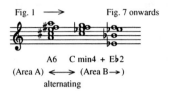

Fig. 1 ⟶   Fig. 7 onwards

      A6   C min4 + E♭2
(Area A) ⟵⟶ (Area B→)
      alternating

Fig. 11 onwards

  + B   A♭   E♭   D♭   D♮   E

Part 12b

Figs. 20–24

  + F♯   F♮   G

adding, some three minutes further on, three more major triads – on F♯, F♮ and G – to complete the formation of triads on all twelve pitch classes. These chromatic sequences have, however, three rather different functions. Firstly, they describe a swift and bumpy ride through the chromatic gamut which, in Part Twelve A, has already included chords on all three pitches – D, E♭ and E♮ – which failed to find a place either as the main key of an individual movement or of one of its separate tonal areas. Secondly, Glass's choice of triads in Part Twelve A has a more specific, and audible, tonal function. Initially moving freely between flat and sharp keys, its final four chords not only include all the above-mentioned roots, D, E♭ and E♮ (plus D♭), but also conclude with E major, the dominant of the A⁶ of Area A to which the completed sequence of Area B now leads. This link between the two alternating Areas A and B brings them together as ultimately a single process of 'preparation' (a chromatic sequence moving from distant tonal terrain to the dominant) and 'resolution' (the tonic A of Part Twelve, and indeed of *Music in Twelve Parts* as a whole). Thirdly, with the aid of such renewed confirmation in the potential of harmonic motion, the cumulatively unfolding procession of chords in Parts 12 A and B taken together creates a powerful sense of dramatic tension and resolution as a fitting climax to a composition several hours long.

Music in Twelve Parts has been viewed as 'a musical lexicon of Seventies minimalism';[82] in 1992, the composer still hoped that it would 'keep his purist fans happy'. But if the consolidation of sonic impact, and the concomitant concern with texture and psycho-acoustics, already redefines the minimalism of *Music with Changing Parts*, its successor's extension and clarification of these render *Music in Twelve Parts* more clearly 'post-minimalist'. Conducted in the context of such a rich display of rhythmic techniques – some old, some new – these tonal discoveries were soon to show their composer the path to a stage work in which even more extended structures would be impelled by the harmonic motion already explored in what is one of Glass's most captivating compositions.

Einstein on the Beach

In the early 1970s, Glass says, he and Robert Wilson 'shared the same community of support'[83] in and around SoHo, and that they 'were bound to meet'. Not for the first time, though, the composer was fortunate in encountering the right person to help him at the right time of his career.

Glass first saw Wilson's work at the Brooklyn Academy of Music in 1973, and met this 'rapidly emerging . . . formidable theater [talent]' at the cast party afterwards. The work he saw, *The Life and Times of Joseph Stalin* (1972), lasts – like its predecessor, *The Life and Times of Sigmund Freud* (1969) – around twelve hours. *Stalin* is a seven-act play which, like other works of his before *Einstein*, Wilson himself called an 'opera'; it ran from 7pm to 7am and had a cast of 144. Expansiveness in one direction is, though, offset by a positively minimalist reduction in another. In Wilson's predominantly visual theatre, the action is sparse and glacially slow; the importance of such texts as exist is minimised rather than emphasised through repetition. When words are used, Wilson was already frequently employing the unusual talents of Christopher Knowles, an autistic boy whose alienation from 'normal' approaches to language clearly struck Wilson as having both practical and metaphorical parallels with his own; outside the theatre, he was also working extensively with handicapped children at this time.

Sheer length forms the most obvious connection between *Music in Twelve Parts* and the theatrical concerns with which Glass was now to become heavily re-engaged in the collaboration on *Einstein*. On the one hand, such drastic extension of theatrical time could be said to aid the creation of an experimental artistic space, a kind of theatre which sought to avoid all the connotations of 'narrative' and even characterisation in a quest for new kinds of experience which were image-based and tended to distort not only 'real time' but also previous kinds of 'theatrical time'. On the other, the construction of such a large edifice clearly necessitated decisions about the ordering, as well as the content, of its building blocks, and decisions about what sort of effect those building blocks would have. Was any cumulative effect to be entirely avoided? And could dramatic notions of the sort already countenanced by Glass in the 'pure' music of *Music in Twelve Parts* play some role?

The drama

Dramatic considerations were, of course, primarily Wilson's concern, and the main artistic thrust of *Einstein on the Beach* has often been interpreted as coming from the theatrical rather than the musical side. (The question of who the real creator of *Einstein* was subsequently contributed to the break-up of the collaboration between Glass and Wilson. Glass was, though, one of several composers involved with Wilson's massive *the CIVIL warS* project in 1984. More recently, the two have worked together again: for instance, on *Monsters of Grace* and *The White Raven*, both premièred in 1998.) The composer's experience of experimental drama, and his understanding of Khatikali theatre, with its (by Western standards) unusual sense of time, gave him both knowledge of, and ideas of his own about, the potential of what Wilson came to call a 'theatre of images'. Besides, *Einstein* is probably unique – even by the standards of experimental theatre of the 1960s and 1970s – for its integration of music, image, dance and speech into what previous terminology can only label a theatrical *Gesamtkunstwerk*.

Glass and Wilson decided at that 1973 party to investigate the possibility of working together, and from the spring of 1974 they met, sometimes weekly, for the next year or so. The work's subject was decided after the composer had rejected his new colleague's earlier suggestions of Hitler and Chaplin as their central focus. Later, Glass was to argue that *Einstein* was the first in a trilogy of operas; this first 'panel' represented not only Einstein himself but also 'science: technology and ecology'.[84] Yet this is probably commercially conceived as well as retrospective; it also implies more common ground between the performance-art-orientated *Einstein* and the more 'regular' operas, *Satyagraha* and *Akhnaten*, which followed. As is clear, the choice of Albert Einstein – the physicist whose discoveries made possible the creation of, among other things, the atom bomb – was to a degree extraneous to Wilson and Glass's main concerns. Wilson, though, saw the work as 'a poetic exploration of Einstein',[85] who is treated as essentially a mythic character. Since the historical Einstein was an amateur fiddle player, a solo violinist occupied a prominent place, visually as well as musically, dressed to look like the scientist as an old man. (In the forty-odd performances of the original 1976 production, this role was taken by Robert Brown; for the first recording – made in the spring of 1977, at the former Big Apple Recording Studios on Greene Street – Paul Zukofsky, the still young but already well-known professional soloist, took over.) While he plays a crucial musical role, this Einstein does not participate in the stage action; occupying a raised dais in the orchestra pit, he is, rather, a witness to the events on stage, and arguably not 'really' the character, imagined or otherwise, at all.

Einstein on the Beach on Wall Street – as it was originally called (for no clear reason) – was conceived from a series of drawings made by Wilson following some general agreement between him and Glass on themes, length and the work's division into four acts, with a total of nine scenes and five connecting sections. The latter Wilson termed 'Knee Plays', explaining that this clarified their 'joining function'.[86] In its first performances, the resulting work lasted almost exactly five-and-a-half hours without intermission. The following description is of the 1976 production, for which, given *Einstein*'s nature, Wilson was naturally designer as well as director.

In *Einstein*, theme and structure are ordered not by narrative, either spoken or even merely mimed, but by a kind of loose association built around three recurring visual images: a train, a trial and something called Field with Spaceship. Act I deals with the train and the trial; Act II with the spaceship and a reworking of the train image, which has now become Night Train. Act III combines the trial with a prison, and follows this with a second Field with Spaceship scene. Act IV is concerned with the radical transmutation of all these images into new ones: the train becomes a building, the trial a bed, and the field now simply a spaceship. These transmutations have been interpreted in terms of Einstein's theory of relativity. It is easy to see how a train, the most commonly used illustration of relativity theory, might form part of such a reading; and it is not hard to read the Act IV Spaceship scene – the work's final 'main' scene, with its wildly flashing lights and belching smoke, its collapsing astronauts and, just to make the point more than merely relatively clear, the equation $E = Mc^2$ on the curtain which then descends – as a vision of nuclear holocaust. On the other hand, the process by which a trial becomes a bed, which itself resembles a beam of light, is more elusive.

While all this can be taken as the main action (however resistant parts of it are to interpretation), the five Knee Plays which form the prologue, interludes and epilogue to the four acts seem of equal significance in both length and dramatic content, even though Knee Play 1 is already in progress as the audience is admitted to the auditorium. The subject matter of these Knee Plays is, though, related only obliquely to that of the 'main' acts; as a result, they are even more difficult to decode. In the Knee Plays, two women (Lucinda Childs and Sheryl Sutton in the first performances) sit at tables placed at the front of the stage to the right; in Knee Play 4 they lie on glass tables, and for the fifth they become Two Lovers sitting on a park bench. Other images counterpoint their action (or inaction): all, like their own movements and words (which here take on greater importance than elsewhere), potentially related to Einstein's achievements, or even to the figure of Einstein himself, in some way.

While image- rather than text-driven, *Einstein* contains important spoken material. This consists of several texts by Knowles, and one each by Samuel M. Johnson (an elderly amateur who auditioned for an acting role and turned out to have a curious creative talent) and Childs (primarily a dancer and choreographer – she was, as we have seen, one of the two women in the Knee Plays – whose work in these areas also contributed much to the original production). These eleven texts are simply read: some are poetic in form, some prose, some a combination of the two. Nothing in their imagery relates in any obvious way to the simultaneous stage action; their respect for grammar, and even straightforward meaning, is some-times only intermittent. The only text (the one by Childs) even to refer to either Einstein or the beach (only the latter, in fact) concerns *avoidance* of the beach. Yet narrative as well as grammatical sense of some sort is by no means entirely avoided in these spoken texts. Sung material, on the other hand, is confined to numbers and *solfège* syllables. The action covers a wide variety of stylised motion and dance, in which some of the singers them-selves took part. For the 1976 performances, Andrew de Groat, who had worked previously with Wilson, choreographed the dance ensembles, while Childs composed her own dance solos. The two remaining original solo roles were taken by Paul Mann (who played a young boy) and the already mentioned Johnson (who played an old man).

The music

Musically, *Einstein on the Beach* is a natural development from *Music in Twelve Parts*. But whereas that work applies a vocabulary of techniques to structures which are still essentially based on rhythmic devices, Glass now turned, as he puts it, 'to problems of harmonic structure or, more accu-rately, structural harmony – new solutions to problems of harmonic usage, where the evolution of material can become the basis of an overall formal structure intrinsic to the music itself'.[87]

Einstein in fact draws on an intervening work for the Philip Glass Ensemble called *Another Look at Harmony*, a large-scale piece in four sections, begun in the spring of 1975. Parts One and Two of this became the basis of the opening scenes of the opera's first two acts, 'the starting points from which additional material and devices were developed'. Though this other work was not completed until 1977, the year after *Einstein*'s première performances, the overlap between the two compositions is considerable, rendering any detailed comment on *Another Look at Harmony* superfluous. The significance of harmony, already established as a newly expressive as well as structural element in *Music in Twelve Parts*, is now accompanied, in *Einstein*, by a tonal plan even more extended and complex than that of the earlier work. This is given as Example 4.16.

The shift of focus towards tonal motion did not, of course, mean that Glass's previous rhythmic and other related technical apparatus had now been abandoned. The continuing use of additive and cyclic processes is often clarified by the extensive use of sung numbers and *solfège*; the solo violin part is also audibly based on such structures. The use of voices in *Music with Changing Parts* and *Music in Twelve Parts* is now extended and formalised, with the sung *solfège* syllables already found in the latter work supplemented with numbers. Both solo and choral singers act more independently of the instrumental ensemble, their roles considerably enhanced from those of the vocalists in the earlier works. This greater conventionality, relatively speaking, is even more noticeable in Glass's reduced interest in psycho-acoustic effects. The larger forces might have suggested new possibilities in this territory; but in fact they encouraged a more familiar separation into vocal and instrumental, melody and accompaniment, foreground and background, than before.

The opera is bounded by a clear cadential progression in C major: a vi–v–i repeating bass line in that key provides the sole material for the Prologue and the chaconne bass above which the framing Knee Plays 1 and 5 unfold their elaborations. While *Einstein* is scarcely 'in C major', individual sections use different tonalities to articulate a totality which, especially when experienced in the theatre, exhibits a surprisingly conventional approach to such matters as proportion and climax. Though C major itself is confined to the Knee Plays, the structural ambiguity of these sections (are they 'main action' or merely 'interludes'?) if anything enhances the importance of this key in the opera as a whole.

Besides, other tonalities in *Einstein* are related to C major. A minor first occurs in Trial (Act I, scene ii) and the immediately following Knee Play 2. In Dance 1 (Act II, scene i), this gives way to a rather unstable D minor that allows A to emerge as its dominant in terms of long-range tonal development. This A/D relationship is replicated later on: in Trial 2/Prison (Act III, scene i), a Phrygian-A tonality acts as a preface to the fairly chromatic

Example 4.16 *Einstein on the Beach*, tonal structure

Prologue   A, G, C repeating bass

Knee Play 1   C major

Act I

Scene 1: Train   a) Pentatonic 'A flat major' (the key signature is three flats, but
                      no D flats, or Gs, occur, and E flat is clearly the dominant, not
                      the tonic)
                      b) Pentatonic 'E flat major' (instrumental)
                      c) F minor modulating constantly to E major

Scene 2: Trial   A minor
                      'rootless' four-chord sequence ('All Men Are Equal')
                      plus two-chord link to

Knee Play 2   A minor alternating with F minor>E major five-chord
                      progression

Act II

Scene 1: Dance 1   D minor (unstable)

Scene 2: Night Train Pentatonic A flat major

Knee Play 3   F minor modulating to E major (both keys and the modulation
                      more ambiguous than in Train 1, but the relationship is
                      clear) alternating with C major (a stepwise contrary-motion
                      version of the original chaconne)

Example 4.16 (*cont.*)

Act III

Scene 1: Trial 2/Prison   Phrygian mode on A

Scene 2: Dance 2   D minor (chromatically inflected)

Knee Play 4   F minor/E major alternating with C major
                      (Knee 4 as a whole is a further variation of Train/Knee 3)

Act IV

Scene 1: Building/Train   Pentatonic 'A flat major'

Scene 2: Bed/Trial   A minor (including organ cadenza),
                      'rootless' four-chord sequence

Scene 3: Spaceship   F minor/E major (more akin again to Train 1)
                      alternating and combining with
                      A minor (but scale patterns only, quickly becoming highly
                      chromatic and soon discernible as a further variation on the F
                      minor/E major sequence rather than on A)

Knee Play 5   C major (as Knee 1)

D minor of the ensuing Dance 2 (Act III, scene ii). The tonality of the Dance scenes – uneasily dissonant though both dances are, in ways untypical of the opera as a whole – suggests that C major, A minor and D minor, together with their modal and chromatic extensions, can be understood as a single group of keys central to *Einstein*'s progress: a view reinforced by the return of A minor in the crucial Bed/Trial (Act IV, scene ii).

Another group of tonalities, however, proves to have greater significance than this. In Train (Act I, scene i), a pentatonic scale (A♭ B♭ D♭ E♭ G♭) is inflected by the emphasis which the bass line gives, first to A♭, then to E♭; this is succeeded by an F-minor arpeggio. A pentatonic/F-minor 'hinge' is used in the lead-back to the entry of the voices in the alternating vocal-plus-instrumental and purely instrumental sections of this scene. It is clear that *Einstein* deploys a group of keys centring around A♭ major/F minor: Night Train (Act II, scene ii) has the same pentatonic character as Train; so has the much later Building/Train (Act IV, scene i). In Train itself, however, the F-minor arpeggio acquires a bass line, B♭ C, and moves, not into F minor, but to an arpeggiated and repeated F-minor/E-major modulation. Despite its initial air of being a mere offshoot of the already established A♭ territory, it is this F-minor/E-major 'cadential pattern' which occupies a central position in the opera's overall structure, integrating local harmonic motion and long-range tonal planning.

Glass calls this five-chord cadential pattern '[t]he most prominent "theme" of the opera';[88] this is given as Example 4.17c. Following its appearance in Train, it occurs in Knee Plays 2, 3 and 4, and furnishes almost the entire basis of Spaceship (Act IV, scene iii). As the composer himself points out, '[w]hat makes the formula distinctive and even useful is . . . the way in which the IV♭ (B♭♭) becomes IV (A) of the new key, thereby making the phrase resolve a half-step lower. This, in turn, provides the leading tone for the original i (F minor). As it is a formula which invites repetition, it is particularly suited to my kind of musical thinking'. This progression's strong character cunningly avoids the potential monotony of having long stretches of music in one key; it derives much of its impact in *Einstein*, indeed, from its sharp contrast with other, more harmonically static, sections.

The F-minor/E-major pattern is limited by its property of looping back on itself, the final arpeggio of E major leading – with an inevitability admittedly enforced more by familiarity through extended repetition than by conformity to the grammatical conventions of tonal music – directly to the return of F minor, thus locking the progression into itself. And in the short term, its function may seem more colouristic than structural: Train (Act I, scene i) returns after about two minutes to its previous alternations.

At the end of this scene, however, the F-minor/E-major 'theme' returns, bringing a finality which the other material could not have done. More importantly, the concluding E major now provides a link, not back to F minor – or, thinking in longer-range terms, to A♭ – as the repetition has by this time taught us to expect, but to the modal A minor of the next scene, Trial. In other words, the F-minor/E-major cadential pattern offers the crucial connection between the two main tonal groups of *Einstein* (C major/A minor/D minor and A♭ major/F minor). The incessant repetitions of this pattern cause E major to take on the role of the dominant, thereby making the arrival of the unambiguous A minor of the Trial scene a natural step. As in the closing stages of *Music in Twelve Parts*, Glass is putting the discoveries of his earlier compositions to good use in the contexts of harmonic progression and tonal resolution, musical drama and long-range structural planning.

This cadential pattern is in fact the last of what the composer calls the three 'themes' which form the basis of the opening Train scene and are developed elsewhere; their deployment offers a good illustration of Glass's basic working methods in *Einstein*. Example 4.17a, based on the combination of two patterns of different lengths, shows, on a simple level, the continued working of cyclic processes in the opera. Example 4.17b, a reworking of this idea, is itself developed further in Building/Train (Act IV, scene i); it demonstrates how Glass continues to construct repeated figures into sequences by means of additive process. Example 4.17c, the F-minor/E-major pattern itself, also functions as the first of five elements which the composer describes as the 'musical material of the opera . . . 5 chords, 4 chords, 3 chords, 2 chords and 1 chord'.[89] The opening F-minor harmony of Example 4.17c provides the starting point for the four-chord pattern, which ends on D major (see Ex. 4.18a). First heard at the end of Trial (Act I, scene ii), it also occurs in Trial 2/Prison (Act III, scene i) and Bed/Trial (Act IV, scene ii). Example 4.18b demonstrates how this is subjected to rhythmic expansion in the first of these three scenes. The three-chord theme (Ex. 4.19a) is reserved for the two Dance scenes (Act II, scene i, and Act III, scene ii) and revolves around D minor. Examples 4.19b and 4.19c show the two-chord and one-chord material: the former oscillating between A-minor^7 and G-minor^7 in Trial 2/Prison (Act III, scene i); the latter outlining A-minor^7 (plus D♮) in the arpeggiated figures to be found in Trial (Act I, scene ii), Trial 2/Prison (Act III, scene i) and Bed/Trial (Act IV, scene ii).

As a further illustration of Glass's structural inventiveness within an individual scene, Knee Play 3's spare, much altered version, for unaccompanied chorus, of the five-chord F-minor/E-major progression is typical

Example 4.17 *Einstein on the Beach*, Train: (a) Figure 2 (First theme); (b) Figure 20 (Second theme); (c) Figure 59 (Third theme; five-chord cadential pattern).

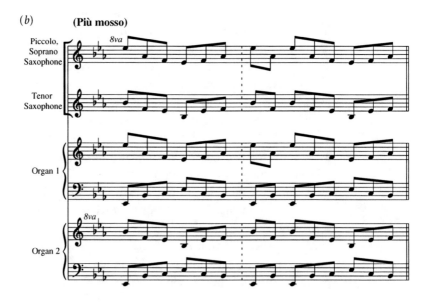

Example 4.17 (*cont.*)

(*c*)

Example 4.18 *Einstein on the Beach*, Trial: (a) Figure 53; (b) Figure 54.

(*a*)

(*b*)

Example 4.19 *Einstein on the Beach*: (a) Dance 1, Figures 1–2; (b) Trial 2/Prison, Figures 11–13; (c) Trial, Figures 20–3.

(a)

(b)

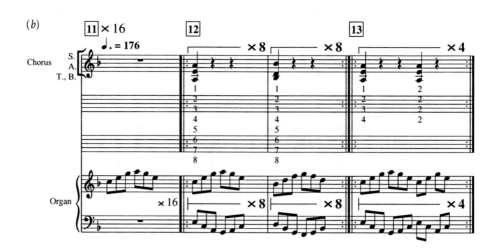

Example 4.19 (*cont.*)

(*c*)

(see Ex. 4.20). What started as a ceaseless round of arpeggiations has now become a rarefied, angular reinterpretation of the plain triads of the original progression strung in an additive process on sung numbers. In between two presentations of an $8+8+8+10$ repetitive scheme, with pauses between each group, comes the variation, again *a cappella*, on the opening chaconne; a reduced version of this also forms a coda. The second presentation of the main section makes further substitutions – the opening F-minor chord, for instance, is reduced simply to a unison C♯ – and is structurally reduced to repetitions of $6+6$.

In Dance 2 (Act III, scene ii), just two scenes later, the spaceship already seen in the earlier Dance scene (Act II, scene i) draws nearer. The positioning of this scene around *Einstein*'s point of Golden Section underlines its pivotal status; the two Dance scenes are, for Glass, 'two pillars equidistant from either end of the opera'. It is here that the three-chord 'theme' (Ex. 4.19a) makes its second and final appearance. By its end, we are almost exactly three-quarters of the way through *Einstein*, according to the performance timings of the 1993 recording. After Knee Play 4, Building/Train (Act IV, scene i) takes up the challenge to find a way forward to a conclusion in such dramatically and musically ambiguous circumstances by displaying the greatest contrast the opera offers between static and developmental harmony. The latter is rendered almost ironic by occupying only the scene's concluding seconds. Before this, for some ten minutes, a single harmony – the pentatonic chord familiar from Train and Night Train – is subjected to an additive rhythmic process on two chords; meanwhile, chords built from these notes swell and die away periodically in the chorus (these are in theory improvised), and woodwind – chiefly a tenor saxophone – improvise around the chord, unconfined to the prevailing pentatony. Surprisingly static by the new harmonic standards *Einstein* has set, in context this scene offers a palpable feeling of expectation. Suddenly, all this ceases, and out of nowhere comes the F-minor/E-major five-chord

Example 4.20 *Einstein on the Beach*, Knee Play 3, Figure 1

progression, played four times – impatiently, urgently – in familiar arpeggiated form by winds and organs.

Bed/Trial (Act IV, scene ii) opens with an organ cadenza that, in the score, consists simply of a few modal scalic passages around A; on the 1993 recording, Riesman plays a two-minute solo that seems deliberately reminiscent of Bach, and even Monteverdi, in its elaborations (an example of stylistic allusion more familiar from recent Glass and Adams). Bed proper then continues with the laid-back, modal A minor of Trial and Knee Play 2, plus the four-chord progression of Example 4.18a, seeming to thwart the denouement Building/Train promised.

A Prelude and Aria now further interrupt the progress of the action: the former a much-reduced version of the A-minor material of Trial for solo organ; the latter an eight-minute vocalise for soprano and organ (see Ex. 4.21), the ethereal, triadically harmonised melody of which – spun over the Trial scene's four-chord progression (Exs. 4.18a and b) – offers something quite new in Glass's music. Then, with Spaceship (Act IV, scene iii), we finally reach the climax for which the previous scenes have prepared us, all the greater in impact for having been so long delayed. The preceding scene has given the wind players the break they needed to make their ascent to the high stage gantry where, amidst the flashing lights and general mayhem of Wilson's representation not merely of space flight but also of nuclear holocaust, they too become part of the action. Musically, Spaceship offers the only possible *dénouement*: a wild fantasy at first based entirely on the five-chord F-minor/E-major progression, now subjected to an extended additive process. The expanding bass line of this underpins the revolving arpeggios of the upper instrumental lines (unbroken except by brief recourse to repeated notes), the chanted numbers of the chorus and the more sustained *solfège* of the solo soprano with an ever more emphatic insistence that this repeated modulation is somehow the key to the whole work. In the later stages of this first section, the chorus abandons its number-chanting for *solfège*.

Example 4.21 *Einstein on the Beach*, Bed/Trial, Figures 35–8

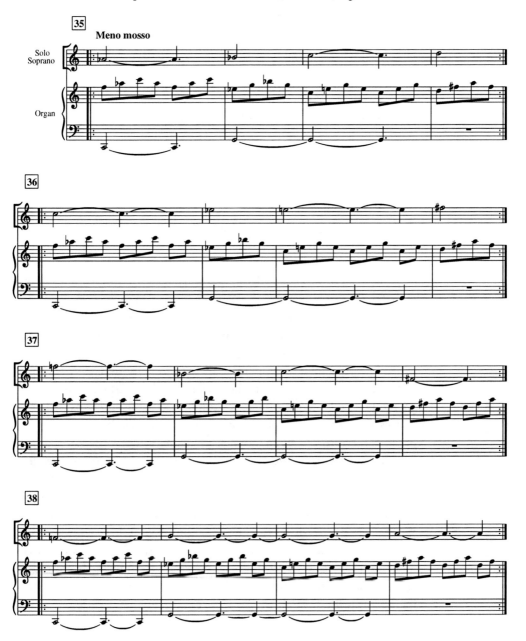

Then, prepared only by the extent to which the concluding E major of this progression retains any shreds of its dominant propensities, instruments alone launch into the fast and furious modal A-minor scales from Trial. Subject first to additive and subtractive process, they then turn more chromatic and plunge back into the F-minor/E-major progression. Chromaticism soon infects the bass line of this as well, eventually causing the loss of the final E-major chord. The repetitions of this version sound at once more regular (four- rather than five-bar sequences) and more awkward (the jump from B^7 to the F-minor triad takes some getting used to). Instrumental chromatic scales in parallel fifths lead to a concluding burst of the full five-chord progression, which takes us to the C major of the final Knee Play 5 and the music with which *Einstein on the Beach* began.

The music of *Einstein* still avoids the full implications of narrative and of thematic structuring, just as it avoids a firm commitment to the directed motion of classical tonality. The capability musical minimalism possesses to move flexibly between different grammars for what remains a reassuringly familiar vocabulary is perhaps demonstrated more completely and more successfully in *Einstein on the Beach* than in any other work by Glass. On the one hand, the larger formal units, as well as the timbres Glass chooses, have an experimental 'rough edge' to them. The opera's large scale, too, still allows it to operate in what its composer calls 'non-colloquial time'. On the other hand, the awakening of interest in harmonic progression and directed motion leads him to notate this music using barred metres and rounded phrasing: for the first time, Glass's music 'hugs' the bar line. Sections are much more clearly demarcated; while this might be considered inevitable with such a long work, it is true of sub-sections within the larger units as well.

A sense of motion, of development, is, moreover, indulgently celebrated in *Einstein*'s overall shaping. Glass – reliant to some degree, of course, on Wilson here, as elsewhere – is almost manipulative in the way he deals with the opera's dramatic unfolding so that, as he says, it 'works towards a finale; you can't miss it. A real finale; a real razzle-dazzle finale', he calls it: 'a piece that left the audience standing'. This is borne out by experience of the opera in the theatre; the last Spaceship scene has, indeed, a terrific feeling of release about it, which is all the greater coming, as it does, after about four hours strung on the tensions of Wilson's static stage pictures and Glass's repetitive patterns. Encountering the work in the theatrical space for which it was conceived – rather than experiencing it on record alone – confirms the impression that *Einstein on the Beach* is another masterpiece of late twentieth-century music.

The composer's increasing interest in tonally directed motion forms the crucial link between his music of the early 1970s, especially the final stages of *Music in Twelve Parts*, and the whole of his later, 'post-minimalist' development. It was this exploration of harmonic motion, however limited at this stage, which was to allow Glass to move into more conventional operatic territory after 1976. For all his previous interest in finding a complementary approach to 'non-narrative' theatre, the composer seems to have come to the conclusion that music-theatre is only sustainable if the stage action is complemented by something resembling familiar tonal motion, no matter how vague, or intermittent. In *Satyagraha* (1980), his first 'proper opera', each scene is constructed on a 'chaconne' bass with harmonic elaborations above it. In the arrival of the chord progression, Glass had forced some rapprochement with functional harmony. In this first really thorough exploration of a vocal line quarried from the chords of a simple tonal progression, he had now discovered a new meaning and purpose for melody: another essential ingredient of opera. In *Satyagraha*, opera singers are required to sing words with quite clear meanings for both character development and plot, even if the text is in Sanskrit – and the plot unchronological. Such expansion, both technically and stylistically, also gave Glass the opportunity to explore further the links with more popular musical forms already established via the sound-world and energy of his ensemble.

Conclusion

Much of Glass's activity since the late 1970s, and a great deal of his influence, can in fact be charted in the arena of rock music and the achievements of a wide popularity for music with a clear beat which also has a tune. The composer's willingness to get involved with the rock world on several levels – to promote his own work on a highly commercial basis, and even as a record producer for other musicians (for instance, Polyrock and The Raybeats in the late 1970s) – has made him much the best known of the four subjects of this book.

Glass was, though, involved with rock from early on. While this initially related to his downtown Manhattan roots, his early European performances, as well as the Chatham Square recordings, gained him a reputation in Britain, West Germany and elsewhere as a seminal influence on the art-rock of the 1970s. The composer's impact on German groups was probably the earliest and in some respects the most significant; among these were Cluster, Kraftwerk, Neu! and the bands involved with what became known as the German wave of 'metronomic' keyboard music. In Germany, too, Glass met Tangerine Dream; the group helped him obtain the contract for Virgin Records which resulted not only in the release of Parts 1 and 2 of *Music in Twelve Parts* in 1975, but also, two years later, of *North Star*.

David Bowie and Brian Eno – who both heard the composer's music in London in 1971 – have been particularly influenced by Glass. Eno's first album with Robert Fripp – *No Pussyfooting* (1973) – is an early example, evidently indebted to the sustained pitches of *Music with Changing Parts*, which was performed in Glass's first London concerts. Eno's 'ambient music' is but one example of the influence of minimalism on his later work. With Bowie, the debt is clearest on the *Low* and *Heroes* albums of 1977, on which Eno was a collaborator. In the 1990s, Glass has written 'symphonic commentaries' on both these. More clearly commercial developments in rock music have also been affected by Glass's early music: for instance, the disco and syntho-pop of the late 1970s, of which Giorgio Moroder's Donna Summer seventeen-minute disco record, 'Love to Love You' of 1975 is probably the most notorious example.

It was only after the tour of *Einstein on the Beach* in 1976 that Glass became seriously involved with Manhattan rock clubs and the then current punk and post-punk movements. From the late 1970s, his ensemble began to play in more 'mainstream' rock venues such as New York's Peppermint Lounge and the Roxy in Los Angeles. Art-rock developments in downtown Manhattan which were influenced by Glass's example, in the 1970s and beyond, include everything from the more obviously rock-orientated band Theoretical Girls to the more experimental work of such composer-performers as Glenn Branca (who early on worked with Theoretical Girls) and Rhys Chatham. Following *Songs from Liquid Days* – his 1986 album of songs with lyrics and vocals provided by a range of major rock and 'alternative' rock singers – Glass's more recent collaborators have included the British artist Richard James, more familiarly known as Aphex Twin.

While Glass has never commanded the respect and attention given to Reich in the Western classical arena, his influence has been felt both there and in developments which, like the composer's own, have sought to cross the boundaries between such categories of music-making. His later operas, in particular, have been staged worldwide, making a particularly strong impression in Germany, where the complete *Einstein–Satyagraha–Akhnaten* trilogy was assembled in Stuttgart in the 1980s. While Michael Nyman has been personally closer to Reich, his root-based chord techniques and vigorous rhythmic style have more in common with Glass. And where Glass and Nyman have led, a whole host of younger composers of all nationalities has followed.

Perhaps the most interesting aspect of Glass's subsequent development has been his ability to work in several musical fields at once, crossing and recrossing the borders normally erected between, for instance, 'concert music' and opera on the one hand, and popular songs, music for films and even television advertising on the other. Practically speaking, the composer has achieved this by taking on more obviously commercial work in order to subsidise his more experimental projects: especially the challenging theatrical and film works such as *1,000 Airplanes on the Roof* (1988) and the operatic setting of the Jean Cocteau film *La Belle et la Bête* (1994). Musically speaking, while it would be foolish to suggest that there is complete uniformity of style between the outputs in each of these territories, the connections between them are more evident than their differences. If the true musical minimalism of the 1960s and early 1970s emerged as a consequence of a realignment of avant-garde, 'cultivated' and 'vernacular' elements which he helped to bring about, then the international, and postmodernist, 'post-minimalism' that has further eroded such previously significant boundaries in the 1980s and 1990s likewise owes much to the example of Philip Glass.

Notes

Introduction

1 From the author's interviews with the composers. Observations of this kind, including direct quotations, which remain unreferenced in this volume are for the most part taken from these sources.

2 Sol Le Witt, 'Paragraphs on Conceptual Art', *Artforum*, 8/5 (June 1967), p. 80.

3 Lawrence Alloway, 'Serial Forms', originally published in the catalogue for the exhibition 'American Sculpture of the 60s' (arranged by Maurice Tuchman at the Los Angeles County Museum, 1967); reprinted in *Topics in American Art Since 1945* (New York: Norton, 1975), p. 95.

4 Tom Johnson, 'The Minimal Slow-Motion Approach: Alvin Lucier and Others', originally published in the *Village Voice*, 30 March 1972; reprinted in *The Voice of New Music: New York City 1972–1982* (Eindhoven: Het Apollohuis, 1989), pp. 31–3.

5 Johnson, *The Voice of New Music*, p. 27.

6 Johnson, 'Philip Glass's New Parts', originally published in the *Village Voice*, 6 April 1972; reprinted in *The Voice of New Music*, pp. 33–5.

7 Johnson, 'LaMonte Young, Steve Reich, Terry Riley, Philip Glass', originally published in the *Village Voice*, 7 September 1972; reprinted in *The Voice of New Music*, pp. 43–5.

8 Originally published in the *Village Voice*, 13 June 1977; reprinted in Johnson, *The Voice of New Music*, pp. 296–8.

9 Michael Nyman, 'Minimal music', *The Spectator*, 221/7320 (Friday 11 October, 1968), pp. 518–19.

10 John Cage, 'COMPOSITION: To Describe the Process of Composition Used in *Music of Changes* and *Imaginary Landscape No. 4*', originally published as part of 'Four Musicians at Work', *trans/formation*, 1/3 (1952); reprinted in *Silence* (Middletown, Conn.: Wesleyan University Press, 1962), p. 59.

11 Michael Nyman (with Hugh Davies and Richard Orton), 'Steve Reich: An Interview with Michael Nyman', *The Musical Times*, 112/1537 (March 1971), p. 229–31.

12 Michael Nyman, 'Believe it or not, melody rides again', *Music and Musicians*, 20/2 (October 1971), p. 28.

13 Michael Nyman, 'SR – mysteries of the phase', *Music and Musicians*, 20/6 (February 1972), pp. 20–1.

14 Michael Nyman, *Experimental Music: Cage and Beyond* (London: Studio Vista/NewYork: Schirmer, 1974).

15 Reported in, for instance, John Rockwell's entry on Glenn Branca in H. Wiley Hitchcock and Stanley Sadie, eds., *The New Grove Dictionary of American*

Music (London: Macmillan/New York: Grove's Dictionaries of Music, 1986), I, p. 285.

16 John Cage, quoted in Daniel Wheeler, *Art Since Mid-Century: 1945 to the Present* (New York: Vendome Press/London:Thames and Hudson, 1991), p. 129.

17 Jonathan W. Bernard, 'The Minimalist Aesthetic in the Plastic Arts and in Music', *Perspectives of New Music*, 31/1 (Winter 1993), p. 126, n. 6.

18 *Ibid.*, p. 105.

19 Morton Feldman, quoted in the composer's promotional leaflet published by Universal Edition, *c.* 1971.

20 Irving Sandler, *American Art of the 1960s* (New York: Harper and Row, 1988), p. 60.

21 Frank Stella, quoted in Bruce Glaser, ed. Lucy R. Lippard, 'Questions to Stella and Judd', *Art News*, 65/5 (September 1966), republished in Gregory Battcock, ed., *Minimal Art: A Critical Anthology* (New York: Dutton, 1968/London: Studio Vista, 1969), p. 158.

22 Kenneth Baker, *Minimalism: Art of Circumstance* (New York: Abbeville Press, 1988), p. 34.

23 Sandler, *American Art of the 1960s*, p. 60.

24 Jasper Johns, quoted in Wheeler, *Art Since Mid-Century*, p. 136.

25 Christin J. Mamiya, *Pop Art and Consumer Culture: American Super Market* (Austin: University of Texas Press, 1992), p. 160.

26 See, for example, 'Avant-Garde and Kitsch', *Partisan Review*, 6/5 (Fall 1939), pp. 34–49.

27 Originally published as one of a number of statements by artists in Barbara Rose and Irving Sandler, eds., 'Sensibility of the Sixties', *Art in America* (January–February 1967), p. 48; reprinted in Sandler, *American Art of the 1960s*, p. 60.

28 Steve Reich, 'Music as a Gradual Process', in Reich, ed. Kaspar Koenig, *Writings about Music* (Halifax, Canada: Nova Scotia College of Art and Design/New York: New York University Press/London: Universal Edition, 1974), pp. 9–11.

29 Michael Nyman, 'Steve Reich: Interview', *Studio International*, 192/984 (November–December 1976), p. 304.

30 Baker, *Minimalism*, p. 43.

31 Barbara Rose, referring to the 'object sculptures' of Judd and Morris, 'ABC Art', *Art in America*, 53/6 (October–November 1965), p. 66. One of the seminal early statements on Minimalism in the fine arts, this article is reprinted in Battcock, ed., *Minimal Art*, pp. 274–97.

32 Frances Colpitt, *Minimal Art: The Critical Perspective* (Ann Arbor: UMI Research Press, 1990), p. 3.

33 In Tim Page, 'Steve Reich, a Former Young Turk, Approaches 50', *New York Times*, 1 June 1986, section 2, p. 23.

34 Philip Glass, quoted in Sheryl Garratt, 'Fun With Monotony', *The Face*, 75 (July 1986), p. 37.

35 Samuel Lipman, 'From Avant-Garde to Pop', in his collection of articles entitled *The House of Music: Art in an Era of Institutions* (Boston: David R. Godine, 1984), p. 48.

36 Richard Toop, 'On Complexity', *Perspectives of New Music*, 31/1 (Winter 1993), p. 44.

37 *Ibid.*, p. 98, n. 6.

38 See William Brooks, 'The Americas, 1945–70', in Robert Morgan, ed., *Modern Times: From World War I to the Present* (Basingstoke: Macmillan, 1993/Englewood Cliffs, N.J: Prentice Hall, 1994), pp. 342–4.

39 This and the following two quotations are taken from Michael Parsons, 'Systems in Art and Music', *The Musical Times*, 127/1604 (October 1976), p. 816.

40 This and the following quotation are taken from Reich, *Writings about Music*, p. 10.

41 Bernard, 'The Minimalist Aesthetic in the Plastic Arts and in Music', p. 97.

42 Reich, *Writings about Music*, p. 10.

43 In interview in Richard Kostelanetz, *The Theatre of Mixed Means: An Introduction to Happenings, Kinetic Environments and Other Mixed-Means Presentations* (New York: Dial Press, 1968/RK Editions, 1980), p. 187.

44 See Robert Carl, 'The Politics of Definition in New Music', *College Music Symposium*, 29 (1989), pp. 101–14.

45 See Kyle Gann, 'Let X = X: Minimalism v. Serialism', *Village Voice*, 24 February 1987, p. 76.

46 Björk, in the course of a Channel 4 TV programme on the arts in the 1990s, August 1998.

47 Quoted in David Lodge, 'Modernism, Antimodernism and Postmodernism', *Working with Structuralism: Essays and Reviews on Nineteenth- and Twentieth-Century Literature* (London: Routledge and Kegan Paul, 1981), p. 9.

48 See, for example, Roland Barthes, 'The Death of the Author', in Barthes, trans. Richard Howard, *The Rustle of Language* (Oxford: Basil Blackwell, 1986), pp. 49–55.

49 Toop, 'On Complexity', p. 97, n. 1.

50 Brian Ferneyhough, in conversation with David Osmond-Smith during the interval of a recording, for BBC Radio Three, of Ferneyhough's *Carceri d'Invenzione* cycle, first broadcast on 18 July 1993.

51 Wim Mertens, trans. J. Hautekiet, *American Minimal Music: La Monte Young, Terry Riley, Steve Reich, Philip Glass* (London: Kahn and Averill/New York: Alexander Broude, 1983), p. 88.

52 Elaine Broad, 'A New X? An Examination of the Aesthetic Foundations of Early Minimalism', *Music Research Forum*, 5 (1990), pp. 51–2; the italics are Broad's.

53 Bernard, 'The Minimalist Aesthetic in the Plastic Arts and in Music', p. 106.

54 This and the following quotations in this paragraph are taken from Timothy

A. Johnson, 'Minimalism: Aesthetic, Style, or Technique?' *The Musical Quarterly*, 78/4 (Winter 1994), pp. 742–3, esp. pp. 742 and 751.

55 See Jonathan Kramer, *The Time of Music: New Meanings, New Temporalities, New Listening Strategies* (New York: Schirmer Books/London: Collier Macmillan, 1988), especially the analysis of Frederic Rzewski's *Les moutons de Panurge*, pp. 388–94.

56 This and the following quotation are taken from John Rockwell, *All American Music: Composition in the Late Twentieth Century* (New York: Alfred A. Knopf, 1983/London: Kahn & Averill, 1985; rev. edn., New York: Da Capo Press, 1997), pp. 3–4.

57 See Russell Jacoby, *The Last Intellectuals: American Culture in the Age of Academe* (New York: Basic Books, 1987).

58 Sally Banes, *Greenwich Village 1963: Avant-Garde Performance and the Effervescent Body* (Durham and London: Duke University Press, 1993), p. 7.

59 *Ibid.*, p. 6. Banes' list occurs on pp. 5–6.

60 Rockwell, *All American Music*, p. 4.

61 For a collection of this author's writings on this subject, see Theodor Adorno, *The Culture Industry: Selected Essays on Mass Culture*, ed. Jay Bernstein (London: Routledge, 1991).

62 See Foster's own introductory essay in Foster, ed. *Postmodern Culture* (London and Sydney: Pluto Press), pp. i–xii.

63 See Keith Potter, 'The Pursuit of the Unimaginable by the Unnarratable, or Some Potentially Telling Developments in Non-Developmental Music', *Contemporary Music Review*, 15/3–4 (1996), pp. 3–11.

64 Lang, in interview with the present author, November 1993.

1 La Monte Young

1 Wim Mertens, trans. J. Hautekiet, *American Minimal Music: La Monte Young, Terry Riley, Steve Reich, Philip Glass* (London: Kahn and Averill/New York: Alexander Broude, 1983), p. 24.

2 The term is used by the composer himself; it is also employed, for instance, by Edward Strickland in *Minimalism: Origins* (Bloomington and Indianapolis: Indiana University Press, 1993).

3 For details of all commercial recordings of Young's music covered in this book, see the Discography.

4 This and all following quotations not individually acknowledged are taken from the author's interviews with the composer.

5 Interview in Richard Kostelanetz, *The Theatre of Mixed Means: An Introduction to Happenings, Kinetic Environments and Other Mixed-Means Presentations* (New York: Dial Press, 1968/RK Editions, 1980), p. 186.

6 Mark Swed, 'La Monte Young Tunes the Piano His Way', *Los Angeles Herald Examiner*, 1 November 1985, p. 36.

7 In Kostelanetz, *The Theatre of Mixed Means*, p. 185.

8 This and the other quotations in this paragraph are taken from correspondence with Young.

9 In Kostelanetz, *The Theatre of Mixed Means*, p. 187.

10 This and the following quotations in this paragraph are taken from unpublished material in the composer's archive.

11 In Kostelanetz, *The Theatre of Mixed Means*, p. 190.

12 *Ibid.*, p. 189.

13 *Ibid.*, p. 188.

14 *Ibid.*, p. 189.

15 This and the quotations in the next two paragraphs are taken from unpublished material and programme notes in the composer's archive.

16 In Kostelanetz, *The Theatre of Mixed Means*, p. 190.

17 This and the following quotations in this paragraph are taken from unpublished material and programme notes in the composer's archive.

18 Taken from the author's correspondence with the composer.

19 This and the quotation in the next paragraph are taken from a programme note in the composer's archive.

20 From a version of the composer's own programme note for *Trio for Strings*.

21 See Dave Smith, 'Following a Straight Line: La Monte Young', *Contact*, 18 (Winter 1977–8), p. 5. Example 1.5 is borrowed, with the permission of its author, from the Corrigenda to this article in *Contact*, 19 (Summer 1978), p. 2.

22 From a version of the composer's own programme note for *Trio for Strings*.

23 Smith, 'Following a Straight Line', p. 4.

24 Strickland, *Minimalism*, p. 124.

25 This and the following quotation, *ibid.*, p. 125.

26 This and all the other quotations in the present paragraph except the last one are taken from Kostelanetz, *The Theatre of Mixed Means*, p. 190.

27 Taken from unpublished material in the composer's archive.

28 This and the other quotations in this and the following paragraph are taken from Kostelanetz, *The Theatre of Mixed Means*, p. 190.

29 Quoted in Robert Palmer, 'A Father Figure for the Avant-Garde', *The Atlantic Monthly*, 247/5 (May 1981), p. 51.

30 From the transcript of an interview with Terry Riley by Neil Strauss, broadcast on WKCR-FM, New York, October 1991, p. 1.

31 This and the following quotations in the present paragraph are taken from the composer's own programme note for *Study I*.

32 This and the following quotation are taken from the composer's own programme note for *Study III*.

33 In Kostelanetz, *The Theatre of Mixed Means*, p. 191.

34 In interview in Cole Gagne, *Soundpieces 2: Interviews with American Composers* (Metuchen, N.J., and London: The Scarecrow Press, 1993), p. 491.

35 In Kostelanetz, *The Theatre of Mixed Means*, p. 191.

36 This and the following two quotations are taken from Kostelanetz, *The Theatre of Mixed Means*, p. 194.

37 From the unpublished notes which constitute the work's score.

38 Taken from unpublished material in the composer's archive.

39 Cornelius Cardew, 'One Sound: La Monte Young', *The Musical Times*, 107/1485 (November 1966), p. 959.

40 Taken from unpublished material in the composer's archive.

41 From a programme note for *Poem* by Michael Parsons, Fluxus retrospective concert, AIR Gallery, London, 23 May 1977.

42 Michael Nyman, *Experimental Music: Cage and Beyond* (London: Studio Vista/New York: Schirmer, 1974), p. 69.

43 Cardew, 'One Sound', p. 959.

44 This and the quotation at the beginning of the next paragraph are taken from unpublished material in the composer's archive.

45 Cardew, 'One Sound', p. 960.

46 This and the following quotation are taken from unpublished material in the composer's archive.

47 Strauss and Riley interview transcript, p. 2.

48 This and the following quotation are taken from Cardew, 'On the Role of the Instructions in the Interpretation of Indeterminate Music', in *Treatise Handbook* (London: Peters Edition, 1971), p. xiv.

49 In Kostelanetz, *The Theatre of Mixed Means*, p. 195.

50 'Lecture 1960', published in Young and Marian Zazeela, *Selected Writings* (Munich: Heiner Friedrich, 1969), no pagination.

51 Henry A. Flynt, Jr., 'Mutations of the Vanguard', in Gino Di Maggio, ed., *Ubi Fluxus Ibi Motus: 1990–1962* (Milan: Nuove Edizione Gabriele Mazzotta, 1990), p. 101.

52 Flynt's 'Mutations of the Vanguard', p. 110, documents these and other gallery-based performances mentioned below.

53 In Kostelanetz, *The Theatre of Mixed Means*, p. 192.

54 Cardew, 'One Sound', p. 959.

55 Transcribed by Young and Zazeela from a telephone conversation with Diane Wakoski, 23 August 1996.

56 From the composer's own programme note for *Piano Pieces for David Tudor #s 1, 2 and 3*.

57 Smith, 'Following a Straight Line', p. 4.

58 Nyman, *Experimental Music*, p. 69.

59 This and the following quotation, *ibid.*, p. 71.

60 Flynt, 'Mutations of the Vanguard', p. 110, and also personal communications with the present author.

61 'John Cage and Roger Reynolds: a Conversation', in R. Dunn, ed., *John Cage* (New York: Henmar Press, 1962), p. 81.

62 This and the following quotation are taken from Flynt, 'Mutations of the Vanguard', pp. 101, 103 and 105.

63 In Kostelanetz, *The Theatre of Mixed Means*, pp. 194–5.

64 This and the following quotation are taken from Douglas Kahn, 'Cage and Fluxus', in Louwrien Wijers, *Fluxus Today and Yesterday* (New York: Dutton, 1993), p. 105.

65 Quoted in *ibid.*, p. 8.

66 For full details of the rather complicated situation surrounding these publications, see Jon Hendricks, *Fluxus Codex* (New York: The Gilbert and Lila Silverman Fluxus Collection/Harry N. Abrams, 1988), pp. 582–6.

67 Quoted in Kahn, 'Cage and Fluxus', p. 101.

68 Flynt, 'Mutations of the Vanguard', p. 99.

69 *Ibid.*, p. 101.

70 *Ibid.*

71 Flynt, 'Essay: Concept Art', in La Monte Young, ed., *An Anthology* (New York: Young and Jackson MacLow, 1963; 2nd edn., Munich: Heiner Friedrich, 1970), unpaginated.

72 Flynt, 'Mutations of the Vanguard', p. 105.

73 La Monte Young and Marian Zazeela, eds., *Selected Writings* (Munich: Heiner Friedrich, 1969).

74 David Farneth, entry on Young in H. Wiley Hitchcock and Stanley Sadie, eds., *The New Grove Dictionary of American Music* (London: Macmillan/New York: Grove's Dictionaries of Music, 1986), IV, p. 579.

75 This and the following two quotations are taken from unpublished material in the composer's archive.

76 Cole Gagne, in interview with Young and Zazeela in *Soundpieces 2: Interviews with American Composers*, p. 493.

77 In Kostelanetz, *The Theatre of Mixed Means*, p. 187.

78 This and the following quotation are taken from the composer's accompanying notes to the recording of *90 XII 9 c. 9.35 – 10.52 PM NYC, The Melodic Version of the Second Dream of The High-Tension Line Stepdown Transformer from The Four Dreams of China*, Gramavision 79467 (1991), unpaginated.

79 From unpublished material in the composer's archive.

80 This and the other quotation in this paragraph, *ibid.*

81 John Perreault, 'La Monte Young's Tracery: The Voice of the Tortoise', *Village Voice*, 22 February 1968, p. 27.

82 From unpublished material in the composer's archive.

83 Alan Licht, 'The History of La Monte Young's Theatre of Eternal Music', *Forced Exposure*, 16 (1990), p. 62.

84 This and the following two quotations are taken from *ibid.*, p. 66.

85 Smith, 'Following a Straight Line', p. 6.

86 Two versions of *Drift Study* – different from the one released on Shandar in 1974 – had been privately released in 1968 and 1969: see the Discography.

87 Smith, 'Following a Straight Line', p. 6.

88 An uncredited quotation in Licht, 'The History of La Monte Young's Theatre of Eternal Music', p. 66.

89 Young and Zazeela, eds., *Selected Writings*, p. 5.

90 Kostelanetz, *The Theatre of Mixed Means*, p. 183.

91 Licht, 'The History of La Monte Young's Theatre of Eternal Music', p. 66.

92 This and the last quotation in this paragraph are taken from the present author's interview with Conrad in February 1995.

93 This and the following quotation are taken from John Corbett, 'Minimal Compact', *The Wire*, 132 (February 1995), p. 35.

94 Tom Johnson, 'In Their "Dream House", Music Becomes a Means of Meditation', *New York Times*, 28 April 1974, section ii, p. 13.

95 Taken from the author's correspondence with Zazeela.

96 All quotations in this paragraph are taken from unpublished material in the composer's archive, some of which has been used as publicity material for the 1990s 'Sound and Light Environment'.

97 This and the following quotations in this paragraph are taken from unpublished material in the composer's archive.

98 Young's accompanying notes to *The Melodic Version of the Second Dream*.

99 This and the following quotations in this paragraph are taken from unpublished material in the composer's archive.

100 Kyle Gann, 'La Monte Young's *The Well-Tuned Piano*', *Perspectives of New Music*, 31/1 (Winter 1993), p. 134.

101 The composer's own 'Notes on *The Well-Tuned Piano*', in the accompanying booklet for the work's recording, Gramavision 18-8701-1 (LP, 1987)/79452 (CD, 1992), p. 7.

102 This and the following quotation are taken from Gann, 'La Monte Young's *The Well-Tuned Piano*', p. 135.

103 *Ibid.*, p. 134.

104 This and all the other quotations in this paragraph are taken from Young, 'Notes on *The Well-Tuned Piano*', p. 8.

105 Daniel Wolf, 'What is *The Well-Tuned Piano*?', accompanying notes to the Gramavision recording, p. 3.

106 Gann, 'La Monte Young's *The Well-Tuned Piano*', pp. 137–8.

107 Cardew, 'One Sound', p. 959.

108 See, for example, her unpublished 'An Axiomatization of Some Minimal Admissible Sets of Concurrent Frequencies Determined by La Monte Young's "Two Systems of Eleven Categories Revised from Vertical Hearing or Hearing in The Present Tense 1967"'.

109 See Uwe Husslein, *Pop Goes Art*, exhibition catalogue (Uppertal: Institut für Pop Kultur, 1990), p. 8, where a 1990 interview with Jonas Mekas is cited in confirmation of this suggestion.

110 In Licht, 'The History of La Monte Young's Theatre of Eternal Music', p. 68.

111 Lou Reed, *Metal Machine Music*, CPL2-1101 (1975); La Monte Young's name is, though, misspelled.

112 Quoted in Jim Aitkin, 'Brian Eno', *Keyboard*, 7 (July 1981), p. 60.

113 Quoted in Palmer, 'A Father Figure for the Avant-Garde', p. 49.

114 For a discussion of the relationship between the minimalism of all four
    subjects of the present book and the more recent developments of Techno,
    see Daniel Caux, 'Des jeux avec les sons: techno et minimalisme', *Artpress*, 9
    (1998), pp. 105–11.

2 Terry Riley

1 This and all following quotations not individually acknowledged are taken
  from the author's interviews with the composer.
2 From Robert Palmer, 'Terry Riley: Doctor of Improvised Surgery', *Downbeat*,
  42/19 (20 November 1975), p. 17.
3 See Edward Strickland, *Minimalism: Origins* (Bloomington and Indianapolis:
  Indiana University Press, 1993), pp. 124 and 143.
4 La Monte Young, ed., *An Anthology* (New York: Young and Jackson MacLow,
  1963; 2nd edn., Munich: Heiner Friedrich, 1970), unpaginated.
5 Cole Gagne, *Soundpieces 2: Interviews with American Composers* (Metuchen,
  N.J., and London: The Scarecrow Press, 1993), p. 238.
6 Interview in Edward Strickland, *American Composers: Dialogues on
  Contemporary Music* (Bloomington and Indianapolis: Indiana University
  Press, 1991), p. 112.
7 See, for example, 'Tentative Programme for the Festival of Very New Music',
  reprinted in H. Sohm, ed., *Happening & Fluxus: Materialen*, catalogue for
  exhibition in the Koelnischer Kunstverein, 6 February 1970 – 6 January 1971,
  unpaginated.
8 This and the following quotation are used, without crediting any source, in
  Keith and Rita Knox, 'Relax and Fully Concentrate: The Time of Terry Riley',
  Friends magazine, 20 February 1970, unpaginated.
9 Quoted in Palmer, 'Terry Riley', p. 17.
10 Interview in William Duckworth, *Talking Music* (New York: Schirmer Books,
   1995), p. 269.
11 *Ibid.*, p. 270.
12 Richard Kostelanetz, *The Theatre of Mixed Means: An Introduction to
   Happenings, Kinetic Environments and Other Mixed-Means Presentations*
   (New York: Dial Press, 1968/RK Editions, 1980), p. 164.
13 This and the following quotation, *ibid.*, p. 168.
14 In Palmer, 'Terry Riley', p. 17.
15 In Duckworth, *Talking Music*, p. 276.
16 In Strickland, *American Composers*, p. 113.
17 In Palmer, 'Terry Riley', pp. 17–18.
18 For details of all commercial recordings of Riley's music covered in this book,
   see the Discography.
19 *In C* is published by the composer.
20 See, for example, Robert P. Morgan, *Twentieth-Century Music: A History of
   Musical Style in Modern Europe and America* (New York and London: W. W.
   Norton, 1991), p. 426.

21 See, notably, Olivier Messiaen, *Le technique de mon langage musicale* (Paris: Alphonse Leduc, 1944); translated into English by John Satterfield as *The Technique of My Musical Language* (Paris: Alphonse Leduc, 1956).

22 See George Russell, *The Lydian Chromatic Concept of Tonal Organization for Improvisation* (Cambridge, Mass.: Concept, 1959).

23 This and the following quotation are taken from Duckworth, *Talking Music*, p. 272.

24 This and the following quotation are taken from *ibid.*, p. 275.

25 Gary Todd has done much to reclaim these tape compositions, and other early performances of Riley's music; these are in the process of being issued on CD by the Cortical Foundation.

26 In Palmer, 'Terry Riley', p. 18.

27 Jon Gibson, accompanying notes to 'Jon Gibson: In Good Company', Point Music 434 873-2 (1992).

28 Michael Nyman, *Experimental Music: Cage and Beyond* (London: Studio Vista/New York: Schirmer, 1974), p. 126.

29 *Ibid.*, p. 124.

30 John Cage, with Alison Knowles, *Notations* (New York: Something Else Press, 1969), p. 204. Though labelled 'Page two', the undated manuscript reproduced here is otherwise identical to the one subsequently published in, for example, the books by Mertens and Nyman.

31 Wim Mertens reproduces the same page in *American Minimal Music* (p. 40), but erroneously entitles it 'Keyboard Studies No. 7'.

32 Riley, in Duckworth, *Talking Music*, p. 275.

33 Uncredited accompanying note to the original recording, Columbia MS 7315 (1969).

34 This and the following quotation are taken from Gagne, *Soundpieces 2*, p. 248.

35 Daniel Caux's accompanying notes to the Shanti recording of *Persian Surgery Dervishes*, Shandar/Shanti 83.501-2 (1972) suggest that only the latter is used.

36 Uncredited accompanying note to the recording of *Descending Moonshine Dervishes*, Kuckuck 047 (1982).

37 Duckworth, *Talking Music*, p. 268.

38 *Ibid.*, p. 269.

39 Alfred Frankenstein, 'Music Like None Other On Earth', *San Francisco Chronicle*, 8 November 1964, p. 28. Part of this was subsequently reprinted on the sleeve of the Columbia recording of *In C*, CBS MK 64565 (1968). The following quotation is taken from this review.

40 David Toop, 'Altered Statesman', *The Wire*, 135 (May 1995), p. 22.

41 Palmer, 'Terry Riley', p. 17.

42 Duckworth, *Talking Music*, p. 266.

3 Steve Reich

1 This and all following quotations not individually acknowledged are taken from the author's interviews with the composer.

2 In Geoff Smith and Nicola Walker Smith, *American Originals: 25 Interviews with Contemporary Composers* (London and Boston: Faber and Faber, 1994), p. 212.

3 For an example of an attempt to investigate this relationship, see Robert Cowan, 'Reich and Wittgenstein: Notes Towards a Synthesis', *Tempo*, 157 (June 1986), pp. 2–7.

4 See, for example, his book, *Music in the Twentieth Century* (New York: Norton, 1966).

5 See, for example, Ludwig Wittgenstein, ed. G. H. von Wright, trans. Peter Winch, *Culture and Value*. (Oxford: Basil Blackwell, 1980), pp. 50 and 50e. The text in question dates from 1946.

6 In Andrew Ford, *Composer to Composer: Conversations about Contemporary Music* (London: Quartet Books, 1993), p. 63.

7 This and the following quotation are taken from Steve Reich, 'Notes on the Ensemble' in *Writings about Music*, ed. Kaspar Koenig (Halifax, Canada: Nova Scotia College of Art and Design/New York: New York University Press/London: Universal Edition, 1974), p. 45.

8 From one of the author's own interviews with Riley.

9 'Notes on Compositions', in Reich, *Writings about Music*, p. 50.

10 See, for example, *ibid.*, p. 50.

11 Emily Wasserman, 'An Interview with Composer Steve Reich', *Artforum*, 10/9 (May 1972), p. 44.

12 'Music as a Gradual Process' may be found in Reich, *Writings about Music*, pp. 9–11. In addition to its initial publication in *Anti-Illusion: Procedures/Materials* (New York: Whitney Museum of American Art, 1969), pp. 56–7, it also appeared in *Source*, 10 (1972), p. 30 (along with *Pendulum Music* and other material also republished in the *Writings*), and in the accompanying notes to the Deutsche Grammophon recording of *Drumming*, *Six Pianos* and *Music for Mallet Instruments, Voices and Organ* (DG 2740-106, 1974). Le Witt's 'Paragraphs on Conceptual Art' may be found in *Artforum*, 8/5 (June 1967), pp. 79–83.

13 This and the following quotation are taken from Steve Reich, '*Wavelength* by Michael Snow', unpublished.

14 Reich, *Writings about Music*, pp. 12–13.

15 For details of all commercial recordings of Reich's music covered in this book, see the Discography.

16 This and the following quotation are taken from Reich, *Writings about Music*, p. 9.

17 Mark Cromar advances this argument in 'Minimal Music: Proposals for a Redefinition', unpublished B.A. dissertation, Oxford University (1986).

18 'Notes on Compositions', in Reich, *Writings about Music*, p. 51.

19 'Steve Reich: An Interview with Michael Nyman', *The Musical Times*, 112/1537 (March 1971), p. 230.

20 'Notes on Compositions', in Reich, *Writings about Music*, p. 51.

21 John Cage, with Alison Knowles, *Notations* (New York: Something Else Press, 1969), p. 178.

22 *Source: The Magazine of the Avant-Garde*, 3 (1968), pp. 69–71.

23 'Appendix: List of Works', in Reich, *Writings about Music*, p. 73.

24 Jon Gibson, accompanying notes to 'Jon Gibson: In Good Company', Point Music 434 873-2 (1992).

25 This and the following quotations in this paragraph are taken from 'Notes on Compositions', in Reich, *Writings about Music*, pp. 51–2.

26 Paul Epstein, 'Pattern Structure and Process in Steve Reich's *Piano Phase*', *The Musical Quarterly*, 72/4 (1986), p. 495.

27 *Ibid.*, p. 498.

28 This and the following quotation are taken from 'Notes on Compositions', in Reich, *Writings about Music*, p. 53.

29 *Ibid.*

30 This and the following quotation are taken from *ibid.*

31 David Behrman, accompanying notes to 'Live/Electric', Columbia MS-7265 (1969).

32 'Slow Motion Sound', in Reich, *Writings about Music*, p. 15.

33 'The Phase Shifting Pulse Gate [etc.]', in *ibid.*, p. 23.

34 This and the following quotation are taken from *ibid.*, p. 25.

35 *Ibid.*, p. 27.

36 *Ibid.*, p. 25.

37 From one of the author's own interviews with Young.

38 From one of the author's own interviews with Riley.

39 Carman Moore, 'Music: Park Place Pianos', *Village Voice*, 23 March 1967, p. 15.

40 See 'Appendix: List of Works', in Reich, *Writings about Music*, p. 73.

41 From one of the author's own interviews with Glass.

42 From one of the author's own interviews with Gibson.

43 *Ibid.*

44 Published, by Boosey and Hawkes, in 1998.

45 Gunther Schuller, *Early Jazz: Its Roots and Musical Development* (New York: Dutton, 1968).

46 A. M. Jones, *Studies in African Music*, 2 vols. (London: Oxford University Press, 1959).

47 'Postscript to a Brief Study of Balinese and African Music', in Reich, *Writings about Music*, p. 38.

48 'Gahu: A Dance of the Ewe Tribe in Ghana', in *ibid.*, p. 35.

49 'Notes on Compositions', in *ibid.*, p. 58.

50 'From Program Notes', in *ibid.*, p. 44.

51 'Postscript to a Brief Study of Balinese and African Music', in *ibid.*, p. 39.

52 Mantle Hood and Jose Maceda, *Music* (Leiden: Brill, 1972), p. 8.

53 See, for example, K. Robert Schwarz, *Minimalism* (London: Phaidon Press, 1996), p. 204.

54 Seven scores – *Piano Phase, Violin Phase, Pendulum Music, Four Organs, Phase*

Patterns, Clapping Music and *Music for Pieces of Wood* – were published by Universal Edition London in that year.

55 In 1983, the composer began an association with Boosey and Hawkes in New York that led first to the availability of several scores in manuscript form and, slowly, to the publication of properly printed scores by that company, especially from the early 1990s.

56 See, for example, in addition to several reviews – and the promotion of the British première of *Drumming* – 'Steve Reich: An Interview with Michael Nyman', and *Experimental Music: Cage and Beyond* (London: Studio Vista/New York: Schirmer, 1974).

57 Though Henahan also wrote one of the earliest sympathetic profiles of Reich to be published in a major newspaper: 'Reich? Philharmonic? Paradiddling?', *New York Times*, 24 October 1971, Section ii, pp. 13 and 26 – a preview article for the 'Prospective Encounter' performance of *Phase Patterns* mentioned above.

58 Johnson's frequent reviews of the composer are collected in *The Voice of New Music: New York City 1972–1982* (Eindhoven: Het Apollohuis, 1989).

59 The first of many reviews of Reich's output by Rockwell is that of the premières of *Six Pianos* and *Music for Mallet Instruments, Voices and Organ*: 'Music: Reich Meditations', *New York Times*, 19 May 1973, Section ii, p. 28.

60 In the accompanying notes to 'Steve Reich: Works: 1965 – 1995', ten-CD boxed set, Nonesuch Records, 7559-79451-2 (1997), p. 24.

61 This and the following quotation are taken from 'Music as a Gradual Process', in Reich, *Writings about Music*, p. 10.

62 This and the quotation from Reich at the beginning of the next paragraph are taken from Michael Nyman, 'Steve Reich: Interview', *Studio International*, 192/6 (November–December 1976), p. 301.

63 'Music as a Gradual Process', in Reich, *Writings about Music*, p. 10.

64 This and the first quotation in the next paragraph are taken from 'Notes on Compositions', in *ibid.*, p. 58.

65 *Ibid.*, p. 61.

66 A revised score is due for publication by Boosey and Hawkes shortly.

67 'Steve Reich' (New York: Boosey and Hawkes, n.d.).

68 This and the following quotation are taken from 'Notes on Compositions', in Reich, *Writings about Music*, p. 58.

69 *Ibid.*, p. 60.

70 This and all the other quotations in this paragraph, *ibid.*, p. 58.

71 Steve Reich, various published programme notes for *Drumming*.

72 *Ibid.*

73 'Notes on Compositions', in Reich, *Writings about Music*, p. 70.

74 *Ibid.*, p. 69.

75 This term seems to have originated not with the composer but in K. Robert Schwarz, 'Steve Reich: Music as a Gradual Process', Part Two, *Perspectives of New Music*, 20 (Fall–Winter 1981/Spring–Summer 1982) pp. 225–86; it is

adopted here as a convenient shorthand with connotations of harmonic motion which seem basically appropriate.

76 This and the following quotation are taken from Steve Reich, accompanying notes to the work's first recording, ECM Records, ECM-1-1129 (1978), unpaginated.

77 This and the following quotation, *ibid.*

78 This and the following quotation, *ibid.*

79 *Ibid.*

80 *Ibid.*

81 Schwarz, 'Steve Reich: Music as a Gradual Process', Part Two, p. 249.

82 Reich, *Writings about Music*, p. 28.

83 This and the following quotation are taken from Ronald Woodley, entry on Reich in Brian Morton and Pamela Collins, eds., *Contemporary Composers* (London: St James Press, 1992), p. 768.

84 This and the following quotation are to be found in Rob Tannenbaum, 'A Meeting of Sound Minds: John Cage and Brian Eno', *Musician*, 83 (September 1985), p. 68.

85 Quoted in Robert Christgau, *Christgau's Guide to Rock Albums of the Seventies* (New Haven, Conn.: Ticknor and Fields, 1981/London: Vermilion, 1982), p. 82.

4 Philip Glass

1 For an account of this, see Philip Glass, *The Music of Philip Glass*, ed. with supplementary material by Robert T. Jones (New York: Harper and Row, 1987)/*Opera on the Beach* (London and Boston: Faber and Faber, 1988), pp. 87–9.

2 For more detailed accounts of the composer's early life, see, in particular, Eve Grimes, 'Interview: Education' (1989) in *Writings on Glass: Essays, Interviews, Criticism*, ed. Richard Kostelanetz (New York: Schirmer Books/London: Prentice Hall International, 1997), pp. 12–36.

3 The composer, quoted in Sheryl Garratt, 'Fun with Monotony', *The Face*, 75 (July 1986), p. 39.

4 The composer, quoted in Robert Matthew-Walker, 'Glass Roots', *CD Review*, 61 (February 1992), p. 18.

5 Joan LaBarbara, 'Philip Glass e Steve Reich: Two from the Steady State School', dual language Italian/English, *Data: pratica e teoria delle arti*, 4/13 (Autumn 1974), pp. 36–9. This unusually detailed article is probably only the second attempt in print to discuss Glass's music from anything resembling a scholarly point of view, the first being Nyman's book, *Experimental Music*. The former is reprinted in Kostelanetz, ed., *Writings on Glass*, pp. 39–45.

6 This and all following quotations not individually acknowledged are taken from the present author's interviews with the composer.

7 Quoted in Robert T. Jones, 'Philip Glass [Musician of the Month]', *High Fidelity/Musical America*, 29/4 (April 1979), p. MA-4.

8 This and the comments attributed to him elsewhere in this chapter are taken from a telephone interview with Kripl in August 1998.

9 This and the following quotation are taken from Glass, ed. Jones, *The Music of Philip Glass/Opera on the Beach*, p. 35.

10 *Ibid.*, p. 19.

11 This and the following two quotations are taken from Glass, ed. Jones, *The Music of Philip Glass/Opera on the Beach*, pp. 35–6.

12 *Ibid.*, p. 16.

13 John Rockwell, 'Philip Glass: The Orient, the Visual Arts and the Evolution of Minimalism', in *All American Music: Composition in the Late Twentieth Century* (New York: Alfred A. Knopf, 1983/London: Kahn and Averill, 1985; rev. edn.: New York: Da Capo Press, 1997), p. 111.

14 Glass, ed. Jones, *The Music of Philip Glass/Opera on the Beach*, p. 17.

15 Quoted in Michael Walsh, 'Making a Joyful Noise', *Time*, 125/26 (1 July 1985), p. 47.

16 Jones, *High Fidelity/Musical America*, p. MA-5.

17 Glass, ed. Jones, *The Music of Philip Glass/Opera on the Beach*, p. 90.

18 Philip Glass and Ravi Shankar, *Passages*, Private Music/BMG 2074-2 P (1990).

19 See Glass, ed. Jones, *The Music of Philip Glass/Opera on the Beach*, pp. 53–4.

20 This and other observations by him below are taken from various conversations with Gibson from August 1986 onwards.

21 In Tim Page, 'A Conversation with Philip Glass and Steve Reich', *Music from the Road: Views and Reviews 1978–1992* (New York and Oxford: Oxford University Press, 1992), p. 67.

22 Gibson, in interview with the present author.

23 Glass, ed. Jones, *The Music of Philip Glass/Opera on the Beach*, p. xiii.

24 In Willoughby Sharp and Liza Bear, 'Phil Glass: An Interview in Two Parts', *Avalanche*, 5 (Summer 1972), p. 33.

25 Lee Breuer and Ann Elizabeth Horton, *A Comic of The Red Horse Animation* (New York, 1976), unpaginated.

26 *Ibid.*

27 Glass, ed. Jones, *The Music of Philip Glass/Opera on the Beach*, p. 8.

28 From a telephone interview with Maleczech in August 1997.

29 In Sharp and Bear, 'Phil Glass', p. 33.

30 Glass, ed. Jones, *The Music of Philip Glass/Opera on the Beach*, p. 7.

31 In Sharp and Bear, 'Phil Glass', p. 28.

32 Barbara Rose, 'ABC Art', *Art in America*, 53/6 (October/November 1965), pp. 57–69; reprinted in Gregory Battcock, ed., *Minimal Art: A Critical Anthology* (New York: Dutton, 1968/London: Studio Vista, 1969), pp. 102–14.

33 Richard Foreman, 'Glass and Snow', *Arts Magazine* (February 1970); reprinted in Kostelanetz, ed., *Writings on Glass*, pp. 80–6. It provides the source for all the quotations in this and the following paragraph.

34 Quoted in Peter Eisenman, 'Interview' (1983), reprinted in Richard Serra,

Writings, Interviews (Chicago and London: University of Chicago Press, 1994), p. 142.

35 Serra, 'Rigging' (1980), reprinted in an edited version in Serra, *Writings, Interviews*, p. 97.

36 Annette Michelson, Richard Serra and Clara Weyergraf, 'The Films of Richard Serra: An Interview' (1979), reprinted in Serra, *Writings, Interviews*, p. 63.

37 Glass, ed. Jones, *The Music of Philip Glass/Opera on the Beach*, p. 23.

38 'Long Beach Island, Word Location', June 1969, Loveladies, New Jersey, reprinted in Serra, *Writings, Interviews*, p. 7.

39 This and the following quotation are taken from Michelson, etc., 'The Films of Serra: An Interview', p. 64.

40 Serra, 'Dialogue with Philip Glass' (1986), reprinted in Kostelanetz, ed., *Writings on Glass*, p. 298.

41 See, for example, Michael Nyman, 'Minimal Music, Determinacy and the New Tonality', *Experimental Music: Cage and Beyond* (London: Studio Vista/New York: Schirmer, 1974), p. 127, and Dave Smith, 'The Music of Phil Glass', *Contact*, 11 (Summer 1975), p. 27.

42 In Keith Potter and Dave Smith, 'Interview with Philip Glass', *Contact*, 13 (Spring 1976), p. 25.

43 See Wim Mertens, trans. J. Hautekiet, *American Minimal Music: La Monte Young, Terry Riley, Steve Reich, Philip Glass* (London: Kahn and Averill/New York: Alexander Broude, 1983), pp. 68–9.

44 Potter and Smith, 'Interview with Philip Glass', p. 28.

45 Glass, ed. Jones, *The Music of Philip Glass/Opera on the Beach*, p. 18.

46 'Music Catalog', in *ibid.*, p. 211.

47 LaBarbara, 'Philip Glass e Steve Reich', p. 36.

48 This and the following quotation are taken from Glass, ed. Jones, *The Music of Philip Glass/Opera on the Beach*, p. 19.

49 LaBarbara, 'Philip Glass e Steve Reich', p. 37.

50 *Ibid.*, p. 37.

51 *Ibid.*, pp. 37 and 39.

52 Quoted in Matthew-Walker, 'Glass Roots', p. 19.

53 LaBarbara, 'Philip Glass e Steve Reich', p. 39.

54 Published by Dunvagen Music in 1984.

55 For details of all commercial recordings of Glass's music covered in this book, see the Discography.

56 Glass, ed. Jones, *The Music of Philip Glass/Opera on the Beach*, p. 20.

57 *Ibid.*, p. 18.

58 In Potter and Smith, 'Interview with Philip Glass', p. 25.

59 Glass, ed. Jones, *The Music of Philip Glass/Opera on the Beach*, pp. 20–1.

60 Reich, in interview with the present author.

61 Gibson, in interview with the present author.

62 Gibson, comment attached to 'PGE Tours and Shows', unpublished

documentation of performances by the Philip Glass Ensemble, compiled by Dan Mather.

63 Nyman, *Experimental Music*, p. 128.

64 Reich, in interview with the present author.

65 Wesley York, 'Form and Process in *Two Pages* of Philip Glass', *Sonus*, 1/2 (Spring 1982), pp. 28–50; reprinted in Thomas DeLio, ed., *Contiguous Lines: Issues and Ideas in the Music of the '60s and '70s* (Lanham, London etc: University Press of America, 1985), pp. 81–106; also reprinted in Kostelanetz, ed. *Writings on Glass*, pp. 60–79.

66 Nyman, *Experimental Music*, p. 128.

67 The precise origin of this quotation is unknown. The present author first saw it in publicity material, produced by the New York company Artservices, for Glass's British tour of *Music in Twelve Parts* in 1975.

68 In Potter and Smith, 'Interview with Philip Glass', p. 26.

69 *Ibid.*, p. 25.

70 Glass, ed. Jones, *The Music of Philip Glass/Opera on the Beach*, p. 8.

71 Taken from Breuer and Horton, *A Comic of The Red Horse Animation*.

72 *Ibid.*

73 John Rockwell, 'There's Nothing Quite Like the Sound of Glass', *New York Times*, 26 May 1974, Section ii, p.11.

74 Smith, 'The Music of Phil Glass', p. 32.

75 In Sharp and Bear, 'Phil Glass', p. 28.

76 Foreman, 'Glass and Snow', pp. 80ff.

77 This and the following quotation are taken from Sharp and Bear, 'Phil Glass', p. 28.

78 *Ibid.*

79 Quoted in Tim Page's accompanying notes to the CD reissue of *Music with Changing Parts*, Elektra/Nonesuch 7559-79325-2 (1994), unpaginated.

80 This and the other quotations in this paragraph are taken from Glass's unpaginated typescript notes for *Music in Twelve Parts*. Probably written in 1974, they form the basis of several programme notes on the work published in 1974–5 and subsequently, including the accompanying notes to the various commercial recordings (see the Discography).

81 In Potter and Smith, 'Interview with Philip Glass', p. 25.

82 This and the following quotation are taken from Mark Pappenheim, 'Shards of Glass', *The Independent*, 11 April 1992, Section ii, p. 28.

83 This and the following two quotations, including the one in the next paragraph, are taken from Glass, ed. Jones, *The Music of Philip Glass/Opera on the Beach*, p. 27.

84 See, for example, *ibid.*, pp. 136ff. It seems that the idea of linking *Einstein on the Beach* with *Satyagraha* (1980) and *Akhnaten* (1984) was motivated primarily by the opportunity this afforded to mount all three works in Stuttgart as a 'trilogy'.

85 Quoted in *ibid.*, p. 32.

86 See, for example, *ibid.*, p. 30. Here the proffered explanation is that 'the "knee" refer[s] to the joining function that humans' anatomical knees perform'.

87 Philip Glass, accompanying notes to the original LP and subsequent CD recordings of *Einstein on the Beach* (1978 and 1993 respectively).

88 This and the quotation in the next paragraph are taken from Glass's accompanying notes, *ibid.*

89 *Ibid.*

Discography

N.B. This discography lists only the works which form the main subject of this book. While it distinguishes between LPs and CDs, particularly since many LPs have subsequently been reissued in CD format, no attempt is made, for the most part, to indicate the subsequent availability in cassette form of any already existing recordings.

La Monte Young

Excerpt from *Drift Study 5 VIII 68 4:37:40 – 5:09:50 PM* (Theatre of Eternal Music): S.M.S. magazine, no. 4 (5′ reel-to-reel audio tape, 1968; reissued on cassette, 1988)

Excerpt from *Drift Study 31 I 69 12:17:33 – 12:49:58 PM* (Theatre of Eternal Music): Aspen magazine, no. 8 (LP, 1969)

Map of 49's Dream The Two Systems of Eleven Sets of Galactic Intervals Ornamental Lightyears Tracery 31 VII 69 10:26 – 10:49 PM Munich, the Volga Delta from *Studies In The Bowed Disc 23 VIII 64 2:50:45 – 3:11 AM* (La Monte Young and Marian Zazeela): [Galerie Heiner Friedrich] Edition X (known as 'The Black LP', 1969)

Drift Study 13 I 73 5:35 – 6:14:03 PM NYC, Map of 49's Dream The Two Systems of Eleven Sets of Galactic Intervals Ornamental Lightyears Tracery 14 VII 73 9:27:27 – 10:15:33 PM NYC (Theatre of Eternal Music): 'Dream House', Disques Shandar 83.510 (LP, 1974)

The Well-Tuned Piano 81 X 25 6:17:50 – 11:18:59 PM NYC (La Monte Young): Gramavision 79452, etc. (5 LPs, CDs and cassette tapes, 1987)

Poem for Chairs, Tables, Benches, etc. 89 VI 8 c. 1:45 – 1:52 AM Paris, the 'Paris Encore' (Theatre of Eternal Music): 'FluxTellus', Tellus, no. 24, Harvestworks (cassette, 1990)

The Melodic Version of The Second Dream of The High-Tension Line Stepdown Transformer from *The Four Dreams of China 90 XII 9 c. 9:35 – 10:52 PM NYC* (Theatre of Eternal Music): Gramavision 79467 (CD, 1991)

Sunday AM [Morning] Blues [1964, edited], *B♭ Dorian Blues* [1963, ed.], *The Well-Tuned Piano* [1964, ed.], *Map of 49's Dream* [1971, ed.] (La Monte Young): RIP, unauthorised bootleg edition, source unknown (2 LPs, *c.* 1992)

Excerpt from *The Well-Tuned Piano 81 X 25 NYC* (La Monte Young): 'Numbers Racket', Just Intonation Network compilation, vol. II, JIN-002 (cassette, 1992)

Five Small Pieces for String Quartet, On Remembering a Naiad [plus works by other composers], (Arditti String Quartet): 'U.S.A.', Disques Montaigne 782010 (CD, 1993)

Young's Dorian Blues in G (La Monte Young and The Forever Bad Blues Band):
'Just Stompin': Live at the Kitchen', Gramavision R279487 (2 CDs, 1993)

Sarabande [plus works by other composers] (John Schneider, guitar; Amy
Schulman, harp): 'Just West Coast: microtonal music for guitar and harp',
Bridge Records BCD 9041 (CD, 1993)

Terry Riley

Untitled Organ (= *Keyboard Study no. 2*), *Dorian Reeds* (Terry Riley): 'Reed
Streams', Mass Art M-131 (LP, 1966)

In C (Center of the Creative and Performing Arts in the State University of New
York at Buffalo/Terry Riley): CBS MK 64565/MS 7178/CBS Classics 61237
(LP, 1968 and later; reissued on CD, 1988)

A Rainbow in Curved Air, Poppy Nogood and the Phantom Band (Terry Riley): CBS
MK 64564/ MS 7315 (LP, 1969; reissued on CD, 1988)

with John Cale, *Church of Anthrax* (John Cale and Terry Riley): CBS 30131/64259
(LP, 1971)

Les Yeux Fermés (Happy Ending) (Terry Riley): [Warner Brothers,] WEA
Filipacchi Music 46 125 U (LP, 1972)

Persian Surgery Dervishes (Terry Riley): Shandar/Shanti 83.501–2 (2 LPs, 1972);
reissued on Robi Droli, New Tone nt 6715 (2 CDs, 1993)

Keyboard Study no. 2, [Pierre Mariétan, *Systemes*] (Groupe Germ): Actuel BYG
529 327 (LP, n.d.)

Le Secret de la Vie (Lifespan) (Terry Riley): Stip 1011 (LP, 1975)

A Rainbow in Curved Air, [Samuel Barber, *Sonata*, Katrina Krimsky, *Specs*, Woody
Shaw, *Katrina Ballerina*, Shaw/Krimsky, *Epilogue*] (Katrina Krimsky):
Transonic 3008 (LP, *c.* 1976)

Shri Camel (Terry Riley): CBS 73 929 (LP, 1980); reissued on CBS 35164 (CD,
1988)

Descending Moonshine Dervishes (Terry Riley): Kuckuck 047 (LP, 1982); reissued
on Celestial Harmonies 12047-2 (CD, 1991)

In C, [David Mingyue Liang, *Music of a Thousand Springs, Zen (Ch'an) of Water*]
(Shanghai Film Orchestra/Wang Yongji, [Wang Zhaoxiang]): Celestial
Harmonies 7689 (CD, 1990)

In C, [Reich, *Six Pianos*] (Piano Circus): Decca, Argo 430 380–2 (CD, 1990)

Tread on the Trail, [Jon Gibson, *Waltz*, John Adams, *Pat's Aria*, Steve Reich, *Reed
Phase*, Terry Jennings, *Terry's G Dorian Blues*, Philip Glass, *Bed*, Gibson, *Song
3*, Glass, *Gradus (For Jon Gibson)* [*sic*], Gibson, *Extensions II*] (Jon Gibson,
plus La Monte Young [Jennings only]): 'Jon Gibson: In Good Company',
Point Music 434 873–2 (CD, 1992)

A 'Terry Riley Archive Series' of recordings is promised by Gary Todd's Cortical
Foundation. Details available from the Cortical Foundation, 23715 West
Malibu Road, #419, Malibu, CA 90265, USA.

Steve Reich

Come Out [plus works by other composers]: 'New Sounds in Electronic Music',
   CBS Odyssey, 32-16-0160 (LP, 1967)

It's Gonna Rain, Violin Phase (Paul Zukofsky, violin): 'Live/Electric', Columbia
   MS-7265 (LP, 1969)

Four Organs, Phase Patterns (Steve Reich and Musicians): Disques Shandar, SR
   10005 (LP, 1971); reissued on Robi Droli, RDC 5018 (CD, 1994)

Drumming (Steve Reich and Musicians): John Gibson and Multiples, Inc. (2 LPs,
   1972). This signed and numbered limited edition of 500, complete with a full
   score, was recorded at the New York Town Hall première performance of the
   work.

Four Organs, [Cage, *Three Dances*] (Ralph Gierson, Roger Kellaway, Tom Raney,
   Steve Reich and Michael Tilson Thomas): Angel, S-36059 (LP, 1973)

Drumming, Music for Mallet Instruments, Voices and Organ, Six Pianos (Steve
   Reich and Musicians): Deutsche Grammophon Gesellschaft, 2740-106 (3
   LPs, 1974)

Music for Eighteen Musicians (Steve Reich and Musicians): ECM Records, ECM-1-
   1129 (LP, 1978; reissued on CD, 1988)

Violin Phase, [*Music for a Large Ensemble, Octet*] (Shem Guibbory, violin, [Steve
   Reich and Musicians]): ECM Records, ECM 1168 (LP, 1980; reissued on CD,
   1989)

Music for Pieces of Wood ('Zene fadarabokra'), [Tibor Szemző, *Vizicsoda* ('Water-
   Wonder'), László Melis, *Etüd három tükörre* ('Etude for Three Mirrors'),
   Frederic Rzewski, *Coming Together*] (Group 180): Hungaroton SLPX 12545
   (LP, 1983); reissued on Hungaroton Classic HCD 12545 (CD, 1995)

Piano Phase, [*Octet*, Béla Faragó, *A pók halála* + *Sírfelirat* ('Death of the
   Spider + Epitaph'), András Soós, *Duett* ('A Duet')] (Group 180):
   Hungaroton SLPX 12799 (LP, 1985)

Melodica, [plus music by twenty-one other composers and improvisers,
   performed by various musicians]: 'Music from Mills: in celebration of the
   Centennial of the Chartering of Mills College 1885–1985', Mills College MC
   001 (3 LPs, 1986)

Six Marimbas, [*Sextet*] (Steve Reich and Musicians): Elektra Nonesuch 7559-
   79138 (LP & CD, 1987)

Come Out, Piano Phase, Clapping Music, It's Gonna Rain (Double Edge, Russ
   Hartenberger & Steve Reich): Elektra Nonesuch 7559-79169 (LP & CD, 1987)

Drumming (Steve Reich and Musicians): Elektra Nonesuch 7559-79170 (2 LPs &
   CD, 1987)

[*The Four Sections*], *Music for Mallet Instruments, Voices and Organ*, ([London
   Symphony Orchestra/Michael Tilson Thomas], Steve Reich and Musicians):
   Elektra Nonesuch 7559-79220 (CD, 1990)

Six Pianos, [Riley, *In C*] (Piano Circus): Decca, Argo 430 380-2 (CD, 1990)

Reed Phase, [plus works by Gibson, Adams, Jennings, Glass and Riley: see Riley,

Tread on the Trail, above] (Jon Gibson, etc.): 'Jon Gibson: In Good Company', Point Music 434 873–2 (CD, 1992)

Music for Mallet Instruments, Voices and Organ, Piano Phase, [*Octet, Sextet*] (Amadinda Percussion Group and Group 180): 'Steve Reich: Another Look at Counterpoint', Amiata Records, ARNR 0393 (CD, 1993)

Four Organs, [Kevin Volans, *Kneeling Dance*; David Lang, *Face So Pale*; Robert Moran, *Three Dances*] (Piano Circus): Decca, Argo 440 294-2 (CD, 1993)

Piano Phase [in version for two marimbas], [István Márta, *Doll's House Story*, László Sáry, *Pebble Playing in a Pot*, John Cage, *Second Construction in Metal*, Traditional African Music, George Hamilton Green, *Log Cabin Blues*, *Charleston Capers, Jovial Jasper*] (Amadinda Percussion Group): Hungaroton Classic HCD 12855, (CD, 1994)

It's Gonna Rain, Come Out, Piano Phase, Four Organs, Drumming, Clapping Music, Music for Eighteen Musicians, [*Eight Lines, Tehillim, The Desert Music, New York Counterpoint, Three Movements, The Four Sections, Electric Counterpoint, Different Trains, The Cave* (excerpts), *City Life, Proverb*] 'Steve Reich: 1965–1995', 10-CD boxed set: Elektra Nonesuch 7559-79451-2 (1997). This sixtieth-birthday compilation includes a valuable interview with the composer by Jonathan Cott and much other useful commentary.

Music for Eighteen Musicians (same recording as above), issued separately: Elektra Nonesuch (CD, 1998)

Philip Glass

Music with Changing Parts (Philip Glass Ensemble): Chatham Square 1001/2 (2 LPs, 1971); reissued on Elektra/Nonesuch 7559-79325-2 (CD, 1994)

Music in Fifths; Music in Similar Motion (Philip Glass Ensemble): Chatham Square 1003 (LP, 1973); reissued (with *Two Pages* & [*Music in*] *Contrary Motion*, see below) on Elektra/Nonesuch 7559-79326-2 (CD, 1994)

Two Pages [plus works by other composers] (Philip Glass and Michael Riesman): Folkways FTS 33902 (LP, 1975)

[*Music in*] *Contrary Motion, Two Pages* (same performance as above) (Philip Glass and electric organ): 'Solo Music', Shandar 83.515 (LP, 1975); reissued (with *Music in Fifths* & *Music in Similar Motion*, see above) on Elektra/Nonesuch 7559-79326-2 (CD, 1994)

Music in Twelve Parts, Parts 1 & 2 (Philip Glass Ensemble): Caroline/Virgin CA 2010 (LP, 1975)

Strung Out, [Giacinto Scelsi, *Anahit*, Iannis Xenakis, *Mikka* and *Mikka 'S'*] (Paul Zukofsky, [unnamed ensemble/Kenneth Moore]): CP² 108 (LP, 1976)

Einstein on the Beach, excerpts (Philip Glass Ensemble, etc.): Tomato TOM-101 (LP, 1978)

Einstein on the Beach (Philip Glass Ensemble, etc.): Tomato TOM-4-2901 (4 LPs, 1979); reissued on 4 LPs & 3 CDs, Sony Masterworks M4K 38875 (1984). Includes extensive notes by Robert Palmer and Philip Glass.

Einstein on the Beach (solo violin music), [Aaron Copland, *Duo for Violin and Piano*, Leo Ornstein, *Sonata for Violin and Piano*, Richard Wernick, *Cadenzas and Variations*] (Gregory Fulkerson, [Robert Shannon and Alan Feinberg]): New World Records NW 313 (LP, 1981)

Music in Twelve Parts (Philip Glass Ensemble): Venture/Virgin 802768995 (6 LPs & 3 CDs, 1988, UK); reissued on Virgin 91311-2 (6 LPs & 3 CDs, 1989, USA)

Einstein on the Beach, extracts (Philip Glass Ensemble), [with music from *Satyagraha* & *Akhnaten*]: 'Songs from the Trilogy', Sony Masterworks MK 45580 (CD, 1987)

Bed (from *Einstein on the Beach*), *Gradus (For Jon Gibson)* [*sic*], [plus works by Gibson, Adams, Reich, Jennings, Glass and Riley: see Riley, *Tread on the Trail*, above] (Jon Gibson, etc.): 'Jon Gibson: In Good Company', Point Music 434 873-2 (CD, 1992)

[Music in] Contrary Motion [with *Dance IV for Organ*, *Mad Rush*, *Dance II for Organ* & *Satyagraha*, Act III conclusion, arr. Michael Riesman] (Donald Joyce, organ): 'Glass Organ Works', BMG Catalyst 09026-61825-2 (CD, 1993)

Einstein on the Beach, 'Bed' (Act IV, scene 2) (Philip Glass Ensemble) [with twelve extracts from later works]: 'The Essential Philip Glass', Sony Masterworks SK 64133 (CD, 1993)

Einstein on the Beach (Philip Glass Ensemble, etc.): Elektra/Nonesuch 7559-79323-2 (3 CDs, 1993)

Music in Twelve Parts (Philip Glass Ensemble): Elektra/Nonesuch 7559-79324-2 (3 CDs, 1996)

Einstein on the Beach 'Spaceship' (Act IV, scene 3), 'Building/Train' (Act IV, scene 1) 'Knee Plays 3 & 5' (Philip Glass Ensemble) [with sixteen extracts from later works]: 'Glassmasters', Sony Masterworks SM3K 62960 (3 CDs, 1997)

Bibliography

This bibliography mainly lists the published material on which this book has drawn directly. No attempt has been made to list the extensive unpublished sources consulted. Reviews and more journalistic articles, of which there are many, have been included only when they seem of especial significance or historical interest from the perspective of the present volume. Like the extensive unpublished sources consulted, these have been detailed in endnotes when quoted in the main text. Accompanying booklet notes to recordings have not been included in this bibliography, though, again, some references to these may be found in endnotes; see also the Discography. Documentary videos and radio programmes have not been included. Studies of musical theory and the more standard textbooks and reference books on twentieth-century music are not included, though some individual dictionary and encyclopaedia entries on the four subjects of this volume are listed. The listed literature on the many other subjects having a more background or peripheral function in the present context – Minimalist art, for instance – is confined to those books and articles, including some of the seminal texts, which this author has found particularly useful for present purposes; for convenience, some are included in their anthologised form.

Adams, John, 'Steve Reich', in *The New Grove Dictionary of American Music,* eds. H. Wiley Hitchcock, H. and Stanley Sadie (London: Macmillan/New York: Grove's Dictionaries of Music, 1986), IX, pp. 23–6

Adorno, Theodor, *The Culture Industry: Selected Essays on Mass Culture,* ed. Jay Bernstein (London: Routledge, 1991)

Ahlgren, C., 'Terry Riley: Music is Path to Heaven', *San Francisco Chronicle,* 17 April 1983

Aikin, J. and Rothstein, J., 'Terry Riley: The Composer of *In C* Explores Indian Sources and Synthesizer Soloing', *Keyboard,* 8/4 (1982), pp. 11–14

Alloway, Lawrence, *Topics in American Art Since 1945* (New York: Norton, 1975)

Amirkhanian, Charles, 'Steve Reich', *Ear [West],* 7 (March–April 1979), Section I, pp. 4–5

Baker, Kenneth, *Minimalism: Art of Circumstance* (New York: Abbeville Press, 1988)

Banes, Sally, *Greenwich Village 1963: Avant-Garde Performance and the Effervescent Body* (Durham, N.C., and London: Duke University Press, 1993)

Battcock, Gregory, ed., *Minimal Art: A Critical Anthology* (New York: Dutton, 1968/London: Studio Vista, 1969)

   Breaking the Sound Barrier: A Critical Anthology of the New Music (New York: Dutton, 1981)

Beard, Rick, and Berlowitz, Leslie Cohen, eds., *Greenwich Village: Culture and Counterculture* (New Brunswick, N.J.: Rutgers University Press/The Museum of the City of New York, 1993)

Berger, Maurice, *Labyrinths: Robert Morris, Minimalism, and the 1960s* (New York: Harper and Row, 1989)

Bernard, Jonathan W., 'The Minimalist Aesthetic in the Plastic Arts and in Music', *Perspectives of New Music*, 31/1 (Winter 1993), pp. 86–132

'Theory, Analysis, and the "Problem" of Minimal Music', in *Concert Music, Rock, and Jazz since 1945: Essays and Analytical Studies*, eds. Elizabeth West Marvin and Richard Hermann (Rochester, NY: University of Rochester Press, 1995), pp. 259–84

Borden, Lizzie, 'The New Dialectic', *Artforum*, 12/7 (1974), pp. 44–8

Brecht, Stefan, *The Theatre of Visions: Robert Wilson* (Frankfurt: Suhrkamp Verlag, 1979)

Breuer, Lee, and Horton, Ann Elizabeth, *A Comic of the Red Horse Animation* (New York: [Mabou Mines], 1976)

Brinkman, R., ed., *Avant-garde Jazz Pop: Tendenzen zwischen Tonalität und Atonalität* (Mainz and London, 1978)

Broad, Elaine, 'A New X? An Examination of the Aesthetic Foundations of Early Minimalism', *Music Research Forum*, 5 (1990), pp. 51–62

Cage, John, *Silence* (Middletown: Wesleyan University Press, 1961)

Cage, John, and Knowles, Alison, *Notations* (New York: Something Else Press, 1969)

Calas, Nicolas, and Elena, *Icons and Images of the Sixties* (New York: Dutton, 1971)

Cardew, Cornelius, 'One Sound: La Monte Young', *The Musical Times*, 107/1485 (November 1966), pp. 959–60

Treatise Handbook (London: Peters Edition, 1971)

Carl, Robert, 'The Politics of Definition in New Music', *College Music Symposium*, 29 (1989), pp. 101–14

Caux, Daniel, 'Des jeux avec les sons: techno et minimalisme', *Artpress*, 9 (1998), pp. 105–11

Chave, Anna C., 'Minimalism and the Rhetoric of Power', *The Arts Magazine*, 64/5 (January 1990), pp. 44–63

Christgau, Robert, *Christgau's Guide to Rock Albums of the Seventies* (New Haven, Conn.: Ticknor and Fields, 1981/London: Vermilion, 1982)

Clarke, Garry E., 'Music', in *The Postmodern Movement: A Handbook of Contemporary Innovation in the Arts,* ed. Stanley Trachtenberg (Westport, Conn., and London: Greenwood Press, 1985), pp. 157–76

Cohn, Richard, 'Transpositional Combination of Beat-Class Sets in Steve Reich's Phase-Shifting Music', *Perspectives of New Music*, 30/1 (1992), pp. 146–77

Colpitt, Frances, *Minimal Art: The Critical Perspective* (Ann Arbor: UMI Research Press, 1990)

Corbett, John, 'Minimal Compact', *The Wire*, 132 (February 1995), pp. 34–5

Cowan, Robert, 'Reich and Wittgenstein: Notes Towards a Synthesis', *Tempo*, 157 (June 1986), pp. 2–7

Crane, Diana, *The Transformation of the Avant-Garde: The New York Art World, 1940–1985* (Chicago and London: University of Chicago Press, 1987)

Danninger, H., 'Destruktion und Heimweh: Anmerkungen zur Neuen Musik Amerikas', *Musica*, 32/1 (1978), pp. 20–5

de la Falaise, Maxime, 'Creating *Einstein on the Beach*: Philip Glass and Robert

Wilson Speak to Maxime de la Falaise', *On the Next Wave: The Audience Magazine of BAM's Next Wave Festival*, 2/4 (1984), pp. 5–9

Dennis, Brian, 'Repetitive and Systemic Music', *The Musical Times*, 115/1582 (December 1974), pp. 1036–8

Di Maggio, Gino, ed., *Ubi Fluxus Ibi Motus: 1990–1962* (Milan: Nuove Edizione Gabriele Mazzotta, 1990)

Dreier, Ruth, 'Minimalism', in *The New Grove Dictionary of American Music,* eds. H. Wiley Hitchcock and Stanley Sadie (London: Macmillan/New York: Grove's Dictionaries of Music, 1986), III, pp. 240–2

Duckworth, William, *Talking Music* (New York: Schirmer Books, 1995)

Duckworth, William, and Fleming, Richard, eds., *Sound and Light: La Monte Young, Marian Zazeela* (Lewisburg, Penn.: Bucknell University Press, 1996)

Dunn, R., ed., *John Cage* (New York: Henmar Press, 1962)

Epstein, Paul, 'Pattern Structure and Process in Steve Reich's *Piano Phase*', *The Musical Quarterly*, 72/4 (1986), pp. 146–77

Farneth, David, 'La Monte Young', in *The New Grove Dictionary of American Music,* eds. H. Wiley Hitchcock and Stanley Sadie (London: Macmillan/New York: Grove's Dictionaries of Music, 1986), IX, pp. 579–81

Fisher, A. J., 'Unmasking Rigor: Composition, Analysis, and the Poetry of Experience', *Perspectives of New Music*, 30/2 (Summer 1992), pp. 6–21

Ford, Andrew, *Composer to Composer: Conversations about Contemporary Music* (London: Quartet Books, 1993)

Foster, Hal, ed., *Postmodern Culture* (London and Sydney: Pluto Press, 1985)

Frascina, Francis, ed., *Pollock and After: The Critical Debate* (New York: Harper and Row, 1985)

Fried, Michael, 'Art and Objecthood', *Artforum*, 8/5 (June 1967), pp. 12–23

Gagne, Cole, *Sonic Transports: New Frontiers In Our Music* (New York: de Falco Books, 1990)

Soundpieces 2: Interviews With American Composers (Metuchen, N.J., and London: The Scarecrow Press, 1993)

Gagne, Cole, and Caras, Tracy, *Soundpieces: Interviews With American Composers* (Metuchen, N.J., and London: The Scarecrow Press, 1982)

Gann, Kyle, 'Let X = X: Minimalism v. Serialism', *Village Voice*, 24 February 1987, p. 76
'La Monte Young's *The Well-Tuned Piano*', *Perspectives of New Music*, 31/1 (Winter 1993), pp. 134–62

Garratt, Sheryl, 'Fun With Monotony' [Interview with Philip Glass], *The Face*, 75 (July 1986), pp. 36–41

Gena, Peter, 'Freedom in Experimental Music: The New York Revolution', *Tri-Quarterly*, 52 (1981), pp. 236–8

Geysen, F., 'Eigen kompositorische bevindingen in vergelijking met het werk van de jonge amerikaanse school', *Adem*, 10/1 (1974), pp. 24–6

Glass, Philip, 'Notes: *Einstein on the Beach*', *Performing Arts Journal*, 2/3 (1978), pp. 63–70

Glass, Philip, ed. with supplementary material by Robert T. Jones, *The Music of Philip Glass* (New York: Harper and Row, 1987)/ *Opera on the Beach* (London and Boston: Faber and Faber, 1988)

Goldberg, Rose Lee, *Performance Art: From Futurism to the Present* (New York: Harry N. Abrams, 1988; originally published as *Performance: Live Art 1909 to the Present*, 1979)

Gordon, Peter, 'Philip Glass: Music of the Moment', *Painted Bride Quarterly*, 4/2 (1977), pp. 56–63

Gottwald, Clytus, 'Signale zwischen Exotik und Industrie: Steve Reich auf der Suche nach einer neuen Identität von Klang und Struktur', *Melos/Neue Zeitschrift für Musik*, o (January-February 1975), pp. 3–6

'Tendenzen der neuen Musik in den USA: György Ligeti im Gesprach mit Clytus Gottwald', *Musik und Bildung*, 8 (February 1976), pp. 57–61

Greenberg, Clement, *Art and Culture* (Boston: Beacon Press, 1961); this collection of the author's articles includes 'Avant-Garde and Kitsch', *Partisan Review*, 6/5 (Fall 1939), pp. 34–49

Henahan, Donal, 'Reich? Philharmonic? Paradiddling?', *New York Times*, 24 October 1971, Section ii, pp. 13 and 26

Hendricks, Jon, *Fluxus Codex* (New York: The Gilbert and Lila Silverman Fluxus Collection/Harry N. Abrams, 1988)

Hitchcock, H. Wiley, 'Minimalism in Art and Music: Origins and Aesthetics', *College Art Journal*, 27 (Summer 1994), pp. 12–18; reprinted in *Classic Essays on Twentieth-Century Music*, eds. Richard Kostelanetz and J. Darby (New York: Schirmer Books, 1996), pp. 303–19

Jacoby, Russell, *The Last Intellectuals: American Culture in the Age of Academe* (New York: Basic Books, 1987)

Jencks, Charles, *What Is Post-Modernism?* (London: Academy Editions/New York: St Martin's Press, 1986; 2nd edn., 1987)

Johnson, Jill, 'Music: La Monte Young', *Village Voice*, 19 November 1964, pp. 14 and 20

Johnson, Timothy A., 'Minimalism: Aesthetic, Style, or Technique?', *The Musical Quarterly*, 78/4 (Winter 1994), pp. 742–73

Johnson, Tom, *The Voice of New Music: New York City 1972–1982* (Eindhoven: Het Apollohuis, 1989)

Jones, Robert T., 'Philip Glass [Musician of the Month]', *High Fidelity/Musical America*, 29/4 (April 1979), pp. MA-4-6

'*Einstein on the Beach*: Return of a Legend', *On the Next Wave: the Audience Magazine of BAM's Next Wave Festival*, 2/4 (1984), pp. 1–4

Judd, Donald, *Complete Writings 1959–1975* (New York: New York University Press, 1975)

Kaye, Nick, *Postmodernism and Performance* (New York: St Martin's Press, 1994)

King, Bruce, ed., *Contemporary American Theatre* (Basingstoke: Macmillan, 1991). Includes a chapter on 'Lee Breuer and Mabou Mines' by S. E. Gontarski, pp. 135–48, and discussion of Robert Wilson and Philip Glass in 'Beyond the Broadway Musical: Crossovers, Confusions and Crisis', pp. 151–76.

Knox, Kenneth, 'The Parametric Music of Terry Riley', *Jazz Monthly*, 13/5 (1967), pp. 9–12

Knox, Kenneth, and Knox, R., 'Relax and Fully Concentrate: The Time of Terry Riley', *Friends Magazine*, 20 February 1970, unpaginated

Kostek, M. C., *The Velvet Underground Handbook* (London: Black Spring Press, 1992)

Kostelanetz, Richard, *The Theatre of Mixed Means: An Introduction to Happenings, Kinetic Environments and Other Mixed-Means Presentations* (New York: Dial Press, 1968/RK Editions, 1980)

Metamorphosis in the Arts: A Critical History of the 1960s (Brooklyn: Assembling Press, 1980)

Kostelanetz, Richard, ed., *Writings on Glass: Essays, Interviews, Criticism* (New York: Schirmer Books/London: Prentice Hall International, 1997). Includes previously published material by Charles Merrell Berg, Thomas Rain Crowe, Peter G. Davis, Paul John Frandsen, Kyle Gann, John Howell, Tom Johnson, John Koopman, Richard Kostelanetz, Allan Kozinn, Art Lange, Robert C. Morgan, Tim Page, Joseph Roddy, Aaron M. Shatzman, Edward Strickland, Mark Swed, Helen Tworkov/Robert Coe, David Walters, in addition to those entries detailed in Chapter 4.

Kozinn, Allan, 'Philip Glass', *Ovation*, 5/1 (1984), pp. 12–14

Kramer, Jonathan D., *The Time of Music: New Meanings, New Temporalities, New Listening Strategies* (New York: Schirmer/London: Collier Macmillan, 1988)

La Barbara, Joan, 'Philip Glass e Steve Reich: Two from the Steady State School', dual language Italian/English, *Data: pratica e teoria delle arti*, 4/13 (Autumn 1974), pp. 36–9; reprinted in Kostelanetz 1997 (see above)

'New Music', *High Fidelity/Musical America*, 27/11 (November 1977), pp. MA 14–15

Lasch, Christopher, *The Minimal Self: Psychic Survival in Troubled Times* (New York and London: W. W. Norton, 1984)

Le Witt, Sol, 'Paragraphs on Conceptual Art', *Artforum*, 8/5 (June 1967), pp. 79–83

Licht, Alan, 'The History of La Monte Young's Theatre of Eternal Music', *Forced Exposure*, 16 (1990), pp. 60–9

Lipman, Samuel, *The House of Music: Art in an Era of Institutions* (Boston: David R. Godine, 1984)

Lippard, Lucy R., ed., *Pop Art* (London: Thames and Hudson, 1966, rev. edns. 1967 and 1970)

Lodge, David, *Working with Structuralism: Essays and Reviews on Nineteenth- and Twentieth-Century Literature* (London: Routledge and Kegan Paul, 1981)

Lovisa, F. R., *Minimal-Music: Entwicklung, Komponisten, Werke* (Darmstadt, 1996)

MacDonald, Ian, 'What is the Use of Minimalism?', *The Face*, 83 (March 1987), pp. 102–09

Mamiya, Christin J., *Pop Art and Consumer Culture: American Super Market* (Austin: University of Texas Press, 1992)

Marranca, Bonnie, *The Theatre of Images* (New York: Drama Books, 1977)

Matthew-Walker, Robert, 'Glass Roots', *CD Review*, 61 (February 1992), pp. 17–21

Mellers, Wilfrid, 'A Minimalist Definition', *The Musical Times*, 125/1696 (June 1984), p. 328

Mertens, Wim, trans. J. Hautekiet, *American Minimal Music: La Monte Young, Terry Riley, Steve Reich, Philip Glass* (London: Kahn and Averill/New York: Alexander Broude, 1983)

Moore, Carman, 'Music: Park Place Electronics', *Village Voice*, 9 June 1966, p. 17
'Music: Park Place Pianos', *Village Voice*, 23 March 1967, p. 15
'Fragments', *Village Voice*, 18 January 1968, pp. 25 and 28
'Music: Zukofsky', *Village Voice*, 1 May 1969, p. 28

Morgan, Robert P., ed., *Modern Times: From World War I to the Present* (Basingstoke: Macmillan, 1993/Englewood Cliffs, N.J: Prentice Hall, 1994). Commentary on minimalism may be found in William Brooks's chapter, 'The Americas, 1945–70', pp. 309–48, the present author's own 'The Current Musical Scene', pp. 349–87, and Michael Tenzer's 'Western Music in the Context of World Music', pp. 388–410.

Morrissey, Lee, ed., *The Kitchen Turns Twenty: A Retrospective Anthology* (New York: The Kitchen/Haleakala, 1992)

Neilson, John, 'La Monte Young', *Creem* (November 1987), p. 44–7.

Nelson, C., ed., *Robert Wilson: The Theatre of Images* (New York: Harper and Row, 1984)

Nicholls, David, *American Experimental Music: 1890–1940* (Cambridge: Cambridge University Press, 1990)
'Transethnicism and the American Experimental Tradition', *The Musical Quarterly*, 80/4 (Winter 1996), pp. 569–94

Norris, Christopher, ed., *Music and the Politics of Culture* (London: Lawrence and Wishart, 1989). Includes Claire Polin's essay, 'Why Minimalism Now?' pp. 226–39.

Nyman, Michael, with Hugh Davies and Richard Orton, 'Steve Reich: An Interview with Michael Nyman', *The Musical Times*, 112/1537 (March 1971), pp. 229–31
'Steve Reich, Phil Glass', *The Musical Times*, 112/1539 (May 1971), pp. 463–4
'SR-mysteries of the phase', *Music and Musicians*, 20/6 (February 1972), pp. 20–1
Experimental Music: Cage and Beyond (London: Studio Vista/New York: Schirmer, 1974; rev. edn., Cambridge: Cambridge University Press 1999)
'Steve Reich: Interview', *Studio International*, 192/6 (November–December 1976), pp. 300–07
'Steve Reich', *Music and Musicians*, 25/5 (January 1977), pp. 18–19
'Against Intellectual Complexity in Music', *October*, 13 (1980), pp. 81–9

O'Grady, Terence J., 'Aesthetic Value in Indeterminate Music', *Musical Quarterly*, 67 (July 1981), pp. 366–81

Oesterreich, Norbert, 'Music with Roots in the Aether', *Perspectives of New Music*, 16 (Fall–Winter 1977), pp. 214–28

Page, Tim, 'Framing the River: A Minimalist Primer', *High Fidelity/Musical America*, 31/11 (November 1981), pp. 64–8 and 117
'The New Romance with Tonality', *New York Times Magazine*, 29 May 1983, pp. 22–5 and 28
'Steve Reich, a Former Young Turk, Approaches 50', *New York Times*, 1 June 1986, Section ii, pp. 23–4

Music from the Road: Views and Reviews 1978–1992 (New York and Oxford: Oxford University Press, 1992)

Palmer, Robert, 'La Monte Young: Lost in the Drone Zone', *Rolling Stone*, 13 February 1975, p. 24

'A Father Figure for the Avant-garde', *The Atlantic*, 247/5 (May 1981), pp. 48–56

'Get Ready for the Music of Harmonics', *New York Times*, 17 July 1983, Section C, p. 17

Parsons, Michael, 'Systems in Art and Music', *The Musical Times*, 117/1604 (October 1976), pp. 815–18

Pincus-Witten, Robert, *Postminimalism into Maximalism: American Art, 1966–1986* (New York: Dutton, 1989)

Porter, Andrew, *Music of Three Seasons: 1974–1977* (New York: Farrar, Straus and Giroux, 1978). A collection of reviews originally published during this period in *The New Yorker* magazine, including 'Many-Colored Glass', a review of one of the Metropolitan Opera House performances of Glass's *Einstein on the Beach*, pp. 459–63.

Potter, Keith, 'Terry Riley Encountered', *Classical Music*, 11 August 1984, p. 17

'The Recent Phases of Steve Reich', *Contact*, 29 (Spring 1985), pp. 28–34

'Steve Reich: Thoughts for his 50th-Birthday Year', *The Musical Times*, 127/1715 (January 1986), pp. 13–17

'Philip Glass', in *The Viking Opera Guide*, ed. Amanda Holden (London: Penguin, 1993), pp. 360–5; reprinted in Holden, ed., *The Penguin Opera Guide* (London: Penguin, 1995), pp. 142–7

'The Pursuit of the Unimaginable by the Unnarratable, or Some Potentially Telling Developments in Non-Developmental Music', *Contemporary Music Review*, 15/ 3–4 (1996), pp. 3–11

Potter, Keith, and Smith, Dave, 'Interview with Philip Glass', *Contact*, 13 (Spring 1976), pp. 25–30

Reich, Steve, *Writings about Music*, ed. Kaspar Koenig (Halifax, Canada: Nova Scotia College of Art and Design/New York: New York University Press/London: Universal Edition, 1974)

'Texture-Space-Survival', *Perspectives of New Music*, 26/2 (Summer 1988), pp. 272–80

Autori Vari: Reich, ed. Enzo Restagno (Turin: Edizioni di Torino, 1994). A much expanded version, in Italian, of *Writings about Music*

Reinhard, J., 'A Conversation with La Monte Young and Marian Zazeela', *Ear*, 7/5 (1982–3), pp. 4–6

Reynolds, Roger, *Mind Models: New Forms of Musical Experience* (New York: Praeger, 1975)

Rockwell, John, 'Boulez and Young: Enormous Gulf or Unwitting Allies?' *Los Angeles Times*, 13 February 1972, p. 38

'Music: Reich Meditations', *New York Times*, 19 May 1973, Section ii, p. 28

'What's New?' *High Fidelity/Musical America*, 23/8 (August 1973), pp. MA 31–2

'There's Nothing Quite Like the Sound of Glass', *New York Times*, 26 May 1974, Section ii, pp. 11 and 21

'The Evolution of Steve Reich', *New York Times*, 14 March 1982, Section ii, pp. 23–4

All American Music: Composition in the Late Twentieth Century (New York: Alfred A. Knopf, 1983/London: Kahn and Averill, 1985; rev. edn., New York: Da Capo Press, 1997)

'"Einstein" Returns Briefly', *New York Times*, 17 December 1984, Section ii

'The Life and Death of Minimalism', *New York Times*, 21 December 1986, Section ii, pp. 1 and 29

'Feldman's Minimalism in Maximal Doses', *New York Times*, 12 January 1992, Section ii, p. 28

Rosenbaum, R., 'Eternal Music in a Dreamhouse Barn', *Village Voice*, 12 February 1970, pp. 5–6 and 63–6

Rothstein, J., 'Terry Riley', *Down Beat*, 48/5 (1981), pp. 26–8

Ruppenthal, Stephen, 'Terry Riley', in *The New Grove Dictionary of American Music*, eds. H. Wiley Hitchcock and Stanley Sadie (London: Macmillan/New York: Grove's Dictionaries of Music, 1986), IX, pp. 48–9

Salzman, Eric, 'The *New York Times* Was Supposed to Print This But Didn't', *Ear Magazine East*, 5 (November–December 1979), pp. 6–7

Sandford, Mariellen R., *Happenings and Other Acts* (London and New York: Routledge, 1995)

Sandler, Irving, *American Art of the 1960s* (New York: Harper and Row, 1988)

Sandow, Gregory, 'Philip Glass', in *The New Grove Dictionary of American Music*, eds. H. Wiley Hitchcock and Stanley Sadie (London: Macmillan/New York: Grove's Dictionaries of Music, 1986), II, pp. 228–30

Sayres, Sohnya, Stephanson, Anders, Aronowitz, Stanley, and Jameson, Fredric, eds. *The 60s Without Apology* (Minneapolis: University of Minnesota Press, in co-operation with *Social Text* 3/3 and 4/1, 1984)

Schaefer, John, *New Sounds: A Listener's Guide to New Music* (New York: Harper and Row, 1987)

Schwarz, David, 'Listening Subjects: Semiotics, Psychoanalysis, and the Music of John Adams and Steve Reich', *Perspectives of New Music*, 31/2 (Summer 1993), pp. 24–56

Schwarz, K. Robert, 'Steve Reich: Music as a Gradual Process', *Perspectives of New Music*, 19 (Fall–Winter 1980/Spring–Summer 1981), pp. 373–92, and 20 (Fall–Winter 1981/Spring–Summer 1982), pp. 225–86

Minimalists (London: Phaidon Press, 1996)

Scott, Derek, 'Postmodernism and Music', in *The Icon Critical Dictionary of Postmodern Thought*, ed. Stuart Sim (Duxford: Icon Books, 1998), pp. 134–46

Serra, Richard, *Writings, Interviews* (Chicago and London: University of Chicago Press, 1994)

Sharp, Willoughby, 'The Phil Glass Ensemble . . . Music in Twelve Parts', *Avalanche*, December 1974 (unnumbered), pp. 39–43

Sharp, Willoughby, and Bear, Liza, 'Phil Glass: An Interview in Two Parts', *Avalanche*, 5 (Summer 1972), pp. 26–35

Shyer, Laurence, *Robert Wilson and His Collaborators* (New York: Theatre Communications Group, 1989)

Smith, Dave, 'The Music of Phil Glass', *Contact*, 11 (Summer 1975), pp. 27–33
   'Following a Straight Line: La Monte Young', *Contact*, 18 (Winter 1977–8), pp.
   4–9
Smith, Geoff, and Smith, Nicola Walker, *American Originals: Interviews with 25 Contemporary Composers* (London and Boston: Faber and Faber, 1994)
Sontag, Susan, ed., *A Barthes Reader* (New York: Hill and Wang, 1982)
Sterritt, David, 'Tradition Reseen: Composer Steve Reich', *Christian Science Monitor*, 23 October 1980, p. 20
Strickland, Edward, *American Composers: Dialogues on Contemporary Music* (Bloomington and Indianapolis: Indiana University Press, 1991)
   Minimalism: Origins (Bloomington and Indianapolis: Indiana University Press, 1993)
Swed, Mark, 'La Monte Young Tunes the Piano His Way', *Los Angeles Herald Examiner*, 1 November 1985, p. 36
Tamm, Eric, *Brian Eno: His Music and the Vertical Color of Sound* (Boston and London: Faber and Faber, 1989)
Taylor, Sean, '*Einstein* on the Stage', Brooklyn Academy of Music programme book (December 1984), p. 3
Terry, Ken, 'La Monte Young – Avant-Garde Visionary Composer and Pianist', *Contemporary Keyboard*, August 1980, p. 16
Toop, David, *Oceans of Sound: Aether Talk, Ambient Sound and Imaginary Worlds* (London: Serpent's Tail, 1995); with two CDs (Virgin Records)
Walsh, Michael, 'Making a Joyful Noise', *Time*, 125/26 (1 July 1985), pp. 47–8
Warburton, Dan, 'A Working Terminology for Minimal Music', *Intégral*, 2 (1988), pp. 135–59
Wasserman, Emily, 'An Interview With Composer Steve Reich', *Artforum*, 10/9 (May 1972), pp. 44–8
Wetzler, Peter, 'Minimal Music', *Ear Magazine East*, 6 (June–July–August 1981), p. 6
Wheeler, Daniel, *Art Since Mid-Century: 1945 to the Present* (New York: Vendome Press/London: Thames and Hudson, 1991)
Wijers, Louwrien, *Fluxus Today and Yesterday* (New York: Dutton, 1993)
Williams, Emmett, and Noel, Ann, eds., *Mr. Fluxus: A Collective Portrait of George Maciunas, 1931–1978* (London: Thames and Hudson, 1997/New York: Thames and Hudson, 1998)
Wilson, Robert, et al., *Einstein on the Beach* (New York: EDS Enterprises, 1976)
Wolf, Daniel J., 'Living and Listening in Real Time', *Interval*, Winter 1982–3, pp.14–26 and Spring 1983, pp. 27–37
Woodley, Ronald, 'Steve Reich', in *Contemporary Composers*, eds. Brian Morton and Pamela Collins (London: St. James Press, 1992), pp. 767–9
Yalkut, Jud, 'Philip Glass and Jon Gibson', *Ear [West]*, 19 (Summer 1981), pp. 4–5
Vidic, Ljerka, 'La Monte Young and Marian Zazeela', *Ear*, 13 (May 1987), pp. 24–6
York, Wesley, 'Form and Process in *Two Pages* of Philip Glass', *Sonus*, 1/2 (Spring 1982), pp. 28–50; reprinted in *Contiguous Lines: Issues and Ideas in the Music of the '60s and '70s*, ed. Thomas, DeLio (Lanham, London, etc.: University Press of America, 1985), pp. 81–106; also reprinted in Kostelanetz 1997 (see above)

Young, La Monte, ed., *An Anthology* (New York: Young and Jackson MacLow, 1963; 2nd edn., Munich: Heiner Friedrich, 1970)

Young, La Monte, and Zazeela, Marian, *Selected Writings* (Munich: Heiner Friedrich, 1969)

Zak, Albin, ed., *The Velvet Underground: Four Decades of Commentary* (London, New York and Sydney: Omnibus Press [Schirmer], 1997)

Zimmermann, Walter, *Desert Plants: Conversations with 23 American Musicians* (Vancouver: Walter Zimmermann and A.R.C. Publications, 1976)

Zimmermann, Walter, ed., *Morton Feldman Essays* (Korpen: Beginner Press, 1985)

Zwerzin, M., 'The Moveable Feast: Philip Glass', *Jazz Forum*, 88 (1984), p. 28

Catalogues

Introduction to *Systemic Painting*, catalogue for the New York Guggenheim Museum exhibition, 1966

Anti-Illusion: Procedures/Materials, catalogue for New York Whitney Museum exhibition (New York: Whitney Museum of American Art, 1969)

New York – Downtown Manhattan – SoHo: Ausstellungen, Theater, Musik, Performance, Video, Film, catalogue for the Akademie der Kunste/Berliner Festwochen exhibition, 5 September – 17 October 1976. Includes a chapter on music by Joan La Barbara, pp. 142–66

'Art and Experimental Music' issue of *Studio International*, 192/984 (November–December 1976)

Haskell, Barbara, *Blam! The Explosion of Pop, Minimalism, and Performance 1958–1964*, catalogue for the New York Whitney Museum exhibition (New York: Norton/Whitney Museum, 1984)

Husslein, Uwe, catalogue for *Pop Goes Art* exhibition, (Uppertal: Institut für Pop Kultur, 1990)

McShine, Kynaston, catalogue for *Primary Structures* exhibition, Jewish Museum, New York, 1966

Phillpot, Clive, and Hendricks, Jon, *Fluxus: Selections from the Gilbert and Lila Silverman Collection*, catalogue for the Museum of Modern Art Library exhibition, New York, 17 November 1988 – 10 March 1989

Rose, Barbara, catalogue article for *A New Aesthetic* exhibition, Washington Gallery of Modern Art, 1967

Rubin, William S., *Frank Stella* (New York: The Museum of Modern Art, 1970)

Sohm, H., ed., *Happening & Fluxus: Materialen*, catalogue for the Koelnischer Kunstverein exhibition, 6 February 1970 – 6 January 1971

Serra, Richard, *Interviews, etc. 1970–1980* (Yonkers: Hudson River Museum, 1980)

Sol Le Witt: Prints, 1970–86, catalogue for Tate Gallery exhibition, London, 17 September – 30 November 1986

Index

Printed in the United States
94673LV00001B/1-40/A

9 780521 015011